Empowerment of Weaker Sections:

Future Planning and Strategies for Rural Development in India

Empowerment of Weaker Sections:

Future Planning and Strategies for Rural Development in India

Prof. K. Vijaya Kumar

SERIALS PUBLICATIONS
NEW DELHI (INDIA)

First Published - 2011

ISBN: 978-81-8387-459-5

Published by

SERIALS PUBLICATIONS
4830/24, Prahlad Street, Ansari Road
Darya Ganj, New Delhi-110002 (India)
Phone : 23245225 Fax : 91-11-23272135
E-mail: serials@sify.com

CONTENTS

SECTION—II

Preface

Our society consists of different categories of people having different economic and social status and strength. Neglected sections which remained away from the main stream of development, are termed as weaker sections. Central and state governments are providing special attention to these sections to enhance their socio-economic status.

The six decades of planning has no doubt helped the country to emerge as a leader in many areas. However there are some apprehensions. Some regard rural development with hostility, believing that it gives rise to distress and tendency to commit suicide, as also to fierce exploitation, economic instability, failure of crops due to natural calamities, increasing poverty, hunger and debt, leading to labour migration and increasing ethnic disparities. Some regard it is a capitalist to destroy the native economy. These angularities have not only persisted with the time bit have also grown and become more sharp, thereby threatening the over all growth achieved so far unless some quick remedial measures are taken up to arrest them.

Social sector planning is now regard as an important tool to counter anomalies. The initiation of a host of social sector programmes stands testimony to the fact that the government is quite concerned about the menace. Thus, for holistic development, development of both economic and social sector is vital because, while economic development provides physical growth and prosperity, social development provides sustainability, which makes both the sectors complementary to each other.

In this backdrop, an attempt has been made through the collection of works, as presented in the book, to elucidate on important issues needed for empowering weaker sections and strategies emphasized for Rural Development.

Prof. K. Vijaya Kumar

FOREWORD

The present publication "Empowerment of Weaker Sections: Future Planning and Strategies for Rural Development in Andhra Pradesh" is brought out by the Department of Sociology, Andhra University, Visakhapatnam, Andhra Pradesh. This is an edited volume of 37 papers presented at a National Seminar.

The seminar was held during 2008, with a focus on the multifaceted outcome of different rural development programmes, which should have lead to a balanced, equitable and sustainable rural development.

All these papers are contributed by academics, professionals and senior research scholars. The papers by and large, are empirical and analytical.

It is a well-known fact that any dialectical approach should provide an insight into the process of development. Agrarian relations always play an important role in rural development. Land reforms as implemented by the Government of India can at best be called a 'paper tiger' as it paid little or no attention to rural development.

Rural development, as an integral part of the overall development of any economy is an important component. In India's efforts towards betterment of living standards of people, it has been in the forefront of development agenda, since late 1970's and is occupying a special place in the policy frame of every five-year plan formulated so far. However, the achievements indicate mixed results. As such, these require appropriate modifications, inclusive of rural empowerment towards transformation of the weaker sections which constitute a major chunk to break away from the dominance of' the existing power centers. It also implies promotion of democratic leadership at the grassroots level by setting up local self-governance without disturbing the working potential of the elected representatives in providing basic needs such as education, healthcare, sanitation, protected water, housing, employment, developing both farming and non-farming activities, so as to generate gainful employment without adversely affecting the environment, generating awareness on legal rights to inculcate values of social security among weaker sections, ensuring a tension-free life for them by promoting communal harmony, cultural activities, enabling the rural poor, particularly the poorest lot by improving their livelihood. In a nutshell, the policy should tackle the twin problem of rural poverty and unemployment and breaking the entangled web.

These papers clearly established that empowerment of weaker sections and rural development programmes are formulated and implemented in a haphazard manner with no perspective plan. Hence, a comprehensive and holistic approach is suggested in the formulation and implementation of these programmes. Further, absence of science and technology components, inadequate management coupled with a weak delivery system is the major obstacle in the implementation of these programmes. As such, the programmes have failed to contribute to a sustainable rural development.

Empowering weaker sections contribute to social development and economic progress in any country, whether developed or under-developed, could be achieved only through properly planned rural development programmes.

The quality and contents of the Volume are quite academic and, is a welcome addition to the existing literature on rural development. It will be useful to policy makers, planners, administrators, extension officials, teachers, students and, to the general public involved in rural development.

BEELA SATYANARAYANA

VICE-CHANCELLOR

M.E.(MD), M.E.(IE), M.Tech.(CST), Ph.D.(HTD)

ACKNOWLEDGEMENT

First of all I express my heart felt thanks to all those who presented papers in the conference. It consists 38 papers contributed by the experts in Rural Development from various parts of India especially from Andhra Pradesh.

I wish to express my deep sense of gratitude to our beloved Vice-chancellor, Prof. B. Satyanarayana who extended co-operation and moral support to me in respect of my academic matters.

I thank late Sri. M.R.B. Narasinga Rao, a retired employee of Andhra University for his academic support and moral support.

I thank Prof. M. Bilmoria Rani, Deputy Coordinator, SAP, Dr. S. Uma Devi, Head, Department of Sociology and Dr. D. Rama Rao, Asst. Professor of Sociology who extended their cooperation and support for conducting national conference.

I thank to Prof. P. Hrushikeseva Rao, Director, School of Distance Education, and teaching staff of distance education who extended their full co-operation in all respects.

I thank Dr. K. Venkat Naidu, Mr. R.V. Prasad, Mr. Ch. Jagan Mohan Rao and Dr. T.S. Raja Kumari working as Research fellows of Department, Special Assistance Programme extended their academic and other assignments related to conference.

I thank to Mr. Teja and Mr. M.N. Gupta to their attentive computer work.

I thank the University Grant Commission for providing the requisite funding for the project.

Finally, express my deep sense of gratitude to the School of Distance Education, Andhra University for facilitating my work and during the project period.

Prof. K. Vijaya Kumar

Section – I

1

ROLE OF DCCBS IN RURAL FINANCE

A Case Study of West Godavari District in Andhra Pradesh

PROF. K. PARAMESWARA RAO

INTRODUCTION

Co-operatives play an important role in the modern age, as an institution to eliminate the middlemen and to serve the interests of the members of the co-operative organizations, formed for the benefit of its members. Provision of agricultural credit constitutes the core component of the cooperative system in India. Co-operatives continue to be considered as highly suitable agencies for financing agriculture and allied activities, not only in India, but also in other developing countries.

In India, more than 545 thousand cooperatives of various types are with membership of nearly 230 million (23 crores). The cooperative movement covers 100 per cent of villages and 75 per cent of rural households. In the field of employment-generation, the cooperatives are playing key role with direct employment generated for more than 11.5 lakhs of people and self-employment generated is around 15 millions.

Agricultural sector can be considered as an important sector, occupying a predominant role in the India economy. Generally, farmers require financial resources for the purpose of agricultural activities in rural areas. Thus, credit needs of the farmers are to be met through various agencies such as institutional as well as non-institutional agencies.

The non-institutional sources are·

1. Money lenders
2. Rich landlords
3. Traders
4. Commission agents

Institutional sources are:

1. Cooperative credit institutions
2. Commercial banks
3. Regional rural banks
4. NABARD
5. Government

The cooperative credit institutions play a unique and important role in the rural credit supply of Indian economy. The cooperative credit structure in India is based on a three tier system consisting of:

1. APEX body of the State level, known as State Cooperative Banks (SCB);
2. At intermediary level, known as District Central Cooperative Banks at district level (DCCB);
3. Primary Agricultural Credit Societies at the base level.

The State Cooperative Bank, being the APEX bank provides financial resources to District Cooperative Central Banks. The APEX bank is closely linked with the Reserve Bank of India (RBI) and NABARD that provides considerable financial assistance to the cooperative credit structure. The District Cooperative Central bank plays an important role in the development of agricultural cooperative credit and other types of societies.

The cheapest and best source of rural credit in India is definitely the Cooperative finance and Primary Agricultural

Credit Society (PACS) are found to work effectively and efficiently in this direction. These PACS are observed to cover nearly 86 per cent of the Indian villages and cater to the credit needs of the country. The federations of PACS working in each district form the Central Cooperative Bank of the district and these are expected to contribute for agricultural and rural development.

A District Central Cooperative Bank is a key financing institution at the district level which shoulders responsibility of meeting the credit needs of different types of cooperatives in the district. It also acts as balancing institution by accepting surplus funds of cooperatives and using this money to meet the credit requirement of needy cooperatives. It is an important link in the three tier agricultural credit structure. Their number has gone up to 367 with total deposits crossing Rs. 75,000 crores mark and loan outstanding at Rs. 65,000 crores. Their branch network has gone up to around 13 thousand. They are playing crucial role in meeting the credit needs of all cooperatives in the district, particularly of primary agricultural credit cooperatives.

Growth of DCC Banks in Andhra Pradesh

The Andhra Pradesh State has presently 22 District Co-operative Central Banks to look after the credit needs of agricultural sector in different districts. These District Co-operative Central Banks having 562 branches are providing employment to nearly 5,300 people. The Krishna District Cooperative Central Bank is observed to be the number one bank in the State in terms of share capital, reserve funds, deposits, loans followed by DCCB at Kakinada, DCCB at Eluru, DCCB at Guntur. The Krishna DCCB, with 54 branches and 455 staff members is catering the credit needs of Krishna district farmers. The bank with a share capital of 52.83 crores and with a deposit of 392.64 crores is observed to disperse loans to the tune of 593.14 crores (outstanding) by 2004. However, the net profitability of the bank is very poor-standing at 0.92 crore. The main reasons is the percentage of NPAS to loans outstanding stood at 19.47. However, the DCCB at Eluru is observed to be the number one bank in terms of net profitability (10.59 crores) by 2004. Further, the percentage of NPAS to outstanding loans is as low as 6.72 per cent compared to other DCCBs in state. Another important feature of the DCCBs of the state is 5 out of 22 banks are running with losses, while only 5 banks are securing net profitability of more than 5 crores. Thus, the progress of the DCCBs of Andhra Pradesh is not exhibiting uniform trend.

The Central Banks form an integral part of the short-term and medium-term cooperative credit delivery system, long-term credit with effect form 01-04-1987, i.e. after implementation of Single Window Credit Delivery Scheme and play a strategic role. They provide a connecting link between the small scattered primaries in the district and the SCB at State level.

The West Godavari district can be divided into three natural regions (i.e. Delta, Upland and Agency Areas). It has an area of 7,742 square kilometers. It has four revenue divisions put together have been divided into 46 revenue mandals, 866 inhabited villages and 35 uninhabited villages and 2,100 hamlets and 8 municipalities.

The district is basically agrarian in character. The district is also having the distinction of being RICE GRANARY of Andhra Pradesh. Paddy is the main crop of the district in both Khariff and Rabi seasons. Paddy farming 61-62 percentage of the total area shown with an average yield of 2,855 Kgs/hectare in the district. The other predominant crops raised in this district are Banana, Sugarcane, Chillies, Coconut, maize, tobacco, Oil palm crop area also increasing day-by-day due to fulfilling the requirement of Oil production factory establishing at Pedavegi. The upland area of the district offers excellent scope for Horticulture Development.

Table 1
West Godavari District Profile at a Glance

Formation	1,925
Area (sq. kms)	7,742
Revenue Divisions	4
Municipalities	8
Mandals	46

Contd....

Villages	887
Population	37,96,144
Density	488
Literacy	73.95 %
Land under cultivation	12.98 lakh hectares
Land under irrigation	5.72 lakh hectares
Source of irrigation canals	63.80 %
Tanks	3.37 %
Tube wells	30.91 %
Other sources	1.92 %
Major crops	Paddy, Sugarcane, Tobacco, Maize, Mango, Banana, Coconut, etc.,

Source: DCCB, Eluru Report

Profile of DCC Bank, Eluru

The DCCB Ltd., Eluru of West Godavari district registered during the year 1918 and commenced its business operations to promote credit needs of agricultural sector and rural development. At present, the bank has 33 branches spread over throughout the district, catering nearly 45 per cent of the agricultural needs of the farming community. The bank provides short-term, medium-term and long-term loans and nearly 75 per cent of its financial assistance go in favour of small medium farmers and weaker sections. Of late, the bank has diversified its lending activities by facilitating gold loans, besides extending loans to small and tiny industry, transport vehicle and rice mills. The bank has been providing loans for rural housing and even participating in Chief Minister's Employment programme for Youth (CMEY).

The bank was recognized in the year 1987, on account of introducing single window credit delivery system in primary Agricultural Development societies.

History of the Bank

The District Cooperative Central Bank Ltd Eluru, was registered on 18-11-1918 and commenced its business from 30-11-1918. The bank was reorganized in the year 1987 on introduction of single window credit delivery system. 8 PADBs were merged with the DCCB. The area of operation of the Bank is confined to the entire West Godavari district with a network of 33 branches. 258 PACS are affiliated to the Bank with an average of 3 villages per PACS (state average 13).

Table 2

There are 667 Societies Affiliated to the Bank as Note Hereunder

Sl. No.	*Type of the Society*	*No.*
1.	Primary Agrl. Coop Credit Societies (includes 53 LSCS and 1 FSCS)	258
2.	Weavers societies	31
3.	Employees Coop. Credit Societies	155
4.	Cooperative Urban Banks	10
5.	Cooperative Consumer Stores	23
6.	Marketing Society	2
7.	Others	187
8.	Government	1
	Total	667

About 4.68 lakhs of people of the district i.e. 12.3 per cent of district population are availing the services of the bank and PACS. Presently, 667 cooperative societies are affiliated to the bank and out of these 667 societies as many as 258 societies are Primary Agricultural Cooperative Credit Societies.

Mobilization of Deposits

The deposits position of the bank is in good progress year to year. The deposits of the bank have been guaranteed by the deposit Insurance and Credit Guarantee Corporation and all deposits are uninsured. All the deposits are being utilized within the district, mainly towards Agricultural & Rural Development. The bank conducts deposits mobilization campaign every year in order to improve the bank's internal resources.

Table 3
The Performance for the Last 10 Years under Mobilization of Deposits is Furnished Hereunder

(Rs. Crores)

Sl.No.	Years	Amount Outstanding
1.	1996 - 1997	89.35
2.	1997 - 1998	92.08
3.	1998 - 1999	131.73
4.	1999 - 2000	172.62
5.	2000 - 2001	214.08
6.	2001 - 2002	217.67
7.	2002 - 2003	219.29
8.	2003 - 2004	240.69
9.	2004 - 2005	259.76
10.	2005 - 2006	270.16
11.	2006 - 2007	284.82

It is also to be mentioned that the DCCB, Eluru is only notified DCCB in the State by the Government of Andhra Pradesh of acceptance of Govt. Deposits vide GOMS No. 43/ Planning (XX55) Dept/.Govt AP, Hyderabad. Despite the Govt. declared as notified DCCB, we are striving hard to mobilize the Govt. deposits from various Govt. departments.

Table 4
Performance of the Deposits of the DCC Bank

Sl. No.	Particulars	2001-02	2002-03	2003-04	2004-05	2005-06	2006-07
1.	Deposits outstanding	21,767	21,928.59	24,068.59	25,976.12	27,016.00	3,482.09
2.	Of which Curren	1,156.29	755.77	1,370.49	3,503.56	3,295.34	3,493.45
	Savings	1,539.49	1,452.36	2,243.57	2,262.24	2,908.18	3,292.60
	Term	19,071.22	19,720.46	20,454.57	20,120.32	20,812.49	21,696.04
	Total	21,767	21,928.69	24,068.69	25,976.12	27,016.00	28,482.09
3.	Out of with						
	Individuals	11,971.71	12,568.71	13,726.78	13,312.43	13,631.76	13,842.51
	Institutions	581.95	901.69	849.08	1,030.40	1,064.81	1,529.49
	Societies	9,213.34	8,457.19	9,492.73	11,633.29	12,319.43	13,110.09
4.	Cost fo funds	7.32 %	6.30 %	5.21 %	5.48 %	4.11 %	4.82 %
5.	Per employee deposits	49.81	51.72	60.02	67.47	75.04	81.84
6.	Per branch deposit	659.61	664.50	729.35	787.16	818.67	863.09
7.	CD ratio of DCCB	203.57	210.38	179.00	173.23	189.37	193.30
8.	Capital adequacy ratio		17.42 %	18.50 %	23.97 %	21.36 %	

It is observed from the Table 5 that the term deposits play an important role. It is noted that per employee deposits increased from 49.81 in 2001-2002 to 81.84 in 2006-07 and also the per branch deposits increased from 659.61 to 863.09 during the period 2001-02, 2006-07 respectively.

Table 5
Proportion of Owner Funds, Deposits and other Borrowings to Total Working Capital

Year	*Owned Funds*	*Deposits*	*Borrowings*
1996 - 1997	30.19 (7.49)	89.35 (22.19)	283.28 (70.32)
1997 - 1998	35.03 (8.00)	92.08 (21.05)	310.46 (70.95)
1998 - 1999	41.23 (8.87)	131.73 (28.38)	291.35 (62.75)
1999 - 2000	48.21 (10.07)	172.62 (36.03)	258.23 (53.90)
2000 - 2001	60.34 (12.01)	214.08 (42.60)	228.13 (45.39)
2001 - 2002	67.72 (12.18)	217.67 (39.16)	270.42 (48.66)
2002 - 2003	81.14 (14.43)	219.29 (38.99)	261.94 (46.58)
2003 - 2004	91.94 (16.02)	240.69 (41.95)	241.10 (42.02)
2004 - 2005	107.60 (41.51)	259.76 (41.51)	258.44 (41.30)
2005 - 2006	119.46 (17.82)	270.16 (40.32)	280.44 (41.86)
2006 - 2007	131.53 (18.20)	284.82 (39.41)	306.32 (42.39)

Source: DCCB Annual Reports

It may be seen from the table that the central bank has made progress in building up owned funds and raising deposits. This is evident from the fact that the proportion of the deposits to working capital has increased from 22.19 per cent in 1996-07 to 39.41 per cent in 2006-07. The borrowings as a proportion to working capital has declined from 70.32 per cent in 1996-97 to 42.32 per cent in 2006-07.

Loans and Advances

The performance of the management of the bank in respect of important loaning operations is evaluated. The DCC bank is providing all types of credit needs of farmers in the form of Seasonal Agricultural Operations (SAO), medium-tem and long-term loans.

(i) *SAO Loans.* During the year 2006-07, the Bank has advanced an amount of Rs. 29391.00 lakhs for Khariff 2006 out of which 1400.00 lakhs to new members. An amount of Rs. 15697.36 lakhs was advanced for Rabi 2006-07, out of which Rs. 124.51 lakhs to new members. The bank has provided loans to the new CKCC holders to the tune of Rs. 15.25 crores during the year 2006-07.

(ii) *Long term loaning.* The bank is financing to minor irrigation, farm mechanization, horticulture, diversified loaning and social forestry purposes. During the year 2003-04, a target of Rs. 2500.00 lakhs was fixed to this Bank and an amount of Rs. 1244.16 lakhs was disbursed; during the year 2004-05, an amount of Rs. 4158.33 lakhs was advanced as against the target of Rs. 5000.00 lakhs. During the year 2005-06, the bank has advanced an amount of Rs. 3913.18 lakhs, as against the target of Rs. 4950 lakhs. In 2006-07 the Bank has advanced Rs. 3403.91 lakhs as against the target of Rs. 1552.81 lakhs.

(iii) *Weavers Finance.* 31 weavers societies are affiliated to the bank. During the year 2000-01, the NABARD has restricted the limit to Rs. 80.65 lakhs to 22 weavers societies. The outstanding as on date is Rs. 269.21 lakhs. During the year 2001-02 the NABARD has sanctioned credit limit to 17 weavers societies for Rs. 51.40 lakhs and Rs. 0.44 lakhs to one society in the year 2002-03. For the year 2004-05, credit limits were sanctioned by NABARD to 9 weavers societies to the tune of Rs. 20.88 lakhs. For the year 2006-07, an amount of Rs. 17.40 lakhs was sanctioned in respect of 10 societies by NABARD under revival packages. The bank has renewed an amount of Rs. 168.51 lakhs to 23 PWCS and Penal Interest and excess interest was waived to an extent of Rs. 60.67 lakhs and Rs. 140.58 lakhs was kept aside and to be recovered in 2 years.

(iv) *Employees Societies.* 155 employees societies are affiliated to the bank. At present, the bank is advancing loans to 130 societies and during 2003-04 advances made comes to Rs. 401.20 lakhs. An amount of Rs. 669.46

lakhs is outstanding as on 31-03-2005. During the year 2005-06, the bank has advanced an amount of Rs. 299.19 lakhs and outstanding stood at Rs. 662.08 lakhs. During the year 2006-07, the bank has advanced Rs. 633.71 lakhs and the outstanding stood at Rs. 922.36 lakhs, as at the end of the year i.e. 31-03-2007.

Table 6
Loans and Advances of the Bank in the Time Series From 1995-96 to 2006-07

(Rs. Crores)

Year	*Crop Loans*	*Long Term Loans*	*Other Loans*	*Total Loans*
1996 - 1997	189.99	124.37	56.62	370.98
1997 - 1998	130.12	145.59	129.57	405.28
1998 - 1999	131.22	146.94	132.17	410.33
1999 - 2000	144.71	143.45	115.39	403.55
2000 - 2001	172.33	130.67	92.96	395.96
2001 - 2002	187.69	127.26	128.17	443.12
2002 - 2003	203.79	122.40	135.16	461.35
2003 - 2004	204.79	117.42	109.51	431.72
2004 - 2005	231.12	137.66	81.20	449.98
2005 - 2006	293.28	155.17	63.18	511.63
006 - 2007	309.49	160.42	80.65	550.56

Source: DCCB Eluru, Annual Reports

Table 7
Loans Issued by the Central Bank

(Percentage Total Loans)

Year	*Crop Loans*	*Long Terms Loans*	*Other Loans*
1996 - 1997	51.22	33.52	15.26
1997 - 1998	32.11	35.92	31.97
1998 - 1999	31.98	35.81	32.21
1999 - 2000	35.86	35.55	28.59
2000 - 2001	43.52	33.00	23.48
2001 - 2002	42.36	28.72	28.92
2002 - 2003	44.17	26.53	29.30
2003 - 2004	47.44	27.19	25.37
2004 - 2005	51.36	30.59	18.05
2005 - 2006	56.21	29.14	14.65

Source: DCCB Eluru, Annual Reports

Table 6 depicts information about loans issued by the Central Bank. The major portion of the loans goes to crop loans 56.21 per cent, long term loans 29.14 and 14.65 per cent to other loans from the total loans in 2006-07. Thus, the bank is serving the agricultural sector through its lending operations. From the table 6 it is observed that the loans issued by the bank increased from Rs. 370.98 crores in 1996-97 to Rs. 550.56 crores by 2006-07.

Crop Loan Operations

Crop loans constitute the core of short-term credit provided to farmers through PACS. The crop loan system is aimed at rationalizing the loan policy of credit cooperatives. The features of crop loan system are:

(a) Loan amount is related to production and needs of the crop grown and the repaying capacity of the grower.

(b) Loan amount is disbursed partly in cash and partly in kind

(c) Seasonality is observed in lending and recovery of loans, and

(d) Credit is linked with marketing.

The crop loan operations considered for the purpose of evaluation of management performance are the fixation of scales of finance for crops.

Medium-Term Agricultural Loan Operations

The medium-term agricultural loans are issued for a period of 3 to 5 years for the identified productive purpose such as purchase of (a) miltch cattle, sheep goats, duck, poultry, (b) bullocks and bullock cars, and (c) pump sets and other agricultural implements, well- repairs, land improvements, etc. These loans are sanctioned on an individual basis, either on the security of land or on the personal security supported by at least one solvent member as surety. The credit limits for the above said purposes are fixed by the Technical group.

Long Term Loans

After implementation of single window service scheme (with effect from 1-4-1987) the provision of multi-term credit and multi-functional services to farmers at one contact point for their accelerated development. So the long term loans are disbursed through PACS by the Central bank.

The long term loans are issued for a period of 5 to 20 years for the identified productive purposes such as animal husbandry schemes like dairy development, sheep rearing and sheep breeding, poultry development, duck rearing, piggery and horticulture like lime, coconut, grapes, cashew, mango, guava, sapota, coffee and in-land fisheries, minor forest, produce and land development. The period of repayment is depending upon the nature of loan, which is ranged from 5 to 20 years.

OTHER TYPES OF ADVANCES

Gold Loans

To cater to the customers needs, the bank has enhanced the individual gold loans limit to a tune of Rs. 2.00 lakhs to each borrower. During the year 2004-05, the bank has advanced an amount of Rs. 626.22 lakhs and during 2005-06 bank has issued Rs. 1355.86 lakhs. The rate of interested charged on gold loans is considerably reduced to 10 % w.e.f. 10-02-2007, not only to agriculturists but also to all other customers. During the year 2006-07, the Bank has advanced an amount of Rs. 2798.10 lakhs and the outstanding stood at Rs. 1717.11 lakhs, as at the end of year 31-3-2007.

Non-farm sector loans:

(i) The bank is advancing non-farm sector loans to small, tiny industries, transport vehicles, paddy harvesters, rice mills, etc under non-farm sector. During the year 2005-06, Rs. 19.86 lakhs were advanced and the outstanding stood at Rs. 41.30 lakhs. During 2006-07, the Bank has advanced Rs. 37.39 lakhs and outstanding stood at Rs. 56.18 lakhs.

(ii) VIDYA NIDHI - Educational loans scheme: Recently a new scheme for extending financial assistance to the students for higher studies is introduced with Rs. 5.00 lakh for the studies within the country and Rs. 10.00 lakhs for education abroad.

(iii) Two & Four wheeler loans: Recently a new scheme for extending financial assistance for purchase of two wheeler was introduced with a unit cost of Rs. 0.40 lakhs for the benefit of salaried employees of government and private sector employees.

Rural Housing Scheme

The bank has launched a special drive for rural housing loans, covering all the areas in the district. During 2005-06, the bank has advanced Rs. 7.82 lakhs and the outstanding stood at Rs. 82.61 lakhs. During the year 2006-07, the bank has advanced an amount of Rs. 40.80 lakhs and the outstanding stood at Rs. 101.13 lakhs as at the end of year i.e. 31-03-2007.

House Mortgage Loans

During the year 1998-99 the bank has diversified its lending activities and started issuing loans under this scheme. The scheme is very encouraging to both the bank and borrowers. The bank has issued house mortgage loans and the outstanding amount is Rs. 354.49 lakhs as on 31-03-2005. During the year 2005-06, the bank has advanced an amount of Rs. 232.28 lakhs. During the year 2006-07, the bank has advanced an amount of Rs. 363.93 lakhs and the outstanding stood at Rs. 619.62 lakhs as at the end of year i.e. 31-03-2007.

Another aspect examined in evaluating the operational performance of the management of the bank is the performance in achieving the targets set by the Registrar for the issue of loans. These targets are considered as the operational goals set for the bank for whose achievements it is exhorted to strive. The performance of the bank in achieving the targets is relatively better in respect of STSAO loans, more so of kharif season.

Recovery Performance of Loans

Recovery performance of the bank for the last many years is very good due to the best cooperation of farming community.

Table 7
The Integrated Recovery Performance (Ended with June) for the Past Years

(Rs. Lakhs)

Year	*Demand*	*Collection*	*Balance*	*Percentage*
1995 - 1996	14890.60	13724.53	1666.07	92.16 %
1996 - 1997	22710.06	21767.96	942.10	95.85 %
1997 - 1998	22811.17	20705.68	2105.49	90.77 %
1998 - 1999	26182.05	23059.23	3122.82	88.07 %
1999 - 2000	26899.55	24608.14	2291.31	91.48 %
2000 - 2001	24610.65	21963.18	2647.47	89.24 %
2001 - 2002	26860.29	24470.47	2389.82	91.10 %
2002 - 2003	25626.87	19814.83	5812.04	77.32 %
2003 - 2004	28494.46	22397.49	6096.97	78.60 %
2004 - 2005	27452.60	23896.97	3555.63	87.05 %
2005 - 2006	30495.31	28064.01	2431.30	92.03 %

Source: DCCB Eluru, Annual Reports

The bank has recorded good recovery performance during the period under study in 1996-97 it was recorded the highest percentage i.e. 95.85 % and in 2005-06 recorded 92.03 per cent. The bank has made recovery arrangements as per the guidelines and calendar activities prepared by APCOB. For this purpose, the bank has allotted all the 33 branches among the nodal officers of the bank duly dividing into nine zones for recovery and monitoring at frequent intervals at branches and PACS levels also.

The bank is moving forward with the following mission. To cater to the agricultural and non-agricultural credit needs of the farmers of the district for sustainable development of rural economy and also to render banking services to the rural as well as urban community and to develop the cooperative sector in the district.

The bank has diversified its activities. The progress and development of the bank can be seen from its banking activities. The special features of the DCC Bank, Eluru are highlighted with the following:

(i) the only DCCB notified by the government of Andhra Pradesh acceptance of government deposits,

(ii) earning profits since 1918 (inception year),

(iii) declaring dividends from its inception,

(iv) A class audit classification since 1975 (28 years continuously),

(v) ranked no. 1 in recovery performance almost every year,

(vi) NABARD best performance award winner for three consecutive years. 1999-2000, 2000-01, 2003-04 and

(vii) first bank in the state to announce 0.50% additional interest on the deposits of women.

The DCCB is motivated by the spirit of service. In the changing economic scenario (LPG) the bank is withstanding by earning profits (in the year 2006-07 earned Rs. 6.86 crores profit) by effective and efficient managerial practices.

The bank is moving forward with the following Mission. To cater to the agricultural and non-agricultural credit needs of the farmers of the district for sustainable development of rural economy and also to render banking services to the rural as well as urban community and to develop the cooperative sector in the district.

2

SOCIAL MOBILIZATION, EMPOWERMENT AND POVERTY REDUCTION

The Case of Rural Andhra Pradesh

PROF. R. RAMAKRISHNA
JAYASHEELA PRAKASH
TATA RAO

INTRODUCTION

Poverty reduction has been a major goal of development policy in India since Independence and achievement of minimum standard of living for all within a reasonable period has been the objective of efforts initiated under the five year plans. Poverty being an outcome of multiple deprivations, empowerment of the poor is considered a critical factor in accelerating poverty reduction. Empowerment is sought to be achieved by giving a role to the poor in governance and development decisions. Economic growth and improvement in real wages, particularly with growth in agriculture which supports considerable part of the population, have impacted upon the proportion of persons in poverty. It is not income growth alone that has brought about poverty reduction through the trickle-down process. There have been direct interventions too for poverty alleviation in India. Employment creation through investment in infrastructure development and pension schemes for the elderly are the recent initiatives. There has also been some shift in the strategy from individual approach to community-based approach and to social mobilization, because improving the livelihood of the poor is gaining some momentum. Social mobilization envisages education and organization of the poor, for improved socio-economic status through collective efforts.

Karmakar K.G. (1998), Puhazhendi V and K.J.S Satyasai (2000), Pallavi Chavan and Ramakumar R (2002), Ramakrishna. R, (2001, 2003, 2004, 2005) and Susil Sirivardana (2001) in their studies have systematically analysed empowerment of weaker sections. The present study endeavors to examine the incidence of poverty among sample households. An attempt is also made in the study to outline the concept, strategy and process of social mobilization and empowerment aimed at sustainable poverty alleviation.

Objectives of the Study

1. To examine the effect of micro credit on employment, income and intensity of poverty among sample households.
2. To analyse the impact of micro credit on social - economic and nutritional empowerment of sample households.

Methodology

Multistage sampling technique is used in the selection of units in the study area. Accordingly, at the first stage, Visakhapatnam district one of the backward districts in the north coastal Andhra Pradesh is selected purposively. In the second stage of sampling, out of the 42 mandals, Anakapalli mandalam was selected for the study. Selection of the mandal was done keeping in the view that it should satisfy the two criteria viz, a) cover the maximum number of poor households and b) cover the maximum coverage of SHG households. The third stage of sampling covered the selection of villages. The fourth stage of sampling involved the selection of households. In all, 300 households were selected for the study by using random sampling technique. While 200 of these households are the members of SHGs, the remaining 100 are out of the converge of Self Help Groups (NSHG). These two groups of sample households has been chosen keeping in view the probability proportion to their actual number in the total number of poor households in the study area. A survey is conducted during the period from 1st May 2007 to 30th June 2007.

Socio-economic Profile of the Respondents

The socio-economic profile of the sample households shows that a majority of the heads of households of the SHG households are in the age group 25-35. For a majority of the SHG households the family size is four and below. In the literacy levels of the heads of the households, the SHG households have more literates than the NSHG households. The percentage of earners to the total family members in the SHG households is higher than that in the NSHG households and the dependency ratio is lower in the SHG households than in the NSHG households. These differences may be due to empowerment of the poor through SHG - Bank linkage programme (see tables 1-4).

Employment, Income and Poverty among Rural Poor

The proportion of persons employed in the Usual Principal Status Concept (UPS) and Usual Principal Subsidiary Status (UPSS) is higher among the SHG households than the NSHG households indicating the positive effect on employment pattern of the micro credit. Apart from the magnitude of employment, the analysis on the occupational pattern of the workers showed that, in the SHG households the majority of the workers are depending on cultivation and on other self-employment activities like live-stock and trade and commerce followed by casual labour. Whereas in the NSHG households majority of the workers are depending on causal labour (agricultural and non-agricultural), followed by cultivation etc. This implies that there is an occupational shift towards non-farm or off-farm activities through micro credit. The estimates of proportion of usually unemployed as per UPSS approach for SHG and NSHG households indicate that due to micro credit the unemployment among the rural poor could be reduced (See tables 5-8).

The distribution of households according to income range showed that around 25 per cent of the SHG households are in the income group of more than Rs. 20,000/- per year as against only less than 10 per cent in case of the NSHG households. It clearly indicated that there are income variations between these two categories of households and can be inferred that the SHG households are in a better position due to availability of micro credit facility. The analysis of the source-wise income distribution showed that in the SHG households, the major source of income is from other sources, which includes, trade and commerce, professions, household industry etc., whereas in the NSHG households they mostly depend on wage income. It can be concluded that due to micro credit, the increased employment opportunities in trade and commerce resulted in the increase of income levels. The above conclusion can be substantiated by a comparative analysis of the source-wise distribution of per capita income. The significance of the increase in levels of income due to micro credit is examined with the help of Z-test. The results showed that the differences in household income and per capita income between the SHG and the NSHG households are statistically significant. The household income as well as per capita income of the SHG households is higher than that of the NSHG households. It can be inferred from the above analysis that households which participated in groups are able to make significant improvements in their incomes compared to the households that do not have the group help (See tables 9 & 10).

With regard to the poverty, there are several studies conducted by individual researchers, which tried to estimate poverty by using different methods. The planning Commission takes into consideration the monthly per capita expenditure norm to estimate the poverty. Having wide methodological differences in the methodology used for fixing the norm to identify the poverty line, all the estimates showed that the incidence of poverty is on a decline in India. In this study also monthly per capita expenditure as a measure of standard of living is used for the analysis of poverty. The official poverty line is adjusted to the year 2000-2001 by using the Consumer Price Index for Rural Labourers. Accordingly the estimated poverty line of Rs. 264.36/- is taken for the rural areas in this study. The three measures of Poverty Head Count Ratio, Poverty Gap Ratio and Modified Sen's Index of poverty were used to estimate poverty for the two groups of households.

Head Count Ratio

For the SHGs as a whole, about 41.5 per cent of total households are found to be below the poverty line, while this picture is accounted for by 67 per cent in case of the NSHG. Based on the above facts, it can be concluded that the incidence of poverty among the NSHG households is comparatively higher than the SHG households (see table-11).

The Poverty Gap Ratio

From the table-11, the estimates of Sen's poverty gap ratio clearly indicate the poverty, as a fraction of total expenditure needed to support every one in the population at the poverty line. Thus, the larger the estimate, the larger is the requirement of resources to guarantee the entire population an expenditure equivalent to the poverty line. Moreover, its smaller empirical results, when analyzed, helped us in deriving the following inferences. The results of this poverty measure shows that, the poverty gap ratio was found to be higher in the NSHG households.

Modified Sen's Index of Poverty

As said earlier, Sen's modified poverty measure overcomes the limitation of his earlier measure, viz., poverty gap ratio. The later measure suffers from the limitation of being insensitive redistribution of income among poor. The modified Sen's Index of Poverty overcomes this drawback modified measure of poverty lie between zero and unity. It assumes zero value when every one's income is above the poverty line and becomes unity when everyone has zero income. Thereby we may infer that the lower the value of this measure, the closer is the distribution of the poor to the poverty line and vice versa. The measure of Sen's Index of Poverty assumed value close to 0 in both the SHG and the NSHG groups (0.0044 for the SHG and 0.0118 for the NSHG) (see table-11) .This indicates that the distribution of the poor is closer to the poverty line.

The empirical results show that the incidence of poverty is less in the SHG households compared to NSHG households. A lower Poverty Gap Ratio was found in the SHG households compared to the NSHG households. The Modified Sen's Index of poverty indicated that the distribution of the poor is closer to the poverty line in both the groups of households. To sum up, according to all the three measures of poverty, SHG households are in a better position than the NSHG households.

Socio-economic and Nutritional Empowerment of the Respondents

Social mobilization envisages education and organization of the poor for improved socio-economic status through collective efforts. In this dynamic process, the poor will be empowered enough to come out of the dependency syndrome as well as poverty. As a means of empowerment, the Social Mobilization (SM) process involves continuous awareness campaigns among the poor by facilitators/social animators so that the poor can participate in the development process and thereby access the basic amenities and resources for socio-economic betterment. Empowerment is a complex process by which the marginalized become aware of the power dynamics at work in the life context and develop skills and capacity for gaining some control over their lives without infringing upon the rights of others (Rowlands, 1997).

Strategies to Social Mobilization

The strategies to SM, range from 'Welfarist' to 'Development' to 'Empowerment'. A few development interventions emphasized on the 'access' dimension and creation of more opportunities to land, credit, education, and health services. Also, some institutional reforms like land reforms and reservations in government jobs and local self-governments for the socially disadvantaged have been introduced for facilitating active participation of the poor in key decisions and exercise of greater control over resources. However, a gradual shift in government strategies is evident from its changed stance and role that is, from 'provider of services' to 'facilitator of processes' initiated by the poor to break the vicious circle of poverty and dependency. Economic interventions, viz., employment as a means for enhancing people's capacity to participate and credit support have been the entry points largely opted by NGOs and GOs for social mobilization and poverty reduction during the 1980s and 1990s in India. 'Entrepreneurship development' and 'linking SHGs to financial institutions' have been the two most crucial events in their development strategy for sustainable poverty reduction.

Process of Social mobilization and Empowerment

Strengthening of people's institutions like the Panchayat Raj Institutions (PRIs) Village Organizations (VOs) and Community Based Organisations (CBOs); enhancing the quality of governance through decentralization of development process, and earmarking larger allocations for social development have been the key elements of the strategy for achieving the Plan objective of growth with social justice. These institutions are expected to improve the quality of delivery of development goods and in the process make governments more responsive and responsible.

The Ninth Five Year Plan has made a qualitative shift in its approach from 'welfare' to 'empowerment' for ensuring the well-being of the disadvantaged. Economic independence and self-reliance through employment and income generating activities and group action have been the main planks. Therefore, it can be inferred that the ingredients essential for the social mobilization process for empowerment and poverty reduction, viz., creation of an enabling environment, building up the capacities of facilitating agencies, creation of opportunities for social and economic development and social protection measures, are well articulated in the Plan documents.

SOCIAL EMPOWERMENT

Education

Women's education is the most important indicator for social empowerment. Women need education in order to improve their knowledge in various fields such as political, economic, social and others. If a woman is educated in the family, then she will be able to play a successful role in her family. Above all, education is the means, which would improve the status and position of women in general. The details of households regarding female literacy is presented in the tables 12 A, B & C. The data presented in the Table-12A revealed that majority (66 per cent) of the households are literates in SHG than in N-SHG households. It was observed that almost half of the women are illiterates in N-SHG households (47 per cent) may be due to lack of empowerment. The Table-12B shows that majority (55 per cent) of the SHG households are in the literacy level of 6th to 10th standard than in N-SHG. (50 per cent). The Table-12C shows that almost all the female members in N-SHG group are studying in government schools. Whereas in SHG group around 15 per cent of the members are studying in private schools.

ECONOMIC EMPOWERMENT

Savings

Savings supplements family income and improve their standard of living. The distributions of households by monthly savings are presented in Table-13. The data shows that majority (85 per cent) of households are in the monthly savings range of Rs. 50-100 in SHG households. However, no single household was reported savings in N-SHG households. The distribution of households by utilization of additional income generated in their family is presented in Table-14. It shows that majority of households (33 per cent) used their income for better health care and education for their children, followed by 20 per cent towards loan repayment and 17 per cent for social functions.

Decision-making

Our main concerns are to examine women's empowerment and to identity the factors associated with variation in the indicators of women's empowerment in the household. Under what conditions do women feel more empowered and under what conditions do women feel less empowered? It is examined and presented in the Table-15. The results shows that wife appears to be the most important decision-maker in SHG and husband in N-SHG with regard to their children's schooling and other issues also.

NUTRITIONAL EMPOWERMENT

Health Status

The national statistics on Health shows that majority of family members suffer from malnutrition resulting in health problems. The Table-16 shows the health problems of family members in the study area. More than 50 per cent of the family members suffer from health problems in NSHG households. Whereas in the case of SHG, only 33 per cent of the members suffering with health problems. Among the health problems, the family members reporting improper eyesight are high (14 per cent) followed by 'Fatigue', 'growth failure' and 'oedema' in both the households.

Nutritional Status

Among the various indicators, nutritional status of family members acquires greater importance. The Table-17A shows that the children suffering with nutritional deficiency is more in NSHG households (60 per cent) than in SHG (53 per cent). And the data from table 17B shows that the adults suffering with nutritional deficiency is relatively more in NSHG households (55 per cent) than in SHG (43 per cent).

Member's Views on Social, Economic and Nutritional Empowerment

It is observed from the Table-18 that as compared to NSHG households, those covered under SHG fared better in respect of socio-economic empowerment and nutritional development. If the SHGs are allowed to develop links with bank branches; the access to credit for the poor would improve.

Summary and Recommendations

Our study has clearly brought to the fore that the SHG experiment has increased, to some extent, their employment pattern, income levels and borrowing performance towards formal sources of credit. Further, the SHG experiment has reduced the intensity of poverty among sample households. It is further observed that as compared to N-SHG households, those who covered under SHG fared better in respect of socio-economic empowerment and nutritional development.

The growth of SHGs in the country demonstrates the willingness of the poor to pay for the credit and other financial services rendered by NGO's and credit institutions without depending on any kind of subsidy from the Government agency. In a market-oriented economy, this is a healthy attitude. There is an apprehension that the launching of various Government programmes, under which the SHGs are to be promoted as well as subsidized by DRDA, may hamper the development of micro-credit system as it promotes a subsidy culture, which goes against the philosophy of micro-credit. This aspect needs to be examined in the light of the feed back obtained and if warranted the modalities may have to be refined as to provide a conducive environment for the growth of micro-credit system in India.

The future policy concerns therefore, should revolve around the issues such as human poverty including nutritional and social deprivations and human rights. So we need to strengthen the existing institutions, even while striving to build newer institutions, especially that of the poor. This institutional network can help in protecting the poor from market and non market risks. Since constitutional sanction was accorded to Panchayat Raj Institutions (PRIs) as decentralized democratic local governance institutions, building the capacities of PRIs and the civil society organizations assumes critical significance (R. Radhakrishna and Shovan Ray, 2005).

Table 1
Distribution of Heads of Households by Age Composition

Groups of Households	Age Composition (Years)					
	Below 25	25-35	35-45	45-55	Above 55	Total
SHG	11 (5.50)	71 (35.50)	62 (31.00)	38 (19.00)	18 (9.00)	200 (100.00)
NSHG	2 (2.00)	28 (28.00)	39 (39.00)	22 (22.00)	9 (9.00)	100 (100.00)

Table 2
Distribution of Households by Size of the Family

Groups of Households	Family Size			
	4 and below	5 & 6	7 & above	Total
SHG	23 (61.50)	63 (34.50)	14 (7.00)	200 (100.00)
NSHG	52 (52.00)	40 (40.00)	8 (8.00)	100 (100.00)

Table 3
Distribution of Heads of Households by Literacy Level

Groups of Households	Literacy Level				
	Illiterates	Primary	Secondary	Higher	Total
SHG	91 (45.50)	37 (18.50)	57 (28.50)	15 (7.50)	200 (100.00)
NSHG	49 (49.00)	27 (27.00)	21 (21.00)	3 (3.00)	100 (100.00)

Table 4

Distribution of the Family Members by Earning Status

Groups of Households	*Earners*				*Non-Earners*					
	Male	*Female*	*Children*	*Total*	*Male*	*Female*	*Children*	*Total*	*Total*	*Dependency Ratio*
SHG	250 (28.28)	154 (17.42)	7 (0.79)	411 (46.49)	129 (14.59)	100 (11.31)	244 (27.60)	473 (53.51)	884 (100.00)	1.15
NSHG	129 (28.73)	64 (14.25)	5 (1.11)	198 (44.10)	91 (20.27)	58 (12.92)	102 (22.72)	251 (55.90)	449 (100.00)	1.27

Table 5
Worker - Population Ratio (Usual Status)

Groups of Households	*No. of Persons*	*No. of Persons Employed for Greater Part of the Year*	*No. of Persons Employed Per 1000 Persons*
SHG	884	142	160
NSHG	449	67	149

Table 6
Worker - Population Ratio (Usual Principal Status)

Groups of Households	*No. of Persons*	*No. of Persons Employed for Greater Part of the Year*	*No. of Persons Employed Per 1000 Persons*
SHG	884	381	431
NSHG	449	166	370

Table 7
Occupational Distribution of Workers among Groups
(as % of Total Workers)

Sl. No	*Occupation*	*SHG*		*NSHG*	
		Main	*Secondary*	*Main*	*Secondary*
1.	Cultivation	35.77	0.73	27.78	-
2.	Agricultural Labour	24.57	21.65	42.42	14.65
3.	Non-agricultural Labour	10.22	5.35	10.10	3.03
4.	Live Stock	7.54	14.60	1.01	11.62
5.	Trade and Commerce	9.25	2.92	6.57	0.51
6.	Profession	8.27	-	8.59	-
7.	Household Industry	0.73	-	2.02	-
8.	Industry	0.49		0.51	
9.	Salaried People	3.16	-	1.01	-
10.	Nil	-	54.74	-	69.70
11.	Total	100.00	100.00	100.00	100.00

Note: In SHG total workers are 411 & in NSHG total workers are 198.

Table 8
No. of Persons Unemployed Per 1000 Persons (UPSS)

Groups of Households	*No. of Persons*	*No. of Persons Unemployed for Greater Part of the Year*	*No. of Persons Unemployed Per 1000 Persons*
SHG	884	30	34
NSHG	449	32	71

Table 9
Distribution of the Sample Households by Annual Household Income Groups

Type of Household	*Below <10000*	*10000-20000*	*20000-30000*	*30000 Above*	*Total*
SHG	52 (26.00)	95 (47.50)	41 (20.50)	12 (6.00)	200 (100.00)
NSHG	46 (46.00)	43 (43.00)	10 (10.00)	1 (1.00)	100 (100.00)

Table 10
Average Per Capita Income by Source

	Wage Income					
Type of Household	*Agri-cultural*	*Non-Agri-cultural*	*Culti-vation*	*Live Stock*	*Other Income*	*Total*
SHG	879.04	525.89	317.76	498.35	1729.09	3950.13
NSHG	1154.97	516.35	303.15	229.74	662.65	2866.77

Table 11
Group-wise Estimates of Three Poverty Measures

Groups of Households	*Head Count Ratio*	*Poverty Gap Ratio*	*Modified Sen's Index of Poverty*
SHG	41.5	11.80	0.0044
NSHG	67	15.72	0.0118

Note: Head Count Ratio and Poverty Gap Ratio are expressed as percentages

Table 12A
Female Literates in the Households

Literacy Status	*SHG*	*N-SHG*
Illiterates	127 (33.69)	82 (47.13)
Literates	250 (66.31)	92 (52.87)
Total	377 (100.0)	174 (100.0)

Note: Figures in brackets are percentages

Table 12B
Female Literacy Level

Literacy Status	*SHG*	*N-SHG*
Upto 5	82 (32.4)	35 (38.04)
6-10	139 (55.6)	46 (50.00)
11 and above	29 (11.6)	11 (11.95)
Total	250 (100.0)	92 (100.0)

Note: Figures in brackets are percentages

Table 12C
Place of Schooling Among Females

Place of School	*SHG*				*N-SHG*			
	Upto 5	*6-10*	*11 and above*	*All*	*Upto 5*	*6-10*	*11 and above*	*All*
Balwadi	1 (1.21)			1 1	-	-	-	-
Government School	66 (80.49)	123 (88.48)	22 (75.86)	211	33 (94.28)	43 (93.47)	11 (100.0)	87
Private School	15 (18.29)	16 (11.51)	7 (24.13)	38	2 (5.71)	3 (6.52)	-	5
Total	82 (100.0)	139 (100.0)	29 (100.0)	250	35 (100.0)	46 (100.0)	11 (100.0)	92

Note: Figures in brackets are percentages

Table 13
Distribution of Households by Monthly Savings

Monthly Savings (In Rupees)	*SHG*	*N- SHG*
Nill	-	100 (100.0)
Less than 50	10 (5.0)	-
50 - 100	170 (85.0)	-
100 - 150	20 (10.0)	-
150 & above	-	-
Total	200 (100.0)	100 (100.0)

Figures in brackets are percentages

Table 14
Distribution of the Households by Utilization of Additional Income Generated

Items	*SHG*
Nutritious food for the family	6.8
Purchase of household durables	4.0
Towards loan repayment	20.0
Minor repairs to house	4.4
Better health care	18.0
Better clothing	4.0
Better education for the children	15.2
Social functions	17.2
Purchase of household durables + purchase of house site	10.4
Total	100

Table 15
Who makes Decisions in the Households

Decision Making	*SHG*				*N-SHG*			
	Wife	*Hus-band*	*Both*	*Elderly people*	*Wife*	*Hus-band*	*Both*	*Elderly people*
Whether the boy should go to school	121 (60.5)	25 (12.5)	13 (6.5)	41 (20.5)	47 (47.0)	51 (51.0)	-	2 (2.0)
Whether the girl should go to school	89 (44.5)	59 (29.5)	15 (7.5)	37 (18.5)	19 (19.0)	34 (34.0)	9 (9.0)	38 (38.0)
Whether the female member should work	73 (36.5)	69 (34.5)	37 (18.5)	21 (10.5)	15 (15.0)	39 (39.0)	5 (5.0)	41 (41.0)
Regarding Loans	36 (18.0)	51 (25.5)	96 (48.4)	17 (8.5)	10 (10.0)	44 (44.0)	34 (34.0)	12 (12.0)
Regarding Purchase of Household items	60 (30.0)	27 (13.5)	98 (49.0)	15 (7.5)	32 (32.0)	39 (39.0)	29 (29.0)	- -

Figures in brackets are percentages

Table 16
Distribution of the Family Members Suffering with Health Problems

Nature of Health Problem	*SHG*	*N-SHG*
Oedema	40 (4.52)	39 (8.68)
Growth failure	25 (2.82)	38 (8.46)
Fatigue	110 (12.44)	85 (18.93)
Improper eye sight	118 (13.34)	64 (14.25)
Nil	591 (66.85)	223 (49.66)
Total	884	449

Figures in brackets are percentages

Table17A

Distribution of the Children Suffering with Nutritional Deficiency

Nutritional deficiency	*SHG*	*N-SHG*
Anemia	61 (24.30)	23 (21.49)
B-complex deficiency	36 (14.34)	19 (17.75)
Vitamin-A deficiency	35 (13.94)	22 (20.56)
Nil	103 (41.03)	43 (40.18)
Total	251	107

Figures in brackets are percentages

Table 17B

Distribution of the Adults Suffering with Nutritional Deficiency

Nutritional deficiency	*SHG*	*N-SHG*
Anemia	95 (15.08)	59 (17.25)
B-complex deficiency	90 (14.17)	52 (15.20)
Vitamin-A deficiency	87 (13.72)	74 (21.63)
Nil	361 (57.01)	157 (45.90)
Total	633	342

Figures in brackets are percentages

Table 18

Distribution of Member's Views Regarding Impact of Involvement of Social Empowerment and Economic Development

(In Percentages)

Items	*SHG*	*N-SHG*
Adoption of small family norm	84.0	64.0
Access to information about Government programmes	86.8	48.8
Improvement in children's education	94.8	62.4
Education of girl child improved	72.8	53.6

Contd....

Items	*SHG*	*N-SHG*
Improvement in sanitation	76.4	52.0
Discontinuation of child labour employment	63.2	29.6
Access to markets	87.2	40.0
Increase in bargaining power	84.8	38.4
Increase in self confidence	65.2	28.8
Increase in self employment potential	78.0	37.6
Increase in marketing & communication skills	80.4	36.0
Improvement in decision making	86.8	72.8
Early marriage discontinued	84.4	60.8
Nutritional status improved	84.0	64.0
Able to sign	85.2	36.8
Banking habits improved	85.2	38.4
Improvement in credit worthiness	69.2	26.4
Better productive skills	82.0	53.6
Mobility	74.8	51.2
Better awareness of health	84.0	73.6

Note: SHG households-200; N-SHG households-100

References

Karmakar K.G. (1998), "Rural Credit and Self-Help Groups: Micro Finance Needs and Concepts in India", Sage Publications, New Delhi.

Pallavi Chavan and R Ramakumar (2002), "Micro Credit and Rural Poverty-An Analysis of Empirical Evidence", Economic and Political Weekly, March 9.

Puhazhendi V. and K.J.S. Satyasai (2000), "Micro Credit for the Rural People: An Impact Evaluation", Study Report, National Bank for Agriculture and Rural Development, Mumbai.

Radhakrishna and Shovan Roy (2005), "Handbook of Poverty in India-Perspectives Policies and Programmes" Oxford University Press.

Ramakrishna. R. (2001), "Credit needs of the rural poor and the role of SHGs", Indian Journal of Agricultural Economics, No. July-Sept. Vol. 56 (3).

Ramakrishna R. (2003), "Micro credit for rural poor through SHGs", Co-operative Perspective, Journal of Co-operative Management, Vol. 38(3), Oct-Dec.

Ramakrishna R. (2004), "Empowering rural women trough Self Help Groups", Indira Devi. M.(Ed), Strategies for Sustainability of Self Help Groups, Visakhapatnam: A.U. Press and Publications, P. 163-170.

Ramakrishna R. (2004), "Developing Grass Root Organisations for Sustainability of Self-Help Groups" Indira Devi. M.(Ed), Strategies for Sustainability of Self Help Groups, Visakhapatnam: A.U. Press and Publications, pp. 71-76.

Ramakrishna R. (2005), "Empowerment of Women through Sustainability of Micro Finance", Co-operative Perspective, Journal of Co-operative Management, Vol. 39 (4), Jan-March. pp. 1-8.

Rowlands J. (1997), "Questioning Empowerment: Working with Women in Honduras", Oxford, UK.

Susil, Sirivardana (2001), "The core Methodology of Social Mobilisation in Women's Empowerment as a Transformative strategy for Poverty Eradication", SAPNA Regional Centre, New Delhi.

3

Minor Irrigation Projects and Their Impact on Agriculture Land of Anantapur District, Andhra Pradesh

Prof. M. Sambasivarao
Dr. G. Venkataramana
Mr. A. Madhavasekhar

Introduction

Minor irrigation Projects serve objects of effective storage, utilization and conservation of water resources in dry areas like Anantapur district. They are mainly intended for stabilization, improvement and expansion of irrigation water of dry lands in chronic drought prone areas. They are of significant important for storage of, little rain water precipitated in dry land areas, soil moisture conservation and stabilization of food and non food crops. By and large the important sources of minor irrigation are ponds, tanks, canals, surface wells, dug wells and deep bore wells.

Study Area

Anantapur district covers an area of about 19,125 km^2 and is geographically located in Southwestern part of Andhra

Pradesh in between 130.40[1] and 150.15[1] North latitudes and 76° 50[1] and 78° 30[1] East longitudes. Topographically the district is divided into three major regions namely the Northern and North Western rolling plains consisting of black soil plains with altitudinal variations of 150 to 300 meters above MSL, the central undulating plains with peoriments and Pedi plains consisting of poor red sandy soils with altitudinal variations of 300 to 600 meters above MSL and Southern and Southeastern uplands with altitudinal variation of 600 to 900 meters above MSL. The total population of the district is 36, 40,478 (2001 census). The district is divided as three major revenue divisions, 63 mandals and 964 villages. The district receives an average annual rainfall of about 558 mm.

Objectives

The main objectives of the study are

1. To map the ponds and tanks distributed in the district using survey of Sandi topographic sheets and IRS (IB) Geocoded data on scale 1:50,000.
2. To study the distributions of well irrigation in the district.
3. To study the cropping pattern and ground water conditions prevailed under minor irrigation projects.
4. To analyze the soil samples under the minor irrigation projects ayacut areas.
5. To assess the impact of minor irrigation projects on agricultural lands of the Anantapur district.

Methodology

The survey of pride topographic sheets (1:50,000) IRS (IB) Geocoded data on scale 1:50,000 have been used base maps to prepare the ponds and tanks distribution in the Anantapur district. The data on minor irrigation projects has been collected from irrigation Department, Anantapur district and the extent of ayacut area under each tank has been mapped using IRS-IB data. The cropping pattern data collected under each minor irrigation has been used to analyse the crop diversification and cropping interest. The ground water levels collected over a period of ten years under each minor irrigation tank are analyzed to study the ground water level variations, fluctuations, and recharge into the subsurface zones. The soil samples collected from the selected ayacut areas are used to study the extent of alkalinity and salinity. Finally the impact assessment studies are carried out for selected ayacut areas of the tanks to throw light on the significance and role of minor irrigation on agricultural land and a few suggestions are made for optimum utilization and conservation of minor irrigation tanks and ayacut areas.

Physical Characteristics of Anantapur District

Physiographical the Anantapur district is divided into three major zones namely hilly terrain, modulating terrain and rolling plains. The altitude and slope varies from one zone to the other and are disturbed in the study area. Geologically the district is composed of two import geological zones namely Achaeans consisting of granites terrain and Proterozac formations. The major part of the district is composed of unclassified granites gneisses with schistose formations. The Northeastern part of the district is comprised of protrusion formations. Recent aluminum is found along major river valleys. The major river flowing through the district is Pennar. The Hagari or Vedavathi River flows in North-south diversion in Northwestern part of the district. The Chitravathi and Papagni are the tributaries of Pennar River. The Anantapur district rivers an average annual rainfall of about 558 mm. The monthly analysis of rainfall is less than 10 mm in January, February, March and December months. It varies from 10 mm to 50 mm in April, May, June, July and November months and 50 mm to 100 mm in August and October months. The average monthly rainfall exceeds 100mm in October month. The rainfall intensity is low in January, February, March and December months, moderate in April, May, June, July and November months, high in August and October months and very high in September months. The rainfall variability is low in August, September and October months. Rainfall ratios are high in January, February, March, April, November and December months. The rainfall ratio is low in September and in other months it is moderate to high. The average annual surface non-off of the district is 83.49 mm and accounts to 14.94% of the annual is 69.85 mm and amounts to 12.50% of the annual rainfall of the district.

Tank Irrigation in the Anatapur District

There are about 1,482 tanks well distributed in the district. The concentration of tank irrigation is very high in the Southern part of Upper Pennar Basin. Out of total 1,482 tanks 1,071 are under the control of Panchayaraj with an ayacut area of about 21,919 hectares. There are 411 tanks under the control of Irrigation Department with an ayacut area of about 47,601 hectares. The total ayacut area under the 1,482 tanks is 69,520 hectares of land.

The analysis of spatial distribution of tanks reveals that the maximum number of 82 tanks is found in Gorantla mandal and the minimum number of 02 tanks is found in D.Hirehal mandal. There is no tank in Vidapankal mandal. The numbers of tanks are more than 50 in five mandals, 40 to 50 tanks in six mandals, 30 to 40 tanks in six mandals, 20 to 30 tanks in ten mandals, 10 to 20 tanks in twenty two mandals and less than 10 tanks in four mandals.

Well Irrigation in Anantapur District

There are about 60,811 wells and 13,480 bore wells in the Anantapur district. About 55,177 electric and oil motor pump sets are used for extraction of ground water from 60,811 wells of the Anantapur district. Under well irrigation about 167,155 hectares of land is irrigated. The maximum number of 5,952 wells and bore wells are found in Tadimarri mandal. The minimum number of 234 wells and bore wells are found in Pamidi mandal. There are two mandals with more than 4,000 wells and bore wells in the district. They are Narpala and Tadimarri. In about 24 mandals the number of wells and bore wells vary from 2,000 to 4,000. In about 28 mandals the number of wells and bore wells vary from 1,000 to 2,000 and in 9 mandals the number of wells and bore wells are less than 1,000.

Cropping Pattern in the Anantapur District

The total cultivated area of the district is about 7,62,978 hectares of land which account for 39.89 % of the total area of the district. The ground nut is the first ranking crop and is cultivated in 486,735 hectares of land. The second rank in the district is Jowar. It is cultivated in 58,574 hectares of land. The third ranking crop is pulses. It is cultivated in 57,150 hectares. The fourth ranking crop is Korra. It is cultivated in 46,832 hectares. The paddy is fifth ranking crop and is cultivated in 37,297 hectares. The sixth ranking crop is bajra. It is cultivated in 30,852 hectares. The seventh ranking crop is ragi and is cultivated in 15,651 hectors. The eight ranking crop is cotton soils. The ninth ranking crop is fruits and vegetables. They are grown in 14,829 hectares. In majority of the mandals the mono crop prevails and it is dominated by ground nut. Paddy crop is cultivated under canal, tank and well irrigation.

Ground Water Conditions under Minor Irrigation of the Anantapur District

The ground water levels under well irrigation are falling steeply and vary from 15 to 20 meters from the ground levels, due to continuous extraction of ground water have dried up. The deep bore wells have dried up in the pediments and Pedi plain zones due to continuous droughts. About 55 drought years have been reported up the last hundred years. Due to low high extraction the farmers have to go to deep bore wells to a depth of about 150 meters to 200 meters.

Under tank and canal irrigation the ground water levels of return flow. Due to hard rock terrain ground water is restricted to weathered, proctored, faulted and fissured zones.

Effects on Soils

The soil samples have been analyzed in the canal, tank and well irrigation areas of the district to study the distribution of alkalinity and salinity. Under land and tank irrigation majority of the soils have been transformed into alkaline and saline soils due to day conditions prevailed in the district. It has been found that majority of the soils under canal and tanks have been effected by the problem is found high in irrigated black soil plains. Salt encrustation is found on the top layers of the soils. Due to alkaline and saline effects the yield and productivity is very much deteriorated. In valley fills under well irrigation the soils are transformed into alkaline soils. The alkalinity and salinity soils can be reclaimed by adding required quality of gypsum, mulching and through plugging and draining out of salts in saline effected soils.

Impact Assessment under Minor Irrigation

Due to continuous irrigation of water the soils are affected by alkalinity and salinity under canal, tank and well irrigation. The salt encrustation is due to dry conditions prevailed, high evapotranspiration and high deficit. The soils have to be reclaimed adopting soil conservation and soil reclamation practices. Under well irrigation the motors are burnt due to fluctuating voltage of electricity. Due to over extraction majority of the wells are dried up. Due to continuous drought occurrence the recharge is very much reclaimed. Finally it is concluded that under canal, well and tank irrigation the soils are affected by alkalinity and salinity. There is a need for micro mapping of soils affected by saline and alkaline soils and the officers of Agriculture department have to suggest suitable measures to reclaim the soils and increase the yield and production of various crops cultivated in the district, micro irrigation practices can be adopted.

4

Extension & Community Development Through Universities

Dr. P. Visawanadha Gupta
Mr. G. Srinivas Rao

Introduction

This is the Age of Extension. In all developing countries, the fruits of knowledge, research and new skills have yet to reach millions of people who need it, who will be profited by it and whose contribution to the productive apparatus is immense. In this age of highly advanced technology, we are talking of appropriate technology for the rural and tribal areas, so that they are not deprived of the wherewithal of their existence by the mighty currents of sophisticated production techniques. Appropriate technology is a means to promote individual and community self-reliance through a swadeshi movement.

Not only, in this country, but in all other developing countries, it is the cities and the urban areas which have gained importance and derived the advantages of the four decades of development initiated by the United Nations and other International agencies. Now, we have changed our outlook and we are seriously thinking of Rural Development which will arrest the culture of too much urbanization and its attendant evils. In the world, the present perspective of all governments, is concerned with the well being of the common man.

Dr. Malcolm, S. Adiseshaiah, in his presidential address to IAPL Conference, pointed out that "when we talk about rural development, we are talking about National Development, as in rural development 80 per cent of the people supplying 70-per cent of the country's work-force and contributing 60 per cent of the National Product Income is involved. To attain the goal of rural development and abolition of un-employment within ten years, the need is (i) wider ownership of rural assets and (ii) a learning system which can help each rural unit to identify those resources in which it has comparative advantage and that no village exists which does not have some such resources. This is the kind of innovative learning system which the goals of rural development system which can extend the benefits of knowledge and modern skills to the nook and corners of rural areas in various parts of country".

As the UGC (1977) pamphlet on a policy frame on "Development of Higher Education in India points out that the university system has to discharge adequately its responsibilities to the entire educational system and to the society as a whole, it must assume extension as the third important responsibility and give it the same status as research and teaching". All universities and colleges should develop close relationship of mutual services and support with their local communities.

The University Grant Commission (UGC), New Delhi framed the guidelines to extend the work on priority basis on the following aspects:

- Human rights and rights of vulnerable groups;
- Life-long and Continuing Education programme at grass-root level;
- Community harmony and peace education;
- Women empowerment through continuing education programme;

- Social, environmental and gender issues;
- Panchayats that strengthen of local governance;
- Health education for the community;

University can be considered as a resource base with a wide variety of departments functioning as teaching units and also as knowledge - generating units through research at various levels. When University has a large number of departments in Humanities, Social Sciences, Natural Sciences, Physical Sciences, Earth Sciences, Technology and Engineering, its obligation for extension is much more as extension can operate at various levels. (1) Extension to other educational institutions at the lower level like colleges, high schools and primary schools; (2) Extension to other public institutions like industries (small, medium and big), business houses, trade and commercial undertakings, transport and banking institutions and Government institutions (like Panchayats, Municipalities, urban development authorities) and training institutes; (3) Extension to rural areas to increase their knowledge to improve skill, increase productivity on different fronts, change their attitudes and thus finally bringing a new philosophy of Development (change for better) and social action.

The above strategy gives the scope and extent of extension activity that can be carried by the University system and colleges. The University system with it brain-power should look deeper into the problems of society and each university system should initiate a philosophy of reconstruction, development growth, changes and lead the rest of humanity including the government, the local gentry, the business and industrial organizations including Municipalities, Zilla Parishads, Panchayats and the Development departments and Welfare departments working at various levels. Unless and until the University system comes away drawn from its ivory tower and jumps into a philosophy of action, there is no redemption for the enormous funds which we spend on various items of teaching, research and administration. They are not delivering the necessary goods at the present moment in the history of our nation.

The problems of the present-day society are directly traceable to the lack a social philosophy of development sharing and utilizing of the existing resources to the largest extent of cooperation at various levels, coordination, reduction in the inequalities of income, productive and worthwhile programmes for generation of wealth, distribution of wealth, increasing the incomes of the lower categories and thus reducing the poverty levels of the poorest of the poor and wholesale reconstruction of societal-based equality, fraternity, patriotism, national pride coupled with international outlook.

Need for Extension

The typical Indian community is lacking not only material resources, but also human resources as well. When it comes to the question of community leadership, there is a vacuum which is actually a condition brought about by adult illiteracy and the inaccessibility of education to any but a small minority of youth. And those who studied successfully at high level, do not remain in their own communities for various obvious reasons. Therefore, higher education has only a marginal impact on the local needs of manpower. The process of search for leadership in the community naturally leads to a closer examination of the human resources available there. Hence, the alternative model of higher education is called the extension education or community education or community college (Ramakrishanan: 1980) may well services the purposes pointed out earlier.

The primary focus of concern for the 'extension education' is the community and its problems. Since a formal educational system cannot cater to the varied local needs, extension education can serve the varied complementary needs of the local community along with education. It must be a catalyst for self-employment and a locus for the varied community needs. The community schools or extension education depends for its success not upon theories or upon building theories, but upon people. Theories help, but the basic humanitarian concept upon which the community school depends for its success is more than a theory.

Taking education thus to the community is the goal of extension education. This new kind of education serving the entire community by breaking the access barriers has made life-long learning a reality. But serving the entire community through community college is of course not an easy task. A difficult task like this can be accomplished only by greater mobilization, organization and planning at the community level for its development and service involving the community in which it is located or initiated. Recognition by the agency of extension education of its place in the community will have its effect on the curriculum, where social relevance is desirable, and on the responsibility and participation not only of parents and pupils but also of wider public. In return of the services and facilities which the agency of extension education is able to offer to the community, the agency will benefit by sharing the community facilities. This in turn may lead to further integration with other fields of education and youth work. In generating desirable changes in human behavior in a given community, extension education adopts both informal and non-formal methods.

Need for Community College

The establishment of community colleges in urban, rural and tribal areas one way speeds up the objectives of extension education. The courses offered in the community college have to be in multi-dimensional nature to cater to the immediate needs of the local communities. The students who studied in the community colleges should be trained as agents at social change, get self-employed or employed in the community and become useful and worthy citizens of society. The curriculum should include a large extent of liberal studies, so that they can develop an analytical mind and begin to observe and understand the social process in and around the society. They should be able to create a new social order of peace, contentment, cooperation and dedication to work and share their knowledge and skills with other members of the society. They should be able to motivate the community in its scientific, literacy, cultural and artistic activities. The daily activity of the students, curriculum, instruction and teaching learning process should be monitored and framed towards community service. Then only the objective will be realized.

If we trace the present malaise in our society and look to the international scene, we find that we have to attend to the following tasks immediately both in terms of short and long-range view-points initiating strategies of action on a war footing:

1. Creation of Ecological balance: Already we see that some areas of the country are not receiving enough rain-fall which can be traced to man's indiscriminate thinking with population pressure and urbanization.
2. Creation of new energy system and reviving the old energy systems in our villages: We suffer frequently due to inadequate supply of electric power, diesel, oil, kerosene, gas, firewood and charcoal. We have to plan at once to the need of boosting social forestry and economic forestry in all the banjar lands, village boundaries, covering hillocks into green pastures and raising of quick growing plants.
3. Making best of existing water resources and discovery of ground water resources, we should not and cannot waste our water. Every drop of water should be utilized properly. Hence, water management, crop rotation, multiple cropping use of underground water resources, research in the use of arid and saline lands for cultivation becomes important.
4. The white revolution: The green revolution has come. In consonance with development and use of land resources, the existing cattle wealth should be improved and the new varieties of Zersy, Murrah Swiss brown cattle development program should be encouraged.
5. Subsidiary occupations and village industries: All encouragement should be given for development of Poultry, Piggery, Sheep units, silk industry, village crafts, handicrafts, palm jiggery, fruit preservation and canning and handicraft products.

6. We would develop intermediate technology where training youth with adequate skills with the help of financial institutions can start units for manufacture of soap, hair oils, tooth pastes, leather goods, lime kilns, cement, bricks, textiles and handlooms which should be taken away from high industry.
7. Abolition of illiteracy, ill-health and creation of scientific temper in society.
8. Creation of new social ethic for building youth power and a philosophy of development should be promoted.

There are many more things that a university set-up of college can take up for extension work though proper planning with schedules for 1 year, 2 years, 5 years and 10 years and gradually extend the extent of service it can render. It can extend the area of operations and the number of departments (staff and students) that can be actively involved in the service of society. Here, the research scholars from the various departments of science, social science, engineering and technology can play vital roles.

We will mention a few areas which University departments can take up as a long range plan for the next 5 years or for the next decade. The departments of Botany, Zoology, Ecology, Environmental Science can jointly take up a scheme of education villagers in social and economic forestry, water management, crop rotation, plant protection, agro-industries, fisheries development and ecological balance. They can select a group of 5 or 6 villages and concentrate their attention in bringing change by involving local youth, women and village elders.

The departments of Physiology, Bio-chemistry and Pharmacy can take up extension in the field of foods, balanced diet, food preservation, healthy life, environmental sanitation and so on. The departments of Geology, Meteorology, Geo-physics and Geo-Engineering can take up schemes for exploration of minerals, ground water, soil analysis, soil mechanics, setting of brick kilns, etc. The departments of Physics, Chemistry, Engineering and Technology can take up development and use of alternative sources of energy, exploring new sources of energy and familiarity and use of Bio-gas, solar energy, wind use of waste materials, preparation of sanitary pits and compost pits, use of chemical fertilizers and natural manures.

The departments of Economics, Applied Economics, Sociology, Social Work, Anthropology, Education and Psychology can appoint teams to make a study of socio-economic conditions, social and psychological problems, they can hold discussions and arrive at alternative strategies for social action, community service, community work and community planning. Formal education and adult education to improve their knowledge skills change their attitudes and behavior patterns for their social good, economic development and betterment. There should be continuity in education and social action.

The University administration can also extend its activities by training persons in office procedures, office management, typing, short hand administration of small undertakings and other worth-while and useful activities

The University as a whole, should move, so that the Philosophy of extension permeates into all the departments and the staff, students and research scholars can plan and work out different strategies and undertake action programmes at suitable intervals of time. The motto "where there is a will, there is a way", can be implemented by suitably altering the time of admission, the vacations and the examination schedules, so that suitable programmes can plan throughout the year and also during vacations.

The Indian Association for Adult Education, the Indian University Association for Continuing Education, the UGC and the State Departments of Higher Education by having a regional conference and identify one nodal university in each state for exploring the extension activities for a period of 5 years. The UGC may earmark some fund to every department of the University to spend at least 10 per cent of its budget for extension work. Every State Government of Higher Education in addition to nodal university and one or two colleges in the backward region to undertake extension activities, and share their experiences with others. The report should contain the approach they adopt towards extension, what action programmes were implemented, what were the difficulties faced, what was the outcome, so that the universities and the colleges can get feedback regularly and try to improve their extension services each year and also step up the pace of extension and gain more experience. Thus, extension can gain ground slowly and steadily in the portals of the University and make headway in the coming decades.

References

Adavi Reddy, A. (1971), "Extension Education", Srilakshmi Pres, Bapatla.

Myrdal, Gunnar (1968), "Asian Drama: A Inquiry into the Poverty of Nations" 20th Century Fund, New York.

Ramakrishnan, G. (1980), "A Community College for India" The institute for Development Education, Madras.

Subba Rao D. and Vasudeva Rao. BS (1984), "Adult and Continuing Education: Some Perspectives" Rural Development Publications, Andhra Pradesh.

5

STATUS OF RURAL HOUSING IN INDIA

The Role of Financial Institutions in Providing Finance to the Rural People

DR. S. PULLA RAO
MRS. P. USHA

INTRODUCTION

Proper housing is considered by many as basic need. It is a basic necessary that cannot be denied in a fair and equitable society. Respiratory disorders among rural population in India are often the result of unfavorable housing and poor living conditions. According to the National Family Health Survey, conducted in 2000 by the government only 19 per cent of the rural population lives in pucca (strong) houses, while the remaining live in kutcha (weak) and semi-pucca houses with mud walls and thatched roofs. The proportion of rural households living in kutcha structures was 17 per cent in 2004[1]. Eighty per cent of the houses in the villages do not have toilet facilities. Cooking is usually done inside the house and under inadequate ventilation with biomass such as dried cow dung, firewood, dry weeds or crop residue.

India is a nation of villages. Rural India, which comprises 5.5 lakh villages and encompasses three fourths of India's population, is characterized by low-income level. The Indian Government and the World Bank, on the basis of per capita consumption expenditure of Rs. 356 per month or Rs.11.70 per day, estimated that less than 30 percent of the nation is poor and 70 per cent of the poor (225 million) live in the villages[2]. As per the 2001 census, 71 per cent of the total population of India live in the rural areas where the problem of housing shortage and the lack of civic amenities have become a serious cause for concern. The data released by the census of India on Houses, Households, Amenities and Assets for 2001 indicate that total number of households in rural areas is 138.27 million as against the availability of 135.05 million houses of which nearly 11.40 million houses were non-serviceable kutcha (temporary) houses needing replacement. Thus it is considered that the requirement of houses in rural areas as 14.6 million[3].

Although many rural people are migrating to cities, three out of four of India's poor people live in the vast rural parts of the country. For more than 21 per cent of them, poverty is a chronic condition. A major cause of poverty among rural people in India is lack of access for both individuals and communities to productive assets and financial resources[4].

The present study aims at review the current status of housing in rural India with a view to assess the prospects for its growth. This paper makes an attempt to examine the existing housing shortage in rural Indian economy. The main objectives of the study are:

(a) to focus on the growth and composition of rural housing stock,

(b) to forecast the likely magnitude of housing shortage in rural areas,

(c) to examine the role of financial institutions in providing housing finance to the rural people.

Rural housing is of immense economic and social importance. Five decades of development planning in India has been unable to ensure a decent living for a large number of people residing in rural areas. Despite many large scale rural development schemes, the absolute number of people in poverty has not declined substantially. Lack of inadequate basic infrastructure both social and physical continues to remain a major constraint to progress in numerous villages and their inhabitations.

Rural India Critical Socio-Economic Indicators

The critical socio-economic indicators like adequate water supply, electricity etc., reflects the current status of housing facilities of the rural poor.

Table 1
Rural India Critical Socio-Economic Indicators

Sl. No.	*Development Indicators*	*Overall*	*Rural*	*Urban*
1.	People below poverty line (%)	26.10	27.10	23.62
2.	Pucca House (%)	-	29.20	70.70
3.	Houses with electricity (%)	55.8	43.52	87.6
4.	Houses with latrines (%)	36.4	21.92	73.7
5.	Houses connecting for waste water (%)	46.4	34.2	77.9
6.	Tap	36.7	24.3	68.7
7.	Hand pump	35.7	43.2	16.2
8.	Tube well	5.6	5.7	5.1

Source : Census of India 2001.

According to the census of India 2001, the rural people live below poverty line was estimated at 27.10 per cent as against 23.62 per cent in urban areas. It is observed that the percentage of pucca houses available to the rural people is accounted for only 29.20 per cent as against 70.70 per cent in case of the urban people. The houses with electricity are estimated at 43.52 per cent. Regarding the basic needs like latrines and provision for the disposal of waste water, it is observed that the houses with latrines is estimated at 21.92 per cent and houses connecting for waste water is estimated at 34.2 per cent. 24.3 per cent rural houses are having the provision of water supply through taps and 43.2 per cent through hand pumps and 5.7 per cent houses are getting water from tube wells.

Rural Housing Shortage

Table 2
Rural Households, Usable Housing Stock and Housing Shortages/Gaps in 1991 and 2001 (In Millions)

Sl. No.	Particulars	Year 1991	Year 2001
1.	Households	113.5	137.0
2.	Usable Housing Stock	92.9	111.5
3.	Housing shortage	20.6	25.5
		(21.2)	(26.5)

Source: A Hand Book of Housing Statistics of NBO

According to the estimates of NBO report on Housing statistics, in 1991 out of the estimated households of 113.5 million, the usable housing stock is accounted for 92.9 million and the housing shortage is estimated at 20.6 millions. The gap is further increased in 2001. Out of 137.0 million households the usable housing stock is only 111.5 millions and housing shortage accounted at 25.5 millions.

According to 'India Rural Infrastructure Report-2007', "housing disadvantage is not only limited to the SC/ST or economically weaker sections but to a much larger proportion of rural households. Many of the groups barred from accessing good housing in rural areas have been constrained either by low income or by their ineligibility in formal lending market"

Role of Government in Promotion of Rural Housing

Keeping in view the shortage of houses especially in rural areas, and the need to provide housing for all citizens, Government of India has taken a number of initiatives to improve the availability of houses in rural areas. The approach has been bi-pronged by making budgetary provision for upgradation of unserviceable kutcha houses and by providing credit with subsidy for certain sections of the poor. Emphasis has also been laid on use of cost effective, disaster resistant and environment friendly technologies in rural housing.

The Indira Awas Yojana (IAY) is the flagship rural housing programme of the Government being implemented since 1985-86 to provide assistance to Below Poverty Line (BPL) households belonging to Scheduled Caste and Scheduled Tribe (SC/ST) families, freed bonded laborers and also to non-SC /ST households of rural BPL, families of ex-servicemen/ paramilitary forces killed in action. The ceiling on assistance under IAY is Rs.25,000 per unit for plain areas and Rs. 27,500 for hilly/difficult areas and for up gradation of kutcha house into pucca (permanent) house is Rs.12,500.The funds under the scheme shared between center and the States in the ratio of 75.25; Union Territories are provided 100% Central assistance. Under the programme, upto March 2004, 114.78 lakh houses have been constructed in the last two decades involving an expenditure of approximately Rs. 20022.89 crore.

The other important schemes implemented by the Government are:

1. Credit-cum-Subsidy Scheme for Rural Housing launched in April 1999, which was merged with IAY from April 2004.
2. Golden Jubilee Rural Housing Finance Scheme introduced in 1997.
3. Innovation Scheme for Rural Housing and Habitat Development being implemented on project basis since 1999-2000.
4. Rural Building Centers launched in April 1999 with the objective of technology transfer/dissemination of information.
5. National Mission for Rural Housing and Habitat to facilitate introduction of science and technology inputs.
6. Equity support to HUDCO to meet the requirement of economically weaker households in rural areas.

Rural Housing schemes of the Government at Central and State level are mainly variants of the IAY. The schemes altogether have managed to touch only a miniscule segment of the population and despite a growing budgetary allocation, have not been able to make a dent in the total rural housing shortage in the country. The emphasis has been on the "provision" of house to the houseless and very little emphasis is laid on the overall habitat planning and development in the villages.

INITIATIVES MADE BY NATIONAL HOUSING BANK

To address the housing credit needs of the rural borrowers, the Golden Jubilee Rural Housing Finance Scheme (GJRHFS) formulated by the National Housing (NHB) in 1997 was launched on the occasion of the Golden Jubilee of the country's independence. The scheme aimed to address the problem of housing shortage in rural areas through improved access to institutional housing finance that would enable an individual to build a modest house or improve or add to his existing dwelling unit. The scheme is implemented through Scheduled Public Sector Commercial Banks, Scheduled State Cooperative Banks, Regional Rural Banks and dedicated housing finance companies viz., Housing Finance Companies, Apex Cooperative Housing Finance Societies and through Agriculture & Rural Development Banks.

During the first year of operation of the scheme (1997-98), the national target of 50,000 was fully achieved and the targets were increased in a phased manner to 275000 by 2005-06. During the period 1997-2006, approximately a total of 16.44 lakh dwelling units were financed against the target of 16.00 lakh units indicating achievement of 103%. Refinance from NHB is offered up to a maximum of Rs.15 lakh per unit for new dwelling units; refinance is also extended for up-gradation/repairs to existing units. To encourage flow of funds to rural sector, NHB offered 0.50% concession over the normal refinance rates availed by commercial banks and HFCs. Refinance availed of by commercial banks under GJRHFS during 2003-04, 2004-05 and 2005-06 amounted to Rs.700.00 crore, Rs.1981.52 crore and Rs.1690.00 crore, respectively.

Refinance assistance extended by NHB to various Primary Lending Institutions under the GJRHFS shows progressively rising trend and formed about 50% of the total refinance assistance during the last three years, as shown in the table below.

Year	*Total Refinance Disbursement*	*Disbursement Under GJRHFS*	*% Age of GJRHFS Disbursement to Total Disbursement*
2001-02	1024.80	222.20	21.70
2002-03	2709.72	335.96	12.39
2003-04	3252.89	1730.54	52.28
2004-05	8062.24	3536.16	47.14
2005-06	5632.39	2609.85	48.25

Source: Report of the Working Group on Rural Habitat 2007.

Rural housing has been identified as a key focus of NHB's future strategy and NHB has been working on various initiatives to address the issue of rural housing. Considering housing not just a shelter but as an excellent platform for income generating activity. NHB has promoted the concept of Productive Housing Rural Areas (PHIRA), as a single point delivery for housing and productive loan. The housing component of this composite loan will be eligible for 100 per cent refinance, while the productive component of the loan would be loan from the financing bank.

A study conducted by NHB on the performance of the GJRHFS identified the following constraints faced by Primary Lending Institutions for financing rural housing. Absence of clear land title, difficulty in assessing the income of rural borrowers, limited tax benefits for the lenders and borrowers, limited reach particularly in respect of HFCs, limited housing loan products for the rural segment and need for flexibility in application of prudential norms. NHB has taken up these constraints with individual banks for extending loans relying on evidence like village Panchayat tax paid receipts, power bill etc., and taking suitable declaration that the owners do not have the little deeds in their names but in fact they are the bonafide owners, without insisting on marketable title, which has since been adopted by two banks.

Rural Housing Finance Provided by NABARD

Recognizing the importance of housing in rural areas, NABARD made refinancing for rural housing as an eligible activity in the year 2001-02. Under the Rural Housing Scheme, NABARD extends refinance to banks for provision of loans to individuals / cooperative housing societies. Rural Housing has emerged as an important segment under Rural Non-Farm Sector, forming about 50% of refinance provided for Non-farm Sector. During 2004-05 and 2005-06, the annual disbursements for rural housing have averaged Rs.1260 crore; cumulative disbursement during the last five years up to 31 March 2006 was Rs.4821.36 crore; agency-wise break up has been as indicated in the following table.

Table 3
Agency-wise Disbursement For Rural Housing by NABARD 2001-02 to 2005-06

(Rs.In Crore)

Agency	*2001-02*	*2002-03*	*2003-04*	*2004-05*	*2005-06*	*Cumulative As on 1 March 2006*
CBs	99.39	40.83	138.47	109.09	291.61	679.42
	(19.80)	(5.30)	(13.44)	(8.54)	(23.47)	(14.09)
RRBs	124.10	270.56	295.21	401.51	192.65	1284.03
	(24.73)	(35.16)	(28.65)	(31.44)	(15.50)	(26.63)
SCARDBs	164.70	242.41	245.80	412.24	368.69	1433.84
	(32.82)	(31.50)	(23.85)	(32.28)	(29.67)	(29.94)
SCBs	96.25	214.98	342.89	351.07	385.27	1390.46
	(19.18)	(27.94)	(33.28)	(27.49)	(31.00)	(28.84)
Sch.PUCBs/	17.42	0.74	7.86	3.03	4.56	33.61
ADFCs	(3.47)	(0.78)	(0.78)	(0.24)	(0.37)	(0.70)
Total	501.86	769.53	1030.23	1242.80	1242.80	4821.36

(Figures un brackets indicate percentage to total)

Source: Report of the Working Group on Rural Habitat 2007.

All the refinance disbursements for Rural Housing have been under Automatic Refinance Facility. Under rural housing refinance scheme for individuals, the ceiling on the cost of the dwelling unit is Rs.20 lakh and the quantum of bank loan, Rs.15 lakh. For renovation, the limit is Rs. 5 lakh. Cumulatively up to 31 March 2006, refinance assistance for 3,08,484 new housing units (with an average cost of Rs. 1.25lakh) and for 2,56,798 houses under Renovation/Repairs (with average cost of Rs.0.50 lakh) has been provided.

Efforts by NGOs and Micro-Finance Institutions

NGOs use grant funds, loan assistance from Government Schemes, Habitat for Humanity, onward lending finance from Commercial banks and HUDCO/HDFC and NABARD in combinations of loan and grant to develop housing in rural areas. NGOs have been found to operate in an integrated manner treating rural housing as part of rural development in a comprehensive way. The experiences of houses delivery by NGOs such as Gram Vikas, Development Alternatives and ODTF indicate that NGO facilitated finance for housing is integrated with technical support services that ensure quality of the house, delivery of basic amenities, promotion of eco-friendly construction technologies and livelihood support systems.

The role of Micro-Finance Institutions (MFIs) in rural housing finance is steadily growing Credit for housing has been a small component of the product offerings of various MFIs such as BASIX and SHARE and is mainly restricted to small loans for house improvement and for shorter periods of three to five years. SEWA's experience of loans to women members of its Self-Help Groups for house improvement is an example of successful delivery of housing credit. NGOs and MFIs have played an important role in the delivery of rural housing. NGOs such as SEWA, BASIX, SHARE, PRADAN and Myrda have assisted Government in developing institutions that link formal finance to rural populations.

The government, including adopting models of successful barefoot banking to the rural environment, puts several proposals forward. The government has announced several rural housing schemes that seek to take the prevailing low interest regime to the villages. Income and seasonal fluctuations linked to agricultural operations often influence the repayment capacity and pattern of borrowers from rural India. The National Housing Bank in consultation with the RBI will identify ways of introducing an element of flexibility for repayment in line with harvesting seasons and other conditions peculiar to rural areas.

References

1. Government of India Report (2004).
2. Government of India Report on Poverty.
3. Report of the working Group on Rural Habitat.
4. Report of IFAD On Rural Poverty in India (2007).
5. Census of India (2001).
6. A Hand Book of Housing statistics NBO.
7. Report of the Working Group on Rural Habitat (2007).

6

Gandhian Perspective on Rural Development

Dr. P. Kishore Kumar
K. Tirumalamba

Introduction

Rural Development as a concept has a long history and has gained popularity in recent years, particularly, since 1970s. It is an elastic concept and everyone interprets it in his own way. But, the broad consensus is that Rural Development implies all-round development of rural areas. It implies a process of economic, political and social transformation of an agrarian rural society[1].

In the context of the developing countries, Rural Development is viewed as an attempt to improving the living conditions of the rural people. The development policies of the third-world during 1950s and early 1960s, centered on growth maximization and the poor were expected to gain from the 'trickle down' of the benefits resulting from overall rapid growth[2]. However, despite an impressive economic growth in most of the developing countries during this period, problems of rural poverty and unemployment remain all-pervasive, intense and intricate[3].

This called for a change in the concept and strategy of Rural Development. As a result, since early 1970s, such terms as 'redistribution with growth' and 'growth with social justice' became very popular and the concept of people's participation in the process of development began to be emphasized. The change of emphasis made Rural Development more broad-based[4].

Rural Development has emerged as a distinctive field of policy and practice and of research, in the last decade and half. As a strategy, it is defined by its concern with equity objectives of various kinds, especially, the reduction of inequalities in income and provision of employment, access to public goods and services and alleviation of poverty. It is this distributional issue which has marked out "Rural Development" as a distinct field, because an overwhelming majority of poor people in the developing countries of Asia and Africa, live in rural areas[5].

In view of the enormity, nature, complexities and urgency of the Rural Development problems, most of the developing nations initiated development programmes which led to the creation of a number of new institutions-political, economic, social and administrative. While creating these institutions, greater attention was paid to people's institutions. The reasons behind this was that the programmes of development were to be carried out not only by the State bureaucracy, but also through active and effective people's participation. Besides, effective people's institutions have to be created to promote political development and social justice. Thus, local institution is necessary, if not sufficient, condition for the accelerated Rural Development[6].

The element of participation is central to Rural Development. It responds to the need to mobilize and use more effectively all the resources available or potentiality available in rural areas of labour, skills, saving, land, fisheries, forests, livestock and water. Even with substantially increased help from government, most of the resources required for broad-based rural development will have to be found in rural areas? Rural Development is not merely the agricultural development but rural transformation as a whole which includes development of all facets of human resources like social, economic, cultural, spiritual etc. Therefore Rural Development has to be viewed in its totality rather than its being a fragmented approach[8].

Importance of Rural Development

Development of rural areas and rural people has been the central concern of development planning in India. Rural India, which encompasses three-fourths of the country's population, is characterized, by low income levels, not even adequate to ensure a quality of life compatible with physical well-being[9]. Rural Development, therefore, occupies an important place in the agenda for national development. It is, in fact, a strategy to improve the economic and social life of a specific group of people-the rural poor[10].

The politico-economic and socio-cultural structural disabilities threaten the development of rural poor. This has aggravated the problem of poverty, which has manifested itself in various forms, i.e. unemployment, inequality, malnutrition, growth of slums and ignorance. The growing poverty, which undermines planned development, is much more severe in rural than urban areas and has become the biggest bottleneck in national development.

The success of some of the developing countries in eliminating destitution and unemployment through a system of communes attracted the attention of policymakers around the world. Government and International agencies started a search for alternative collectivist models; this led to many 'reformist' experiments in Rural Development. Since Rural Development holds the key to nation-building, it can transform rural society from traditional isolation to integration with the mainstream of national life. It will evolve a new society with a built-in value system by raising the social, economic and cultural values of rural people through basic infrastructural amenities.

Finally, due to lack of resources and little or no bargaining power, the owners of small, scattered and unorganized rural enterprises are exploited to the hilt vis-à-vis those to whom they sell their products and from whom they purchase raw materials, etc. These small rural entrepreneurs can be protected from exploitation and their financial conditions can be improved only through Rural Development in the form of price support, credit facilities, insurance, etc.

Conceptual Analysis of Rural Development

Since 1970s, the concept of Rural Development has undergone a change and has become more comprehensive. The World Bank defines Rural Development as a strategy designed to improve the economic and social life of specific group of people, that is, the rural poor. It involves the extending benefits of development to the poorest among those who are living in the rural areas. This group includes a mix of activities, including projects to raise agricultural output, create new employment, improve, health and education, expand communication and improve housing. Thus, the World Bank defines Rural Development in terms of an improvement of the economic and social life of the rural poor[11].

Thus, Rural Development is, of late, viewed as a strategy to bring about improvement in the economic and social life of the rural poor. It implies both economic betterment of people as well as greater social transformation. It encompasses a spectrum of activities and human mobilization to make people stand on their own feet and break away from all structural disabilities which claim them to condition in which they may live in[12].

Rural Development: Gandhian Perspective

To Gandhi, salvation of India could come only through the Rural Development. The soul of India lives in villages. Gandhi's approach to Rural Development is holistic and people centered. Among the early pioneers of Rural Development, Mahatma Gandhi occupies a significant place. As against the localized village uplift movements of Tagore and Braynes, Gandhi attracted the attention of the entire country. His first experiment in rural reconstruction was at Champaran in 1916.

People at Champaran live in utter poverty and ignorance. The root cause of poverty, according to Gandhi, was the ignorance of the people. So, he started the mass education programme with the help of some devoted workers. Champaran was the first laboratory where Gandhi forged not only his political weapon but also his rural reconstruction programme. From 1918 onwards, Gandhi rose to new heights and become an uncrowned king of India. He launched the Swadeshi movement to save the decaying indigenous products. Gandhi wants an idle preacher. He was an example. He himself settled in a village called Segoan near Wardha in April 1936. There he taught the people the spirit of self-help. The Gandhian programme of rural reconstruction included the following points: Use of khadi, development of village industries, socio-economic equality, communal unity, removal of untouchability, prohibition, equal status for women and adoption of basic education.

Gandhi, 'the born democrat', wanted to build the structure of the pure democracy 'inch by inch', directly from below. He wanted to make each village 'a complete republic, independent of its neighbors for its vital wants, and yet interdependent for many others in which dependence is necessity'. He was convinced that 'if all Indian villages could come up to the ideal, India would be free from most of its worries'.

Today everyone is talking in terms of Rural Development. Gandhiji did not approve of the Western civilization, which is urban for the entire world. He said that 'a big country with a teeming population, with an ancient rural tradition, which has hitherto answered its purpose, need not, must not copy the Western model. What is good for one nation situated in one condition is not necessarily good enough for another differently situated". So he advocated a rural style of life and culture based on neighborliness and sharing. His mission was to build a nonviolent culture and civilization which could only be built on self-reliant and self contained villages'[13].

According to Gandhiji, Rural Development is the natural development and Rural Development of better human relations, is different from city development which results in alienation of the individual from his surroundings, ultimately leading to frustration and destruction[14].

Gandhi therefore determined to work for small rural communities, wherein propel will cooperate with one another and give aid to those who lack the resources for growth and development. He spoke and wrote about Village Swaraj. He said, 'the Swaraj of my dreams is the poor man's Swaraj. The necessaries of life should be enjoyed by you in common with thus enjoyed by the princes and the moneyed men. But that does not mean that you should have palaces like theirs. They are not necessary for happiness. You are I, would be lost in them. But you ought to get all the ordinary amenities of life that a rich man enjoys. I have not the slightest doubt that Swaraj is not Poorna Swaraj until these amenities are guaranteed to you under it"[15].

Gandhiji's concept of Rural Development emerge out from what he said in "India of My Dreams". It follows: I shall strive for a constitution, which will release India from all thralldom and patronage, and give her, if need be, the right to sin. I shall work for India, in which the poorest shall feel that it is their country in whose making they have an effective voice: an India in which there shall be no high class and low class of people; an India in which all communities shall live in perfect harmony. There can be no room in such an India for the course of unsociability or the curst of the intoxicating drinks and drugs. Women will enjoy the same right as men. Since we shall be at peace with all the rest of the world, neither exploiting, nor being exploited, we should have the smallest army imaginable. All interests not in conflict with the interests of the dumb millions will be scrupulously respected, whether foreign or indigenous. Personally, I hate distinction between foreign and indigenous. This is the India of my dreams... I shall be satisfied with nothing less"[16].

Gandhi placed Rural Development at the core of India's future destiny-not rural development visualized microcosmically but in terms of the development of each of its numerous villages to full potential. Gandhi not only expected most of them to continue living in villages but wanted them to do so to give legitimacy to people's participation[17].

The Gandhian perspectives on Rural Development is based on the following values and premises:

1. Real India is found not in its cities, but in its villages.
2. The revival of villages is possible only when the villagers are no more exploited. Exploitation of villagers by city-dwellers was 'violence' in Gandhi's opinion.
3. Simple living and high thinking, employing voluntary reduction of materialistic wants, and pursuit of moral and spiritual principles of life.
4. Dignity of labour, every one must earn his bread by physical labour and one who labours must necessarily get his subsistence.
5. Preference to the use of indigenous (Swadeshi) products, services and institutions.
6. Balance between the needs and the means... Gandhiji believed that non-violence and truth could not be sustained unless a balance between the needs and the means was maintained.

According to Gandhi, Village Development should be carried on through means and resources of the village without government help. Gandhi also believed in the overall development of the village people, including more, material and social development, keeping their natural requirements and circumstances in mind. Participation of the local people in the developmental process is necessary and unavoidable.

Summing Up

Rural Development is not as simple as it looks on paper. Capabilities have to be built up, suitable structures have to be valued, changes have to be brought about in the administrative, technical and political arena. Equally important is kindling the zeal and enthusiasm of the people. But the most important agents to make Rural Development a success are the political and administrative will to decentralize decision making powers to the lower levels on Gandhian-line with a clear policy enunciation, full political support, and needed administrative infrastructure. It is expected that the goals of real Swaraj will be achieved by fulfilling the dream of the Father of the Nation. It is high time for both our policymakers and the people, to turn the torch within so that they may be inspired to adopt the Gandhian way, if not for any other consideration, but for its pragmatic strength to solve our present day maladies of rural India. There is need to reiterate Gandhian values, and instead of merely garlanding the portraits of Gandhiji, India must translate his ideals into real life and make rural India free from hunger, poverty and exploitation.

References

1. Sau, Sachinandan (1998), "Approaches to Rural Development Problems: A Review with Speical reference to India' in Rural Development Theories and Experience (cds, Sachinandan Sau), Alllied Publsihers, New Delhi, p. 10.
2. Datta, Prabhat (1998), Major Issues in the Development Debate; Lessons in Empowerment from India, Kanishka Publishers, p. 119.
3. Mishra, S.N and Mishra, Swita (2002), Decentralised Governance, Shipra, New Delhi, p. 1
4. Datta, Prabhat, ibid
5. Sau, Sachinandan, op.cit., p. 11
6. Bajpai, Ashok (1997), Panchayati Raj and Rural Development, Sahitya Prakashan, Delhi, p. 5
7. Mishra, S.N. and Sharma Kushal (1983), Problems and Prospects of Rural Development in India, Uppal Publishing House, New Delhi, pp. 3-4.
8. Jha, L.K. (1998), 'Planning for Rural Transformation in Eastern India: An Integrated Approach" in Rural Development in India: Problems and Prospects (ed. Ugra Mohan Jha), Anmol Publications, New Delhi, p. 105.
9. Dasgupta, K.R. (1997), Rural Development Programmes in India- Concepts and Strategies in Kurukshetra, Vol. XIV, No.11, August, p. 29.
10. Mishra, S.N. and Mishra, Sweta, op. cit., p. 63.

11. Maheshwari, S.R. (1985), Rural Development in India, Sage Publications, New Delhi, p. 18

12. Mishra, S.N. and Mishra, Sweta, op. cit., p. 66

13. Arunachalam K. (1981), Gandhian Approach to Rural Development, Sarvodaya Bakkiya Pannai, Madurai, Preface.

14. Ibid., p. 17

15. Gandhi, M.K. (1962), India of My Dreams, Navajivan Publishing House, Ahmedabad, p. 6

16. Asraf Ali and Mishra S.N. (1996), Public Administration: A New Paradigm, Cadplan publisher and Distributor, New Delhi, pp. 313 - 314

17. Sighn Kartar (1999), Rural Development Principles, Policies and Management, Sage, New Delhi. pp. 85 - 86.

7

Rural India : Gandhian Approach

Dr. M.V.S.S. Prakasa Rao
Mr. H. Subhramanyam

Introduction

Development implies a change that is desirable. Since what is desirable at a particular time, place and in a particular culture, may not be desirable at other places, or at other times at the same place and in the same culture milieu. It is difficult to derive a universally acceptable definition of development. The term 'rural development' connotes overall development of rural areas with a view to improve the quality of life of rural people. The new economic view of development considers, reduction or elimination of Illiteracy, poverty, inequality and unemployment as an important index of development.

Since time immemorial, India still continues to be and will remain in the foreseeable future, as a land of village communities. As a matter of fact, the village was the basic unit of administration, as far as the Vedic Age is concerned. There is a reference to 'gramini' (village) in the Rig Veda. The predominantly rural character of India's national economy is reflected in the very high proportion of its population living in rural areas. It was 89 per cent in 1901, 83 per cent in 1951, 80 per cent in 1971, seventy four per cent in 1991 and around 70 per cent in 2001 census are living in rural and tribal areas, i.e. more than 700 million of its people living in rural areas, and with the rural sector contributing about 29 per cent of its Gross Domestic Product. No strategy of socio-economic development for India that neglects rural people and rural areas can be successful.

The rural sector occupies an important place in Indian economy. About 74 per cent of India's population live in its 5,80,000 or so villages, and about two-thirds of the country's population is dependent on agriculture and allied activities for its livelihood. Agricultural and allied activities had contributed about 29 per cent of India's Gross Domestic Product at factor cost in 1994-95 at current prices. It is also an important source of foreign exchange and raw materials for India's major agro-industries, and a large market for industrial products. Thus, the rural sector forms the basic foundation of India's economy. No programme of national development can ever succeed, if it is not built on this foundation.

Gandhiji advocated the ideals of truth, non-violence and moral values to achieve the ultimate truth of self-realization. He is a devotee of Naturalism, when he speaks about the development of the child according to his nature and he becomes a Pragmatist when he advocates learning by doing and learning by experience. All these lead to an integration, so essential to effective education and development of the total personality of an individual.

Basic Education

Gandhiji's scheme of education is known as 'Basic Education'. Its curriculum is activity-centered. Its aim is to prepare the child for practical work, conduct experiments and do research, so that he is able to develop himself physically, mentally and spiritually and become a useful member of society. In this activity centered curriculum, Gandhiji included Mother-tongue, Basic Craft, Arithmetic, Sociology, General Science, Art Music and other like subjects.

The Basic Education, as originally conceived, was to cover the education of children from seven to fourteen. On the basis of experience and further thinking, Gandhiji extended both the scope and content of Basic Education. Addressing Basic Education workers at Sevagram, he said that we must participate in the homes of the children. We must educate their parents. Basic Education must become literally education for life. Gandhiji explained this new conception of Basic Education as education for life and through life. He stated that the scope of Basic Education has to be extended. It should include the education of everybody at every stage of life.

Development-Different Strategies

Development is a complex process, which is affected by economic and non economic factors. The importance of non-economic factors in development was duly recognized by the classical school. John Stuart Mill thought that non-economics factors, like beliefs, habits of thought, customs and institutions play an important role in economic development, and he attributed the backwardness of underdeveloped countries to the despotic and anti-progressive character of their customs, institutions, and beliefs.

For example in India large part of the credit for bringing about the Green Revolution goes to the United States Agency for International Development (USAID) that helped India, both financially and technically, in setting up modern land-grant type State Agricultural universities in the 1960s, and trained its agricultural scientists in American land-grant agricultural universities. Similarly, the operation flood programme that is credited with modernizing India's dairy industry also benefited a lot from food aid in the form of skimmed milk powder and butter oil, first from the World Food Programme of FAO, and then from the European Economic Community (EEC).

There is a need for the government to accord a very high priority, next only to defense, to rural development and to formulate a comprehensive national rural development policy, guaranteeing a reasonably satisfactory level of living to everyone in the sector, and liberating them from their servitude to the rich and the elite. Both public and private investment in the sector needs to be stepped up in order to increase the factor productivity in the sector, and improve the quality of life of rural people. Public investment is needed for creating and strengthening basic infrastructure, and private investment for expanding income and employment - generating activities.

The non-agriculture sub sector of the rural sector has been increasing at a faster rate than the agricultural sub sector in the recent past, and has a vast potential to provide employment opportunities to rural people in the future. Looking towards the twenty-first century, we must slow the process of the urban spread, with its emphasis on labour-intensive and small-scale enterprises, widen income opportunities for the poor, including small farmers, the landless and women, enabling them to even out extreme fluctuations in their incomes.

Consequences of Development

The whole structure of national societies and of international society is therefore relevant to the development of people. There are few societies, which can be said to serve this purpose; there are few, if any which both accept and are orgnaised to serve social justice, in what has been called the Revolution of Rising Expectations.

The greatest advances in technology and economic growth have been achieved under capitalism. But the decisions pertaining to what goods shall be produced, and how they shall be produced are made by a small number of people who have control over land and capital. The determining factor in their decision-making is whether the activity will yield profit, power, or prestige to them, as owners of land or capital. The needs of humankind are secondary, if they are considered at all.

Challenges and Opportunities

Achieving food security has so far been the overriding goal of agricultural policy in India. The introduction and rapid spread of high yielding varieties in the late sixties and early seventies resulted in a steady growth of output of food grains. The present crop yield in India is very low as compared to the undeveloped countries. The yield gap could be bridged only through a comprehensive integrated National Agricultural Policy emphasizing, inter alia, increased public and private investment in agriculture, widespread use of appropriate new technologies, and producer-oriented price policies and professionally- managed programmes. If the average cereal yield in India can be increased to the level of the world average, India can become the world's number one nation in terms of food grain production. Therefore, the biggest challenge before India is how to increase its crop yields to the world average level.

Liberalization has opened up new opportunities for Indian farmers to benefit from higher world prices for their produce, and lower prices for some of the inputs. Export orientation has brought in its wake the need for high tech projects and for exploring international markets for exportable commodities. The assessment of credit demand, appraisal, and instruments of financing high tech sector requires concomitant institutional innovations for which a beginning has been made with the establishment of agricultural development finance companies.

Rural Economy-Indian Scenario

India's economy can be thought of as comprising of two main sectors, namely, the rural sector and the non-rural sector. The rural sector is in turn, composed of two main sub-sectors, i.e., the agricultural sub-sector comprises of agriculture and allied economic activities such as crop husbandry, animal husbandry and dairying, fisheries, poultry and forestry. The non-agriculture sub sector consists of economic activities relating to industry, business and services. Industry here refers to co-enterprises, trading to general goods, small shops, petty traders, etc., where as services refer to transport, communications, banking input supply, marketing of farm and non-farm produce, etc. The main stakeholders of the rural sector include farmers agricultural and non-agricultural labourers, artisans, traders, moneylenders, and those engaged in providing such services as transport communication processing, banking and education and extension.

Rural Poverty

Rural poverty is the opposite of the term 'rural development'. It implies lack of development, or underdevelopment, and therefore the knowledge of its measures also is as important as that of measures of rural development.

Rural poverty is a world wide problem; it exists in both developing and developed countries of the world. Over one billion people in the world are estimated to be living in poverty. The incidence of poverty is highly uneven among the regions of the world, among countries within those regions, as among localities within those countries. Nearly half of the world's poor live in South Asia, a region that accounts for roughly 30 per cent of the world's population. Alleviation of poverty has been an important objective of development policies and programmes formulated all over the world, including India.

Rural Development-Gandhian Model

Gandhiji's approach to India's rural development was holistic and people-centered. It was rooted in this conviction in the tenets of truth, non-violence and the goodness of human beings. Influenced as he was by Tolstoy, Ruskin and the teachings of the Gita, he placed more emphasis on moral and spiritual values than economic motives as a means of over all development.

Values Underlying the Model

Gandhian model of rural development is based on the following values and premises:

1. Real India is found not in its cities, but in its villages.
2. The revival of villages is possible only when the village is exploited no more. Exploitation of villagers by city dwellers was "violence", in Gandhiji's opinion.

3. Simple living and high thinking , implying voluntary reduction of materialistic wants, and pursuit of moral and spiritual principles of life.
4. Dignity of labour: everyone must earn his bread by physical labour, and one who labours must necessarily get his subsistence.
5. Preference to the use of indigenous (Swadeshi) products, service and institutions.
6. Balance between the ends and the means: Gandhiji believed that non-violence as the end and the means was maintained.

Principal Components of the Model

The principal components of the Gandhian model are as follows:

Self-Sufficient Village Economy

Gandhiji's concept of self-sufficiency was not a narrow one, nor was it that of selfishness or arrogance. He realized the need for villagers to get those things from outside the village, which they could not produce in the village.

Decentralisation

Gandhiji believed that human happiness with mental and moral development should be the supreme goal of society, and that this goal should be achieved through decentralisation of political and economic powers.

Khadi and Village Industries

For Gândhi, Khadi was an instrument of decentralization of production and distribution of the basic necessities of life, and of ensuring 'work to all'. He also favoured the promotion of other village industries, such as hand-grinding, hand-pounding, soap-making, paper-making, metal-making, oilseed-crushing, tanning etc. He advocated the use of manual labour, but he appreciated the role of new technologies, if they were appropriate, indigenous, and did not affect the level of employment and standard of living.

IMPLEMENTING STRATEGY

Gandhiji prescribed the following institutional structure and instruments for implementing his strategy, namely, panchayatraj, cooperatives, trusteeship, and Nai Taleem (New Education). A brief description of each of these instruments follows.

Panchayatraj

Gandhiji envisaged that each village in India would be a republic, where the village panchayat would have the full power of managing its affairs, including defense. He expected the panchayat to perform the legislative, executive and judicial functions necessary for smooth functioning of the village economy. Various development activities such as education, health and sanitation would also be taken up by the village panchayat. It is good and in conformity with Gandhian views, that India now has made panchayatraj institutions statutory bodies by passing the 73rd (Constitution) Amendment Act, 1992. It is hoped that Gandhiji's dream of local self-governance through village panchayats would now be fulfilled.

Co-operatives

Gandhiji saw a great virtue in cooperation as an instrument of rural development. He assigned specific roles to cooperatives in the fields of agriculture, commending the promotion of cooperative farming and thereby preventing further fragmentation of landholding. He also advocated the establishment of other type of cooperatives, such as credit cooperatives, weavers and spinner's cooperatives and dairy cooperatives up to the expectations of Gandhi. India now has the world's largest network of cooperatives which occupy an important place in India's rural economy. The Operation Flood Programme is a living example of what cooperatives can do to promote agricultural and rural development in India.

Trusteeship

Gandhiji considered trusteeship is an instrument of transforming the capitalist order of society into an egalitarian one. In his opinion, all the land belonged to god, that is the community, and therefore he advocated that land and other natural resources should be collectively owned by, and operated for, the welfare of the community. Landlords should merely be trustees of land and other natural resources and capital assets. He saw in the principles of trusteeship a non-violent method of persuading landowners to donate their land voluntarily for community welfare purposes, and of avoiding class conflicts.

Nai Taleem

Gandhiji had no faith in modern education, which emphasized only literacy and acquisition of information. In his opinion , modern education was debauchery of the mind Hence he developed a new system of appropriate education and training, which he called Nai taleem. He believed that Nai taleem would help to develop the full potential of children and adults, through full development of their bodies, minds and spirits. He wanted to see Nai Taleem to be self-supporting and practice-oriented.

Conclusions & Suggestions

India has rich human resources. This has been amply demonstrated by what Indians have achieved in all fields of human endeavour, including science and technology. What is needed now is a long term policy for development of human resources through education, training, health care, and empowerment and creation of a congenial socio-economic institutional (including legal), and political environment for the fullest possible utilization of the vast, untapped reservoirs of human power and ingenuity. Human resources are inexhaustible and renewable, and, hence, the only resources which can sustain development forever. Our axiom in the twenty-first century should be human beings are both the end and the means of development, which include:

1. Elementary education: Hundred per cent enrolment in the age-group up to 14 years by 1990. It would be supplemented with non-formal education.

- Hundred per cent coverage of adults in the age-group of 15 to 35 by 2010 through Non-Formal Education.
- Provision of compulsory and free education at elementary stage.
- Provision of adult education centers, CECS and rural library services.

2. Rural Health: One community health volunteer for a population of 1000 or a village by 2010, establishment of one for 3000 in tribal and hilly areas by 2000 AD. Establishment of one community health centre for a population of one lakh or one CD Block by 2000 AD.
   - Provision of sanitary (including drainage and disposal of wastes) and public health measures.
   - Provision for the control of Malaria and other diseases.
   - Provision of drinking water supplies.
   - Provision of medical aid for the ailing.
   - Antenatal care of expectant mothers and midwifery services.
3. Rural water supply: Linking all remaining villages with a population of 1500 and above and 50 per cent of the total number of villages with population of 1000 to 1500 by 1990.
4. Rural Electrification: At least 60 per cent of the villages in each State and Union Territory to be electrified by 1990.
5. Housing to landless labour: Provision of housing assistance to all landless labour households by 1990. Assistance includes house site, construction materials, drinking water facility for a cluster of houses and approach road. Encouragement of improved rural housing on a self-help basis.
6. Rural Agriculture:
   - Reclamation of available virgin and waste land.
   - Provision of water for agriculture through various channels.

- Development of rural electrification.
- Promotion of improved agricultural techniques and land utilization.
- Provision of quality seeds.
- Promotion of veterinary aid.
- Promotion of marketing and credit facilities.
- Promotion of home economics.
- Encouragement of the use of natural and compost manures.
- Provision of improved agricultural implements

7. Communication Net Work: Provision of roads and transport services.
8. Encouragement of employment through trade auxiliary and welfare services.

Suggestions

Hence keeping the view of the above Gandhian model towards the development of rural areas, it is observed that the foremost is development of rural villages in building the national economy and development. Even in the threshold of the 21st Century, Gandhian model is more appropriate for the developing country like India. The following suggestions are made, keeping in view, while preparing and planning a model for Gram Swaraj.

1. Strengthening the impulses of modernization for the achievement of economic and technological self-reliance.
2. There is a significant need of reduction in the incidence of poverty and unemployment.
3. Improving the quality of life of the people with special reference to the economically and socially-challenged population through a Minimum Needs Programme.
4. Promoting policies to control the growth of population through voluntary acceptance of the small family norm.
5. Promoting the active involvement of all sections of the people in the process of development through

appropriate education, communication and institutional strategies.

REFERENCES

Adelman, Irma and C.T. Morris, (1967), Society Politics and Economic Development. Baltimore: Johns Hopkins University Press.

Chand, Ramesh, (1997), 'Important Liberalization and Indian Agriculture: the challenge and strategy', New Delhi: National Centre for Agricultural Economics and Policy Research, Policy Paper 6.

Dandekar, V.M. and Nilakanth Rath, (1971), Poverty in India. Pune: Indian School of Political Economy.

Desai, D.K. (1983), Management in Rural Development. New Delhi: oxford and IBH. Deshpande, D.V.M.K. Mudgal and K.K. Gupta. 1996. 'Regional Rural Banks at Cross Roads', Working Paper 9. Lucknow: Bankers Institute of Rural Development.

Doornvos, Martin, Frank van Dorsten, Manoshi Mitra and Piet Terhal, (1990), Dairy Aid and Development: India's separation Flood Indo-Dutch Studies on Development Alternatives, 3. New Delhi/New Bury Park/London: Sage Publications.

Guptha, S.P. (1995), 'Economic Reform and its Impact on Poor', in the Economic and political Weekly, 3 June, 1295-1313.

Krishnaji, N. (1997), 'Human Poverty Index: A Critique', in the Economic and Political Weekly, 30, August: 2202-5.

Kumar, Nalini. (1997), 'Operation Flood: Literature Review and Reconciliation', Occasional Publication, No-13. Anand: Institute of Rural Management.

World Bank (1997), World Bank Development Report 1997. Delhi: Oxford University Press.

Katar Singh, Rural Development, Principles, Policies and Management, Sage Publications, New Delhi.

V.R. Taneja (1987), Educational Thought and Practice, Published by Sterling Publishers Private Limited, New Delhi - 110020.

N.R. Swaroop Saxena (2005), Principles of Education, Published by R.Lall Book Depot, Meerut - 250001.

8

Rural Infrastructure Development

A Key Area in Rural Development

Dr. J. Ramu Naidu

Introduction

The Indian economy has undergone a remarkable transformation over the past two decades. The growth rate of average incomes has increased from 1¼ per cent prior to 1980 to 7 % by 2006. Prosperity of a country depends directly upon the development of agriculture and industry. Agricultural production, however, requires irrigation, power, credit, transport facilities, etc. Industrial production requires not only machinery and equipment but also skilled man-power, management, energy, banking and insurance facilities, transport services which include railways, roads, and shipping, communication facilities, etc. All these facilities and services which help in industrial and agricultural production constitute collectively the infrastructure of an economy. The development and expansion of these facilities are an essential pre-condition for increasing agricultural and industrial production in a country.

An attempt is made in this paper to review the existing literature regarding infrastructural facilities in India often refereed to as economic and social overheads. These consist of

(i) Irrigation, including flood control and command area development;

(ii) Energy: coal, electricity, oil and non-conventional sources;

(iii) Transport: Railways, roads, shipping and civil aviation;

(iv) Communications: Posts and telegraphs, telephones, telecommunications, etc.

(v) Banking, finance and insurance;

(vi) Science and technology;

(vii) Social overheads: health and hygiene and education.

Economic development of a country depends very much on the availability of its infrastructural facilities, particularly in the development of agriculture and industry sectors which depend on its infrastructure. The infrastructural facilities include various economic and social overhead viz., energy, irrigation, transportation, communication, banking, finance and insurance. Science and Technology and other social overheads like education and healthy environment. All these facilities jointly constitute the infrastructure of the country. Like other countries the development process of India put much emphasis on the growth of infrastructure. A relationship between infrastructure development and economic development of a country has long been recognized (World Development Report, 1994). Infrastructure development may effect production and consumption directly and create many positive and negative externalities. Therefore, it is essential to look at the relationship between infrastructure and economic development process. The main focus of this paper is to examine the impact of infrastructure on economic growth and quality of life. Infrastructure has strong forward and backward linkages within the economy. It affects economic development process both at the production and consumption levels. In the case of production, it contributes to economic growth in various ways such as by reducing input costs, by increasing the productivity of other factors like capital and labour, by providing more job opportunities and by attracting foreign and local investment. On the other hand, at the consumption level, it contributes to the quality of life of households through providing clean water, sanitation, electricity, transport and communication facilities which increase the real income level of households on the one hand and to help to reduce environmental pollution on the other (Abdhul Ghafoor, 2000). However, it must be kept in mind that the contribution of infrastructure to economic growth and quality of life can only be achieved by its efficient as and the value of services generated, not just through the existence and creation of physical facilities.

With high rates of economic growth and low public sector investment, India s infrastructure is in short supply and potentially a major constraint on future growth. To alleviate fiscal constraints and improve infrastructure productivity, the government is turning increasingly to the private sector to finance and run infrastructure projects. In some infrastructure sectors in which the regulatory environment is conducive to private sector involvement, performance has improved significantly. However, although infrastructure policy is moving in the right direction in some sectors, there are still a number of ways in which the regulatory environment could be improved further. This chapter outlines a range of policy initiatives that would increase private sector participation and improve infrastructure service delivery to international standards. It begins by discussing the role of public-private partnerships in the provision of infrastructure services before moving on to review the regulatory environment in a number of infrastructure sectors with a focus on regulatory settings that constrain competition.

India is predominantly an agricultural country. Agriculture forms the core sector of Indian economy. Since independence, a large number of schemes for rural development have been launched from time to time. Though, all these schemes and policies have brought considerable exchanges in agro-economic scenes of rural area, yet the fruits of development have been shared unequally. The economic opportunities are strongly shaped by access to infrastructure. There is solid evidence that infrastructure investments broaden opportunities for the people and communities by integrating them into regional and national systems of production and commerce improving their access to public services. The availability of infrastructure facilities in rural areas helps in reducing degree of poverty, increase in agricultural productivity and wages as well as the growth of non-agricultural activities in the rural area. Against this background of the well-accepted linkage between rural infrastructure programme of the Government of India are examined.

Rural infrastructure comprises rural roads, rural housing and rural electrification. Rural road connectivity is an extremely important aspect of rural development. A centrally sponsored scheme has been launched called the Pradhan Mantri Gram Sadak Yojana (PMGSY) which seeks to provide connectivity of all unconnected habitations in rural areas with a population of more than 500 persons through good all-weather roads by the end of the Tenth Plan period. In respect of All States and Desert areas, the objective would be to connect habitations with population of 250 persons and above. In order to achieve the objective of the programme, a requirement of Rs. 60,000 crore has been estimated. The available source of funds, for the present, is the 50 per cent share of the cess on High Speed Diesel (HSD), amounting to approximately Rs. 2500 crore per annum. For the year 2001-02, a sum of Rs. 2500 crore has been earmarked for the PMGSY. Project proposal for Rs.4273 crore pertaining to 26 states and two Union territories have been cleared. While projects worth twice the amount of allocation have been cleared during the current year, actual release in 2001-02 would be limited to this year's allocation and next year's releases will be made from April 2002 onwards depending on the progress of the works.

According to the 1991 census, around 3.1 million households are without shelter and another 10.31 million households reside in unserviceable kutcha houses. Considering the magnitude of the problem, a National

Housing Habitat Policy was announced in 1998 which aims at providing, housing for all and facilitates construction of 20 lakh additional housing units 913 lakh in rural areas and 7 lakh in urban areas annually with an emphasis on extending benefits to the poor and deprived. Government is committed to the goal of ensuring shelter for all by the end of Tenth Plan period. For achieving these objectives, a comprehensive action plan for rural housing has been prepared (Annexure-I). The objective of the Indira Gandhi Awas Yojana (IAY) is to provide assistance to the below-poverty-level households (BPL) belonging to scheduled caste, scheduled tribe and free bonded labour categories.

The central assistance under the IAY for 2001-02 is Rs.1618 crore for construction up-gradation of 1.3 million houses. So far, an amount of Rs. 1098 cores has been released during 2001-02. The Pradhan Mantri Gramodya Yojana is part of the comprehensive Pradhan Mantri Gramodya Yojana introduced during 2000-01 to achieve the objectives of sustainable human development at the village level. During 2001-02 Rs.280 crore has been made available for implementing the Rural Shelter component of PMGY. An amount of Rs. 126 crore has been released so far during 2001-02 to meet the requirement of EWS and LIG groups in rural areas and to improve the outreach of housing finance in rural areas, the equity support to HUDCO has been increased from 5 crores to 355 crores during the Ninth Five Year Plan. The entire amount of Rs. 150 crores has been released.

At present, there are about 80000 villages which still remain to be electrified and which are concentrated in nine States. In order to achieve the national goal of village electrification by 2007, village electrification has now been included under Pradhan Mantri Gramodya Yojana (PMGY) as basic minimum service for 2001-02. Under the scheme, an allocation of Rs. 418.59 crore has been made to the States for carrying out rural electrification. The States have the flexibility to allocate additional funds available. Under different components of PMGY. The first instalment equivalent to 50 per cent of the total allocation to various States has been released by the middle of January 2001.

Annexure–1

Action plan for Rural Housing:

(i) Provision of up gradation of unserviceable kutcha houses in Indira Awas Yojana (IAY) in addition to new construction.

(ii) Pradhan mantra Gramodaya Yojana Gramin Awas.

(iii) Credit-cum subsidy scheme for rural housing.

(iv) Innovative scheme for Rural Housing and Habitat Development.

(v) Rural Building Centres.

(vi) Enhancement of equity contribution by Ministry of Rural Development to HUDCO.

(vii) Samagra Awas Yojana.

(viii) National Mission for rural Housing and Habitat.

Serious Shortcomings

But all is not well with the infrastructural facilities at present. The rate of progress, despite being fast, has not made the quantum of infrastructure adequate. Moreover, the mix of different infrastructural components remains satisfactory. Their utilization is also not upto to the mark.

One important weakness of the country's rural infrastructure at present is its smallness as compared to its needs. This is particularly true in the fields of transport and power. The inadequacy is also sharply brought out by the fact that as yet large many villages remain without electricity.

There is again a greater inadequacy in respect of some infrastructural facilities. In the development of inland waterways, for instance, much remains to be done. Road transport, the most important medium of the village development is still very insufficient. Electricity generation capacity is far less than needed.

There is, again, much inadequacy of infrastructure in the field of technology for the promotion of activities for the upliftment of the weaker sections, for backward areas, for dry lands and small farming etc.

Another shortcoming of the existing infrastructure is both under-utilized and improperly used. Sometimes, there is an inadequate demand due to failures in other sectors, or there is a lack of proper coordination in the other sectors in respect of their demands. Quite often, the inefficiency is caused by the inadequacy in the maintenance (repairs, replacements, etc) of the infrastructure. Many installations have become weak in their output for lack of modernization or up gradation of their technology.

Suggested Measures

In view of the above mentioned shortcomings, it is necessary that the growth of infrastructure is accelerated and its quality upgraded. These objectives can be achieved by increasing investments in this sector and by improving its performance.

The first and the foremost solution lie in sharply stepping up of investment in rural infrastructure. This measure alone till help in raising significantly the growth-rate of the economy. The expert group on Commercialization of infrastructure projects (1996) of the World Bank's shows that in large many countries, it has been found that a one per cent rise in infrastructure goes wit a one per cent increase in the Gross Domestic Product (GDP). In providing for the infrastructure, the public sector will have to be the major contributor because of such reasons as: large and huge capital investment, long gestation periods, externalities, high risks and low rates of return. The State is also facing serious problem sin respect of the debts it has incurred on this account. With public sector units not doing well, interest payments are eating away a substantial portion of government revenues. In view of the above, the private sector will have to be associated as an important supplementary source of finance and builder of infrastructure. The finances can be drawn both from the domestic sources and foreign sources. The foreign investors, in particular, those making direct investments, can provide large funds for this sector. Additionally, the private sector can provide the much-needed expertise for efficient management and modern technologies for cost-effective construction of infrastructure projects.

Improving Performance

It is also essential that the rural infrastructure delivers its services in the most efficient way, so that the costs of growth of the economy are the least possible and the benefits flowing from it, the best attainable. This requires first that the technologies used to build the infrastructure are the most advanced. It is also necessary that the stock of infrastructure is well maintained and the necessary repairs and replacements made as and when needed. The allocations of investments in the different sectors of infrastructure are in right proportions and also it is necessary that these allocations change with the changing patterns of demand for their services.

References

Abdul Kalam, A.P.J. with Rajan YS (1998), India 2020-A Vision for the New Millenium, Penguin Books, New Delhi.

Abdul Ghaffor (2000), Public Infrastructure Performance in Developing Countries, Ashgate Publications,

Agrawal A.N. (2005), Indian Economy-Problems of Development and Planning, New Age International (P) Ltd., New Delhi

India (2006), (A Reference Annual) Ministry of Information and Broadcasting, Govt. of India, New Delhi.

Khan N.A. (2004), Infrastructure for Economic Development (A comparative study of India and Malasia), Anmol Publications Pvt. Ltd., New Delhi.

Misra S.K. and Puri V.K. (2007), Indian Economy-Its Development Experience, Himalaya Publishing House, New Delhi.

Rao T.V. (2006), Human Resource Development-Experiences & Interventions, Strategies, Sage Publications, New Delhi.

Ruddar, Datt K.P.M. Sundaram (2008), Indian Economy, S. Chand and Company Ltd., New Delhi.

World Development Report, (1994), United Nations.

World Bank Publication, (1989), Environmental Management & Economic Development.

9

NRHMj A Rural Health Reform

Y. Divya Rupa
Dr. K. Mary Sujatha

Introduction

Since Independence, the country has created a vast public health infrastructure on Public Health Centres (PHCs) and Community Health Centres (CHCs). There is also a health care provide (Auxiliary Nurse, Midwives, Male Health Workers, Lady Health Assistants). Yet, this vast infrastructure is able to cater to only 20 per cent of them, while 80 per cent of health care needs are still being provided by the private sector. Poor are suffering from long-standing health care problems. Most of the Health problems that people suffer in rural areas and in urban areas are preventable and easily treatable. With this view, the Government of India had launched NRHM (National Rural Health Mission).

Recognizing the importance of health in the process of economic and social development and improving the quality of life of our citizens, the Government of India has resolved to launch the National Rural Health Mission to carry out necessary architectural correction in the basic health care delivery system. The mission adopts a synergetic approach by relating health to determinants of good health, viz. segments of nutrition, sanitation, hygiene and safe drinking water. The goal of the mission is to improve the availability of and access to quality healthcare by people, especially for those residing in rural area, the poor, women and children.

Present paper throws light on various components involved in NRHM, which has been launched in April 2005 by Government of India.

Methodology

Present paper is a content analysis, which analyses NRHM (2005-2012) Mission Document.

Objectives

Following specific objectives are intended to analyze the NRHM Document:

- Status of public health
- Vision and goals of NRHM
- Components of the Mission
- Role of State Government
- Funding Mechanisms
- Expected outcomes

Status of Pubic Health

Public health expenditure in India has declined from 1.3 per cent of GDP in 1990 to 0.9 per cent of GDP in 1999. The Union Budgetary allocation for health in 1.3 per cent, while the State's budgetary allocation is 5.5 per cent.

Union Government contribution to public health expenditure is 15 per cent, while States contribution is about 85 per cent. Lack of community ownership of Public Health Programmes inspects levels of efficiency, accountability and effectiveness and lack of integration of sanitation, hygiene, nutrition and drinking waster issues which are rampant. There are striking regional inequalities in health care sector. Population Stabilization is still challenge, especially in states with weak demographic indicators.

Over 40 per cent of hospitalized Indians borrow heavily (or) sell assets to cover hospital expenses. Over 25 per cent of hospitalized Indians fall below poverty line expenses.

Vision and Goals of Mission

The National Rural Health Mission (2005-12) seeks to provide effective health care to rural population throughout the country with special focus on 18 States, which have weak public health indicators and/or weak infrastructure.

The Mission is an articulation of the commitment of the Government to raise public spending on health from 0.9 per cent of GDP to 2.3 per cent of GDP.

It aims to undertake architectural correction of the health system to enable it to effectively handle increased allocation, as promised under the National Common Minimum Programme and promote policies that strengthen pubic health management and service delivery in the country.

It aims at effective integration of health concerns with determinants of health like sanitation and hygiene, nutrition, and safe drinking water through a district plan for health. It seeks to improve aces of healthcare for rural people, especially poor women and children, to equitable, affordable, accountable and effective primary health care.

Goals of NRHM

- Reduction in Infant Mortality Rate (IMR) and Maternal Mortality Rate (MMR);
- Universal access to public health services such as women's health, child health, water, sanitation and hygiene, immunization and nutrition;
- Prevention and control of communicable and non-communicable diseases, including locally endemic diseases;
- Access to integrated comprehensive primary health care;
- Population stabilization, gender and demographic balance;

- Revitalize local health traditions and mainstream AYUSH;
- Promotion of healthy life styles;

There are certain strategies to achieve the goals of NRHM. They are:

- Train and enhance capacity of Panchayat Raj Institutions (PRIs) to own and manage public health services
- Health plan for each village through village health committee of the Panchayat
- Provision of 24 hour service in 50 per cent PHCs by addressing shortage of doctors in high focus States, through mainstream AYUSH man power.
- The duration of NRHM will be from 2005-2012, the total allocation for the development of family welfare has been linked from Rs. 8420 crores to Rs. 10820 crores proposals for the year 2005-06.

Components and Institutional Mechanism of NRHM

To implement the NRHM, there are certain components, which need to be understood. They are:

- Accredited Social Health Activities (ASHA);
- Strengthening sub-centres;
- Strengthening Primary Health Centres;
- Strengthening CHCs for first referral care;
- District Health Plan;
- Converging Sanitation and Hygiene under NRHM;
- Strengthening Disease Control programmes;
- Pubic private partnership for Public Health Goals, including regulation of private sector;
- New Health Financing mechanism;
- Reorienting Health/Medical education to support rural Health issues.

Institutional Mechanism

- Village Health and Sanitation Samiti (at village level consisting of Panchayat representatives, ANM/MPW, Anaganwadi worker, teacher ASHA, community health volunteers);
- Rogi Kalyan Samiti (or equivalent) for community management of public hospitals;
- District Health Mission, under the Leadership of Zilla Parishad with district Health Head as convener and all relevant departments, NGOs, private professional etc., represented in it.
- State Health Mission, chaired by Chief Minister and Co-chaired by Health Minister and while State Healthy Secretary as convener representation of related departments, NGOs, private professionals
- Integration of departments of health and family welfare, at National and State Level;
- Standing mentoring group shall guide and oversee the implementation of ASHA initiative;

Role of State Government under NRHM

The Mission covers the entire country. The 18 high focus States are: Uttar Pradesh, Bihar, Rajasthan, Madhya Pradesh, Orissa, Uttaranchal, Jharkand, Manipur, Meghalaya, Tripura, Nagaland, Mizoram, Himachal Pradesh and Jammu & Kashmir.

Government of India would provide funding for key components in these 18 high focus States. Other states would fund interventions like ASHA, Programme Management Unit (PMU), and upgradation of SC/PHC/CHC through Integrated Financial Envelope (IFC).

NRHM would prioritize funding for addressing Inter State and Intra-district disparities in terms of health India structure and indicators.

All States should sign MOU with Government of India, including their commitment to increase contribution to public Health Budget (preferably by 10 per cent each year).

Increased devolution to Panchayat Raj Institutions as per 73rd Constitution (Amendment) Act, and performance benchmarks for release of funds.

Funding Mechanisms of NRHM

The NRHM is conceived as an umbrella programme subsuming the existing programmes of health and family welfare, including the RCH-II, National Diseases Control Programme for Malaria, TB, Kala Azar, Filaria, Blindness and Iodine Deficiency and Integrated Disease Surveillance Programme.

The outlay of the NRHM for 2005-06 is in the range of Rs. 6700 crores. The Mission envisages additionally of 30 per cent over existing Annual Budgeting outlays, every year, to fulfill the mandate of National Common Minimum Programme to raise the outlays for public Health from 0.9 per cent of GDP to 2.3 per cent of GDP.

The outlay for NRHM shall accordingly be determined in the Annual Budgeting exercise.

The States are expected to raise their contributions to Pubic Health Budget by minimum 10 per cent per annum to support the Mission activities.

Expected Outcomes

The NRHM has been launched with some major outcomes. They are both at National level and Community level.

National Level

- Infant Mortality Rate reduced to 30/1000 live births.
- Maternal Mortality Rate reduced to 100/100000.
- Total Fertility Rate reduced to 2.1.
- Malaria mortality reduction rate: 50% upto 2010, additional 10% by 2012.
- Kala Azar mortality reduction rate: 100% by 2010 and sustaining elimination until 2012.
- Filaria/Microfilaria reduction rate: 70% by 2010, 80% by 2012 and elimination by 2015.

- Dengue mortality reduction rate: 50% by 2010 and sustaining at that level until 2012.
- Japanese Encephalitis mortality reduction rate: 50% by 2010 and sustaining at that level until 2012.
- Cataract Operation: Increasing to 46 lakhs per year until 2012.
- Leprosy prevalence rate: reduce from 1.8/10000 in 2005 to less than 1/10000 thereafter.
- Tuberculosis DOTS services: Maintain 85% care rate through entire mission period.
- Upgrading community health centers to Indian Public Health standards.
- Increase utilization of First Referral Units from less than 20% to 75%.
- Engaging 250000 female Accredited Social Health Activists (ASHAs) in 10 States.

Community Level

- Availability to trained community level worker at village level, with a drug for generic ailments
- Health Day at Anganwadi level on a fixed day/month for provision of immunization, anti/post-natal checkups and services related to mother and child healthcare, including nutrition.
- Availability of generic drugs for common ailments at Sub-centers and Hospital level.
- Good hospital care through assured availability of doctors, drugs and quality services at PHC/CHC level.
- Improved access to Universal Immunization through induction of Auto Disabled Syringes, alternate vaccine delivery and improved mobilization services under the programme
- Improved facilities for institutional delivery through provision of referral, transport, escort and improved

hospital care subsidized under the Janani Suraksha Yojana (JSY) for the below poverty line families.

- Availability of assured healthcare at reduced financial risk through pilots of Community Health Insurance under the Mission
- Provision of households toilets
- Improved outreach services through mobile medical units at district level

Conclusion

The prestigious Mission of Government of India in the Health Care has great challenges. The Mission of NRHM is a revolutionary reform and a boon for Rural Health Sector. Hope India may attain to the status of health for all by 2010.

10

RURAL BANKING IN INDIA

An Overview of the Recent Trends, Regulations and the Revolutions

E.V.P.A.S. PALLAVI
P.S. RAVINDRA

INTRODUCTION

A well-sequenced and calibrated process of financial sector reform introduced in the early 1990s has resulted in a competitive and resilient banking sector. The total business of the Indian banking industry has gone up by more than seven times from Rs. 5,984 billion in 1994-95 to Rs 45,372 billion in 2006-07. Now, India enjoys being one of the best regulatory and supervisory systems for its banking sector amongst the emerging market economies.

The introduction of social and development banking policy entailed a radical shift from prevalent practice in respect of the objective and functioning of commercial banks. It was only after 1969 that a multi-institutional approach to credit provision in the countryside became policy, with commercial banks, rural banks and cooperative institutions establishing wide geographical and functional reach in the Indian countryside. The Reserve Bank of India (RBI) issued specific directives with respect to social and development banking. Similarly, in 1975, the Government established by ordinance and then legislation, a new network of rural financial institutions called the Regional Rural Banks (RRBs).

The Review of Rural Banking

RRBs were created on the basis of recommendations by a working group on commercial credit, also called the Narasimham Committee, and were intended to "combine the cooperatives' local feel and familiarity with the business acumen of commercial banks" Initially, the number of such banks expanded rapidly, and covered 476 districts by 1987. The late 1970s and early 1980s, were a period when the rhetoric of land reform was finally discarded by the ruling classes themselves, and a period when the major instruments of official anti-poverty policy were programmes for the creation of employment.

The most important new scheme of this phase was, of course, the Integrated Rural Development Programme or IRDP, a scheme for the creation of productive income-bearing assets among the poor through the allocation of subsidized credit. The IRDP was initiated in 1978-79 as a pilot project and extended to all rural blocks of the country in 1980. There is much writing on the failure of IRDP to create long-term income-bearing assets in the hands of asset-poor rural households. Among the many reasons for this failure were the absence of agrarian reform and decentralized institutions of democratic government, the inadequacy of public infrastructure and public provisioning of support services and the persistence of employment-insecurity and poverty in rural society. Nevertheless, the IRDP strategy did lead to a significant transfer of funds to the rural poor. This also involved an expansion and consolidation of the institutional infrastructure of rural banking. "Even ardent critics of India's growth strategy," wrote a noted scholar of India's banking system, "would admit that what the country achieved in the area of financial sector development before the present reform process began, particularly after bank nationalization, was unparalleled in financial history".

The policy objectives of the current phase are encapsulated in the Report of the Committee on the Financial System, which was chaired, ironically, by the same person who recommended the establishment of Regional Rural Banks, M. Narasimham (RBI, 1991). In its very first paragraph, the report called for "a vibrant and competitive financial system...to sustain the ongoing reform in the structural aspects of the real economy." The Committee said that redistributive objectives "should use the instrumentality of the fiscal rather than the credit system" and, accordingly, that "directed credit programmes should be phased out." It also recommended that interest rates be deregulated, that capital adequacy norms be changed (to "compete with banks globally"), that branch licensing policy be revoked, that a new institutional structure that is "market-driven and based on profitability" be created, and that the part played by private Indian and foreign banks be enlarged. Let us make it clear that, before the 1990s, the banking system was open to much criticism, particularly of its bureaucratic failures, its insensitivity to the social and economic contexts in which it functioned, and class and regional inequalities in lending patterns.

The Realities of Rural Credit

The reality for the expansion of rural branches all over the State is mostly to impose ceilings on interest rates, and setting guidelines for the sectoral allocation of credit. Rural credit was an important component of the 'Green Revolution' package; the first post nationalization phase of expansion in rural banking saw a substantial growth in credit advances for agriculture. Specifically, a target of 40 per cent of advances for the "priority sectors," namely, agriculture and allied activities, and small-scale and cottage industries, was set for commercial banks. Advances to the countryside increased substantially, although they were, as was the Green Revolution itself, biased in respect of regions, crops and classes.

Development of the rural credit delivery system in the country has metamorphosed from monopoly of cooperatives to the induction of commercial banks and establishment of regional rural banks for improving the outreach and ensuring access to credit in rural areas. With the implementation of financial sector reforms, the accent is on ensuring the financial health of the system. Innovations in rural credit delivery had an impact on agricultural production and reduction of poverty due to increased flow of credit. Accelerating the pace of capital formation in agriculture, infrastructure development with focus on transportation and marketing, ensuring credit discipline will enable the rural sector to absorb more credit from institutional sources.

Ensuring access to credit in the rural areas for augmenting agricultural production, alleviating poverty and improving the efficiency of the rural credit delivery system has been an area of focus in the planning process in our country. Various measures initiated to improve the outreach of credit institutions, besides enhancing capital formation and production in agriculture, have been instrumental in alleviating poverty in the country. The changing economic scenario coupled with emerging segmentation of the rural credit markets pose new challenges to the rural credit delivery system. Financial sector reforms which seek to minimize governmental controls on credit institutions impose stringent accounting norms and give freedom to banks from mandatory rural lending may create conditions not auguring well for rural development, especially for the vulnerable sections.

The Regulations of Rural Banking since 1969

The period from 1969 to the present can be characterised as representing, broadly speaking, three phases in banking policy vis-à-vis the Indian countryside. The first was the period following the nationalization of India's 14 major commercial banks in 1969. This was also the early phase of the 'Green Revolution' in rural India, and one of the objectives of the nationalization of banks was for the state to gain access to new liquidity, particularly among rich farmers, in the countryside. The declared objectives of the new policy with respect to rural banking-what came to be known as "social and development banking"-were (i) to provide banking services in previously unbanked or under-banked rural areas; (ii) to provide substantial credit to specific activities, including agriculture and cottage industries; and (iii) to provide credit to certain disadvantaged groups such as, Dalit and Scheduled Tribe households. The two main crops that gained from the Green Revolution, as is well recognized, were wheat and rice.

Financial liberalization after 1991 decimated the formal system of institutional credit in rural India. It represented a clear and explicit reversal of the policy of social and development banking, such as it was, and contributed in no small way to the extreme deprivation and distress of which the rural poor in India have been victims over the last decade. It is well known that the burden of indebtedness in rural India is very great, and that despite major structural changes in credit institutions and forms of rural credit in the post-Independence period, the exploitation of the rural masses in the credit market is one of the most pervasive and persistent features of rural life in India. Rural households need credit for a variety of reasons. They need credit to meet short-term requirements of working capital and for long-term investment in agriculture and other income-bearing activities. These include expenditure on food, housing, health and education. In the Indian context, another important purpose of borrowing is to meet expenses on a variety of social obligations and rituals.

The Real Problems of Rural Credit

Historically, there have been four major problems with respect to the supply of credit to the Indian countryside. Firstly, the supply of formal sector credit to the countryside as a whole has been inadequate. Secondly, rural credit markets in India themselves have been very imperfect and fragmented. Thirdly, as the foregoing suggests, the distribution of formal sector credit has been unequal, particularly with respect to region and class, caste and gender in the countryside. Formal sector credit needs specially to reach backward areas, income poor households, people of the oppressed castes and tribes, and women. Fourthly, the major source of credit to rural households, particularly income-poor working households, has been the informal sector.

Given the abysmal spread of formal credit facilities in the country, and more so in village India, it's hardly surprising that both the Government as well as the Reserve Bank of India are both talking of universal financial access or "financial inclusion" nowadays. That's perhaps why, a South India - based PSU bank is planning to adopt the union territory of Pondicherry for "financial inclusion". The problem, however, is that unless this goes hand-in-hand with the overall development of village India, it's akin to growing grass without roots. Since financial inclusion means access to financial services, the best indicator is the proportion of families with a bank account. In the United Kingdom, about 5 per cent of the populations do not have bank accounts. In Australia, about 7-8 per cent of the populations do not do banking.

The latest Report of the National Sample Survey Organisation on village facilities -conducted in July-December 2007 - revealed that there were no post offices in over 78 per cent of India's villages and only one-third of all villages were within two km of a telegraph office/PCO/e-mail facility. The situation has not dramatically changed since then. Look at some other parameters of social infrastructure. One-fourth of the villages do not have access to electricity; non-conventional forms of energy are available in less than 12 per cent of villages; tap water is used for drinking in about 18 per cent of villages and 55 per cent of them get their drinking water mainly from tube-wells or hand-pumps. What's more, 54 per cent of the villages are more than five km away from the nearest primary health centre and 27 per cent are more than 10 km away from it. Only 10 per cent of the villages have a medicine shop and 20 per cent a private clinic or doctor. One-third of the villages do not have pre-primary schools and 28 per cent do not have primary schools. Finally, co-operative societies exist only in 30 per cent of Indian villages. Financial inclusion alone cannot do the trick for the rural masses until social exclusion is taken care of. Access to health, education and pucca roads is as important as access to a bank account and credit. However, urban India presents a different picture. Even in Mumbai, millions of people are financially excluded, although they have access to social infrastructure.

The Revolutions in Rural Banking

In the banking sector, out of the total 67,897 branches in the country (2002) 47.7 per cent are in rural India (32,443). The average population served by a bank branch is 15,000. If one includes the rural cooperative banks, the average could be lower still - 12,800. The numbers compare favourably with Indonesia and Mexico. However about 58 per cent of the rural households do not have a bank account and only 21 per cent have access to credit from a formal source and also 70 per cent of marginal farmers have no deposit account, 87 per cent have no formal credit. Only a little over 1 per cent of rural households can rely on a loan from a financial intermediary to finance unforeseen expenses.

In 2002, the number of rural deposits was 30.2 per cent of the total deposits in the banking system (Rs 13.30 crore out of Rs 43.99 crore). However, the amount of deposits mopped up in rural India is only 14 per cent of the total deposit liability of the system (Rs.1,59,423 crore out of Rs.11,23,393 crore). Similarly, there are 2.51 crore rural advance accounts, which is 44.5 per cent of the total number of advance accounts. However, the share of rural pockets in the total credit kitty is only 14 per cent (Rs.92,789 crore out of Rs.6,55,993 crore). As a whole 18 per cent of the rural population has bank account, as against these the bank account in urban India is 103 per cent.

This is a welcome initiative, if we want to reduce rural India's dependence on non-formal financial sources like local money lenders, hit funds, bashes and so on. A 1997 PricewaterhouseCoopers study said that the dependence of low-income households on informal sources is as high as 78 per cent. Branch banking in rural India is a loss-making proposition and existing regulations prevent the entry of agents mobilising deposits or selling loans. In this context, the combination of the Internet kiosk and a local language ATM can revolutionise the landscape of rural banking without violating the letter of the law. They can do what 196 regional rural banks and four local area banks have been unable to achieve. At a parallel level, the rural population can be reached out to through non-government organisations and micro-finance institutions.

The pilot programme of India's first rainfall insurance programme was conducted in July 2003, in Mahabubnagar, Andhra Pradesh, when a local area bank bought a bulk insurance policy from ICICI Lombard, the bank's general insurance arm, and sold around 200 individual policies for groundnut and castor farmers. Since then, the cover has been extended to 50 soya farmers in Madhya Pradesh and 600 acres of paddy crop in Aligarh in Uttar Pradesh. The message is quite clear. An innovative approach to rural lending can do what the government's continuous pressure on the banking system for expanding the base of kisan credit cards and good old guidelines for agricultural lending cannot.

The Recent Trends and Opportunities

Thousands of people from rural areas across 12 States are likely to get their social security pension and wages paid under the National Rural Employment Guarantee Act (NREGA) scheme with the help of mobiles over the coming few months. In Andhra Pradesh alone, for instance, 250,000 people have registered for mobile banking services. The State government is rolling out a programme to enroll three million people by the end of 2008. Mobile banking pilots and full-scale operations are being conducted across 12 States, and the entire ecosystem is being managed by the government with the help of the Reserve Bank of India, banks, leading telecom operators and technology implementation partners.

Mobile banking, which is catching up fast in the cities and hinterland, is not only helping the government to take a step forward towards fulfilling its aim of having one bank account for every household, but also saving it crores of rupees by way of reduced transaction costs. While the government incurs a transaction cost of Rs.12-13 for every Rs. 100 it sells out, mobile banking helps it reduce the cost to a mere Rs. 2. RBI estimates that around 40 per cent of Indians lack access to formal financial services and are largely 'unbanked'. For instance, the AP government has tied up with banks like the State Bank of India, Union Bank of India, Axis Bank, Andhra Bank, State Bank of Hyderabad, Andhra Pradesh Grameen Vikas Bank, and Punjab National Bank.

The mobile acts as a branch of the bank by storing a database of customers. It also has a smartcard, which biometrically stores the identity of the customer such as name, address, photograph, fingerprint templates and relevant details of the savings or loan accounts held by the issuing bank. Customers get a secure electronic identity via phone or smartcard, while agents take deposits and dispense cash.

State Bank of India, the country's largest bank, recently announced that it would shift its focus to Rural India to boost the retail portfolio. According to its Chairman, there is business opportunity in rural India. A large pool of high net worth individuals, traders, entrepreneurs, processing industries, marketing and warehousing agencies, market intermediaries, professionals, educational institutions, plantations and so on provides a wide range of business avenues and market for these institutions to diversify the risks and also seek growth. Many economists and policy-makers increasingly believe that future growth of the domestic economy to a large extent will depend on the robust performance of the agriculture and rural sector. The manufacturing and service sectors cannot sustain the economy's growth if the rural sector underperforms.

The rural sector needs timely credit. Due to the failure of the organised sector to make an impact in bridging the credit gap, the informal credit sector has been thriving and is able to lend as high as 24-36 per cent per annum depending on the borrowers' risk profile. The concepts of lending based on credit history and risk perception being implemented in the organised sector now have been in vogue in Rural India's informal credit sector for long. If banks can offer housing and car loans through simple procedures in urban markets, greater acceleration in development can be achieved through such direct incentives as exemption of tax on all private sector employment generation activities in the rural sector. As banking is the engine of growth, it would be worthwhile to exempt rural earnings from tax.

The Union Budget for 2006-07 highlighted a number of schemes for rural India including creating opportunities for rural employment and a National Rural Health Mission. It has also asked banks to give farm credit at 7 per cent to bring more farmers under the organised credit net. The Finance Ministry has proposed to ask banks to increase the level of farm credit to Rs.1,75,000 crore in 2006-07, an increase of about Rs.33,500 crore. In addition, banks are being asked to bring 50 lakh more farmers into the banking fold. The potential, no doubt, is tremendous.

CONCLUSION

The Development of the rural credit delivery system in the country has metamorphosed from monopoly of cooperatives to the induction of commercial banks and establishment of regional rural banks for improving the outreach and ensuring access to credit in rural areas. With the implementation of financial sector reforms, the accent is on ensuring the financial health of the system. Innovations in rural credit delivery had an impact on agricultural production and reduction of poverty due to increased flow of credit. Accelerating the pace of capital formation in agriculture, infrastructure development with focus on transportation and marketing, ensuring credit discipline will enable the rural sector to absorb more credit from institutional sources. The focus should be on strategies that are required for tackling issues such as sustainability and viability, operational efficiency, recovery performance, small farmer coverage and balanced sectoral development.

REFERENCES

Chandrasekhar, C.P., and Ray, Sujit Kumar (2004), "Financial Sector Reform and the Transformation of Banking" in Ramachandran and Swaminathan.

Jagan Mohan, V., "Regional Rural Banks (RRBs): The Vehicles for Bridging the Banking Divide," State Bank of India Monthly Review, XLIII, Jan., pp. 21-41.

Ramachandran, V.K., and Swaminathan, Madhur, "Rural Banking and Landless Labour Households, Institutional Reform and Rural Credit Markets in India," Journal of Agrarian Change, 2, 4, Oct., pp. 502-544.

Rangarajan, (Jan. 1997), C. "Role of Non-Governmental Organisations in Rural Credit Delivery System", Reserve Bank of India Bulletin, Reserve Bank of India, Bombay.

Rupa Rege Nitsure, (Dec. 2007), "Welcome Global Banks? Trends and Opportunities in the Indian Banking Industry, The Indian Banker, Volume II No. 12, p. 14.

Shetty, (Aug. 2004), S.L. "Performance of Commercial Banks since Nationalisation of Major Banks", Economic and Political Weekly, 13, nos. 31, 32 and 33.

11

RURAL MARKETING IN INDIA: THE CORPORATE SCENARIO

DR. ISRAEL RAJU VURAM
MR. MOHIDEEN A.K.

INTRODUCTION

The importance of rural marketing can be understood from the fact that today modern inputs like diesel, electricity, fertilizers, pesticides and seeds account for as much as 70 per cent of the total cash costs and 23 per cent of the total costs incurred by the farmers in the Green Revolution areas. Further the percentages were higher at 81 and 38 for small farmers owning 1.85 hectares of land.

Rural marketing in India is not much developed as there are many hindrances in the area of market, product design and positioning, pricing, distribution and promotion. Companies need to understand rural marketing in a broader manner not only to survive and grow in their business, but also as a means to the development of rural economy. However, rural India had its own set of problems like illiteracy, early childhood marriages, lack of access to birth control measures, poverty etc., that are interdependent on each other. There are also large numbers of daily wage earners and most of the people depended on the vagaries of monsoon. Inadequate infrastructure like non-availability of gas supply, frequent power cuts, improper sanitary conditions, inaccessible areas are the other common features of rural areas.

One needs to have a strategic view of the rural markets so as to know and understand the markets well. In the context of rural marketing one has to understand the manipulation of marketing mix has to be properly understood in terms of product usage. Product usage is central to price, distribution, promotion, branding, company image and more important farmer economics. Thus, any strategy in rural marketing should be given due attention and importance by understanding the product usage, all elements of marketing mix can be better organized and managed.

The Concept

Indian agricultural industry has been growing at a tremendous pace in the last few decades. The rural areas are consuming a large number of industrial and urban manufactured products. The rural agricultural production and consumption process plays a predominant role in developing the Indian economy. This has designed a new way for understanding a new process called 'Rural Marketing'. Rural marketing is different from agricultural marketing, which signifies marketing of rural products to the urban consumer or institutional markets. On the other hand, Rural Marketing basically deals with delivering manufactured or processed inputs or services to rural producers, the demand for which is basically a derived outcome.

The concept of rural marketing has to be distinguished from Agricultural marketing. Marketing is the process of identifying and satisfying customers' needs and providing them with adequate after sales service. Rural marketing scientists also term it as developmental marketing, as the process of rural marketing involves an urban to rural activity, which in turn is characterized by various peculiarities in terms of nature of market, products and processes. Rural marketing differs from agricultural or consumer products marketing in terms of the nature of transactions, which includes participants, products, modalities, norms and outcomes. The participants in case of Rural Marketing would also be different as they include input manufacturers, dealers, farmers, opinion makers, government agencies and traders. The existing approach to the rural markets has viewed the markets as a homogeneous one, but, in practice, there is significant buyer and user differences across regions as well as within that which require a differential treatment of the marketing problems. These differences could be in terms of the type of farmers, type of crops and other agro-climatic conditions. One has to understand the market norms in agricultural input so as to devise good marketing strategies and to avoid unethical practices, which distort the marketing environment. Many of the inputs used for production process have implications for food, health and environmental sectors. Rural marketing needs to combine concerns for profit with a concern for the society, besides being titled towards profit. Rural market for agricultural inputs is a case of market pull and not market push. Most of the jobs of marketing and selling is left to the local dealers and retailers. The market for input gets interlocked with other markets like output, consumer goods, money and labour.

Around the world, over 4 billion people survived in rural areas that came to more than 60 per cent of the total population. In India also, the ratio of rural to urban population was slightly higher than the world's ratio with 70 per cent of them living in rural areas. They domiciled in nearly 6,27,000 villages, spread over 3.2 million sq. km. This growing affluence along with good monsoon and the increased agriculture output, increased the total disposable income of rural consumers to 58 per cent with two-thirds of middle income households being in the rural market. It is predicted by industry analysts that by 2009-10, the urban households are projected to grow by 4 per cent, while the rural households are expected to grow by 11 per cent. If the rural income rose by 1 per cent, then the buying power would correspondingly increase by about Rs.10,000 crore. The colour televisions, refrigerators, air-conditioners and microwaves have become a household sight in villages and small townships that were long thought of as a luxury and domain of urbanites.

The Core Strategic Aspects

In most of the rural areas in different parts of the country, there is considerable awareness on various latest products that are available in the market. This has been possible due to the penetration of cable and satellite channels that have brought down the world at the finger tips of the common man. The media influenced the mindset of the rural consumer to such an extent that people who had money started purchasing the products unmindful of the costs, just to satisfy their needs as well as their ego. But, the growth of rural market could be attributed to many other reasons that in one way increased the sales as well as the profits of the companies.

Some of the important causes for the growth of rural markets are:

1. The rise in disposable income of the rural families;
2. The economic boom;
3. Timely rains;
4. Rural population involved themselves in business other than agriculture;
5. Increase white-collar jobs in nearby towns;
6. Commercialization of agriculture;
7. Saturation of the urban markets;
8. Media penetration in rural areas (particularly satellite channels);
9. Globalization
10. Economic liberalization;
11. Revolution in the Information Technology;
12. Women empowerment;
13. Improving infrastructure.

However, there was a significant role of the corporate

enterprises simultaneously in the development of rural market. Their timely intervention into the rural areas, their appropriate planning, their perception and identification about the growth of rural markets and the use of marketing strategies, all have equally contributed for the progress of rural markets. Even though corporate houses were hedged with so many problems in the rural areas, they saw a galore of opportunities in the rural market and converted all the pessimistic characteristics of the rural market into affirmative attributes. They satisfied themselves with the availability of limited infrastructure, saw a sign of prosperity rather than fear during the entry of competitors into the rural markets, showed excitement at the availability of satellite channels in the rural households, visualized their cash bells ringing with the increase in purchasing power of the rural masses that came equivalent to their urban counterparts. They traced a constant rise in the demand for those products that were once confined mostly to the urban houses. But, blame it on the kind of awareness created by the companies-people started using the products for other purposes as seen earlier.

In many villages, one can see today the alternate use of the products other than for their actual purpose. People in the State of Bihar feed the cattle with Horlicks as a health drink to fatten them! Similarly, people in Punjab use washing machine not for washing clothes but to make frothy lassi in huge quantities! Animals are rubbed with Iodex on their skins to relieve them from muscular pains after a day's hard work. Paints meant for houses are used on the horns of cattle for easy identification and theft prevention! The weavers in North India wear condoms on their fingers as gloves to weave fine threads, while its lubrication allows them fine control on threads and protect their sensitive fingers! If companies felt happy with their increased sales and profits through this means and thought that they captured the rural markets, then it is time for them to review their marketing strategies. They should understand that these results do not coincide with the application of the marketing tools and the technical expertise that are generally used to satisfy the customers as well as the company objectives. The implications of 4Ps of marketing mix or the use of 4As for successful rural marketing have produced wrong results.

Developmental marketing refers to taking up marketing programmes keeping the development objective in mind and using various managerial and other inputs of marketing to achieve these objectives. A prerequisite for developmental marketing is Development Market Research, which can be termed as the application of marketing research tools and techniques to the problems of development. The research tools of marketing like product testing, tests marketing, concept testing and media testing or message test and focus groups are used in this work. Developmental marketing has started to find its roots in India, where researchers are using focus groups and products tests to learn more about rural markets and products needs and USPs (Unique Selling Proposition) can be tried out. Media rural marketing uses both kinds of media, i.e., the traditional media as well as the modern media. The traditional media includes puppetry, drama, folk theatre, e.g. tamsaha (role play of different characters by one or two persons), nautanki (short skits with songs and poetry), street plays, folk songs, wall paintings and proverbs. Marketer uses traditional media as it is more accessible, personalized, familiar and carries a high potential for change. The modern media includes the print media, the television and the radio USPs.

Some of the USPs of the companies engaged in rural marketing are given below. Mahindra Tractors 'Mera Desh Mera Gaon' (My country my village) Tafe Tractors-'Grameen Bharat ki Dhadkan', Tafe ka Massey Ferguson (The heart beat of rural India its Tafe's Massey Ferguson) Swaraj Tractors-'Pragati aur Khush-hali ke liye' (For development and happiness) Escorts- 'Nayi technique ke sath, Bharosa Jeevan bhar Ka' (A life long trust with new techniques) Eicher-'Ghazab ki takat, ghazab ki shaan' (Incredible strength, Incredible pride) Sun Seeds- 'Grow with Sun' ICI Karate Insecticide-'Keedon ka Maha-kaal, Phasal Ka Pehredaar' (Insects enemy, protector of the crops). Pesticide India 'Desh ke liye Phasal Anek, Keedon ke Naash ke liye Foratox Sirf Ek' (Numerous crops for the country but only for destroying pests i.e.

Foratox). Thus the companies use different formats to influence the target audience in order to produce the desired results.

There are several limitations of rural marketing in the Indian context. This leads to the need for extension services to supplement the efforts of the firms engaged in rural marketing. The various extension services could include credit facilities, competitions among the farmers, educating the farmers regarding the appropriate agricultural practices, etc. Extension services would thus play a crucial role in the development of rural marketing in India.

The Corporate Contribution

In 2005, Hindustan Lever Limited had a contribution of Rs. 5,000 crore from the rural market that was a whopping 50 per cent of its total sales turnover. Another large corporate house LG Electronics that had a total turnover of Rs. 4,500 crore had a share of 55 per cent from the rural and semi-urban market. With such kind of contribution from the rural India, corporate houses perceived great opportunity in the rural markets and tapped the countryside to enlarge their market share.

Rural marketing is the much talked about subject for the business establishments-especially the FMCG and the consumer durable industry. Many of them who had earlier ignored this segment due to lot of investment requirements and low returns have again started foraying into it and targeted the rural masses. They attempted all the feasible approaches to sell the products to the rural consumers that met their lifestyles and living standards. Several large companies like HLL, ITC, Coca-Cola, LG, Britannia, Philips, Colgate-Palmolive etc., penetrated aggressively into the rural markets and spent heavily in the rural areas. Some of them even invested money to create separate sales and marketing teams exclusively for rural markets. They also appointed specialist agencies who could advise them on rural marketing.

In order to reap the benefits of, the economies of the scale, a rural marketer has to resort to bundling of inputs. 'Bundling of Inputs' is the process by which the marketer would provide a bundle of products to the retailer so that he can meet the requirements of the farmers in one place. The village level co-operatives and other agencies can play an effective role in the distribution of inputs. Establishing linkages with financial agencies and other input sellers can help greatly as the bank credit plays an important role by making the purchase possible. Management of Demand A marketer apart from maintaining good supplies in terms of quality and quantity also has to focus on the demand side of the operations also. Continuous market research should be undertaken to assess the buyer's needs and problems so that continuous improvements and innovations can be undertaken for a sustainable market performance.

There is a need to build partnership with rural clients for a sustainable business relationship and sustainable marketing relationship. There should be a long-term relationship between the firms and farmers for agro business projects, which are risky, long drawn and technical in nature. Partnership is required in rural marketing business so as to award distributorship to local groups and individuals employing locals, staff secondment in local projects, preferential purchase of local product, training to locals and discount on product supplies in some areas. Rural marketing firms can work with NGOs also because NGOs have better linkages and understanding of the local communities and their problems. Nagarjuna fertilizers and Chemicals Ltd has set up an agro output division which is known as FMS (Farm Management Service) which provides packages to the farmers right from soil testing to post harvest stage of the crop system. The FMS aims at enhancing farm productivity optimizing cost of production, improving economic returns to farmers and enhancing the cost of production and enhancing the produce quality.

Conclusion

The rural India that has lot of money with it definitely offers a great potential for the companies where the chances of outnumbering the urban areas in all aspects are very high.

But only those companies would survive at these places and win over the rural consumers who can spend time and money on understanding the needs of them and come up with innovative ideas. The companies should also strive to give more focus to the rural market in order to make it a market leader. This can happen only with the firm commitment of the top management and extension of full support to the marketing personnel by each and every department of the organization. Rural marketing in India has still a long way to go, rural marketers have to understand the fact that rural marketing in India has a tremendous potential in our country. Rural marketers should understand this fact and try to tap the huge untapped potential in our country.

References

Aaker J.L. (1999), "The Malleable Self: The role of self-expression in Persuasion", Journal of Marketing Research, Vol. 36, pp. 45-57.

Bhushan Ratna (2003), "The Rural Conundrum", The Hindu Businessline.

B.S. Corporate Bureau (2003), "Corporate Turn to rural India for growth"' Business Standard, August 21.

Iyengar Hansa (2004), "Indian Rural Markets–A Snapshot", Marketing Mastermind, December 2004.

Jain Sunil (2005), "Why rural markets are the key", Business Standard.

www.rediff.com/money/2005/jun/02inter.htm

www.indiauntouched.com/blog/archives/2004/12/rural_poverty_o.html.

Section – II

12

Empowerment of Women in Rural A.P. : A Sociological Study

Dr. M. Bilmoria Rani
Ch. Jagan Mohan Rao

Introduction

India is a country where 70 per cent of the population relies on agriculture and agro based industries, and majority of them live in rural areas. The country's largest reservoir of human resources is thus constituted by the people living in rural areas. The country's welfare and its development predominantly depend upon the socio-economic well-being of the rural people. Keeping this in view the government has made a concerted effort for the development of rural areas through its Five Year Plans. The strategies adopted are innovative, realistic and are finely shaped to tune the aspirations of people. But it is unfortunate to note that though the country is the largest democracy in the world, many inequalities prevailed among different social and economic groups, whether they are Scheduled Castes, Tribes, or women, as to their access to development. Efforts were made on for quite sometime to provide needful opportunities for weaker sections to get access to development avenues, yet the results were not quiet encouraging. However, it is heartening to observe that the recent past has been witnessing a sea change in terms of efforts to empower weaker sections, particularly in terms of targeting appropriate communities and the strategies adopted. Several of the initiatives promoted, especially for women including the rural women has indeed note worthy. This paper deals with the nature of women's participation in rural socio-economic life and their lack of recognition; and various governmental efforts to improve the living conditions of women and to empower them with skills, and efficiencies to become active partakers in developmental activities in rural areas on par with men, and measures to improve the quality of programmes.

The world-wide situation shows that women in rural areas are leading a very meager life. Statistics indicate that nearly 70 per cent (1.3 billion) of the world's poor people are represented by women, and they receive only 10 per cent of the income though they produce 50 per cent of the food. Not only is this but their access to resources lesser than that being enjoyed by men. In recent times many countries have noticed that women play a major role in agricultural activities. In Sub-Saharan Africa or the Caribbean region, for example, 60 to 80 per cent of the basic food stuffs are produced by women; whereas in Asia over 50 per cent of the labour in rice cultivation is represented by women; and in Pacific or Latin America the complex agricultural system including the home gardens etc., are handled predominantly with greater responsibility by women. Women also shoulder greater responsibility in rearing livestock, and performing a wide range of post-harvest operations like storage, handling, food processing, marketing etc. besides playing many other domestic and community roles (Srivastava, S. 2007).

In India over 350 million people living below the poverty line are women and majority of them live in rural areas (70.2 per cent). These women, particularly those belong to backward communities and lower castes are mostly illiterates, untrained and have very low social and economic status. As much as 89.5 per cent of the women labour is employed in agricultural and allied industrial sectors. This situation holds good even in the state of Andhra Pradesh where 72.9 per cent of women live in rural areas.

In India and in the state Andhra Pradesh traditionally all the household members in rural areas frequently play gender and age specific roles, and they put all their combined efforts in agricultural operations, agro-based trading and wage labour. But the contributions of women in agricultural work are more than that of their counterparts (Devi, R.1992, Abraham, G, 2001). Further women almost and always rely on manual labour using only their own energy, whereas men perform agricultural operations by adopting machinery and animals (buffaloes). The number of tasks performed and time spent by women in agriculture and its related work are greater than that of men. For e.g. in Indian Himalayas the rural woman work for 3485 hours a year in one hector farm while man works for 1212 hours and a pair of bullocks for 1064 hours. It shows that a year's farm work handled by woman is equal to that of one man and two bullocks. Another study on time and energy spent by men and women on agricultural work found that 53 per cent of human hours per household are contributed by women as compared to 31 per cent by men (Coonrod 1998). In the state of Andhra Pradesh also women work hard in agriculture and its related sectors (Govt. of A.P). Her work in agriculture ranges from sowing transplanting, weeding irrigation, transporting organic manure and transferring it to the fields, harvesting, threshing, grading to assembling of the produce. Adding to this, as a home maker she attends to different domestic activities like that of cooking, caring, managing fuel and water for the home, carrying heavy loads of fodder and fuel wood, looking after domestic animals, chaffing the fodder, cleaning the animal houses, preparing the animal feed, milking animals, filling the manure pits, making cow dung cakes etc. All these activities keep woman busy from morning till late in the night. Studies show that the work day of an woman agricultural labourer during the agricultural season lasts for 15 hours, whereas her male counterpart work for 7 to 8 hours (Coonrod, C. S. 1998).

Further it is found that while doing the agricultural work women almost always rely on manual labour using only their own energy, while men adopt machinery and animal energy in attending to the agricultural operations.

It is interesting to note that since ages though women have contributed much of their roles in agricultural work and in the domestic activities, their participation remained without much recognition. One of the reasons for this might be that the nature of women's work is largely based on human energy rather than involving any implement as is used by men and subsequently considering their work as unskilled, less productive (Coonrod, C.S. 1998). By and large women remain as invisible workers. Women are marginalized because they are powerless in economic, social and political activities. Social, political and family structures do not include women in decision making. Moreover among the lower sections women are subjected to lot of economic exploitation and social oppression. They face excess burden of poverty because of their much concern for the survival of their dependents in the family. To meet at least the minimum needs of their dependents they work for long hours to the extent of neglecting their own food and health. Adding to this the existing patriarchal values and intra- household gender specific disparities in distributing system in terms of income, resource, consumption and time etc., are aggravating the burden of poverty on the rural women. All these socio-cultural and economic imbalances have negative impact on woman's personality system causing low self esteem, dejected attitudes and negative thinking in them which in a way directly or indirectly affects the entire family structure and economy in rural areas. Of late the government has come to recognise the seriousness of the situation and bestowed its interest to work for the cause of the poor women in rural areas.

The gender dimension on development approaches at conceptual level has come in to existence since 1940's uncovering several distinct areas of gender bias. Many have felt that though male farmers are generally regarded as the backbone of the agricultural system, in reality (as the available evidences show that) women remain as the backbone of the family structure as well as the rural economy and hence the true development is possible only when the welfare of the women are taken care. Thanks to the efforts of various non-governmental organizations including women's organizations, many conferences, and the UN conventions at Cairo and Beizing the woman's development perspective was emerged to tackle the problem of gender inequalities. But the strategy adopted by planners was not in favour of women and moreover they served to reinforce the existing gender inequalities. Many researchers felt that such drawback might be due to the planners' failure to understand the nature of gender inequalities or their unconscious gender prejudices (Boserup 1970). Some others contend that the prevailing model is both capitalistic and patriarchal in nature (Studad see in Sushila Jain 2005). The fact nevertheless remains as it is and women have not received a fair deal from development endeavour. The development community realized that the 'tickle down' approach to development is of not effective and they contended a strong case for devising a gender sensitive strategy of development and a gender responsive index of development. The whole thrust was on treating women as partners in development rather than as mere beneficiaries of it. The plea was for the recognition of woman's economic agency in economic development i.e., her productive role over and above her reproductive role. This remained as the main thrust in the UN Decade for Women and prominence was given to woman empowerment in all areas of social, economic and political life.

The empowerment concept gained much importance in the minds social scientists including sociologists and various experts connected with the development programmes. Ishmail in 20th century Meis (1991.89) explained that empowerment is an idea that 'manifests itself at all levels of societal interactions. It is found in giving voice to the disenfranchised in allowing the week and the marginalized to have access to the tools and the materials they need forge their own destines. It is regarded as a process which involves active participation of institutions and the 'actors'. On the part of the institutions the right environment and structure has to be set up to create circumstances where a woman can use her faculties and abilities to fully actualize her potential. On the part of the actor i.e., from the point of woman this process enables her to get access to those modes and medium of expression of her self and self actualization and through that she can achieve empowerment. Thus empowerment is considered as an important tool for social development that can be achieved when the society recognizes woman as one among the social partners, provide them equal rights, felicitate them with equal education, health, and out of all these allow them to participate equally and effectively (Vijaya Kumar 2002, Sushma Jain 2005). Some scholars like Sundar Raj felt that the process of empowering woman is a positive discrimination. It implies a positive role and participation of women in development not only for the benefit of themselves but for the benefit of the society as a whole (2005.51). The empowerment entails five levels of gender equality such as material welfare, access to resources, and benefits, conscientization, and participation in decision making process (See Long We in Sushma Jain 2005.26). Further it is necessary that all these aspects should be taken care in a coordinated manner because different forms of inequality are mutually reinforcing and their remedies have similar inter connections. Thus we can say that the empowerment of women including rural woman is a complex process which involves multi-dimensional approach (George 2005.26).

In India the process of women empowerment has gone through several stages right from the inception of its importance in the minds of the policy makers and development programmers. During 1960s and 1970s the governmental policies and programmes are concerned mainly with the provision of welfare services to women rather than equipping them with skills. Nevertheless all the policies have worked together to pave a way for women's empowerment. Initially through establishing women's association the rural poor women were given training in nutrition, safe drinking water, household management, child care, tailoring, embroidery etc. This subsequently shifted women from the stereotyped traditional roles to organize themselves into groups to make use of their leisure time activities more meaningful and for their self development. During 1970 and 1980 which was declared as Women's Decades special interest was bestowed towards the women's issues. Many women organizations have felt that credit and savings play an important role in increasing women's income and to bring them together to address wider gender issues. There was a greater shift took place in the development thinking from rapid economic growth to poverty elimination and creating productive efficiency in the people. This subsequently resulted in identifying women as agents and partners of development. Keeping poor women as target groups various development programmes were launched and as a part of them women were given access for employment and loan facilities, and housing and other schemes. Poverty targeted micro finance institutions like Grameena Banks were emerged with a focus on empowerment of poor in the rural areas. In 1990s depending on the evidence of high female repayment rates and the rising influence of gender lobbies within donor agencies and NGOs there was a greater emphasis on targeting women in micro finance programmes. The main contention here was that women's access to savings and credit facilities and their decision about what is being done with savings and credit strengthens their say in economic decisions of the household. This enables women to increase expenditure on the wellbeing of themselves and their children. Women's control over decision making was also seen as benefiting men through preventing leakage of household income to unproductive and harmful activities. Other welfare interventions were advocated in addition to micro finance, typically nutrition, health and literacy campaign to further decrease the vulnerability and to improve women's skills(Singh, B.N.2006 A major step was taken during 1990s to facilitate women to take active participation in decision making at the gross root level. The Constitutional Amendments (73rd and 74th amendments) enabled women to have 33 per cent reservation at the grass root's democracy. Panchayat Raj institutions acted as effective vehicles for the political empowerment of women in rural areas. In the state of Andhra Pradesh there are more than the statutory 33 per cent of Panchat Raj seats are represented by women members (Himanshu Jha and Kumar 2005).

In 2000s the government has made serious efforts to create an environment where women could freely exercise their rights both within and outside the household i.e., in their work places as well on par with men. The year 2001 is declared as the 'Year of Women Empowerment'. The National policy for Empowerment of woman was framed in 2001, and the National Plan of Action for empowerment of women came into existence since 10th Five Year Plan. The policy makers outlined various strategies for social and economic empowerment of women and gender justice. In almost all poverty alleviation programmes women component was incorporated. Special programmes for women like Sarva Siksha Abhiyan and Mahila Samaky etc. were launched.

The UN conference in Beizing in 1995 has recognized that more than a quarter of the world population is represented by rural women and they play a key role in food production and food security, and their contributions to the well being of their families and to the development of rural economies. In view of these facts the UN has declared that every year October 15th be celebrated as the World Rural Woman's Day. The main objective of the Day is to provide rural women and their organizations with a main focus on: (i) to raise the rural woman's profile; (ii) sensitise both governments and the public to their crucial, yet largely unorganized roles and (iii) promote action in their support.

The Government through the Ministry of Rural Development has implemented several programmes exclusively for rural poor women. Funds were earmarked as "women component" to ensure the flow of adequate resources for their development activities. To mention a few following are some of the noteworthy programmes:

SGSY

The Swarnajayanti Gram Swarozgar Yojana is a holistic programme. It covers various aspects of self-employment programmes such as organization of the poor self-help groups, training, credit, technology, infra structure and marketing. Under this programme the stress is laid on that 50 per cent of the groups formed in each block should be exclusively for women. Women are encouraged in the practice of thrift and credit which enable them to become self-reliant. Through providing assistance in the form of Revolving Fund, Bank Credit and subsidy, the yojana seeks to integrate women in the economy by providing increasing opportunities of self-reliant.

JGSY

The Jawarhar Gram Samridhi Yojana was launched with an intention to create demand driven community village infrastructure and to generate supplementary employment for the unemployed rural poor. Under this programme 30 per cent of the employment opportunities are reserved for poor women living in below poverty line families.

IAY

The Indira Awas Yojana was implemented with a main focus on providing assistance for the construction of houses of people 'Below the Poverty Line' in rural areas. Under this scheme, priority is extended to widows. In the state of Andhra Pradesh an historical turning point could be witnessed in the construction of houses for the weaker sections enhancing from 4 lakhs houses to 20 lakh houses a year. Further under this scheme the houses are allotted in the name of women members of the household or alternatively in the joint names of husband and wife.

NSAP

The National Social Assistance Programme is the one where a significant step towards introducing a National Policy for Social Assistance was taken. This was implemented with a major focus on women who are living in "Below the Poverty line'.

This programme covers 3 components—the National Old Age Pension Scheme, the National Family Benefit Scheme and the National Maternity Benefit Scheme. The National Maternity Benefit Scheme is exclusively aimed at assisting expectant mothers by providing them Rs.500/- each for the first two live births.

Under the National Oldage Pension scheme, Central assistance of Rs. 75 per month is provided to women who have little or no regular means of subsistence for their own sources of income or through financial support from the family members. The State of Andhra Pradesh has enhanced this amount from Rs.75/- to Rs.200/- per month for the aged, destitute women and disabled.

Under the National Family Benefit Scheme the Central assistance of Rs.10,000/- is extended to the bereaved family in the case of death of the primary bread winner due to natural /accidental causes. Women are also included as beneficiaries under this scheme.

RSRP

The Restructured Centrally sponsored Rural Sanitation Programme aimed at the construction of village sanitary complexes exclusively for women to ensure privacy/dignity.

ARWSP

Under the Rural water supply programme, training is being afforded to women to enable them to play an active role in using and maintaining hand pumps for the supply of drinking water. Women are also represented in Village level committees and are actively involved in the selection of sites for hand pumps and other sources.

DWCRA

The erstwhile scheme of Development of Women and Children in Rural areas now merged with the SGSY. The main aim of this scheme is to raise the income level of women of poor households so as to enable organized participation by them in social development for economic self-reliance. The primary thrust was the formation of groups of 10-50 women from poor households at the village level for delivery of services like credit and skill training and cash and infrastructure support for self-employment.

The state of Andhra Pradesh stands as the foremost state in taking firm interest in the implementation of various development programmes for the rural poor and marginalized women. The state has recognized the importance of women in rural life and conducted various experiments by adopting different strategies of development. The State has adopted Self-Help Group approach extensively as a primary tool of poverty alleviation and empowerment of women in rural areas. The reasons for adopting SHG approach is that the participation of women in self help groups and their access to micro credit will enhance their life in many aspects - economic, physical, socio-cultural, political and psychological aspect.

The self-help group is the one where a small group of women come together with an intention to find a solution for their common problem such as livelihood generation with a degree of self-suffiency. In all there are more than 4.8 million women in the state are mobilized into self-help groups. Homogeneous groups of women would choose and collectively undertake an economic activity suited to their skills and resources supplemented by the state matching grants. The state has encouraged women self-help groups to take up marketing of agricultural produce and various other goods (for e.g. pickles, papads, handicrafts etc.) and provided marketing facilities towards this end. The number and structure of the women self-help groups have been scaled up. Accordingly the sate has focused on identifying, developing and promoting alternative approaches to increase women's access to and control over the means of making a living on a sustainable and long term bases. Through opening various venues the state has widened the choices for women and their capacity building to take advantage of new economic opportunities.

The State has implemented Indira Kranti Patham, a noteworthy scheme which is first of its kind in the country, to empower women financially. Under this various programs are sponsored exclusively for more than three million of women living below the poverty line in rural areas. These programmes have addressed several issues like child labour, girl child education, and high drop out rates, etc. Through the Rajiv Arogya Sri Pathakam the state is extending its helping hand to many poor women to meet their critical health issues which can not be otherwise solved because of its greater financial burden. The recently announce Rajiv Insurance Scheme also will help women in one way or the other to shoulder the responsibility of their households when unwelcoming incidence i.e., the death of bread winners -takes place in their families.

From the above discussion it is clear that the development of any rural community is justifiable only when all the neglected sections including women are taken into consideration and given due importance while framing and implementing the policies in the country. Further for a better understanding of the needs and issues of the rural marginalized and poor women it is necessary that the state should adopt systemic approach, and in the largest background of socio-economic, cultural and geographical set up the policies and programmes should be framed for women. The state of Andhra Pradesh not doubt is doing a commendable work towards the empowerment of rural women. But in order to keep the pace with the fast developments in the world at large and in India in particular as to the adaptation of science and technology in socio-economic developments , the state has to develop different strategies touching different modules for the empowerment of the rural women This will facilitate the women to get acquaint with the latest knowledge, skills and to incorporate the same in their day to day agricultural operations and its related services as well as in other productive activities.

The state has to conduct often training programmes, workshops and exposure programmes for all the development personnel in order to facilitate them to share their experiences, problems and to sort out a further plan of action with necessary modifications, if any. Over and above all this, the personnel should have proper perspective that the development in rural areas is an initiative rather than merely a government's routine action.. Not only this but they should have positive attitude towards women in general and the marginalized sections of women in rural areas in particular and should give up their traditionally digested gender biased attitude. They should work with great identity , burden and moral commitment in their heart for the socially and economically marginalized women. The inner abilities, and skills of women -whether they are significant or not must be respected, honoured. This will facilitate confidence building in women and their co-operation in the programmes. All the departments/ institutions which are associated with the rural poor women and their development programmes should work together with one mind and one spirit.

Further since much of the funds allocated for rural development in general and women's development are going waste because of the unbearable bureaucracy, terrible inefficiency and corruption at all levels (as is being witnessing in day to day news papers), the government should keep constant vigilance on the functionaries at all levels, and should take severe action against those who involves in misusing of power, misappropriation of funds, and/or misbehaving with women.

All the development organizations should adequately encourage and support women in taking active participation in planning and decision making in their concerned developmental activities. Steps should be taken for the establishment of associations and net work of rural women; involvement of existing women's association in committees and partnerships, encouraging women's groups to apply for funding for development initiatives, linking up women's association with development organization etc.

References

Arunachalam, J. et al. (2006), Empowerment Rural Women in India, New Delhi: Rawat.

Abraham, G. (2001), "Empowerment of Women in Rural-India", Paper presented in Conference on Empowerment of Women in Developing Countries, New Mexico USA, April, 26-27

Coonard, C.S. (1998), "Chronic Hunger-the Status of Woman in India", Woman in Panchyat Raj: Change Agents for a new future for India.

Devi, R. (1992), How Poor are Women in Rural India? Asia Pacific Jr. Rural Development, July 2(1).

Government of Andhra Pradesh (2001), "Rural Livelihood Project", www/Rural Women empowerment in

Kumar, K.V. & Vanaja Rani, S. (2001), "Empowerment and women-a Myth or Reality", in Social Change, Vol. 31:3

Rani, Bilmoria, M. (2004), "Women Self-help and Sustainability Development: the Need, Hurdles and Strategies" in Strategies for Sustainability of Self-help Groups, Dr. Indira Devi, M., (Ed) Visakhapatnam: A.U. Press. Andhra Pradesh

Singh, B.N. (2006), Rural Development and Women, New Delhi: Vista International Pub., House

Srivastava, S. (2007), Women Empowerment: Encyclopedia of Women & Development, Vol. 3, New Delhi: Common Wealth.

U.N. Population (2001), Population Parameters of Rural Information Network Development, www./undp.org./popin.

13

Status of Women in India and Abroad

Prof. E. Nagabhushuna Rao
K. Geetanjali

Introduction

In this paper, an attempt is made to review the status of women from different countries, including India with an objective to suggest some concrete measures for the improvement of the status of women, in general, and rural women, in particular, on par with men.

U.S.A has the distinction of giving birth to the Women's Rights Movement for the first time, which soon spread to different parts of the globe encompassing countries shaped by different histories, faiths and political structures. The Women's Liberation Movement was started in the late 60's by Betty Friedman and Gloria Steiman, as a consequence upon various atrocities on women like high divorce rate, child abuse, drug addiction, loneliness, teenage motherhood etc.

In the European countries, the overall status of the women is quite bright. In many countries, women have entered politics and reached to the highest position in their government. Some of them are the British Prime Minister Margarete Thatcher, the Norwegian Prime Minister Gro-Brundtland, Parliamentary President of East Germany, Sabene Bergnenn-Pohl etc. All these powerful women have raised the status of women in their respective count.

In the history of the Federal Republic of Germany, for the first time, men and women were declared to be equal in the eyes of the law when its Constitution came into force in 1949. But the law and reality are still worlds apart. The working women of Germany like their sisters in other countries, bear the triple burden of job, housework and children.

The status of women in West Asia and other Muslim Countries is still subdued and low. Following the Iranian revolution in 1979, which swept away the progressive legislation passed under the Shahs, extremists in many Islamic countries have reduced the legal rights of women. In Iran, under Khomeini, woman's mere presence in public is regarded as seditious. Wearing the 'hejab' (Burkha) became mandatory. All state run crèches were closed and the working women were forced to be unemployed and go inside the home to produce sons for the holy war that Iran had to fight to save Islam worldwide. In Egypt, Sudan and Algeria, the status of women is still depressing and they are treated like slaves. The modified Islam religion has marginalized the status of women more in these countries.

The African women really put forward strenuous and hazardous works that too even against poor wages and infectious condition by toiling in the agricultural land, making sweating efforts in the hazardous condition of mines, and doing back-breaking jobs in trading houses in towns. This, when added to their unpaid household works, leaves African women, quite tired and exhausted every day. To add fuel to the fire in some Countries of Africa, the relatives of the women strip them of their inheritance from their husbands. The problems of women in Africa are aggravated by drought and socio-economic crisis, which result in diminishing quantities of food availability that too at high prices leaving the women to remain hungry often.

In China, still the feudalistic attitude prevails which favours sons and regards daughter as a temporary member of the family, an extra mouth to feed and another dowry to pay continues. So the female infanticide continues still. However, the women in China have come a long way. Their socio-economic condition has developed considerably over the last 40 years. They can be found working in every field, be it in science, technology, politics or academics, says Mrs. Zhang ye, wife of the Chinese ambassador to India (Reported in Hindustan Times, Delhi, 1st March 1992).

Chinese Government is encouraging women to enjoy equal rights with men. Though Mao Zedong had remarked that "women hold up half the sky", but in reality, China's 550 million women population pass through a miserable time from their birth onwards. A baby boy is considered as "ten thousand ounces of gold", whereas a baby girl is called merely "a thousand ounces of gold", (Quoted from the Book, Sinha, Anjana Maitra, "Women in a Changing Society", 1993). This status becomes evident when we examine the number of women present in the ruling political party, i.e., communist party where the women are only 14 per cent.

Japan represented a truly patriarchal form of family system, in which women occupied completely subordinate position. Despite governmental endeavours and legislations to promote the status of women in the society, still the women of Japan are second class citizens. Traditional values discourage women from becoming independent minded. They are demoralized by men, when they try to climb up the political business or bureaucratic leaders. Under pressures of traditional values, the women in Japan have dual role to play-both at home and office. The Japanese men rarely help in the domestic works, thus making it difficult for Japanese wives to work outside to earn after managing the entire works of home and children. Unless the Japanese men ease the workload on women, the status of women cannot improve at all.

A country which has the distinction of giving the first women Prime Minister to the world (Sirimavo Bandarnaike,

1960), Sri Lanka offers its women a relatively high status in the society. Women in Sri Lanka are increasingly participating in a number of private and public domains, including Parliamentary politics, education, law and social justice. Several reasons account for the relatively higher status enjoyed by Sri Lankan Women, as compared to other South Asian countries. First, the high female literacy rate; secondly, the main religion of the country, i.e., Buddhism advocates positive attitude towards the women. Despite that still the women workers are not free from exploitation at home, as men are invariably the bosses and woman has to take the entire domestic responsibility to carry on. However, a Sri Lankan women's status is better than that of her Indian counterparts.

Ms. Benazir Bhutto created history by being sworn in as the first woman Prime Minister of Pakistan and the first ever Muslim Woman Head of State in the modern world. Although she could become quite powerful in Pakistan's politics, still she could not dare to repeal the Hooded ordinance and declare the Federal "Shariat" courts in Pakistan redundant for fear of incurring the wrath of orthodox Muslim mullahs, fundamentalists and other political allies.

As it was told, after the Hooded ordinance was passed, rape cases against women have increased and most of them were reported to be done by family male members. Adultery and rape cases are treated as similar offences under this law. The evidence that two women are equal to one man, the age of marriage of girl has been lowered to 13 years, women are prohibited from participating in spectator sports in Pakistan etc. are clear expressions of discrimination against women.

A study of women's role in television and radio in five countries, i.e., India, Egypt, Nigeria, Canada and Ecuador proves that women have a long way to go, if they are to make any meaningful impact on the society by climbing upto the key management and policy making positions.

After Independence in India, many efforts have been made to improve the status of women. By amendment of Child Marriage Restraint Act, 1929 in 1989, the girls age of marriage has been raised to 18 years. Hindu Marriage Act and Divorce

Act, 1955, and Special Marriage Act, 1954, have permitted the women to marry away from the restrictions of religion, caste and to break the bond of marriage, if so required. Now polygamy has been made illegal and the widow remarriage got legally approved. The Hindu Succession Act, 1956, has empowered the Hindu women to get property rights as equal to men. Medical Termination of Pregnancy Act, 1971 has checked the unmarried/unwanted motherhood.

In every field and level of education now the women of middle class are seen. And they are now found in every occupation and earning as men for their livelihood. In political and social activities, their participation is increasing because rigid restrictions on their mobility and interaction with males outside the house have been reduced considerably. As a consequence, their social awareness, self respect, and desire to prove their ability as equal, or even better than men is becoming stronger and are frequently manifested in all fields of activities in recent days. In joint families, women's status has significantly improved and sometimes she becomes the determining person in the family. Thus, after the achievement of freedom, the status of Indian women has improved significantly as Srinivas (1978) concludes.

Despite all this, as Desai (1977) stated that, which can't be denied is that in most of the rural families and tabooist urban families, status of women has not yet improved much. Still, outdated caste system, Kulin Vivah, giving marriage in own caste, dowry system etc. exist among the urban lower middle class, middle class and sometimes upper class families and all classes in rural areas. Aggravation of these blind believes and system became more prominent and frightful where there are financial/economic problems.

The following majors can be put forward to uplift the status of women in general and rural women, in particular.

1. Women should be educated as it will broaden their outlook and make them aware of their rights, responsibilities and duties in society.
2. Women should be encouraged to be economically independent.

3. They should be encouraged to participate at an increasing rate in Panchyati Raj Institutions (PRIs), politics, administration and all such works which they can perform as their male counterparts.
4. They should be given equal benefits and respect in work places.
5. There should be general awareness among women about their problems and more women's organizations should be promoted.

However, the Government should not be dormant after enacting different Acts and rules to prohibit atrocities on women but should make the administrative machineries vigilant and alert to see that these are implemented whenever and wherever any such Acts like female infanticide, amniocentesis, child marriage and dowry deaths occur. Punitive measures should be taken against the criminals and victims should be properly compensated. In case of failure to do so the concerned officials should be made accountable and steps against them should also be taken, forthwith.

In conclusion, we may note that despite several laws and regulations passed to uplift the status of women, they are still regarded as second-class citizens and are discriminated against, more specifically the rural women.

14

Globalisation and Its Impact on Weaker Section Women Students in Higher Education

Dr. B. Ratna Kumari
Ms. Zilani Begum

Introduction

The women's emancipation movement in the western world started in the nineteenth century with an attack against the exclusion of women from higher education. After considerable struggle and determined efforts by leaders of the movement, the universities in the west gave grudging consent to women's entry to the formal establishment of higher education. The University of London opened its gates to women in 1878. The traditional universities of Oxford and Cambridge, being more conservative, delayed admitting women to their degrees till after the First World War, though they were permitted to appear at the examinations from 1872 in Cambridge and from 1884 in Oxford. American and European universities were equally if not more grudging in welcoming women into their fraternity. The appointment of women on the, faculties of the universities met with even stronger resistance, and with a few exceptions, really happened only after the Second World War. It may come as new to many in India that women were not appointed as full professors in American Universities till very recently, and their scales of pay were also lower than men.

Present paper focus attention on weaker section women higher education and empowerment in the light of globalization process.

In 2000-2001, out of total enrolment in higher education, 33, 06,410 were women i.e. contributing to 39.4 per cent. In the year 2001-2002, total enrolment (provisional) of women student in higher education was 35,14,000 i.e. 39,84 per cent as against the total enrolment of 40,000 in 1950-51. Further against 100 enrolled, only 14 women were pursuing higher education during 1950-51, which has increased, to 66 in 2001-02.

The technological course at undergraduate level for women in Women University were introduced to provide opportunities for women in important technological areas and also to reduce gender imbalance in the sphere of Engineering & Technology. In this connection the present study made an attempt to study the impact of globalization processes on weaker sections.

Objectives

The present study examines the growth of Empowerment of weaker sections women students in Higher Education in Andhra University Visakhapatnam at micro level and examines whether the globalization processes has promoted weaker section women students in Andhra University.

The objectives of the study are as follows:

- To analyze the Socio-Economic profile of weaker sections women in higher Education.
- To asses the Study expenditure levels of weaker sections women student in Higher education in the context of globalization process.

- To study aspirations of the weaker sections women students with relevance to empowerment and economic security.
- To suggest some policy options for weaker sections women empowerment through higher education in Andhra Pradesh.

Data Collection

To collect the data, well structural questionnaires were administered on 378 women students of Andhra University, Visakhapatnam.

Analysis

To analyze the data, appropriate statistical tools were used.

Table 1
Distribution of Respondent Women by Their Age

Age of Respondent	*Frequency*	*Per cent*
15-20	49	13.0
21-25	321	84.9
26-30	6	1.6
31-35	2	0.5
Total	378	100.0

The table-1 explains that the distribution of the age of the respondent women. Out of the total respondents 84.9 per cent of respondent are in 21-25 years age group 13 per cent of the respondents are in 15-20 years age group. 1.6 per cent of the respondents are in 26-30 years of age group. A small per centage (0.5) respondent is in 31-35 years and above age group.

Table 2
Distribution of Respondent Women by Their Religion

Religion	*Frequency*	*Per cent*
Christian	20	5.3
Hindu	355	93.9
Islam	3	0.8
Total	378	100.0

The table-2 explains that the distribution religion of the respondents. The table indicates out of the total 93 per cent of them are Hindus and 5.3 per cent of them are Christians and 0.8 per cent of the respondents are Muslims.

Table 3
Distribution of Respondent Women by Their Caste

Caste	*Frequency*	*Per cent*
SC	81	21.4
ST	19	5.0
OC	103	27.2
BC	175	46.3
Total	378	100.0

The table-3 explains that the distribution of respondent women by their caste. Out of the total respondents 46.3 per cent belong to BC, 27.2 per cent of the respondent belongs to OC, 21.4 per cent of the respondent belongs to the SC and a small (5.0) per cent of them are STs.

Table 4
Distribution of Respondent Women by Their Marital Status

Marital Status	*Frequency*	*Per cent*
Married	14	3.7
Un-married	364	96.3
Total	378	100.0

The table-4 explains about respondent women Martial Status. 96.3 per cent respondents were un-married and 3.7 per cent of respondents were married.

Table 5
Distribution of Respondent Women by Their Languages Known

Languages You Known	*Frequency*	*Per cent*
Telugu	62	16.4
English	14	3.7
Telugu-English	254	67.2
Hindi-Telugu-English	47	12.4
Others	1	0.3
Total	378	100.0

The table-5 indicates about the languages known by the respondents. Out of the total respondents 67.2 per cent knows Telugu and English, 16.4 per cent knows Telugu only, 12.4 per cent knows Telugu, English and Hindi and a small (0.3) per cent knows other languages.

Table 6
Distribution of the Respondent Women by Their Parent's Occupation

Occupation of the Parent	*Father*	*Mother*	*Husband*	*Total (%)*
Agricultural labours	72	3	2	77 (20.37)
farmer	107	-	-	107 (28.37)
Private employee	27	1	-	28 (7.41)
Govt. Service	88	3	-	11 (24.07)
Self Employee	35	1	1	37 (9.80)
Others	35	3	-	38 (10.05)
Total	364	11	3	378 (100)

Table 6 indicates the respondent women parental occupational status. 20.37 per cent parents are agricultural laboures. 28.37 per cent of them are farmers. 7.41 per cent of parents are private employees. 24.07 per cent are in government service. 9.80 per cent of parents are involved in self employment. 10.05 per cent of parents are involved in other activities.

Table 7
Distribution of Respondent Women by Their Course Duration

Years of course	*Frequency*	*Per cent*
two years course	313	82.8
three years course	41	10.8
four years course	2	0.5
one years course	19	5.0
five years course	3	0.8
Total	378	100.0

The table-7 explains the respondent women course duration in the university. It reveals that, 82.8 per cent respondents are studying 2 years course, 10.8 per cent are in three years course, 5.0 per cent of them are doing one year course 0.8 and 0.5 per cent of respondent are doing five years and four years course respectively.

Table 8
Distribution of Respondent Women by Their Medium of Study

Medium	*Frequency*	*Per cent*
Telugu	121	32.0
English	255	67.5
Hindi	2	0.5
Total	378	100.0

The table-8 explains that the number of respondents women by their medium of Study. Out of the total respondents, from 67.5 per cent are studying in English medium, 32.0 per cent are studying in Telugu medium only and a small (0.5) per cent in Hindi medium.

Table 9
Distributions of Respondent Women by Their Purpose for Join This Course

Why Did You Join This Course	*Frequency*	*Per cent*
To get employment	250	66.1
No alternative	8	2.1
Seat allotted	12	3.2
Self-motivation	108	28.6
Total	378	100.0

Table-9 explains that the distributions of respondent women by their purpose for join this course. Out of the total, 66.1 respondents answered to get employment, 28.6 per cent respondents are by self-motivation, 3.2 per cent respondents joined as the seat was allotted and a small (2.1) per cent reported as they have no other alternative to do.

Table 10
Distribution of Respondent Women by Their Opinion on Expenditure on Education

Do you feel Expenditure on Education is High	*Frequency*	*Per cent*
Yes	285	75.4
No	93	24.6
Total	378	100.0

Table-10 explains that, 75.4 per cent of respondent women felt that expenditure on education is high. 24.6 per cent of respondent women opinion about expenditure on education is not high.

Table 10.1
If Yes-What are the Reasons?

If Yes-What are the Reasons	*Frequency*	*Per cent*
private institutions entry in to he	103	27.2
globalization processes	67	17.7
to read in English medium	20	5.3
Less grants from central government	96	25.4
None	92	24.3
Total	378	100.0

Out of 378 respondents, 285 (75.4) per cent of women opined that, the expenditure on education is high. The reasons they have mentioned are 27.2 per cent of them felt that, the entry of private institutes, 17.7 per cent of them opined that, because of globalization process, 25.4 per cent of them felt that, insufficient grants from central government for education also makes the expenditure on education as high. 5.3 per cent of them opined that, medium of instruction as English also one of the reason for high expenditure on education. 24.3 per cent of them did not mention any specific reason.

Table 11
Distribution of Respondent Women by Their Source of Expenses

How Did You Meet Your Expenses	*Frequency*	*Per cent*
Father/mothers income	307	81.2
Relatives help	34	9.0
Private lenders	12	3.2
Banks loans	25	6.6
Total	378	100.0

The table-11 reveals that, respondent women source of expenses for their higher studies. 81.2 per cent of respondents meet their expenses from father/mother income, 9.0 per cent seek help from relatives and 3.2 per cent take loans from private lenders. 6.6 per cent of them take loans from banks.

Table 12
Distribution of Respondent Women by Amount Paid for Their Studies

(2/3 Years Courses; Rs)

How Much Amount You Paid for Your Studies	*Frequency*	*Per cent*
1,000 - 10,000	157	41.5
11,000 - 20,000	58	15.3
21,000 - 30,000	34	9.0
31,000 - 40,000	39	10.3
41,000 - 50,000	51	13.5
51,000 - Above	39	10.3
Total	378	100.0

Table-12 reveals that, the amount paid by the respondent women for their studies (course). 41.5 per cent reported that they have spent Rs.1,000-10,000 for their course. 15.3 per cent have reported that, the incurred expenditure on their course was Rs.11,000-20,000. 9.0 per cent reported that they have spent Rs.21,000-30,000 for their course. 10.3 per cent reported that, they have spent Rs.31,000-40,000 for their course. 13.5 per cent have reported that, they have spent Rs.41,000-50,000 and 10.3 per cent of them have spent more than 50 thousand.

Table 13
Distribution of Respondent Women by Kind of Preference for Course

What Kind of Courses You Like to Prefer	*Frequency*	*Per cent*
income oriented	53	14.0
knowledge oriented	110	29.1
skill oriented	94	24.9
training oriented	15	4.0
employment oriented	106	28.0
Total	378	100.0

Table 13 explains that, the respondent women's preference of the course. 14.0 per cent preferred to study income oriented course. 29.1 per cent preferred knowledge oriented courses. 24.9 per cent preferred skill oriented courses, 4.0 per cent wants training oriented courses and 28.0 per cent of them preferred employment oriented courses.

Table 14
Distribution of Respondent Women by Their Order of Generation in Attaining Higher Education

Are You First Generation in the Family to Attain Higher Education	*Frequency*	*Per cent*
Yes	238	63.0
No	140	37.0
Total	378	100.0

Table 14 reveals that, 63.0 per cent of respondent women are first generation in their family to pursue higher education. 37.0 per cent of them are not the first generation who pursues higher education.

Table 15
Distribution of Respondent Women Opinion About Higher Education for Girls

Why There is More Entry of Girls in Higher Education	*Frequency*	*Per cent*
self-motivation	152	40.2
to get good job	168	44.4
to get knowledge	50	13.2
Better martial alliance	4	1.1
Others	4	1.1
Total	378	100.0

Table-15 explains about respondent women opinion about higher education for girls. 40.2 per cent have expressed that, the higher education gives self motivation for their lives. 44.2 per cent felt that by doing higher studies they may get good job, 13.2 per cent felt that, higher studies increase their knowledge. Very little per cent 1.1 each felt that by doing higher studies they may get martial alliance and other reasons.

Table 16
Distribution of Respondent Women by Their Opinion About Gender Bias in Education System

Do You Feel Gender Bias in The Present Education System	*Frequency*	*Per cent*
Yes	134	35.4
No	244	64.6
Total	378	100.0

Table-16 explains about respondent women opinion on gender bias in education system 35.4 per cent reported that, there is gender bias in education system. 64.6 per cent felt that there is no gender bias.

Table 17
Distributions of Respondent Women by Their Awareness on Globalization

What is Globalization	*Frequency*	*Per cent*
boarder less economy	95	25.1
networking with markets institutions	110	29.1
trade without barriers	76	20.1
opened economy	97	25.7
Total	378	100.0

Table 17 explains about respondent women's awareness on globalization. 29.1 per cent felt that globalization is networking with markets/institutions. 20.1 per cent felt that, it's a trade without barriers. 25.7 felt that it is an open economy.

Table 18
Distributions of Respondent Women by Their Awareness on Globalization and its Impact on Expenses on Higher Education

Do You Feel Globalization Processes has Increased the Expenses on the HE	*Frequency*	*Per cent*
Yes	297	78.6
No	81	21.4
Total	378	100.0

Table-18 reveals that, 78.6 per cent of respondent women felt that, the globalization process has increased expenses on Higher Education. 21.4 per cent felt that, the process of globalization has not increased the Higher Education expenses.

FINDINGS

- Out of the total respondent 84.9 per cent of respondents are in 21-25 years age group 13 per cent of the respondents are in 15-20 years age group. 1.6 per cent of the respondents are in 26-30 years of age group. Small per centage (0.5) respondents are in 31-35 years and above age group.
- 93 per cent of them are Hindus and 5.3 per cent of the respondents are Christians and 0.8 per cent of the respondents are Muslims.
- Out of the total respondents 46.3 per cent belong to BC, 27.2 per cent of the respondent belongs to OC, 21.4 per cent of the respondent belongs to the SC and a small 5.0 per cent of them are STs.
- Out of the total respondents 96.3 per cent respondent were un-married and 3.7 per cent of respondents were married.
- Out of the total respondents 67.2 per cent knows Telugu and English, 16.4 per cent knows Telugu only, 12.4 per cent knows Telugu, English and Hindi and a small 0.3 per cent knows other languages.
- 20.37 per cent parents are agricultural laboures. 28.37 per cent of them are farmers. 7.41 per cent of parents are private employees. 24.07 per cent are in government service. 9.80 per cent of parents are involved in self employment. 10.05 per cent of parents are involved in other activities.
- Data reveals that, 82.8 per cent respondents are studying 2 years course, 10.8 per cent are in three years course, 5.0 per cent of them are doing one year

course 0.8 and 0.5 per cent of respondent are doing five years and four years course respectively.

- Out of the total respondents 67.5 per cent are studying in English medium, 32.0 per cent are studying in Telugu medium only and a small (0.5) per cent are in Hindi medium.
- Out of the total respondents 66.1 per cent joined the course to get a job, 28.6 per cent joined by self-motivation, 3.2 per cent joined as they have obtained/ secured a seat in the course, a small 2.1 per cent have joined as they do not have any other alternative to do.
- 81.2 per cent of respondent meet their expenses from father/mother income, 9.0 per cent seek help from relatives and 3.2 per cent take loans from private lenders. 6.6 per cent of them take loans from banks.
- 41.5 per cent reported that they have spent Rs.1,000-10,000 for their course. 15.3 per cent have reported that, the incurred expenditure on their course was Rs.11,000-20,000. 9.0 per cent reported that they have spent Rs.21,000-30,000 for their course. 10.3 per cent reported that, they have spent Rs.31,000-40,000 for their course.
- 14.0 per cent preferred to study income oriented course. 29.1 per cent preferred knowledge oriented courses. 24.9 per cent preferred skill oriented courses, 4.0 per cent wants training oriented courses and 28.0 per cent of them preferred employment oriented courses.
- Respondent women students' opinion about higher education for girls. 40.2 per cent have expressed that, the higher education gives self motivation for their lives. 44.2 per cent felt that by doing higher studies they may get good job, 13.2 per cent felt that, higher studies increase their knowledge. Very little per cent 1.1 each felt that by doing higher studies they may get martial alliance and some other reasons.

- Respondent women students opinion on gender bias in education system 35.4 per cent reported that, there is gender bias in education system. 64.6 per cent felt that there is no gender bias.
- Respondent women students awareness on globalization. 29.1 per cent felt that globalization is networking with markets/ institutions. 20.1 per cent felt that, it's a trade without barriers. 25.7 per cent felt that, it is an open economy.
- Awareness on globalization and its impact on expenses on Higher Education 78.6 per cent of respondent women felt that, the globalization process has increased expenses on Higher Education. 21.4 per cent felt that, the process of globalization has not increased the Higher Education expenses.

CONCLUSION

Globalization process has both positive and negative impact on women higher education in general and weaker section women in particular. Higher education has to undergo some modifications and the admission approaches need to be modified in order to get admission for more number of weaker section women in higher education arena. The impact of globalization has also given boost for weaker sections women students. However higher education has positive as well as negative impact on women empowerment processes.

15

A Study of the Tribal Children Mainstreamed From Residential Bridge Course Camps in the Srikakulam District

Dr. M. Venkata Rao

Introduction

Education is an important instrument of social change. It is essential for individual as well as social development. Indian Constitution enshrines justice, social, economic and political equality of status and opportunity to all the Country men, may be through equality. International Commission on Education for twenty first century (1996) has rightly observed, education must now be viewed as a part of a new approach to problems in which it is not simply one of many means towards development, but one of the constituent elements and one of its essential goals.

In India, several programmes were implemented to educate the vulnerable and weaker sections. As a result, education is becoming one of the chief gateways to a wide variety of jobs, has stimulated a new competition among various groups to achieve mobility. Primary Education is a well recognized sector which is essential for sustainable development of a country. The terms of access, equality and quality are the key points for the sustainable development.

The Directive Principles of State Policy enshrined in Article-45 emphasized that "the State shall endeavour to provide free and compulsory education for all children until they complete the age of fourteen years".

The Directive Principles contained in Article-46 of the Constitution mention that "the State shall promote with special care the educational and economic interests of the weaker sections of the people and in particular, of the Scheduled Castes and Scheduled Tribes, and shall protect them from social justice and all forms of exploitation".

In India, the traditional caste system was based on fourfold Varna system, placing the Brahmins at the top and the Sudras at the bottom. Ghurye (1969:306) describes 'the Scheduled Caste' as 'depressed class' and they are regarded as the 'fifth order' of the Hindu Caste System. Dushkin (1972:172) opined that the depressed classes include all untouchables whether of milder or more severe degree of untouchability".

The term "Scheduled Caste" was first used by the Simon Commission in Section 309 of the Government of India Act, 1935. Further, the Madras Removal Social Disabilities Act, 1938 made several provisions to SCs. Article-17 abolished the practice of untouchability. Article 15 (2) puts an end to any disability, liability, restriction or condition emanating on grounds of religion, race, caste, sex, place of birth or any of them with regard to access to shops, hotels and use of wells, tanks, places of public resort. Article (29) (2) of the Constitution also prohibits the denial of admission to an applicant, by any educational institution receiving government aid on grounds of either religion, race, caste, or language.

Further, the Constitution provided guidelines for preparing a list of castes to be scheduled for the purpose. The list of SCs was notified by the President in 1950. Chandra Sekhar Bhat (1984) mentioned that the problem of Scheduled Caste may, therefore, be looked at from two angles: first, the problems of the untouchables and, secondly, those of the low-ranking castes above the untouchables.

Articles 330, 332, 335, 338 to 342 and the entire fifth and sixth schedules of the Commission deal with special provisions for the implementation of the objectives set forth in Article-46. Then the government initiated welfare programmes on the basis of Constitutional provisions, in the fields of the education, employment and political participation.

Objectives of the Study

1. to know various provisions for the development of SC children in Rural Areas.
2. to analyse the rates of literacy, enrolment status, dropout situation among SC children.
3. to know the range of participation of SC children in the activities at elementary level.
4. to find out the socio-economic reasons of educational backwardness among SC children.

METHODOLOGY

The study was conducted in Narasannapeta Mandal of Srikakulam District of Andhra Pradesh. After a preliminary survey of the sample area, SC children were selected purposively within the purview of primary schools. School Complex is a group covering 9-10 schools in the Mandal to facilitate the academic and administrative activities. 50 SC children are identified in one School Complex area i.e. from 10 schools and the children are separately interviewed with the help of structured interview schedule. Informal interviews were conducted among the parents to know the reasons and other data. Data regarding the progress of the children are recorded from the respective Head Masters of the schools. The achievement of general children (other than SC children) is also taken into consideration for a comparative analysis. Secondary data were also collected from various Government records for a consolidated analysis.

Provisions for SCs in Five Year Plans

The development programmes were launched during First Plan (1951-56) pertaining to all sections of the population, including SCs, OBCs and Minorities. The notion of 'equality of opportunities' was advocated between the second and third plans (1956-66). Social justice to weaker sections was greatly stressed in the fourth and fifth plans (1969-78). Special Component Plan (SCP) for SCs to obtain more benefits has been provided in Annual Plan (1979-80).

The Sixth Plan (1980-85) emphasized pooling of resources from all the other developmental sectors for the benefit of SCs. The formation of National Scheduled Castes and Scheduled Tribes Finance and Development Corporation (NSFDC) in 1989 was an important achievement during the Seventh Plan Period (1985-90).

The Eighth Plan (1992-97) marked the recognition of all forms of oppression and SCs and their socio-economic improvement. Three Apex bodies were set up during this plan period. i) The National Backward Classes Finance and Development Corporation (1992), ii) The National Minorities Development and Finance Corporation (1994-95), iii) National Safai Karmachari Finance and Development Corporation (1996-97). The Ninth Plan (1997-2002) has mentioned the need to empower the Socially Disadvantaged Groups ie., SCs, OBCs and other Minorities.

Educational Provisions

The government initiated several educational provisions to the SC children. They are pre-matric and post-matric scholarships, stipends, exemption from tuition and exam fee, midday meals, coaching schemes, residential and social welfare schools, hostels etc. The Scheme of Special Educational Development Programmes for SC girls belonging to low literacy districts was introduced in 1996-97. As a result, the project spread across 48 districts in Bihar, Madhya Pradesh, Rajasthan, Uttar Pradesh (Chatterjee, 2000).

PROTECTION OF WEAKER SECTIONS

Special legislations were made under the guidance of the Ministry of Social Justice and Empowerment, Government of India. The problems of untouchability and atrocities against SCs were recorded. With the effective implementation of the Protection of Civil Rights (PCR) Act,1955 and the Scheduled Castes and the Scheduled Tribes (Prevention of Atrocities) Act, 1989. Scavengers were rehabilitated through the efforts of Government and Non-Government Organisations. For this, the National Scheme of Liberation and Rehabilitation of Scavengers and the Dependents was modified in 1998.

Four Statutory Commissions were set up to safeguard the rights and interests of SCs. i) National Commission for SCs and STs, ii) National Commission for Safai Karamcharis, iii) National Commission for Backward Classes, iv) National Commission for Minorities.

POPULATION

Table 1
Population and Decadal Growth Rate of SCs and Total Population (1971-2001)

(Figures in Millions)

	Population		*Decadal Growth Rate*	
Census Year	*Total*	*SC's*	*Total*	*SC's*
(1)	*(2)*	*(3)*	*(4)*	*(5)*
1971	542.1	80.0 (14.6)	24.8	24.2
1981	683.4	104.7 (15.3)	24.7	30.9
1991	846.3	138.2 (16.8)	23.9	32.0
2001	1028.6	179.7 (17.5)	21.3	30.0

Source : Census of India, GoI.

The trends of population among SCs were analysed during 1971-2001. The proportion of SC population has increased from 14.6 per cent in 1971 to 17.5 per cent in 2001. The decadal growth rate for SCs is nearly 30.0 per cent and it was more than the decadal growth rate 21.0 per cent.

Literacy among Scheduled Castes

Though the Government is providing various provisions, the educational status in respect of SC children is significantly lower as compared to others. Several programmes - Operation Black Board (OBB), Andhra Pradesh Primary Education Programme (APPEP), District Primary Education Programme (DPEP), Sarva Siksha Abhayan (SSA) were implemented to universalize the educational opportunities. Further, several learning strategies were also developed through the specific programmes like Quality Improvement Programme (QIP) during 2003-04, Children Language Improvement Programme (CLIP) during 2004-06. Presently, Children Learning Acceleration Programme for Sustainability (CLAPS) incorporated in primary education during 2006-07 as a part of Sarva Siksha Abhayan (SSA) to develop competency based learning strategies among the children of primary classes.

Table 2
Literacy Rates of SCs and Total Population (1971-2001)

Category	*1971*	*1981*	*1991*	*2001*
(1)	*(2)*	*(3)*	*(4)*	*(5)*
Total population	29.45	36.23	52.21	65.38
SCs	14.67	21.38	37.41	54.69
Gap	14.78	14.85	14.80	10.69

Source: Census of India , GoI.

The literacy rate is significantly lower in rural than urban areas. As far as concerning to the rural areas in India, the literacy rate increased from 18.3 per cent in 1951 to 65.4 per cent in 2001. However, the literacy rate among SCs increased from 14.7 per cent in 1951 to 54.7 per cent in 2001. The percentage of literacy rate among SC males and females is 54.7 and 41.9 per cent during 2001 (GoI 2005). The gap between the general literacy rate and SC population is 10.7 per cent. The literate rate of Andhra Pradesh is 61.2 per cent and

Srikakulam (district of the study area) is 56.0 respectively. The rate of literacy among SCs in Andhra Pradesh is around 52.0 per cent and it is 48.0 per cent in the study area (Srikakulam dt.).

The gradual development in terms of literacy seen among SCs. To the extent to which the members of the SCs enter these open occupations they are becoming a part of the new system of stratification based on achievement and class (Rao 1979).

Enrolment of SC Children

Table 3

Gross Enrolment Ratio (GER) During 2002-03

Unit	*Primary*			*Upper Primary*			*Secondary*		
	Boys	*Girls*	*Total*	*Boys*	*Girls*	*Total*	*Boys*	*Girls*	*Total*
(1)	*(2)*	*(3)*	*(4)*	*(5)*	*(6)*	*(7)*	*(8)*	*(9)*	*(10)*
India(All)	97.5	93.1	95.4	65.3	56.2	61.0	85.4	79.3	82.5
SCs	101.6	89.4	95.6	63.2	48.6	56.3	87.1	74.4	81.1
A.P.(All)	98.6	95.2	96.8	69.2	59.8	63.5	87.5	81.4	83.5
SCs	108.5	108.3	108.4	71.5	62.1	66.9	94.3	91.1	92.7

Source: Selected Educational Statistics, 2002-03.

The Gross Enrolment Ratio of SC children is around 95.6 at the primary level , 85.4 at the upper primary level and it is 81.0 concerning to the age group of 6-14 years during 2002-03. Regarding the Andhra Pradesh State, the Gross Enrolment Ratio among SC primary children is 108.5, secondary children is 66.97 and it is 92.1 concerning to age group of 6-14 years. GER among SC children in the study area (Srikakulam dt.) is 101.4 at primary level. It is observed that the enrolment rate is increasing year by year especially among SC children due to the efforts of district level activities as a part of Sarva Siksha Abhayan (SSA). Hence, the status of SC Children is better in terms of enrolment, when compared to the earlier.

Duggel (1992) stated that there is close relationship between enrolment and educational achievement of the parents. Khan and Chopra (1964) emphasized the relation between the social status and educational achievement. Hence, the similar observation is also recorded in the study area where enrolment rates are higher among general castes than Scheduled Castes.

Dropout Situation

The Gross Drop-out Rate represent the percentage of pupils who dropout from a given grade or cycle or level of education in a given school year. The method used to calculate Gross Drop-out Rates is known as the Apparent Cohort Method (NCERT Report 2006).

Table 4
Dropout Rates at Primary, Upper Primary and Secondary Stages 2002-03

Unit	*Primary*			*Upper Primary*			*Secondary*		
	Boys	*Girls*	*Total*	*Boys*	*Girls*	*Total*	*Boys*	*Girls*	*Total*
(1)	*(2)*	*(3)*	*(4)*	*(5)*	*(6)*	*(7)*	*(8)*	*(9)*	*(10)*
India (All)	35.9	33.7	34.9	52.3	53.5	52.8	60.7	65.0	62.7
SCs	38.7	37.2	37.9	55.4	57.8	56.6	65.3	69.7	67.5
A.P (All)	36.7	32.1	34.3	54.1	57.8	55.8	62.3	68.1	65.7
SCs	41.7	41.8	41.7	58.1	62.0	59.9	67.9	70.8	70.0

Source: Selected Educational Statistics, 2002-03.

The general dropout rate was gradually decreased from 64.9 per cent in 1960-61 to 35.0 per cent in 2002-03 in primary classes; 78.3 to 52.8 per cent in the upper primary classes; 82.5 (1980-81) to 62.6 (2002-03) in the secondary classes. The dropout rate of SC children is 34.89 (I-V classes); 52.79 (I-VIII) and 62.58 (I-X) in India.

The dropout rate of SC children in A.P. is 41.71 per cent at primary (I-V); 59.91 per cent at upper primary (I-VIII) and 69.95 per cent at secondary level (I-X) during 2002-03. It is estimated to decline upto 35.0 per cent at primary level by the end of 2006.

At the district level (study area) the dropout rate is around 17.0 per cent among SC children in primary classes during 2006-07. It is gradually decreasing trend in the study area due to the special drives of enrolment and other educational activities by the DPEP/SSA. The local reasons of dropout situation as delivered by the teachers in the study area are the impact of migration of parents and relatives, local festivals, jataras, ill health, marriages etc. Hence, the socio-economic factors which influence the achievement of the children are to be analysed.

Socio-Economic Reasons

The socio-economic factors such as illiteracy of the parents, occupational background, parental, poverty, etc., have an impact on the achievement of children in primary classes.

Table 5

Socio-Economic Background of the SC Children in the Study Area

Socio-Economic Variable	*No. of Children (N = 50)*	*Percentage*
(1)	*(2)*	*(3)*
Type of Family:		
Joint	03	6.0
Nuclear	47	94.0
Type of House:		
Pucca	09	18.0
Kutcha	22	44.0
Thatched	19	38.0
Educational background:		
Education of the father:		
Illiterate	29	58.0
Primary	10	20.0
Middle	07	14.0
SSC and above	04	8.0
Education of the mother:		
Illiterate	32	64.0
Primary	08	16.0
Middle	05	10.0
SSC and above	05	10.0
Parental Care:		
Both father/mother alive	29	58.0
Only father alive	06	12.0
Only mother alive	05	10.0
Both father/mother not alive	02	4.0
Divorced/Separated	08	16.0

Contd....

Socio-Economic Variable	No. of Children (N = 50)	Percentage
(1)	(2)	(3)
Occupational background:		
Cultivation	05	10.0
Agricultural labour	11	22.0
Wage labour	25	50.0
Lease of fruit trees	07	14.0
Others	02	4.0

Table-5 shows the socio-economic background of the SC children in the study area. Majority of them are from nuclear families and kutcha dwellings. We can observe that the literacy of their fathers and mothers effect the career of their children. Higher proportion (58.0 per cent) of their fathers and 64.0 per cent of their mothers are uneducated, only 26.0 per cent are with primary education.

There are vast majority of illiterate and literate persons at lower levels of education among SCs. A striking trend is that the pace of human capital formation in terms of educational stock is found to be quite higher among the weaker sections (Biradar and Jayasheela, 2006).

Regarding the occupational patterns, majority of them (66.6 per cent) are wage labourers; 16.0 per cent are cultivators, 14.0 per cent are in fruit tree growing. Wages in agriculture are very low in the study area. As a result, they are migrating towards the better employment opportunities which adjust their family economy. There is a shift of SC workers from agricultural to non-agricultural activities due to the lower wages. The income levels of the workers are increased and further it contributes to a decline in the incidence of poverty in rural areas (Bagalkoti, 2004). Family occupation wields a great leverage on the future economic life in the matter of acceptance or rejection of educational opportunities (Acharya and Deepak 2005).

The economic condition of the family is an indispensable element in educational attainment of a child (Sachidananda and Sinha 1989). Similarly, the studies of Sundaram and Tendulkar, 2003, Thorat 2005 and GoI 2005 the incidence of poverty is higher in rural areas especially among the social groups - SCs and STs.

Regarding the parental care, 58.0 per cent of the SC children have their parents (father and mother); 12.0 per cent have only with their father and 10.0 per cent have only mother alive; 4.0 per cent have lost both of their parents; 16.0 of their parents are divorced/separated. Out of 50 SC children as many as 32 (66.0 per cent) are absent often to their schools because their parents decision to send them to their relatives house due to the seasonal migration. Hence, the parental care towards the development of their children is very much influenced. The studies of primary education also reveals that the loss of parental care is positively correlated with the enrolment and attendance (Acharya and Deepak, 2005, Dhingra, Mahas and Sethi 2007). According to Edwards and Redfern(1988) parental involvement in reading not only has positive influence on the children but also the parent's knowledge base is enhanced. The participation of parents in educating the children has a positively influence on the academic achievement of their children (Gene and Stoneman, 1995).

It is noticed from the study area that the support of parents and family among the SC children with reference to the primary education is to be taken care of.

Status of SC Children in Class-room Transaction

The children at primary classes are graded into ABCD categories as a part of the programme-Children Learning Acceleration Programme for Sustainability (CLAPS). Children have to achieve 10 competencies in 5 subjects namely, Telugu, Maths, Social, Science and English. The marks assigned to each grade are as follows: 80 and more-A grade; 60-79-B grade; 40-59-C grade and less than 40-D grade.

Table 6
Achievement of SC Children at Primary Level

Marks	*Grade*	*No. of Children*	*Percentage*
(1)	(2)	(3)	(4)
80 marks and more	A	08	16.0
60-79 marks	B	08	16.0
40-59 marks	C	14	28.0
Less than 40 marks	D	20	40.0

Source: School Records in the Study Area

Data on the gradation of SC children pertaining to the academic year of 2006-07 describes that there are only 16.0 per cent of A grade children; 16.0 per cent of B grade; 28.0 per cent of C grade; and 40.0 per cent of D grade children in their respective primary classes. It implies that majority (68.0 per cent) of them are backward in the classroom transaction. While enquiring the respective teachers about their under achievement, they expressed that majority of the SC children are not able to follow their instructions in maintaining the notes, home work etc. This is due to their home-level environmental reasons like father drunkard, daily quarrelsome situation, peer group influence etc. Further, most of the children are not having adequate health status and are suffering from anemia, followed by skin allergies. The studies of Panda (1982) and Devi (1985) also revealed that home conditions and environment blocks the achievement of the SC children in the school.

Similarly, the involvement in the classroom transaction was also recorded, while organizing the study. The involvement of SC children in the classroom activities pertaining to the learning is also dubious and some of them are isolated in which they cannot respond as other general children. The gradation of other children is taken into consideration for a comparison. Data revealed that the majority of other children are in A and B grade and only 20.0 per cent of them are in C and D grade. Hence, it is observed that the Non-SC children have scored higher marks than that of their counterparts. The studies of Acharya and Deepak

(2005) also observed similar conclusions that the rate of achievement of SC children is very low when compared to the general students.

Conclusions

It is observed that number of educational programmes are organized to attain the goals of quality and sustainability among all groups. In India, the proportion of SCs in the total population account for 17.4 per cent. The literacy rate among SCs is 54.69 per cent and it is lower than the general Indian literacy rate (65.30). Every effort is being made to improve the literacy levels among weaker sections especially Scheduled Castes to reduce the present gap of 10.69 per cent. Free education, special reservations in jobs, residential welfare schools and colleges, coaching facilities for various CETs like 21st Century Gurukulas etc are organized for the upliftment of SC students.

However, the achievement of SC children at primary level seems to be very low when compared to the general category children. Providing a good quality of primary education leads to sustainability and it can arrest the dropout situation among weaker sections. The level of educational attainment, therefore, plays a 'linchpin' role in reducing the incidence of poverty as well as improving the health status of the socially marginalized and economically disadvantaged sections of the society (Biradar and Jayasheela, 2006).

The government has initiated several innovative activities in primary education as a part of Sarva Siksha Abhayan (SSA) objectives. The facilities like construction of new school buildings, mid day meal programme, pre-school education centers etc. definitely promote the rates of enrolment and retention of children to attain the objective of Universalization of Elementary Education (UEE). The status of SC children in primary education needs to be taken care. They could not utilize the available opportunities as other children due to the home level reasons, poverty stricken conditions etc.

The present study also observed that the performance of SC children in primary education is directly proportional to their economic condition or parental background. The efforts of the government has to reach the grass-root level to sanskritize the SC children. Accordingly, the government has to modify the activities at primary level to benefit the children of Scheduled Castes.

References

Acharya, T. and Deepak., (2005), Factors Influencing the Educational Achievements of the Scheduled Caste and General Caste Students of Cuttack Municipality Corporation, Orissa: Journal of Social Sciences Vol. 10(3): 215-222.

Bagalkoti, S.T., (2004), Growth of Rural Non-Farm Activities in India: Spatial and Temporal Analysis in P.Purushotham (ed.), Non-Farm Employment, NIRD, Hyderabad.

Bhat, Chandrasekhar, (1984), Ethnicity and Mobility: Concept publishing Company, New Delhi.

Biradar, R.K., and Jayasheela, (2006), Effects of Educational Inequality Among Social Group in Rural India: Journal of Rural Development, Vol. 26 No (3) 339-407, NIRD, Hyderabad.

Chatterjee, S.K., (2000), Educational Development of Scheduled Caste, Looking Ahead: Gyan publishers, New Delhi.

Devi, Rajpute, (1985), Barriers in Primary Education of Scheduled Caste Students, Unpublished Ph.D. Thesis (Education), Benaras Hindu University, Benaras.

Dhingra, R., Manhas and N. Sethi, (2007), Involvement of Parents in School Related Activities: Journal of Social Science., Vol 15(2):161-167.

Duggal, J., (1992), Access of Scheduled Castes Girls to Elementary Education in Rural Haryana: A Study of Socio-Economic Problems in Universalisation of Elementary Education Unpublished Ph.D. Thesis, Jamia Milha Islamia, New Delhi.

Dushkin, Lelah, (1972), Scheduled caste Politics in Michael Mahar (ed.) The Untouchables in Contemporary India, Tucson, University of Arizona Press.

Edwards, V. and Redfern, A. (1988), At Home in School Parent Participation in Primary Education London: Routledge.

Gene, H.B. and Stoneman, Z. (1995), Linking Family Processes and Academic Competence Among Rural African American Youth: Journal of Marriage and Family, 57 : 567-579.

Ghurye, G.S., (1969), Caste and Race in India, Bombay: Popular Prakashan.

Government of India (GoI)., (2005), The Report of the Task Group on Development of Scheduled Castes and Scheduled Tribes, Planning Commission, GoI, New Delhi.

Khan, M.B., (1996), Parental Involvement in Education Possibilities and Limitations: The School Community Journal pp. 57-68.

Panda, M.D, (1982), The Relationship of Parental Life Style to Intellectual Achievement Responsibility Adjustment and Cognitive Performance Among Under Privileged Children, Unpublished Ph.D. Thesis (Psychology), Utkal University, Bhubaneswar.

Rao, M.S.A., (1979), Social Movements and Social Transformation, Madras: Macmillan.

Sachidananda and P. Sinha, (1989), Education and Disadvantaged: Uppal Publishing House, New Delhi.

Sundaram, K. and S.D. Tendulkar., (2003), Poverty Among Social and Economic Groups in India in 1990s Economic and Political Weekly 38 (50).

Thorat, Sukhadeo., (2005), Affirmative Actions Policy in India: Dimension, Progress and Issues a paper presented at the workshop on 'Addressing Inequality: Policies for Inclusive Development' organized by Inter-Regional Inequality facility held at UNECA, Addis Ababa, July, 2005.

16

Socio-Economic and Political Background of Women Panchayat Leaderrs

A Case Study of Polaki Mandal in Srikakulam District (AP)

Dr. Rama Rao Darmana
Dr. Rajeswari Gulipilli

Introduction

The seventy-third Constitutional Amendment 1992 which not only gave a new lease of life to the Panchayat system of India but also ensured at least 33 per cent of the total seats at the three tiers of local governments both rural and urban areas for women Gram Panchayats at the village level, block Panchayats at the intermediate level, and district Panchayat, at the district level. The 73rd amendment has led to first empowerment of women. In Andhra Pradesh, Karnataka and Maharashtra, women had contested in elections, occupied observed positions and contributed to effective functioning of the Panchayats even before the implementation of 73rd amendments. A number of micro studies have documented the profile and experience of these women and perceptions about their new role.

Elections to the local bodies held recently in the state of Andhra Pradesh. In this context, it is proposed to study and examine the nature, and character of women Panchayat leadership in a specific locality, in the backward district of Srikakulam in the state of Andhra Pradesh. The present paper seeks to examine empowerment of Panchayat leaders in the selected mandal of Polaki in the district of Srikakulam.

Objectives

The following are the main objectives of the study:

(a) To study the significance of the Panchayat Raj system of local self government in general and the reservation of seats for women members and the implications there on in particular.

(b) To understand the nature of women Panchayat leadership and the alleged "Proxy" nature of the women contestants in the selected Mandal.

(c) To assess the roles played by factors like caste, party, money and faction etc., in the election of women leaders.

(d) To examine the social, economic and political background of the elected women contenders and their nearest rivals.

(e) To analyze the implications arising from the reservation of seats for women members and the problems faced by them in discharging their functions as elected members.

Methodology

Both primary and secondary data was used in the present study. Primary data was collected from the concerned electoral officer, news clippings and political activities while the secondary data was obtained from the elected women Panchayat members and the public through a structured and unstructured questionnaire. The study involves extensive field survey in the Polaki Mandal of Srikakulam district not only to gather relevant data by means of interviews, questionnaire etc., but also to record the perceptions of the officials and the public. Efforts are also made to obtain first-hand information on selected parameters and cross-check the same for objectivity. Tabular analysis is followed wherever necessary in analyzing the socio-economic and political indices relating to the elected women representatives of the selected Mandal.

Review of Literature

There is a very rich literature on Panchayat Raj in the form of book, committee reports and publishing of articles in various journals.

Jain et al, (1985) examined the structure and suitability of the institutional arrangements that have been made for the delivery of rural development programmes, especially to the poor. The authors concluded that poverty and inequality are on the increase.

Sabib and Swinder (1986) made an attempt to provide a comprehensive and objective analysis of both the rural and urban segments of Local government.

Singh (1986) discussed the three-tier structure of Panchayat Raj and their functioning in his article. "Revitalization of Panchayat".

Mishra (1989) revealed that various countries have different to achieve the target of rural development, in Indian context. Further, he examined the three-tier system and stresses the need of people's participation in policy formulation and its implementation.

Hirway (1989) in her article, "Panchayat Raj cross roads" the concept of Panchyat Raj was discussed. She analyzed the experience of different states and drawn lessons from these experiences.

Desai (1990) analysed the relevant problems of function, finances, management and organization of programmes initiated to improve the living conditions of the rural people.

According to Pinto, rural development has gone a long a way from CDP of the fifties to anti-poverty programmes of the eighties.

Kirti Kumar emphasized that in order to strengthen women's empowerment, female literacy has to be promoted.

The state of Andhra Pradesh was one of the first two states (Rajasthan being the other state) to implement the system of local self-government in India. Andhra Pradesh along with other states in the country not only adopted the 73rd Amendment but also conducted elections to the local bodies twice first in 1994 and again in the year 2001.

Socio-Economic Background of Women Panchayati Leader in Srikakulam District

The women leaders were classified into three groups as per their designation as ward members of the Panchayat, Sarpanch and MPTC. Majority 117 (84.78 %) of them are ward members followed 12 are Sarpanch and remaining 9 (6.52 %) are MPTCs.

Profile of the Women

Caste: In the social group classification of the women leaders, backward castes ward members constitute 36.75 per cent followed by SC/ST (32.48 %) and open category (30.77 %). In case of Sarpanches, all the Sarpanches are from backward communities only and in case of MPTC, majority 8 (88.89 %) of the women leaders are also from backward community only, one woman leader belongs to SC/ST community.

Education: Among the ward members majority of them are illiterates while few of them had their secondary education. With regard to the Sarpanches category majority of them had their secondary education, while very few of them had their primary education.

Age: Among the ward members, majority 31 (26.50 %) of them fall in the 26-35 age group, while few of them are in the above 55 age group. In case of Sarpanches, majority 8 (66.7%) of them belong to 26-35 age group but relatively few of them are in the 46-55 age group.

Occupation: Among ward members majority of them are doing agricultural and allied works and few of them are artisans. With regard to Sarpanches majority of them are doing agriculture and allied works and only one person is doing small business.

Land: Among the ward members, nearly two fifth of them are landless and only 9.40 per cent of them own large size land holding. While it come to Sarpanches, 55.56 per cent of the own medium size land holding and only 44.44 per cent of them own large size landholdings.

Case Studies of Selected Women Representatives and Their Responses

Case studies are found to be more effective means to obtain the understanding of the life situations. Hence an attempt is made to study the individual cases of a few women leaders. Observation, dialogue and participation in their life situations helped us to understand the virtual functioning of village women leaders.

A common picture is that of women representatives functioning as proxy candidates under the close observation and supervision of their guardians (majority -husbands). Prominent men, generally ex-presidents of panchayats and cooperatives, retired government functionaries and members of political parties made their wives or sisters or close relatives contest in the elections against the reserved panchayats, they started as ' de facto' leaders. They were conducting the panchayat meetings and running the panchayat administration.

Case-I: Linguberi Ramanamma wife of Sriramulu is a MPTC member of Talasamudram of Srikakulam district. Majority of the people are wishing to vote congress party. She won the seat with a margin of 670 votes.

Case-II: Surapu Nageswaramma wife of Shivarama Krishna Prasad is a MPTC of Gollalavalasa. She belongs to Santhalaxmipuram panchayat. Majority of the population belongs to only one community. She won the seat with a margin of more than 800 votes.

Case-III: Karimi Umakumari wife of Rajeswara Rao who is a MPTC member of Polaki village won the elections against

Venkata Appalanaidu a male candidate with a majority of 350 votes. This MPTC distinct feature i.e. it was ruled by her husband as MPP. She and her husband has a good quality of service motto towards the people and their welfare. She has studied up to intermediate and well experienced in the politics.

Case-IV: Bhavana Tirupathamma wife of Prasada Rao elected as a Village Sarpanche of Thalasmudram panchayat of Srikakulam district.

Case-V: Rayala Suvarna, is Gathalavalasa Sarpanch. She was a good social worker and has work motto. Due to inefficiency of the previous Sarpanch she won the seat.

Case-VI: Danthi Padmavathi, wife of Venkata Ramana belongs to Piruvada Village was elected as a Sarpanch. Previous Sarpanch's husband did some illegal activities and miss-utilized the funds of the Panchayat. Her husband has good talkative power and doing good things for the welfare of the society. She takes the decision with the help of her husband. It shows that there is no women empowerment.

Case-VII: Panchireddy Santhamma, wife of Jaganmohan Rao was elected as a Sarpanch of Gollalavalasa village panchayat. She is the second wife of Jaganmohan Rao. Her husband's first wife was recently expired. Due to some sympathy she won the Sarpanch seat.

Case studies of Ward Members

Case-1: Smt Pasina Thulasamma is the 3rd ward member of Gollalavalasa village panchayat. She worked as a social worker. She is a well known person in the congress party at the grass root level. She is very talkative.

Case-2: With regard to Gangivalasa Panchayat, 4th ward member is Korrayai Suramma. She belongs to Telugu Desam Political Party. She won the seat with the familiarity in the party and there is no influence of her husband and there is no impact of the others.

Case-3: In Belamara Palavalasa village panchayat, Chintu Saraswathi was elected as member for the 1st ward. She was sister-in-law of the sarpanch. She was elected with the majority of 80 votes against Gorle Narayanamma who belongs to Telugu Desam Party.

Case-4: Mrs. Linguberi Punnamma is the 7th ward member in Belamara Palavalasa village Panchayat. She was elected on the dominance of her caste Srisaina in the village. She won with the majority of 20 votes against Kallapalli Jayamma.

Special Case Studies

Case-5: In Dola village panchayat, three wards were given the women reservation, but for all the wards women were unanimously elected. These women are not exercising their power but their husbands or relatives are exercising the power.

Case-6: In Eduluvalasa village panchayat, Sarpanch Bora Krishnaveni, MPTC Bora Bhavani and all the ten ward members were women only. They were unanimously elected. But all the wards were occupied by women only because of the influence of their husbands or relatives or village heads. These women were not able to exercise their power but their husbands or relatives or villages heads are exercising the power.

Public Perceptions about Women Panchayati Leadership

Leadership of women at the grassroots level, in general, is unsatisfactory. During the field work the researcher noticed that some women leaders are very active and committed. This situation is definitely an encouraging one. Training of women to become responsible leaders will add momentum to the already existing encouraging trend.

Viewed from a macro-level, women's leadership in the rural political scene also reveals an unhappy situation. But micro-level studies help us to identify some women activists. Studies found that some women chairpersons of Mandala Parishads in Andhra Pradesh (33 % of the offices of chairpersons of Mandal Parishad and Zilla Parishads in

Andhra Pradesh is reserved for women) are functioning as effective leaders. A number of women participated in the election campaign of these chairpersons. As pointed out in the national perspective plan for women, power and access to position of decision making and authority are critical pre-requisites for women's equality in the processes of nation building.

For the purpose of the present study we have selected 200 respondents from different occupation like agriculture, teachers, housewives and business and also different age groups from 18 years to above 45 years to record their perceptions about women panchayat leaders. The sample contained 82 female and 118 male respondents.

Gender: Majority 118 (59.0 %) of the sample members are male category and remaining 82 (41.0 %) of the respondents are female category.

Age: Majority 81 (40.5 %) of the sample members belong to 26-35 years of the age followed by 66 (33.0%) are above 35 years and 53 (26.5 %) are below 25 years of the age.

Need of Women Leadership

77 per cent gave positive responses indicating that women leadership is imperative for the healthy functioning of the Panchyat Raj institution. The respondents felt that the women participation is indispensable not only for the effective functioning of the Panchayat Raj institutions, but also solve problems like health, sanitation and primary education. The rational behind such a perception is that Women are better motivators than men.

16 per cent of Sarpanches, MPTCs, ZPTCs and MPPs are efficient and 48 per cent of MPTCs, ZPTCs and MPPs are inefficient in discharging their functions. While 36 per cent of the respondents felt that they unable to say anything 86.5 per cent of the total sample felt that the women leaders do not enjoy freedom to exercise their powers and functions, whereas 13.5 per cent of the total sample admitted that women were having freedom in exercising their powers and functions in Panchayati Raj Institutions.

More than three fourths or 77.0 % respondents believed that women leaders are invariably influenced in decision-making by their family members. Only 23 per cent of total sample opined that women leaders take their own decision in matters regard to local bodies. Illiteracy is one of the main drawbacks in performing their duties. 79 per cent of the total respondents believed that illiteracy is the root cause for the poor performance of women leaders. Nearly 21 per cent of the total sample are of the view that performance is not linked to literacy levels.

In the opinion of the respondents the performance of the majority of the scheduled caste women leaders was very poor and below average. It is observed that the low literacy rate among dalit women leaders could account for their poor performance. It is significant to know that 13.5 % of the respondent believed that the dalit Sarpanches were ignorant of their powers and the village leaders majority of who belonged to forward castes dominated functions. It is very important that almost all the women leaders especially at the grass-root level need training is necessary to enable them to function more effectively. It is observed that the husbands of women Sarpanches and functionaries attended the training camps rather than the actual representatives.

The need for training is more for women because of their lower literacy and less exposure to public affairs and dealings with the public and officials. Training should be continuous and spread over different phases rather than a one-time exercise. The new tasks for training are call for awareness, knowledge and skills, understanding of administrative procedures and sensitivity to the problems of society.

Conclusion

The 73rd Amendment, is a milestone in the history of legislation, which has ensured the coming of women to the leadership and decision making positions, and it has made such a role mandatory and universal in the whole of India. The women chairpersons Sarpanches and even voters have still to prove themselves.

According to various micro-studies including our own observations from the field about 80 to 90 per cent women attend the Panchayati meetings regularly. Given their sheer numbers, one might conclude the democracy has become more, participatory than before at least at the grassroots level. The socio economic background of these women showed that majority of them come from the lower income group particularly at the village Panchayati level. They get outside support in terms of NGO intervention, women's groups, or any other social or political movement, the women become relatively more vocal and their knowledge about the functioning of the Panchayati increase. Women not only take up issues relating to basic needs - drinking water, availability of doctors and teachers in the villages, which is dear to them, but also general developmental activities for e.g. to augment income of the Panchayati, irrigation facilities for the Paddy field.

The 2001 elections to local bodies in Andhra Pradesh ushered a new era of silent social revolution in one of the predominantly rural and agricultural states of India. The present study made an attempt of understand the nature character and problems of elected women village Sarpanches in the districts of Srikakulam in the state of Andhra Pradesh.

The village Sarpanches were quite unhappy with the system of village secretaries. The presidents complained that the village secretaries were over bearing and dominating to say the least. Whenever inspections are conducted, secretaries use the occasion to pressurize and give them more trouble to the Sarpanches of the village Panchayati. The Sarpanches were of the view that rotation in reservation of village presidentship was not good for the development of the village. They felt that no leader would concentrate on village development if the rotation system continues.

It is said that about one million women have come to active politics as a result of the reservation. If we assume that on an average three women contest for one seat, about three million women are involved in the political process and they become aware of the grass roots institutions. Moreover, it is noticed that women in the village become the main campaigners for the women candidates fallout of that is noticed that women particularly in the rural areas have become restless and desire to get engaged in certain economically gainful activities. It is encouraging that many self help groups have been formed in different parts of rural areas.

In addition to that more women than men attended the ward sabha (a smaller unit of Gram sabha). They get familiar with the words like Block Development Office, District Magistrate etc., so a ground has been created to mobilize women of the rural India to seek the gender justice in the more vigorous way.

The 73rd Amendment has created an opportunity for large number of rural women to take part-in the public institutions. In many places women have been functioning well and have engendered the development process although in a limited sense. The family has accepted the new role and even the relationship between husband and wife has been altered. The myth of being a proxy woman gets disproved according to my study. The husband wife relationship has become relatively more egalitarian. This has led mobilization of rural women to a great extent. They are becoming restless. The elected women prove to be the role model for the women. Thus we find that the 73rd Amendment has an empowering impact on the women where women's labour is still marginalized and the rural hierarchies remain unchallenged, to a large extent. The entry of women into politics in such a big way is in itself a radical change. Despite the constraints, they are playing an extremely important role, which needs to be recognized.

17

Empowerment of Rural Women

Dr. A. Lavanya Kumari
B. Mohan Rao

Introduction

Women constitute a little less than 50 per cent of the total population of India. But women, particularly the rural poor women, are the most underprivileged from the point of view of empowerment. In 1991, the Female Work Participation Rate was very low at 23.3 as against 51.6 for males. The 2001 Census results indicate the continuing differential Work Participation Rate between females and males. Females accounted for only 18.4 per cent of the total employment of the public and private sectors put together in the year 2003. The Tenth Five year Plan (2002-07) adopted 'Empowerment of Women' as an important approach for ensuring women their rightful place in society as agents of socio-economic development of the country.

Objectives

- To study the need for empowerment of rural women,

- To know the importance of empowerment of rural women and
- To suggest the suitable measures to improve the empowerment of rural women.

NEED FOR EMPOWERMENT OF RURAL WOMEN

There is need for empowerment of rural women in order to promote gender equality; women are to be encouraged as agents to bring change in society.

All their capabilities are to be utilized for betterment of women. Instead of concentrating on women's issues like freedom, it is better to concentrate on increasing the capabilities of rural women. As Amartya Sen put it "Nothing arguably, is a important today in the political economy of development as an adequate recognition of political, economic and social participation of women". The word 'Empowerment' captures the sense of gaining control over their lives, participating and decision-making.

The concept of empowerment in general, described as 'a process, which enables individual or group to change of power in social, economic and political relations in the society". It has been more specifically described in the context of empowerment of women in Bangladesh as, 'freedom of choice for self fulfillment and self development as well as equal access to domestic and community resources, opportunities and power. In most definitions to empowerment, there runs a thread of commonality. 'more freedom' leads to 'greater control' and 'self-fulfillment'.

The women community has long been delaminated, degenerated and disempowered by the male dominated society. For making good such created deficiency, the rural women folk now deserve all sorts of social and economic and political empowerment. This discriminatory attitude has constrained their freedom, mobility that consequently led for the denial of opportunities for the development of their personalities. That is why; rural women have lagged behind in the fields of education, skills development and employment.

The Importance of Empowerment of Rural Women

Women get an independent income only when they enter into economic activities. Women work continuously throughout the day but they do not get any incomes as they possess enormous use value but not exchange value. Women empowerment has been one of the most important item in the agenda of National development.

The roles that rural women play in agriculture vary from region to region and country to country. In many developing countries hit by the economic ravages of the 1980s, women, especially very poor women are now working 60-90 hours a week in order to maintain their meager living standards in a decade ago. They play a major part in sowing, weeding, application of fertilizers, and pesticides, harvesting, threshing, food processing, transportations and marketing. Rural women carry out various operations from farm jobs to marketing produce and business. In animal husbandry, women seem to monopolize almost all operations such as feeding and watering of animals, cleaning of sheds, fodder collection and coking grain for cattle. Women participate equally with men in making livestock products. Women are involved in decision-making both individually and jointly with their husbands.

Traditionally women played an important role in fish handling and processing in India. The involvement of women in fisheries is limited to auctioning of fish, catching of fish by hand picking, retail marketing, net mending and processing of fish. There is considerable gender based division of labour in the fishing communities as with many parts of the world the women are mainly restricted to land based activities. Such activities might, in addition to housework, include fish processing and trade. The majority of women in coastal fishing villages are involved in household level activities curing small pelagics and some are involved in the trade of fresh and dried fish through local markets. Women are also engaged as seasonal agricultural labour and for working in saltpans.

The IRDP and its allied programmes such as TRYSEM, DWCRA and MWS have been restructured into a single self-employment programme called "Swarnajayanthi Grama Swarojgar Yojana" (SGSY), which has been launched since 1999. It develops the rural poor through self-employment with their own efforts. SGSY improve the skills of the rural poor and to enable them to utilize the local resources effectively and efficiently. It gives importance to Self Help Groups and thereby enhance the self-confidence of rural women and develop them economically, and to bring about social change. It created some dynamism among the rural women in the society.

Women in rural India are involved in myriad activities, ranging from growing crop production to the management of household resources. It is also important to keep that in mind the fact that women also spend a substantial part of their time in the management of livestock agriculture, dairying, fishing and poultry, etc.

SUGGESTIONS

To improve the status of rural women and overcome all the problems of rural women, the Government has strictly implemented the policies like National plan of action for women, 1976, setting up of National Commission for Rural Women, Parliamentary Committee as empowerment of rural women.

Rural development programmes for rural women must provide them with ownership of land, better credit facilities, agricultural inputs, extension services, skill upgradation, in production and marketing, knowledge of technology, communication skills, and confidence to emerge as leaders of rural development the planners, policy makers, and the social activists, must take this reality into account and aim at bringing improvements in the conditions of poor rural women. Therefore, it is suggested that the Government and NGOs should take predication for more participation of rural women.

CONCLUSION

Women in rural areas are the major work force in different sectors and play a significant role in domestic socio-economic sphere in the rural areas. But still, they are deprived of family wealth and stay aside from major decision making on family matters. When women become empowered society develops towards betterment. It is a fact that policy makers in India are increasingly aware of this problem and have launched several innovative schemes for rural women empowerment, not only through Government agencies, but also through Non-Governmental Organizations (NGOs).

REFERENCES

Vanitha Chethan and Krishnamurthy "Women in Rural Development through SGSY" edited by Kiran Prasad, The Women Press, Delhi-110009.

Deshpande, L.K., (1987), "Planning for Fuller Employment-A Review", in P.R. Brahmananda and V.R. Panchamukhi(ed), The Development Process of the Indian Economy, Himalaya Publishing House, Bombay.

Karl, (1995), "Women and Empowerment Participation and Decision-making", Zed books Ltd. London and New Jersey.

18

Empowerment of Rural Women Through Education

G. Vidyavathi
P. Tirumaleswara Rao
Dr. T. Sharon Raju

Introduction

The poorer sections of the rural tribal women should be the focus of discussion categorizing the rural women into three groups, namely, landless Agricultural labourers; traditional artisans; and others, such as, fisherwomen, the group made the following observations and recommendations;

The concept of development should include knowledge and awareness of the right of women, various inputs of knowledge with regard to health, nutrition, child care, family life, mother craft; and knowledge of organizational skills, which would bring about a change in the total quality of their lives.

A methodology should be evolved for conducting adult education programmer and for motivating and retaining learners in the functional literacy programmes.

An in-depth study should be taken up to identify the needs and problems of the target groups, and appropriate educational materials should be prepared.

The agricultural universities should be involved in all the programmes of adult education for the target groups and the UGC should come forward to fully support these Programmes of education and extension. The Indian agricultural research institutes should also contribute significantly in these programmes.

Various developmental agencies working in rural and tribal areas should cooperate in the programmes of adult education and all the information relevant to the target group should be disseminated through the adult education functionaries.

The programmes should give special attention to social, economic and educational problems of women belonging to scheduled castes and scheduled tribes.

Women should become equal partners in development. Women should be made aware of the existing situation along with their rights and role in society and also about the various developmental programmes intended for them in their districts, blocks, villages, etc.

Various groups and officials need to be oriented and educated regarding women's problems and needs. Effective co-ordination is needed among various officials so that adequate linkages can be established between different developmental departments and officials. The groups needing orientation are: opinion leaders in villages, educated girls and women, educated youth and women, panchayat members and especially women members, mahila mandals, bank officers, B.D.Os and other functionaries at the block level; district planning cells of all departments, such as, health, social welfare, education, agriculture, rural development and information and broadcasting.

With the introduction of modern and new technology, jobs, which were traditionally being done by women, are being taken over by men, pointing to the need for equipping rural female working force with permanent skills so that they can come above the poverty level. Income generating programmes, through which such integration is to be done, should not be fragments of ill-defined skill learning programmes, but they should brought out with, carefully, economically viable skill in human resource development programmes.

More and more voluntary agencies should be encouraged to go into the interiors of the country, especially tribal areas. Only voluntary agencies which are motivated, can help in the effective implementation of various programmes and schemes of the Government.

Rural libraries should be set up for neo-literate women. Women should have access to reading materials, so that they can cultivate and retain their interest in reading and writing, avoiding relapse into illiteracy and improve their quality of life.

Rural radio broadcasts and telecasts should give names and addresses of officials/agencies that can be contacted for assistance relating to each development programme.

A simple list of welfare movements organized in the country should be made available to women in every district in the State, as soon as possible.

There should be a continuous review of the implementation of the programmes through a closely-knit monitoring and evaluation system.

It is observed that although the importance of Women's education had been emphasized from time to time by various Committees, a lot remained to be done quantitatively and qualitatively. Keeping in view the magnitude of the problem of women's education, the participants recommended that both formal and non-formal approaches should be used for tackling it. The various factors responsible for the low educational development of women, it is observed, could be divided into the following three categories:

Economic: This was considered as the most important factor for the non-participation of women in educational programmes. Girls, it was pointed out, begin to contribute to the family's income from a very early age. They look after their younger siblings and do household work to enable their parents to go out to earn a living, thus indirectly supplementing the family's income.

Social: Customs and practices like purdah and early marriage deter women from participating in educational activities. Besides, the attitude widen prevalent towards girls education, especially among the rural poor, is also not favorable.

The role of the girls, it is believed, is limited to the four walls of the house, and education is considered to be of no use for them.

Parental Attitude due to cultural and social customs, parents are reluctant to send their daughters to school.

The following observations and recommendations were made with regard to the promotion of women's education:

Motivation is the driving force, which urges an individual to strive after an objective, whatever be the obstructions on the way. Hence, adult education programmes to be a success must make sense to the learners and meet their felt needs. For otherwise not only will the adult women themselves reject the programmes but will also dissuade their daughters from joining them.

Health and Nutrition Education for Women

The lively and interesting discussion of the participants concluded in the following observations and recommendations:

It was generally felt that the existing health and nutrition education component for women in adult education programmes needs to be strengthened, expanded and updated.

It was pointed out that the women of our country are still suffering from poor health, malnutrition, infectious diseases, particularly gastrointestinal diseases, anemia, worm-infestations respiratory tract diseases as well as psychological and emotional problems for which they require education. They are also ignorant about correct methods of cooking, balanced diet, importance of vegetables, personal hygiene, sanitation, cleanliness of the home and environment and about maternal care and the care of the growing child. The participants felt that adolescent girls being potential mothers also need to be educated in matters of health and nutrition. Women are ignorant and illiterate and there is a lack of health consciousness, as well as health facilities and counseling specially directed towards the care of women. Women tend to spend more money on items of lower priority and thus are ignorant about household budgeting.

The members agreed that intensive education needs to be carried out to promote breast- feeding. It was felt that women need to be educated about proper feeding and warning practices, proper health and hygiene in child care, importance of immunization, spacing of children, knowledge about common ailments in children and their prevention, promotion of use of indigenous and Ayurvedic remedies and importance of personality development of child.

Points regarding improvement in the methods and techniques of adult education of women were also made. The gaps and lapses in adult education programme were reviewed and it was suggested that a multi-directional approach should be taken, coordinating the adult education programmes, such as medical and health programmes being conducted by Departments of preventive and social medicine, pediatrics, obstetrics and gynaecology, family planning programmes, MCH Centres, PHC centers and other University departments, such as, home science, sociology, economics and psychology. An integrated approach was considered to be important to avoid confusion and duplication among the target groups. Extensive use of audio-visual aids by securing aids from Central Health Education Bureau, transfer of aids from Central Government institutions to adult education centres and use of mass media to the maximum were recommended. It was further suggested that training and refresher courses for adult education workers should be held more frequently.

Social Awareness of Rural Women

The Group after a stimulating discussion came to the following conclusions:

Literacy, awareness and functionality need not follow any sequential order. The order may change from situation to situation.

Even though it is not likely that with the increase in the level of literacy, the level of superstition will decrease, awareness required for decreasing superstition has to be created in the learners.

Awareness is a pre-requisite to development. Participation of rural women in developmental programmes can be ensured only by creating in them an awareness about the assistance provided by the development agencies.

In order to enable rural women to perform their functions as mother, wife and individual they must be made aware of the components constituting their participation in social life.

To enable the rural women to plan their family life it is essential to make them aware of the facilities and methods at their command. Rural women have to be trained in critical and analytical thinking so that they can develop their discretionary faculty. To enable the rural women to exercise their right of franchise they have to be made aware of the Indian democratic system.

Rural women should be made aware of the legal provisions and rules enacted for their betterment. They have to be made aware of the fact that the Constitution has granted equal protection to men and women. They have to be made aware of their civic rights especially of those relating to

(a) equality before law,

(b) equal pay for men and women,

(c) special provisions for women,

(d) equality of opportunity in the matter of public appointment,

(e) marriage,

(f) maintenance,

(g) adoption and

(h) succession.

In order that the rural women may be able to liberate themselves from poverty and exploit tics they have to be made aware of the how and why of their present economic status, viz.:

(a) Why is that we are poor?

(b) Who is responsible for our poverty?

(c) Can we get ride of the poverty?

(d) How?

Rural women should be helped to the higher level of awareness required for bringing about a desirable change in the structure of the society.

Reformative approach cannot help to create awareness among the rural women. Conscientisation alone can help to stimulate the learners' thinking, leading to social change.

Creating of awareness takes time. This cannot be achieved fully within the duration fixed for the adult education programme. This has to be a continuing process.

In order to create awareness, to impart skills and to bring about attitudinal change among the women of the rural and tribal areas, adult education functionaries from among the women of the respective areas have to be identified and trained.

In selecting adult education functionaries for the rural/ tribal women, social commitment should be preferred to educational qualifications. All universities of India should take up the responsibility of training the trainees in the field of adult education.

Women carry heavy workloads, yet their contribution to national development goes unnoticed. Women are "faceless, voiceless, and invisible". Our school text books also have a sex bias. They represent girls and women as passive and only fulfilling roles of wife and mother.

Huge sums of money are spent in India on the education of the middle and upper castes. The money allocated for the services to the poor goes for the salaries of the educated. Yet many of these paid persons function very poorly. Thus the literacy and deprivation among the low-income groups increases.

More girls than boys suffer from this handicap. Therefore the non-formal education aimed at illiterate girls from low income families should be encouraged so that every Indian girl gets a chance to dispel ignorance. To face life with self-confidence women and girls must develop skills to become economically independent, otherwise they will be enslaved forever.

Most women and girls have in decisions which affect their lives always be subjected to others, specially men.

If women are forced to work at home and outside should they continue to carry a double burden.

Will men give a helping hand to women in child rearing and household tasks if not forced by circumstances? Will Indian women discourage boys from learning housekeeping jobs which will lead to their non-participation as adults?

Non-Formal Education Programme:

Need for Education

India's literacy rate has increased from 16.6 per cent in 1951 to 36.17 per cent in 1981. The literacy among men is 46.74 per cent while among women it is only 24.88 per cent. However, facilities for education do not keep pace with the rise in population, hence the number of illiterate increase every decade. Majority of these are women.

About twenty per cent of our children never enter schools. While around 50 per cent of the children who join schools leave in the first year, 60 per cent drop out before std. V while 75 per cent drop out before std. VII. Due to a lack of follow-up and dearth of easy reading material many lapse into illiteracy.

Reasons for Lack of Education

Poverty is the main cause for keeping boys and girls from schools though education is free in many states children have to earn to meet basic needs. Sickness or death of parents means an end of schooling for many.

The formal education offered in our schools do not prepare children for agricultural work. Often rural Youth, when literate, these traditional jobs are lowly or have a low status. Therefore parents are afraid to send them to school.

Many schools are at great distances from the place where the children live. In backward areas of many states a large number of schools do not function due to inadequate supervision on the part of teachers Children from low castes often do not fit into the culture of the school Also fear of corporal punishment from teachers discourages children to return to school.

PROBLEMS OF GIRLS

The proportion of boys to girls in education is as follows:

- Primary level 5:2,
- Secondary level 3:1,
- University level 4:1.

Therefore there is tremendous need for educating girls to make them aware that there is something beyond the domain of a home and a kitchen. Girls also take charge of younger brothers and sisters while parents work, others look after cattle and household chores.

In rural and jungle areas schools are far away from home, and parents are reluctant to send their girls to co-educational schools. In many places schools exclusively for girls do not exist. Child marriage means an end to education of girls in several regions.

MEDICAL OPINION ABOUT WOMAN'S EDUCATION

No one in India dreams that woman's education has a medical aspect. Many doctors in the West have sufficiently studied the problems of women and they have come to certain definite conclusions. Sir James Critchton Browne, M.D. who says that the differences between sexes are involved in every organ and tissue. He also deprecates the present relentless zeal of inter-sexual competition, concerning the results of which it is appalling to speculate from a medical point of view. "Girls," he says, "Suffer far more change and instability, at the onset of puberty than boys," He finds head-aches far too common among young girls from ten to seventeen, advocates the abolition of evening study, finds danger than the ovum and sperm-cell may have their activity so reduced before meeting that the infant comes to life old and without a fair chance.

Many eminent and renowned doctors in the West advocate that the higher education of girls, wishing to become mothers and wives, should be completed before the age of 18 or 19 and they should then enter married life. Late marriages and postponement of marriage are generally discouraged by medical authorities. Thus the medical aspect should be considered as one of the fundamental principles of woman's education.

The entrance in Government service depends on a medical certificate of physical fitness. Insurance companies generally accept lives after they are recommended by doctors. Schools and colleges alone seem to ignore the recommendations of doctors regarding education of women.

The Doctrine of Individual Freedom in Marriage, Education and Occupations

In every-day conversation no one uses them in their true sense. Economic Independence is considered more valuable now-a-days than married life. There are many guardians and parents in India, who think that their widowed daughters would be quite better off in case they spend their lives in hospitals and schools earning their livelihood.

These daughters are often child-widows and there are hundreds of them in India and the guardians of such girls do not attach any importance to the career of a wife and mother.

Public opinion considers that a child-widow is bringing about her self-development by becoming a nurse, a teacher or a doctor. The general education given to women in India is quite identical with that of men and schools and colleges are doing level best in helping women to achieve economic independence. Very few persons have as yet realized that the principle of self-determination, if logically applied to marriage, would annihilate the homes as a social institution. Marriage, in India, is considered as a sacrifice and a compromise both on the part of the bride and the bridegroom.

CO-EDUCATION

Many eminent educationists in India consider co-education, as a kind of consummation devoutly to be wished for in all schools and college in India. Separate education is now looked down upon as a kind of slavery and the go-ahead women and girls of India consider co-education as their birth-right. Eminent reformers in India look to co-education as the greatest educational reform of the modern times.

Co-educationalizing primary schools in India would take years and would require an all-India propaganda to bring about this desired reform in education. For the present not even one per cent primary schools are coeducational and public opinion is adverse even to this reform.

Co-education is not an educational reform but it is merely a social experiment. The Imparting of knowledge is not in any way easier when and female students constitute one single class. Co-education makes boys more refined and cultured and makes girls more study in their every day behavior. Co-education has certain economical and social advantages. In case sufficient girl students are not available, it is waste of money to maintain a separate school for such girls.

19

Empowerment of Rural Woman in Andhra Pradesh

H.V.A. Meenakshi

Introduction

First We Know About What is Empowerment?

The triple handicap and empowerment is not single country in the world." where men and woman enjoy completely equal opportunities "means in education, political, socio, cultural, earnings, health, etc. that we call empowerment and also one of the ideology that is decision making improve the women status equal to men. That is why we must change attitudes and policies the aim must be given each and every human being grater freedom to make chooses about their own lives.

Who Are the Rural Women?

Rural woman from schedule caste and schedule tribe (STs, also known as girijans are mountain people carry a triple handicap-as woman as rural persons and schedule caste and schedule tribe. It is for this reason that the alternative strategy under study, which seeks to help the "poorest of the poor specifically targets the rural woman.

Methodology

Present paper focus attention on empowerment levels of woman in rural India. For this following objectives were specified.

Objectives

1. To understand the status of rural woman in India and Andhra Pradesh.
2. To understand the empowerment levels of rural woman in Andhra Pradesh.
3. To examine varies programs and schemes initiated by government for rural woman enlistment.
4. Impact of rural woman the empowerment strategy and independent assessment of aware strategy and why aware is successful reasons.
5. Some select case studies and conclusions.

Analysis

For the present paper secondary data from varies authentic sources have been collected.

Status of Rural Woman in India

At first summery of findings in second section the status of woman in as certain then, issues regarding women's development in the contest of nation raised are debated finally away in through out to integrate the woman of village under study with the main stream of change and transformation. In terms of every sector indices of developments social economic status woman have fared worse than man.

Woman constitute 70 % of the world's poor populations of 1.3 billion, they produce 50 % of food world wide but receive only 10 % of the incomes.

India presented at the 4th world conference on women at Beijing in 1995 observed that percentage of women among the extremely poor is disproportionately large adding that "intra-house hold inequalities can be significant necessitating special attention for poor women these realities of the women handicaps are not generally reflected in economic models of development which disregard gender" desegregated statistics indicated. Examples: earnings, health, education, politics, socio cultural factors.

As Rural Woman

If the reality is that lag behind man in terms of every set of socio-economic indicators in spite of gender inequalities being one of the constitutional mandates, The same kind of imbalances mark the urban rural divide also, with a greater percentage of the rural population falling below the poverty line since the rural sector accounts for 72.8 % of the economy (1991 census) this inequality has significant implications for focusing on the rural sector in development policy (comparison of rural and urban).

Literacy Level of Women

Literacy has been recognized as a basic human right it's availability is a key aspect in the determination of woman development. The female literacy rate is always low when compare to male literacy rate. In 1961 AP female literacy rate is a low as 12.3 %. It reached 15.65 % in 1971, 24.16% in 1981 and 35.72 % in 1991. how suddenly improved to 51.02 in 2001 it is to be noticed that the female literacy rate was never equal to male literacy rate which clearly indicates gender inequalities further rural-urban and cast wise variation can be noticed regard to female literacy rate in 1991 in AP rural female literacy rate was 23.92 % while it was 56.41 % in urban areas. More ever SC female literacy rate in rural areaas69.19% and it is 7.29 % for ST woman thus SC & ST woman stands last in regard to literacy.

Table 1

Year	*Residence*	*Male*	*Female*	*Percentage*
1961	Rural	25.14	8.45	16.85
	Urban	53.62	29.33	41.78
	Total	20.19	12.03	21.19
1971	Rural	27.31	10.92	19.19
	Urban	57.30	36.31	47.08
	Total	33.18	15.75	24.57
1981	Rural	32.25	14.08	23.24
	Urban	61.89	41.55	51.99
	Total	39.26	20.39	29.94
1991	Rural	47.28	23.92	35.74
	Urban	75.81	56.41	66.32
	Total	55.13	32.72	44.09
2001	Rural	66.13	44.36	55.33
	Urban	83.21	69.34	76.39
	Total	70.85	51.17	61.11

Source: 50 years of A.P

Health Status

The health status of woman also shows considerable variation in urban and rural areas the health indicators such as birth rate death rate infant mortality immunization of children, woman body mass index <18.5 and percentage of children survival under weight were taken for the present paper the birth rate is 21 in rural areas where as it is 19 in urban areas death rate is 9 it is 5 in urban areas here the strengthening of health care providers in rural areas need to addressed. IMR rates are very high in rural areas 67/1000 & it is 33/1000 live births in urban areas.

Table 2
Rural Urban Differentials in Health in AP

Health indicators	*Rural*	*Urban*
Birth rate	21	19
Death rate	9	5
Infant mortality rate	67	33
% of children receiving all vaccinations	54	73
% of women with BMI <18.5	43.2	19.7
% of children survival under weight	2.1	0.4

Table 3

	AP	*India*
Rural population (as % of total population 1991)	·73.2	74.3
Life expectancy at birth (1989-1993)		
Rural	59.7	58
Urban	64.2	64.9
Female rate	33	39
Annul population growth rate (1981-1991)	23.91	23.56
% of under nourished Sc children	50.6	57.5
% of children attending school(1992-1993)	63.3	67.5
SC literacy	32	37
Under 5 mortality rate(1992-1993)	91.2	
% of SC population (1991)	15.93	16.48
% of house holds with drinking water with pump/pipe	63.4	68.2
Girls aged 6-14 not attending school (1992-1993)		45.41

Source: National family health survey the progress of Indian status 1995, UNICF March1996

To examine various programmes and schemes initiated by government for rural woman upliftment.

A separate ministry for woman and children was created 1984 issues pertaining to rural woman's advancement were identified by three planning groups of the government of India.

1. IRDP 1976.
2. The national committee on the role and participation of the rural woman in agricultural rural development.

Various Rural Development Schemes

1. IRDP: Integrated Rural Development Programme.
2. DWACRA: Development of Woman and Children of Rural Areas.
3. TRYSEM: Training of Rural Youth For Self Employment.
4. NREP: National Rural Employment Programme.

Non-Economic Measures

Article 15 of the constitution empowers the state to in act legislation to protect woman and promote the welfare the progress of SC/ST.

The word empowerment has been used frequently in recent official pronouncements on the status of women (The country report presented it Beijing in 1995).

They have been other attempts addressing there awareness component of empowerment. Central social welfare board, a voluntary action bureau was started in 1982.

Impact of Rural Woman the Empowerment Strategy and Independent Assessment of Aware Strategy and Why Aware is Successful Reasons

Making woman equal partners in the national development process and equipping them to make informed choices in order to actualize their self-wroth through empowerment or goals to when government is compiied-there is a long way to go but the endeavor A is ceaseless (India country report forth world conference as woman Bejing 1995).

An alternate strategy receiving the convenient ional sequence of development of assistance which is economic assistance first followed by awareness generation and empowerment later was developed by the NGOs this organization create a sustainable pattern development for rural woman empowerment was carried out through two schemes. NGO's known as aware acronym for action for welfare and awaking in rural women. (1) Chaithanya Shakthi Awareness programs; (2) Skills training (3) Chaitanya Nidhi.

To call woman weaker sections is liable; it's men's injustice to women if by strength then indeed is women less brute then men if by strength is meant moral power then woman is immeasurably superior to men the strategy workers because the methodology adopted is one of working with the poor rather than working for the poor- a crucial difference between the convenient ional approaches to the empowerment.

Case Study

Ajmeerachitti hails from suryathanda village, in the Warangalregion

About Ajmeerachitti: She is an illiterate. She earn daily wages as a laborer but it is not enough to live on she have two daughters & a son they cant go to school, they do odd jobs like cleaning, fetching her husband can not go to work and earn, he drinks regularly and tortures her for money for liquor

Ajmeerachitti thoughts before attend under Aware Rural development programme.

Most man, drink that is their habit we can't do anything (that's way she never try to stop drinking of his husband) if children were born to be officers ,they wouldn't have been born as her children (That's way she never tried to their children's education).

Ajmeerachitti after attend under Aware Rural devolepment programme.

She asked for loan to start sheep rearing with that additional income she able to send her children's to school with support of woman's group which was formed in the village chitti was able to put a stop to her husband drinking She declared very happy with the changes which had occurred in her life.

Case Conclusion

Chitti after attending Aware Rural development programme she left inner reverses of strength and get awareness used as a priming strategy for women's empowerment.

Conclusion

As a Government is conducting a number of programmes for the empowerment of rural women, the whole responsibility should not be laid on itself. The domination of men on women should be removed. There must be a change in law according to globalization. Women empowerment cannot be achieved suddenly. It comes gradually with change in generations and there is hope to achieve it in future.

20

PANCHAYATI RAJ AND THE POLITICAL EMPOWERMENT OF BACKWARD CLASSES WOMEN

A Study of Backward Class Women Sarpanches in Anantapur District of A.P.

A. SREENIVASULU
PROF. C. RAMI REDDY
PROF. A.R. DAS

INTRODUCTION

Indian women belong to the most deprived sections of society, having been segregated, exploited and assigned a secondary status of depravity, inferiority vis-à-vis their male counterparts. Backward class women suffer a double deprivation both as women and as women from disadvantaged section belonging to the lower rungs of social ladder.

Underlining the parity of the genders Gandhiji observed that, "Woman is the companion of man, gifted with equal mental capacities, she has the right to participate in the minute details of the activities of man, and she has the same right of freedom and liberty as he by sheer force of a vicious custom, even the most ignorant and worthless men have been enjoying a superiority over women which they do not deserve and ought not to have" (Mahatma Gandhi, 1918).

The social depravity of Backward Caste Women was clearly reflected in terms of socio-economic and political indicators which show them occupying the subservient position in the Indian Society. Along with the Scheduled Castes and Scheduled Tribes, the women were also included among the disadvantaged groups of people in India. The Constitution of India provides equal rights for all the citizens irrespective of socio-economic, religious status, but these provisions couldn't yield results in terms of ensuring mobility of the deprived sections even today decades.

The various aspects of social depravity of Indian women was examined by a number of scholars in terms of sex ratio, life expectancy, literacy (Census of India, 1991), nutrition (Battiwala 1985, Sen and Sen Gupta 1983), in work force participation and with earnings (Mukarjee, 1996) and work time dispositions (Jain 1996), but also in terms of access to power (Mukarjee, 1996). The access to political power controls and guides development programs, if a society's access to political opportunity and participation in political decision making process are important components of capacity-building and also autonomy. The entry of women into the decision-making bodies, it was thought would necessitate restructuring of institutions and would bring solutions to issues pertaining to women's rights.

India as a Welfare State is committed to the welfare and development of its people, in general and of vulnerable sections, in particular, on an egalitarian plane. The government has special concern and commitment for the well being of the socially disadvantaged groups i.e. the Scheduled Caste (SCs), the Scheduled Tribes (STs.), the Other Backward Classes (BCs) and the Minorities. The planning in the post Independent era focused on the social amelioration of the weaker sections through educational and economic upliftment programmes. Women also constituted as belonging to this disadvantaged section. The Constitution of India envisaged providing equality of opportunity to all the citizens through provision of protective discrimination and also political participation. The planned efforts to emancipate women educationally and economically did not yield the desired results over the decades that followed Independence. Beginning with 1980's began the efforts of political empowerment, as it was perceived to give women the needed fillip to an onward surge towards all round development and to a status of respectability and partnership in decision making.

To make political empowerment of women, a reality, the issue of reservation of 1/3 of the seats for women at the grass-root level organization was taken by women's organizations and the social activists. The Government of India passed the 73rd and 74th Amendments, which paved the way for women's political participation at the grass root level Panchayati Raj institutions. It was expected that the Panchayati Raj Institution would ensure political empowerment and a betterment of their social status removing the social and economic discrimination against them.

Empowerment means the process by which power is gained, developed, sized, felicitated or given (Webster's Dictionary). Empowerment may be broadly defined as the control over material assets, intellectual resources and ideology (Battiwala, 1995) Empowerment therefore is a process aimed at changing the nature and direction of systematic forces which marginalized the disadvantaged sections in a given context (Sharma, 1991). Perceptions of being empowered across time dominate a person's life. In India, a low caste woman currently feels empowered when she is given a fair hearing in a public meeting, which comprises of men and women from different social and economic groups.

Empowerment in the human services has emerged from efforts to develop more effective and responsive services of women and other disadvantaged groups. The aim of empowerment is to address the role of powerlessness to play in creating and perpetuating personal social problems. It can be distinguished by its focus on developing critical awareness with increased feelings of collective and self-efficiency, developing skill for personal, inter-personal or social change.

Empowerment in its simple form means the manifestation of the redistribution of power that challenges patriarchal ideology and the male dominance [Chandra, 1997]. It is both a process and the result of the process. It seeks to change the structures and institutions that reinforce and perpetuate it, pave the way for women to gain access to and control of materials as well as information resources.

The concept of Women's empowerment appears to be the result of a number of important critical discussion and dialogues and debates generated by women throughout the world and getting intellectual resources. Control over ideology signifies the ability to generate capacity to propagate, capacity to sustain and institutionalize specific sets of beliefs, principles, values, attitudes, action and behaviours, 'virtually' determining how people perceive, think and function in a given Socio-economic and political environment (Apte, 1995).

The term "Backward Classes" describes the totality of groups entitled of preferential treatment on the basis of their backwardness, viz., the SCs and STs as well as BC, but those accorded special treatment because of temporary or situational disadvantage. Gender discrimination is a universal phenomenon. Both inside and outside the households, women are excluded from position of power. They are denied opportunities to participate in the decision making process. Even when the decisions are to affect their well-being, they are only passive observers. The primary challenge facing women to-day, therefore, is to increase their participation so that they get hold of the situation and become actively involved in the process of decision making (Chandra, 1997).

The Government of A.P. passed executive order in 1963 declaring 139 castes as backward and reserved for them 25 per cent of the seats in educational institutions. This order was struck down by the High Court of Andhra Pradesh on the ground that it was based solely on caste. The sub-committee adopted the following criteria for determining backwardness (1) Poverty, (2) Low level of education, (3) Low standard of living, (4) Place of habitation, (5) Inferiority of occupation, and (6) Low status of caste.

Women's political participation in grassroots and community organisations, in non-government and people's organisations, in feminist's organisations and in workers' movement and in other social and political movements for the transformation of society were witnessed. Women had been at the forefront of the movements for peace, human rights, consumers and others. Women have mobilized in massive numbers to contribute to liberation movements and movements for democracy.

The real empowerment can take place only if women are turned from weaker sex and passive beneficiaries into a valuable human resource of unique strength, and to be integrated in our development efforts. Empowerment of women is strengthening of their innate vitality which can be done through acquirement of knowledge, power and experience. Power is not power to dominate but power to reduce helplessness and effectiveness. No account of Constitutional guarantee of equality will help promote women's social transformation unless they become empowered persons. Realizing women's subjugation and subordination and affirmative discrimination against women, in general, has emerged in the need of their empowerment, both political and economic. Here,. empowerment refers to exercise of powers guaranteed by the Constitution to woman in Panchayati Raj to get rid of different types of socio-economic disabilities.

The legislation in the Amendment of the Constitution (73rd) for entailing the provisions in respect of Panchayati Raj and Municipality is definitely a hall mark for new and effective system of local self government. The late Prime Minister Rajiv Gandhi had embarked upon empowerment of people to have greater say in their own affairs at the gross root levels in addition to the nation and state levels. The concept of empowerment is again embossed on the society, which is a complex organism of multi-level interactions and interrelationships.

One decade has gone by after the provision of political participation to women from disadvantaged sections to take up roles of leadership as Sarpanches at grass-root level democratic institution of Panchayati Raj. The effort has been a step in the right direction. It has to be assessed to what an extent the real political empowerment of the Backward Class women has become a reality? To what extent the egalitarian society has emerged in the caste ridden fabric of rural India? Need to be examined through empirical studies so as to make suitable policy modifications to forge political empowerment and through it the emancipation of the backward sections of the society.

Objectives

This paper examines the political empowerment of Backward Caste women through participation in Panchayati Raj and to know the impact that the political empowerment has wrought in the status of Backward Caste women in grass-root political institutions of Panchayati Raj.

Method of Study

Anantapur district is one the four districts of the backward region of Rayalaseema situated in the state of Andhra Pradesh. Total Panchayats in Anantapur District are 1005. Total women headed Panchayats are 301. Other Caste women and SCs and STs Women put together head 217 Panchayats in the district. The universe for the present study was all the 84 Backward Caste Women who head village Panchayats of Anantapur District. Since the universe was small and manageable, all the respondents were covered in this census survey. The present study was carried out on all the 84 backward caste women Sarpanches occupying the Gram Panchayats in the Anantapur district of Andhra Pradesh.

Findings and Discussions

The empowerment of women through political participation became a reality through passing of the historic 73rd Amendment to the Constitution paving way for the reservation for women in Panchayati Raj to ensure their participation in the decision making process. The active participation of women in the decision making process is to begin at the Gram Panchayat level. It was made that 33 per cent of reservation for women at all tiers of Panchayat so as to get the elected women to safeguard the interests of the village and in particularly of women and children. Adequate training and authority have to be given to them to ensure their effective participation and smooth governance.

Backward Classes women who form sizable portion of the population becoming Sarpanches signaled the dawn of the era of women's political empowerment propelling women for their all round development. The following are the major findings of the study.

1. A majority of women 78.5 per cent of them are in the group age of 20-40 years. It is heartening to know that women in their prime adult age are entering politics, which indicates the enthusiasm and interest they exhibit to come forward to participate in the process of planning for development.
2. It is observable that 63.10 per cent of the respondents are illiterates. It was only 9.52 per cent are with education levels of high school education and above.
3. The overall inference is that all the respondents have minimum of land holdings which is an indicator of their economic status in their rural areas. Based on the sample it is observed that owning a land certainly enhances a person's political stature particularly in the rural areas.
4. The income levels of the families of Backward Caste Sarpanches are in the category lower middle and lower classes.
5. The basic social institutions viz. family and caste continue to be motivating factors for Backward Class women's entry into politics.
6. The respondents clearly indicated that 50 per cent of the respondents had protecting the families interest

as the main consideration forcing their entry, while in the case of 32.14 per cent, rivalry prevalent in the political set up as the reason for their entry into politics.

7. On the whole 76.19 per cent have accepted that they were forced into politics to some extent propelling women for their all round development. The following are the major findings of the study.
8. The process of emergence of backward class women leaders was found to be following the traditional channels of political emergence such as caste, family's standing in the village and of course the new dimension of reservation for gender which was found to be linked to the traditional channels of caste and family status, intertwined with rivalry and factions prevalent in rural areas.
9. In spite of several constraints, these women leaders with limited literacy and exposure to political deliberations in the rural areas have certainly registered moderate levels of success as incumbents of the office of Sarpanches.
10. The reservations, no doubt have helped largely the first generation leaders while the majority of them 78.57 per cent who are either second or third generation leaders, which means that the traditional channels of political emergence and dominance are still prevalent. Reservation or no reservations the rural political elites still rule the rural political institutions
11. The average empowerment score of all the backward caste women leaders indicate an average of 43.56 points which is indicative of certain empowerment among these women, which signals of a positive change in the right direction.
12. The empowerment scores reveal that the opinion on empowerment ascends as their age increases.
13. The highest average was obtained by younger generation of women. The lower scores of the higher

age groups might be due to their pre-occupation with family burden and their experience of the local political scenario for a longer duration.

14. The highest scores of political attitude are noticed among 21.42 per cent of the respondents who are having primary education. Paradoxically respondents with education levels ranging from upper primary level degree have attitude scores which shows declining attitude scores.

In the light of the findings listed above regarding the socio-economic profile and on the emergence and the performance of Backward Caste women leaders of Panchayati Raj, it can concluded that the process of emergence of Backward Caste women leaders is the same as in the case of men from these castes. The channels of emergence of rural leadership through caste, family status are widely operational even in the case of emergence of Backward Caste women leaders. Most of the women are from families with second and third generation of political participation. Therefore they must have had adequate political socialization.

The empowerment of Backward Class women is nothing significant except for these women occupying positions of power. The self appraisal of women leaders reveals that the empowerment they experienced is to large extent moderate considering the fact that women are not totally equipped and free from the influence of the traditional institutions which continue to sway the rural political scenario. No doubt the political reservations have opened the doors of local self government for the women to enter positions of power to partake in the decision making process.

The political empowerment has given the women a sense of confidence and opportunity for interest articulation which would not have been possible without their entry into local self government. Women in political offices, has certainly broken the ice. A beginning has been made in the emancipation of Backward Class women through political empowerment. Given the constraints, the strides made by Backward Class women through Panchayati Raj is certainly an indictor of the socio-political ascendance and indeed a step in the right direction. It is hoped that empowerment of women in general and Backward Class women in particular in the true sense of term, in all its dimensions will be a reality in the coming decades.

SELECT BIBLIOGRAPHY

Ambedkar, S.N., (March 1993), "Panchayati Raj and Grass-root Politics Issues and Perspectives", Journal of Social Development and Justice, Vol. 3.

Andre Beteille, (1999), "Caste, Class and Power".

Mukarjee, R., (1996), "Local Government in Ancient India," Delhi, Motilal Banarsi Das.

India, (1978), Report of Committee on Panchayati Raj Institutions, Chairman, Ashok Mehta, New Delhi, Dept. of Rural Development.

Table 1
Distribution of the Respondents by Age

Sl. No.	*Age Group in Years*	*No. of Respondents*	*Percentage*
1.	20-30	19	22.62
2.	30-40	47	55.95
3.	40-50	16	19.05
4.	50 and above	2	2.38
5.	Total	84	100.00

Table 2
Distribution of the Respondents by Their Level of Education

Sl. No.	*Levels of Education*	*No. of Respondents*	*Percentage*
1	Illiterates	53	63.14
2	Primary	18	21.42
3	Upper Primary	5	5.92
4	High School	6	7.14
5	College	2	2.38
6	Total	84	100.00

Table 3
Distribution of the Respondents by Village Considerations that Forced the L.S.G.

Sl. No.	*Response*	*No. of Respondents*	*Percentage*
1.	Factions	6	7.14
2.	Rivalry	27	32.14
3.	Protecting Family Interest	42	50.00
4.	Any other specify	9	10.71
5.	Total	84	100

Table 4
Age and Empowerment Scores

Sl. No.	*Age Group in Year*	*No. of Respondents*	*Empowerment Scores*
1.	20-30	19 (22.62 %)	45
2.	30-40	47 (55.95 %)	50
3.	40-50	16 (19.05 %)	50
4.	50 and above	2 (2.38 %)	55
5.	Total	84 (100 %)	

Table 6
Education and Political Attitude Scores

Sl. No.	*Levels of Education*	*No. of Respondents*	*Average Attitude Scores*
1	Illiterate	53 (63.10 %)	59
2	Primary	18 (21.42 %)	46
3	Upper Primary	5 (5.92 %)	
4	Secondary	6 (7.14 %)	24
5	Inter	2 (2.38 %)	18
6	Total	84 (100 %)	

21

POPULATION, LITERACY AND EDUCATIONAL STATUS OF SCHEDULED TRIBES IN INDIA

PROF. D. PULLA RAO

INTRODUCTION

The Scheduled Tribes (STs) are the segregated and isolated communities and are concentrated in the states of Orissa, Bihar, Madhya Pradesh, Andhra Pradesh, Maharashtra, Gujarat and Rajasthan, where they constitute about 80 per cent of the total ST population of India. The STs constitute 8.20 per cent of the country's population as per 2001 Census, living mainly in forest and hilly regions. They are sons of soil and live in isolation from other communities. Most of the tribes constitute separate socio-cultural groups having distinct customs, traditions, marriage, kinship and property inheritance system and they live largely in agricultural and pre-agricultural level of technology. Among these tribes, there are food gatherers, hunters, forest land cultivators, shifting cultivators and minor forest produce collectors. The essential characteristics of these communities are primitive traits, geographical isolation, distinctive culture and shyness of contact with outsiders. There are 573 Scheduled Tribes living in different parts of the country, having their own languages different from the one that mostly spoken in the State where they live. There are more than 270 such languages in India. Educational and economic backwardness is also their common feature. They are isolated from the rest of the society due to poor transportation and communication facilities and have remained as educationally, culturally, economically, and socially disadvantaged sections. Being mostly illiterate, they are subjected to all kinds of exploitation-social, economic and political. They comprised of 6.87, 6.82, 7.76, 8.08 and 8.20 per cent of India's population in 1961, 1971, 1981, 1991 and 2001 respectively.

Definition of Tribe

1. A tribe is a collection of families bearing a common name, speaking a common dialect, occupying or professing to occupy a common territory and is not usually endogamous, though originally it might have been so. *Imperial Gazeteer of India*
2. A tribe is a group of people in a primitive or barbarous stage of development acknowledging the authority of a chief and usually regarding themselves as having a common on sector. *Oxford Dictionary*
3. In its simplest form the tribes is a group of bands occupying a contiguous territory or territories and having a feeling of unity deriving form numerous similarities in culture frequent contacts, and a certain community of interest. *Ralpla Linton*
4. A tribe is an independent political division of a population with a common culture. *Lucy Mair*
5. A tribe is a group united by a common name in which the members take a pride by a common language, by a common territory, and by a feeling that all who do not share this name are outsiders, 'enemies' in fact.

   G.W.B. Humtingford

Constitutional Safeguards

After independence the framers of our Constitution have given certain special safety and security to the tribals. These softies and securities provide some protective discrimination to the tribals against the non-tribals. Table-1 shows that which information has been in various Articles and Schedules for Tribes. These are the base for development approach in tribal areas. As a part of two pronged strategy of development and protection, the department of Tribal Welfare has geared up the enforcement machinery for the effective implementation of the protective regulations which were promulgated by the Governor in exercise of powers conferred under Para 5(2) of fifth schedule to the constitution to provide the much needed protection of tribals.

Table 1
Constitution For Scheduled Tribes

Sl. No.	*Article and Schedule*	*Information*
1.	342	Definition of Tribal
2.	46	Educational and economic interests of Scheduled Castes and Tribals
3.	244	Empower the tribal people in tribal areas
4.	339	Welfare Schemes of the STs
5.	275	Funds for tribes to the State Government
6.	330, 332, 334	Provide reservation of seats for STs in the house of the people and the state legislatures
7.	335	Reservation the various services
8.	15, 16, 19	Tribes are also equality of citizens
9.	338	The machinery for implementing the safeguard of the STs and the programmes for their development
10.	5	Powers and lays certain duties on the Governor of every State
11.	6	The way of living

Population Profile of Scheduled Tribes in India

The Census experience indicates that the population of Scheduled Tribe increases faster than overall population of the country. Table-2 shows the overall population of the country for the census period 1951 was 36.1 crores, of which the ST population was 1.9 crores. The decadal growth rate of ST population was high (52.6) in 1961 and the proportion of ST population to overall population was 6.6 per cent. The sex ratio of STs was in a better position at 987 as against to overall sex ratio was 941 in 1961. As per 2001 Census, the overall population increased to 102.8 crores of which STs was 8.4 crores. The decadal growth rate of ST population was high (23.5) as against to overall population (21.5). The proportion of ST population to overall population was 8.2 per cent. The sex ratio of STs was 978, which was higher than the sex ratio of overall population (933) in 2001.

Table 2
Overall and Scheduled Tribe Population and Sex Ratios in India

(In Crores)

Year	Overall Population	Decadal Growth Rate of Overall Population	Scheduled Tribes: Population	Scheduled Tribes: Decadal Growth Rate	% of ST Population of Overall Population	Sex Ratio: Overall	Sex Ratio: ST
1951	36.1	-	1.9	-	5.2	946	988
1961	43.9	21.6	2.9	52.6	6.6	941	987
1971	54.8	24.8	3.8	31.0	6.9	930	985
1981	68.3	24.6	5.2	36.8	7.6	935	983
1991	84.6	23.9	6.8	30.8	8.0	927	972
2001	102.8	21.5	8.4	23.5	8.2	933	978

Source: Selected Educational Statistics, MHRD, GOI, New Delhi, 2002-03.

According to 2001 Census, Scheduled Tribes inhabited allover the country except in Haryana, Punjab, Chandigarh, Delhi and Pondicherry. While the highest concentration of the Scheduled Tribe population is found in the North Eastern states of Mizoram (94.46 %), Nagaland (89.15 %), Meghalaya (85.94 %) and Arunachal Pradesh (64.22%) and in the Union Territories of Lakshadweep (94.51%), and Dadra and Nagar Haveli (62.24%), there are heavy concentrations in the states of Manipur (34.20%), Chhattisgarh (31.76%), Tripura (31.05%), Jharkhand (26.30%), Orissa (22.13%), Sikkim (20.60 %), and Madhya Pradesh (20.27%). The lowest concentration of Scheduled Tribe population is found in the States/UTs of Uttar Pradesh (0.06%), Bihar (0.91%), Tamil Nadu (1.04%), Kerala (1.14%) and Andaman and Nicobar Islands (1.27%) (Table-3).

Table 3
Total Population and Percentage of Scheduled Tribe Population: 2001 Census

S. No.	India/State/Union Territory	Total Population ('000)	Scheduled Tribe Population ('000)	Percentage of ST Population to Total Population
1	2	3	4	5
	INDIA	1,028,610	84,326	8.20
1.	Jammu and Kashmir	10,144	1,106	10.90
2.	Himachal Pradesh	6,078	245	4.02
3.	Punjab	24,359	0	0.00
4.	Chandigarh	901	0	0.00
5.	Uttaranchal	8,489	256	3.02
6.	Haryana	21,145	0	0.00
7.	Delhi	13,851	0	0.00
8.	Rajasthan	56,507	7,098	12.56
9.	Uttar Pradesh	166,198	108	0.06
10.	Bihar	82,999	758	0.91
11.	Sikkim	541	111	20.60
12.	Arunachal Pradesh	1,098	705	64.22
13.	Nagaland	1,990	1,774	89.15
14.	Manipur	2,167	741	34.20
15.	Mizoram	889	839	94.46
16.	Tripura	3,199	993	31.05
17.	Meghalaya	2,319	1,993	85.94
18.	Assam	26,656	3,309	12.41
19.	West Bengal	80,176	4,407	5.50
20.	Jharkhand	26,946	7,087	26.30
21.	Orissa	26,805	8,145	22.13
22.	Chhattisgarh	20,834	6,617	31.76
23.	Madhya Pradesh	60,348	12,233	20.27
24.	Gujarat	50,671	7,481	14.76

Contd....

S. No.	India/State/Union Territory	Total Population ('000)	Scheduled Tribe Population ('000)	Percentage of ST Population to Total Population
1	2	3	4	5
25.	Daman and Diu	158	14	8.85
26.	Dadra & Nagar Haveli	220	137	62.24
27.	Maharashtra	96,879	8,577	8.85
28.	Andhra Pradesh	76,210	5,024	6.59
29.	Karnataka	52,851	3,464	6.55
30.	Goa	1,348	1	0.04
31.	Lakshadweep	61	57	94.51
32.	Kerala	31,841	364	1.14
33.	Tamil Nadu	62,406	651	1.04
34.	Pondicherry	974	0	0.00
35.	Andaman and Nicobar Islands	356	29	1.27

Note: 1. India and Manipur figures exclude those of the three sub-divisions, viz, Mao Maram, Paomata and Purul of Senapati district of Manipur as population census 2001 in these three sub-divisions were cancelled due to technical and administrative reasons although a population census was carried out in these sub-division also as per schedule.

Source: Census of India, 2001.

Literacy Profile of Scheduled Tribes in India

Literacy and level of education are two basic indicators of the level of development achieved by a group or a society. The literacy results in a more awareness besides contributing to the overall improvement of health, hygiene and other social conditions. As per the figures based on the 2001 Census, in the field of literacy, the disparities between males and females are still large. Table - 4 shows the gap between the literacy rates of the overall population and ST population, overall males and ST males and overall females and ST females. It shows how the difference has been persisting since 1961. In 1961 total ST literacy rate was 8.53 per cent as against 23.30 per cent among overall population. The difference in 1961 was 14.77 per cent. In the same year the literacy rate of ST males was 13.83 per cent as against 4.40 per cent among overall males and the difference between ST males and overall males was 26.57 per cent. In the case of female literacy rate it was only 3.16 per cent for ST females as against 15.35 per cent among overall females and the difference was 12.19 per cent.

As per 2001 Census, the literacy rate of total STs increased to 47.10 per cent as against 65.38 per cent among overall population. The difference between the literacy rate of total STs and overall population was 18.28 per cent. The literacy rate of ST males increased to 59.17 per cent as against 75.85 per cent among overall males and the difference was 16.68 per cent. In the case of female literacy rate it was 34.76 per cent of ST females as against 54.16 per cent of overall females and the difference was 19.40 per cent. Understandably, female literacy rates at all points of time are lower than those for males. This is true irrespective of whether one considers STs or overall persons. Also, the disparity in literacy rate between overall population and ST population is higher among females than among males.

Table 4
Gender-wise Literacy Rates of Overall Population and ST Population in India

Year	*Overall Literacy*	*Total ST Literacy*	*Difference*	*Overall Male Literacy*	*ST Male Literacy*	*Difference*	*Overall Female Literacy*	*ST Female Literacy*	*Difference*
1961	23.30	8.53	14.77	40.40	13.83	26.57	15.35	3.16	12.19
1971	34.45	11.30	23.15	45.96	17.63	28.33	21.97	4.85	17.12
1981	43.57	16.35	27.22	56.38	24.52	31.86	29.76	8.04	21.72
1991	52.21	29.60	22.61	64.13	40.65	23.48	39.29	18.19	21.10
2001	65.38	47.10	18.28	75.85	59.17	16.68	54.16	34.76	19.40

Source: Census of India, Relevant Issues.

The literacy rate of STs and overall population by major states of India has shown in Table - 5. It is found that as per the 2001 Census, more than half of the tribal population in the Country is illiterate. The position in this regard is further worsened in the states of Bihar, Andhra Pradesh, Orissa and Madhya Pradesh, which account for more than 30 per cent of total ST population in the Country. In all points of time, the literacy rates of overall population are much higher than that of the STs. The growth in literacy of the STs is very slow compared to overall population from 1961-1991. But the growth in literacy of STs is higher than the overall population from 1991 to 2001.

Table 5
Literacy Rates of Overall and STs by Major States in India

(Per cent)

	Overall					Scheduled Tribe				
State	*1961*	*1971*	*1981*	*1991*	*2001*	*1961*	*1971*	*1981*	*1991*	*2001*
1	2	3	4	5	6	7	8	9	10	11
Andhra Pradesh	21.19	24.57	29.94	44.09	61.11	4.41	5.34	7.82	17.16	37.04
Bihar	18.40	19.94	26.20	38.48	47.53	9.16	11.64	16.99	26.78	28.17
Gujarat	30.45	35.79	43.70	61.29	69.97	11.69	14.12	21.14	36.45	47.74
Karnataka	25.03	31.52	38.46	56.04	67.04	8.15	14.85	20.14	36.01	48.27
Madhya Pradesh	17.13	22.14	27.87	44.20	64.11	5.10	7.62	10.68	21.54	41.16
Maharashtra	29.82	39.18	47.18	64.87	77.27	7.12	11.74	22.29	36.79	55.21
Orissa	21.66	26.18	34.23	49.09	63.61	7.36	9.46	13.96	22.31	37.37
Rajasthan	15.21	19.07	24.38	38.55	61.03	3.97	6.47	10.27	19.44	44.66
West Bengal	29.28	33.20	40.94	57.70	69.22	6.55	8.92	13.21	27.28	43.40
India	2330	34.45	43.57	52.21	65.38	8.53	11.30	16.35	29.60	47.10

Source: Census of India, Relevant Issues.

Number of Recognized Schools and Enrollment of ST Students by Sex in Primary and Upper Primary Education in India:

The educational problems of STs are more serious than that of any other section of the society because of their special geographical and environmental constraints. The enrollment status of ST children in primary and upper primary stages is presented in Table-6.

The enrollment of ST children at primary and upper primary stages corresponds to the proportion of their number in the overall population. Table - 6 shows that during 1990s, the enrollment of ST children including girls at the primary stage has been about 7-9 per cent, which approximates the percentage of their population (8.20 %) in the overall population of India in 2001. But, at upper primary level their enrollment has not been satisfactory. It may be seen that the enrollment of ST children at the upper primary stage varies between 5 and 6 per cent. This data indicate that the progress of education of ST children at upper primary stage is not satisfactory, and sustained efforts have to be made to raise their educational status during the years to come. The government should provide attractive financial incentives to enhance the enrollment of ST children, especially, at upper primary stage in view of their specific problems emerging out of their geographical and environmental location. The total number of primary schools in India increased from 4.94 lakhs in 1980-81 to 6.39 lakhs in 2000-01, in the case of upper primary schools it has increased from 1.18 lakhs in 1980-81 to 2.06 lakhs in 2000-01.

Government should set up more schools in the vicinity of ST habitations. Attempts may be made to utilize the services of voluntary agencies by way of helping them in opening non-formal education centres and pre-primary schools.

Table 6

No. of Recognized Schools and Enrollment of ST Children by Sex in Primary And Upper Primary Education in India

(Figures in '000)

	Primary (Classes I-V)			*Upper Primary (Classes VI-VIII)*		
Year	*No. of Schools*	*Total Enrollment*	*Girls Enrollment*	*No. of Schools*	*Total Enrollment*	*Girls Enrollment*
1978-79	NA	3398 (7.0)	1124 (4.3)	NA	1279 (4.8)	401 (6.8)
1980-81	4.94	4660 (6.3)	1527 (5.4)	1.18	742 (3.6)	205 (3.0)
1985-86	5.29	6580 (7.5)	2406 (6.8)	1.35	1283 (4.7)	390 (4.1)
1990-91	5.61	7869 (8.1)	2911 (7.2)	1.51	1707 (5.0)	576 (4.6)
1995-96	5.9	8794 (8.0)	3608 (7.6)	1.71	2545 (6.2)	938 (5.9)
2000-01	6.39	10995 (9.4)	4665 (9.4)	2.06	3084 (7.2)	1205 (6.9)

* The figures within the parentheses indicate the ST enrollment as per cent of the total enrollment at the corresponding stages.

Sources: (i) Govt. of India, Education of Scheduled Castes and Scheduled Tribes 1988-89, MHRD, Department of Education, New Delhi, 1993. (ii) Govt. of India, Selected Educational Statistics 2002-03, Department of Education, MHRD, New Delhi.

Gross Enrollment Ratios of STs in Primary and Upper Primary Education by Major States in India

The gross enrollment ratio for ST girls and boys for grades I to V and for grades VI to VIII are shown in Table-7. It is note that at grades I to V, the gross enrollment ratio of ST girls and boys in Andhra Pradesh is higher than the gross enrollment ratios of ST girls and boys in Kerala and Tamil Nadu. But at the upper primary stage the gross enrollment ratio of ST girls in Andhra Pradesh declined sharply to 38.5 per cent and is substantially lower than the gross enrollment ratios of ST girls of Kerala (80.8%) and the gross enrollment ratio of ST girls of Tamil Nadu (99.2%). It is interesting to note that both in primary and upper primary stages the gross enrollment ratios of ST boys and girls in Uttar Pradesh is higher than the other states in India. Where as the state of Bihar recorded the lowest gross enrollment ratios for both boys and girls than the other states in the country.

Table 7
Gross Enrollment Ratio of Scheduled Tribe Students by Sex in Primary and Upper Primary Stages by Major States in India: 2002-03

State	*Primary Classes I-V (6-11 Years)*		*Upper Primary Classes VI-VIII (11-14 Years)*	
	Boys	*Girls*	*Boys*	*Girls*
		NORTH EAST		
Meghalaya	90.2	93.0	41.6	51.3
Mizoram	119.3	122.7	78.3	78.0
Nagaland	72.9	70.9	38.0	38.3
EAST				
Bihar	59.6	32.5	18.6	8.5
Orissa	103.4	87.3	38.4	26.6
West Bengal	108.1	94.6	60.5	29.8
		CENTRAL		
Madhya Pradesh	91.9	71.8	41.6	24.6
		WEST		
Gujarat	111.6	107.9	67.8	58.2
Maharashtra	116.6	106.4	72.9	63.8
Rajasthan	118.7	106.4	64.8	31.8

Contd....

State	*Primary Classes I-V (6-11 Years)*		*Upper Primary Classes VI-VIII (11-14 Years)*	
	Boys	*Girls*	*Boys*	*Girls*
		NORTH		
Uttar Pradesh	130.4	124.6	108.6	99.3
Himachal Pradesh	126.5	122.1	100.6	75.9
		SOUTH		
Andhra Pradesh	118.1	113.6	54.3	38.5
Kerala	112.9	107.7	84.6	80.8
Tamil Nadu	105.7	113.2	85.6	99.2
INDIA	104.8	92.3	55.0	40.8

Source: Selected Educational Statistics, G.O.I. Ministry of Human Resource Development, 2002-03.

Drop-Out Rates of ST Students in Primary and Upper Primary Education by Major States in India

Drop-out rate is another important factor which hinders the progress of literacy among the Scheduled Tribes. The drop-out rates of STs by major states has shown in Table-8. It indicate that the drop-out rate of ST girls in Andhra Pradesh of 68.7 per cent at the primary level of education is much higher than the drop-out rate of girls in other states in India. The drop-out rate of ST boys in Bihar of 66.6 per cent at the primary stage is much higher than the drop-out rate of boys in other sates in the country. At upper primary stage of education, the drop-out rate of both girls and boys is increasing. The drop-out rate of 84.3 pr cent for ST girls in Andhra Pradesh is next only to that of Bihar of 85.6 per cent. It is also higher than the national average drop-out rate of girls at 71.2 per cent. The highest drop-out rate of ST boys was 82.4 per cent at upper primary sage in Bihar. It is evident that apart from gender disparities in the gross enrollment ratios and drop-out rates, the gross enrollment ratios is declining and the drop-out rates are increasing for the Tribal students at upper primary level of education, particularly in the Scheduled Tribe girls in Andhra Pradesh. This may be due to the relatively higher poverty levels and lower human development levels in Andhra Pradesh compared to other Southern Sates of Kerala and Tamil Nadu. Most of the Ashram schools are not being maintained properly and are suffering from lack of basic facilities. The location of the schools is not convenient for the students as well as the teachers leading to absenteeism on both sides. The quality of teaching, the attitude of the teachers towards the cultural background of the Tribal students, the number of teachers and the allocation of resources for tribal literacy improvement - all these variables need much to be rectified.

Table 8
State Wise Drop-Out Rates of Scheduled Tribe Students by Sex in Primary and Upper Primary Sages by Major States in India: 2002-03

State	*Primary Classes I-V*		*Upper Primary Classes I-VIII*	
	Boys	*Girls*	*Boys*	*Girls*
		NORTH EAST		
Meghalaya	61.4	59.3	81.1	80.3
Mizoram	55.9	54.9	59.9	56.3
Nagaland	37.4	37.0	42.8	44.2
		EAST		
Bihar	66.6	65.4	82.4	85.6
Orissa	58.0	53.5	77.5	79.1
West Bengal	53.7	59.3	60.7	42.4
		CENTRAL		
Madhya Pradesh	51.9	50.5	65.6	70.2
		WEST		
Gujarat	36.1	43.1	58.3	67.0
Maharashtra	28.8	40.2	61.0	66.4
Rajasthan	50.6	59.9	52.6	73.2
		NORTH		
Uttar Pradesh	31.2	30.0	37.0	36.5
Himachal Pradesh	16.2	21.7	26.8	37.4
		SOUTH		
Andhra Pradesh	63.3	68.7	78.6	84.3
Kerala	2.2	6.0	33.6	40.0
Tamil Nadu	27.2	21.0	57.0	54.4
INDIA	50.8	52.1	66.9	71.2

Source: Selected Educational Statistics, G.O.I. Ministry of Human Resource Development, 2002-03.

Conclusions and Suggestions

Scheduled Tribes being considered as the lowest in the social hierarchy and they were labeled as untouchables as such they were denied all educational opportunities in the past. They are living mainly in forest and hilly regions. Being mostly illiterate, they are being subjected to all kinds of exploitation -social, economic, political and educational. After independence the Government of India provided some constitutional safe guards to the upliftment of Scheduled Tribes in India-social, economic, political and educational. Yet, we could not achieve the desired result.

So, the Government need to undertake some more special measures to encourage the Scheduled Castes and Scheduled Tribes to send their children, especially girl children to schools compulsorily and regularly. The Government should provide attractive financial incentives to enhance the enrollment of the children of STs even in the school stage. Government should set up more schools in the vicinity of Scheduled Tribe habitations. Attempts may be made to utilize the services of voluntary agencies by way of helping the students in opening non-formal education centres and pre-primary schools in the tribal habitations. It is more appropriate to implement some strategies of schooling in tribal areas like mobile schools, alternate intake schools, non-graded schools, mosque schools, learning post schools etc. Attempts shall be made to involve the parents of the tribal children actively in the educational process of the tribal children such that parents will know in quite advance the end results of education and the need to send their children to the schools regularly and punctually.

References

Ambasht, N.K. (1970), A Critical Study of Tribal Education, S. Chand and Co., New Delhi.

Ahmed Aijazuddin, (1984), Education of Scheduled Tribes: Some aspects of inequality, National Institute of Educational Planning and Administration, New Delhi.

Chalam K.S. (1988), Education and Weaker Sections, Inter India Publication, New Delhi.

Das Gupta, N.K. (1963), Problems of Tribal Education and the Santals, Bharatiya Adimjati Sevak Sangh, New Delhi.

Dube, S.C. (1968), "Approaches to Tribal Problems in India", in Vidyarth, L.P. (ed.) Applied Anthropology in India Kitab Mahal, Allahabad.

Ghanshyam Shah. (1984), Economic Differentiations and Tribal identity, Ajanta Publications, Delhi.

Gopinathan Nair, P.R. (1981), Primary Education, Population Growth and Socio-Economic Change, Allied Publishers, New Delhi.

Government of India (1986), National Policy on Education 1986: Programme of Action, New Delhi.

Mishra, B.C. (1996), Education of Tribal Children, Discovery Publishing House, New Delhi.

Naik, J.P. (1975), Elementary Education in India-a Promise to Keep, Allied Publishers, Bombay.

Patel, M.L. (1984), Planning Strategy for Tribal development, Inter-India Publications, New Delhi.

Rajaiah, B. (1987), Economics of Education, Mittal Publication, New Delhi.

Rath, R. (1976), "Problems of Equalization of Educational Opportunities for the Tribal Children", Indian Educational Review, IX (2) NCERT, New Delhi.

Srivastava, L.R.N. (ed.) (1967), "Tribal Education in India", Report of the National Seminar on Tribal Education in India. NCERT, New Delhi.

Section – III

22

Tribal Development Through ITDA Approach

A Sustainable Approach to Development of Tribal in Agency Area

Prof. B. Appa Rao
Mr. A. Sarath
Mr. Susanta Kumar Barik
Miss. K.B.D. Sobha Rani

Introduction

The tribal and indigenous people of India constitute an important segment of the Indian population. They are duly listed in the Constitution, which also accords them special rights and privileges. Both the Government and the Non-Government Organisations (NGOs) have been engaged in their socio-economic development ever since Independence. But the question is, whether the tribals are benefited from the various development interventions and are empowered in the country's federal structure in terms of governance and political participation.

This paper attempts to examine the life and livelihood of the tribals of Paderu agency area with respect to the multiplicity of programmes/schemes floated to and executed in the agency area over the last five years and contextualize the findings to the overall tribal development and empowerment in India. It first examines the tribal situation in the country and gives a critical appraisal of tribal development both by the government and the NGOs in the first section. It also analyses the process of tribal empowerment, particularly through the 73rd Constitutional Amendment and the consequent legislations for tribal self-rule. Section two broadly judges the plans and procedures of government for formation of ITDA's. Section three critically analyses the achievements of ITDA, Paderu and Section four finally, based on the past and present scenarios it tries to spell out roads ahead for tribal empowerment.

Section I: Global Perception of Empowerment Approaches and Strategies

What is Empowerment?

Empowerment is the process of enhancing the capacity of individuals or groups to make choices and to transform those choices into desired actions and outcomes. Central to this process are actions which both build individual and collective assets, and improve the efficiency and fairness of the organizational and institutional context which govern the use of these assets.

The World Bank's 2002, Empowerment Sourcebook, set out to bring together the thinking and practice of empowerment as a first step in developing a better understanding of this component. It identified empowerment as "the expansion of assets and capabilities of poor people to participate in, negotiate with, influence, control, and hold accountable institutions that affect their lives." Building on this, as the Bank and its partners have continued to develop and apply an empowerment framework to their work, and learn from this experience, both ideas and definitions have evolved. This has brought about a definition rooted in both the long academic discourse on power, and one tested and confirmed through applied experience in a number of countries: "Empowerment is the process of increasing the assets and capabilities of individuals or groups to make purposive choices and to transform those choices into desired actions and outcomes."

Empowered people have freedom of choice and action. This in turn enables them to better influence the course of their lives and the decisions which affect them.

However, perceptions of being empowered vary across time, culture and domains of a person's life: in India, a low caste woman currently feels empowered when she is given a fair hearing in a public meeting, which is comprised of men and women from different social and economic groups; in Brazil, in Porto Allegre, citizens-both men and women-feel empowered if they are able to engage in decisions on budget allocations; in Ethiopia, citizens and civil society groups report feeling empowered by consultations undertaken during the preparation of the poverty reduction support program; in the USA, immigrant workers feel empowered through unionization which has allowed them to negotiate working conditions with employers; and in the UK, a battered woman feels empowered when she is freed from the threat of violence and becomes able to make decisions about her own life.

In essence empowerment speaks to self determined change. It implies bringing together the supply and demand sides of development-changing the environment within which poor people live and helping them build and capitalize on their own attributes. Empowerment is a cross-cutting issue. From education and health care to governance and economic policy, activities which seek to empower poor people are expected to increase development opportunities, enhance development outcomes and improve people's quality of life.

Four Areas of Practice

There are thousands of examples of empowerment strategies that have been initiated by poor people themselves and by governments, civil society, and the private sector. Although there is no single institutional model for empowerment, experience shows that certain elements are almost always present when empowerment efforts are successful. The four key elements of empowerment that must underlie institutional reform are:

(a) Access to information.
(b) Inclusion and participation.
(c) Accountability.
(d) Local organizational capacity.

While these four elements are discussed separately, they are closely intertwined and act in synergy. Thus although access to timely information about programs, or about government performance or corruption, is a necessary precondition for action, poor people or citizens more broadly may not take action because there are no institutional mechanisms that demand accountable performance or because the costs of individual action may be too high. Similarly, experience shows that poor people do not participate in activities when they know their participation will make no difference to products being offered or decisions made because there are no mechanisms for holding providers accountable. Even where there are strong local organizations, they may still be disconnected from local governments and the private sector, and lack access to information.

Application of Empowerment

Areas of Practice

Empowering approaches can be applied across a broad range of work. To provide some practical illustrations, the study focuses on applications in five areas:

Provision of Basic Services

Provision of basic services refers to improving poor people's access to and effective use of basic services including health care, education, water, and roads. The government efforts to get resources down to the community level through a variety of institutional models so that the implementation can be carried out by private or public actors, by central agencies, Sectoral agencies, or decentralized authorities of local government, through stand-alone sector projects, or through multisectoral community-driven development projects.

Sector policies and projects necessarily vary in the extent to which they adopt all four elements of empowerment. Although it is difficult to completely disentangle the four empowerment elements, three different strategies for providing effective services to poor people can be highlighted, based on the nature of the good service to be provided and the institutional strategies possible in particular contexts.

The first focuses on improving access to information, primarily by putting information about government performance in the public domain. The second makes use mainly of mechanisms for inclusion/participation. It includes private sector strategies that depend on designing access to basic services that poor people can afford, as well demand-side financing strategies, particularly in education and health. The third focuses on local organizational capacity and includes all four elements of empowerment, which act in synergy.

Examples include a variety of multi-sectoral community-driven development projects, as well as single-sector projects such as those in rural water supply and sanitation of UNICEF, World Bank, NABARD etc.

Improved Local Governance

Improved local governance is critical to better service delivery and greater responsiveness to poor people's priority problems. To improve local governance, local governments with authority and resources need to empower local communities through mechanisms that increase citizen access to information, enable inclusion and participation, increase accountability of governments to citizens, and invest in local organizational capacity. Decentralization and local government reform have so far focused primarily on the supply side of formal systems and not on strengthening the demand side through actions that enable citizens to effectively utilize the space created by new rules and regulations. Experiences in India demonstrate that when space is created by new rules, there is a lack of investment in information dissemination and local organizational capacity of civil society and poor people's organizations. Poor people cannot participate effectively in local governance. There has been insufficient attention to the relationship between citizens and local governments.

Focus on the demand side of improved local governance is just beginning. Although still few, there are some important examples of efforts to increase access to information, design mechanisms for inclusion and participation, and build in mechanisms of accountability to citizens. On the other hand, in the context of local government reform, there do not appear to be any strong cases of investment in strengthening poor people's organizations or other local civil society intermediaries so that they can effectively play the new roles assigned to them.

Improved National Governance

Macroeconomic policy and choices are areas that are just beginning to open to societal engagement. While the ultimate decisions, like all development decisions, involve technical expertise, discussion with those who are affected offers multiple advantages. It helps clarify the causal links and assumptions underlying policy tradeoffs and choices; it leads to discussions about the institutional capacity needed to implement reforms, and alliances that will have to be built with different parts of society; it builds social consensus on the importance of the reform; it gives the reformers room to maneuver against narrower political interests; it educates all involved in the process; and it helps identify and develop needed compensatory mechanisms for the poorest and most adversely affected citizens.

Some progress has been made in demonstrating the value of information tools in the public domain as well as consultative processes. Progress on linking information collected to mechanisms of accountability to poor people and citizens' groups is just beginning. Sector reform loans and credits, as well as budget support loans and credits, assume that local capacity exists at all levels of civil society to collect and analyze information and engage effectively with governments to keep them accountable. None of the budget support loans/credits are directly supported by capacity-building operations.

Public sector reform processes that focus on rationalizing and tracking public expenditures as well as modernizing financial management systems are critical first steps toward internal and public accountability. Public participation and public access to key information in forms that can be understood can further increase government accountability for improved performance.

Participatory processes in the development of national poverty reduction strategies, particularly in connection with the preparation of Poverty Reduction Strategy in low-income countries, have become a central part of efforts to reach societal consensus on priorities for government expenditure as well as for policy reform. These processes can lay the foundation for public accountability to citizens. Since national processes and policies determine poor people's access to resources and opportunities, it is critical that these processes incorporate the four empowerment elements.

Pro-Poor Market Development

Economic empowerment is critical for poor people's wellbeing. Freedom from hunger, adequate income, and security of material assets are central issues in poor people's lives. Even in natural disasters such as floods and earthquakes, poor people often refuse at peril of their lives to leave their meager assets, knowing that lost assets mean a slow but just as certain death.

Poverty and vulnerability will not be reduced without broad-based growth fueled by private sector activity. Economic growth cannot be sustained if poor women and men, who may be 50 percent or more of a country's population, are excluded from optimal engagement in productive activities. Involvement of such large numbers of poor people in more productive livelihoods can only happen when a country's overall domestic investment climate fosters entrepreneurship, job creation, competition, and security of property or benefit rights. This is not enough, however. While the overall business climate for investment is important, micro and small enterprises face constraints and exclusion that are not automatically corrected by improvements in the macro investment climate. Hence the need for "liberalization from below". Poor people are often excluded from equal access to economic opportunity because of regulations, because they lack information, connections, skills, credit, and organization, and because of discrimination. Empowerment strategies can help overcome many of these barriers that prevent poor people's entry into new markets and limit their productivity despite their unremitting hard labor.

Understanding the business investment climate for farmers, micro-entrepreneurs and small and medium businesses-as well as for large firms-is critical to inform policy change that supports economic development and increases productivity, security, and empowerment. Governments can accelerate the development of markets for financial and non-financial services appropriate for poor women and men by promoting innovation in products and delivery mechanisms, and by building institutional capacity.

A market-oriented approach to these services is critical to avoid unsustainable and ineffective public programs. A key component is carefully structured and time-bound subsidies within an overall approach incorporating market features, product innovation, and wide dissemination of institutional innovations.

This section highlights the application of the four empowerment elements to support poor women's and men's entrepreneurship through (a) business development services for micro, small, and medium enterprises, (b) financial services, and (c) microinsurance and housing loans. Local and international NGOs and international agencies have played important roles in supporting innovations by subsidizing research and development, experimentation, and investment in organizational development. However, in almost all cases, achieving financial viability was central in the experimentation.

Access to Justice and Legal Aid

A new generation of judicial and legal reform projects is creating the legal environment for accountable governance and empowering poor people by increasing their access to justice through a mix of strategies. The goal of legal and judicial reform is to build legal systems based on the rule of law, with laws that are publicly known and are enforced in a predictable way and through transparent mechanisms. The rules must apply equally to all citizens, and the State must also be subject to the rules. The quality of legal norms in a society and the manner in which they are administered have direct impacts on the extent to which citizens have a voice in the decision-making process. How state institutions comply with the law greatly affect the daily lives of citizens, particularly poor people who are least able to protect themselves from abuse of their rights. The extent to which a society is law-bound affects its national income as well as its levels of literacy and infant mortality.

Clearly defined property and benefit rights, and confidence that these rights can be fairly and efficiently defended against encroachment, if needed, are critical to induce hundreds of thousands of individuals and groups to make investment decisions that contribute to economic growth and poverty reduction.

SECTION-II: FORMATION OF ITDA AND ITS FUNCTIONALITY

The term 'Scheduled Tribes' first appeared in the Constitution of India. Article 366 (25) defined scheduled tribes as "such tribes or tribal communities or parts of groups within such tribes or tribal communities as are deemed under Article 342 to be Scheduled Tribes for the purposes of this Constitution". Article 342, which is reproduced below, prescribes procedure to be followed in the matter of specification of scheduled tribes.

Thus, the first specification of Scheduled Tribes in relation to a particular State/Union Territory is by a notified order of the President, after consultation with the State governments concerned. These orders can be modified subsequently only through an Act of Parliament. The above Article also provides for listing of Scheduled Tribes State/Union Territory wise and not on an all India basis.

The criterion followed for specification of a community, as scheduled tribe are indications of primitive traits, distinctive culture, geographical isolation, shyness of contact with the community at large, and backwardness. This criterion is not spelt out in the Constitution but has become well established. It subsumes the definitions contained in 1931Census, the Reports of First Backward Classes Commission 1955, the Advisory Committee (Kalelkar), on Revision of SC/ST lists (Lokur Committee), 1965 and the Joint Committee of Parliament on the Scheduled Castes and Scheduled Tribes orders (Amendment) Bill, 1967 (Chanda Committee), 1969.

Target-Led Intervention for Tribal Empowerment through ITDA Approach

The Constitution of India incorporates several special provisions for the promotion of educational and economic interest of Scheduled Tribes and their protection from social injustice and all forms of exploitation. These objectives are sought to be achieved through a strategy, known as, the Tribal Sub-Plan strategy, which was adopted at the beginning of the Fifth Five-Year Plan. The strategy seeks to ensure adequate flow of funds for tribal development from the State Plan allocations, schemes/programmes of Central Ministries/ Departments, financial and Developmental Institutions. The cornerstone of this strategy has been to ensure earmarking of funds for TSP by States/UTs in proportion to the ST population in those State/Uts. Besides the efforts of the States/ UTs and the Central Ministries/Departments to formulate and implement Tribal Sub-Plan for achieving socio-economic development of STs, the Ministry of Tribal Affairs is implementing several schemes and programmes for the benefits of STs.

There are now 194 Integrated Tribal Development Projects (ITDPs) in the country, where the ST population is more than 50 % of the total population of the blocks or groups of block. During the Sixth Plan, pockets outside ITDP areas, having a total population of 10,000 with at least 5,000 scheduled tribes were covered under the Tribal Sub-Plan under Modified Area Development Approach (MADA). So far, 252 MADA pockets have been identified in the country. In addition, 79 clusters with a total population of 5,000 of which 50 per cent are scheduled tribes have been identified.

In order to give more focused attention to the development of Scheduled Tribes, a separate Ministry, known as the Ministry of Tribal Affairs was constituted in October 1999. The new Ministry carved out of the Ministry of Social Justice and Empowerment, is the nodal Ministry for overall policy, planning and coordination of programmes and schemes for the development of Scheduled Tribes.

The Government of Andhra Pradesh has made continuous efforts for tribal development. The Tribal Sub-Plan strategy has brought all government officers and staff working in the sub-plan area under the administrative control of a single agency, the Integrated Tribal Development Agency (ITDA), facilitating better coordination. However, empowerment of tribal communities remains a challenge.

Integrated Tribal Development Agency, Paderu was established in Visakhapatnam District in the year 1975. This ITDA caters to about 5.66 lakhs of Scheduled Tribes spread over in 6,293 Sq.Kms. of area of the District. The ITDA was established to bring about overall development of the tribals in the area. The main Tribes present in the area are Bhagatha, Valmmiki, Kondadora, Kotia, Benthoriya, Yendia, Yerukalas, Nool, Kamara, Khonds, Gadaba and Poorja.

ITDA Roles, Responsibilities and Functional Modalities

The ITDA has the overall responsibility of bringing about the development of the tribals of the area by utilizing its own funds, funds from the external agencies, funds available with various other departments of the Government working in the Sub-Plan Area. The Government of Andhra Pradesh vide G.O.Ms.No.434 has sought to establish a Single Line Administration in the Tribal Sub Plan Areas by empowering one agency, i.e., ITDA to control and co-ordinate the functions of the various departments functioning here. The Project Officer, ITDA, is designated as Joint Collector, Addl.District Magistrate and Additional Agent to Government and has been given powers of these officers in the Government Order mentioned. The Project Officer is given powers to plan, implement, review and co-ordinate the activities of all Departments working in the area. ITDA by itself has a lot of wings directly under its control. These wings are meant for both the Hardware and Software development of the Tribals. The Tribals are basically dependent on the forest and live by collecting forest produce or doing shifting cultivation. With the intervention of the ITDA, settled agriculture has become the order of the day, with more and more tribals coming down for settled agriculture using new varieties of seeds and agriculture implements and methods of cultivation.

The agriculture wing of the ITDA, plans, implements and monitors the development of agriculture in the land owned by the tribals and its activities include distribution of new variety of seeds, agriculture implements, transfer of modern Agricultural packages, and enlightening the people on new crops and cropping patterns. The Horticulture Wing looks after the development of Horticulture and encourages the Tribals to bring their wasteland, degraded land etc. under horticulture crops like Cashew, Mango, etc. The tribals are encouraged to take-up improved varieties and are taught grafting and modern methods of horticulture to improve the productivity and to bring more and more land under productive cultivation.

The Minor Irrigation Wing of the ITDA is responsible for taking up construction of minor irrigation tanks, check-dams, community irrigation wells. Electric Motors, Oil Engines are supplied to the tribal beneficiaries for irrigating their land using water from small rivulets and wells. The ITDA bears the cost for extending electricity supply to the remotest habitation for meeting the consumption requirement as well as using economic purposes.

The Tribal Welfare Engineering Department is responsible for the construction of the buildings - for Schools, Hostels, Offices, etc., construction of Roads, Bridges for connecting interior villages. They also take up the construction of the Lift Irrigation schemes, Check Dams and Irrigation Bore Wells.

The Animal Husbandry section of the ITDA ensures the supply of strong Plough Bullocks for ploughing the lands, Milch Animals like Cows and Buffaloes for milk purposes for consumption as well as sale and distribution of new and improved varieties of poultry, sheep units etc.

The Sericulture wing helps tribals to take up raising mulberry crops and rearing of cocoons. The Girijan Co-operative Corporation, for which the Project Officer is one of the Executive Directors, is responsible for the supply of daily requirements to the tribals in the interior areas at nominal rates, for the purchase of various non-timber minor forest products which are collected by the tribals, for distribution of loans short term and long term credit loans-to the tribal farmers for raising of the crops and for supply of motors etc., The GCC has a monopoly of the purchase of the minor produce from the forest. The shandy inspectors of the GCC are present in local markets to ensure that the poor tribals are not cheated. They ensure the correct price and weighment of the produce collected. The GCC also distributes daily requirements like rice, dal and other essential commodities at the interior village points and they are running fair price shops to help in the public distribution system of the Government.

ITDA is primarily responsible for the development of the health and education of the tribals. ITDA tries to improve the literacy of the tribals by having a set of schools in various interior pockets of the district.

ITDA is the umbrella for the entire agency and hence mandated for provisioning sustainable and integrated development. The intent and performance of the agency area, being the unit of administration, is reviewed for the period of ten years, i.e., 1997-2006 in the following sections.

Section - III: Contextualizing Empowerment Strategies and Approaches to ITDA Plans and Sectoral Achievements - An Overview of Paderu Agency Area

A packaged intervention for a geographically contiguous area is well crafted to suit the need and requirement of the tribals to lead a life with honour, dignity and self-esteem. This section critically examines the functional capability and efficiency of all government schemes executed in the Paderu Agency area with the above-mentioned parameters of empowerment.

Impact on Increased Income of Tribal Families

All the agencies working with the tribals for the development of tribals are guided by the comprehensive guidelines for implementation of economic support schemes vide G.O.M.S. No. 76 for development of Scheduled Tribes in this State. All these interventions are intended to retain a sustainable livelihood basked for the inhabitants. Sustainable livelihood for sustainable development is guided by the following agents:

Economics: "Maintain an acceptable rate of growth in per capita real incomes without depleting the national capital assets stock or the natural environment asset stock (Turner, 1988:20).

Ecology: Improving the quality of human life, while living within the capacity of supporting ecosystem (IUCN/WWF/UNEP (1991:10).

Sociology: Meet the targets of human needs with satisfaction without violating long-term natural resources capacities and standards of environmental quality and social equity (Bartelmus 1994:73).

Composite Development: Meets the needs of the present without compromising the ability of future generations to meet their own needs (Brundtland, 1987:43).

All the Economic Support Schemes for the tribal are guided by the following objectives:

1. To build strong grassroot level institutions of the poor, where the tribal community will actively participate in planning, implementation and monitoring of the programmes and develop greater access to and control over resources to sustain their livelihoods and achieve self-reliance.
2. To provide linkage and convergence of all the resources available under tribal development strategy and all other anti-poverty programmes of the Government for the Tribal Development with a view to reaching out to maximum number of Scheduled Tribes.
3. To provide sustainable livelihood opportunities to the Scheduled Tribes, who are below the poverty line, particularly the poorest of the poor among them, for enhancing their incomes and improving their quality of life.

Strategy Followed in Grounding the ESS (As Circulated by Govt. of India)

1. For development of Scheduled Tribes, Tribal Sub Plan (TSP) Strategy has been followed, since 1975 (V Five Year Plan onwards). For this purpose, the areas of ST concentration have been brought under the purview of following projects:
   (a) Integrated Tribal Development Agency (ITDA): These are generally contiguous large areas of the size of one or more Development Block in which the ST population is 50% or more of the total population.
   (b) Clusters: These are identified pockets of tribal concentration, containing 50 % or more ST population within a total population of about 5,000 or more.
   (c) Primitive Tribal Groups (PTGs): Identified isolated communities among the STs characterized by a

low rate of population, a backward or pre-agricultural level of technology and low levels of literacy.

(d) Dispersed Tribal Groups (DTG): The tribal population other than population of the above said groups is identified as Dispersed Tribal Groups.

2. The Government of India has issued revised guidelines where it has directed that long-term area-specific micro planning, by taking into consideration ITDAs and the Clusters therein as geographical units, should be taken up under SCA to TSP. Multidisciplinary agencies could be entrusted with the task of preparing such long term plans indicating estimates of the flow of funds from the State Plan (TSP), the Central Plan (SCA to TSP) and through the Grant-in-aid under Article 275(1) of the Constitution.
3. Various project staff implementing the schemes developed a strong conviction that the Tribals have tremendous potential and willingness to help themselves and participate as active partners in their development rather than mere recipients of benefits. This approach would empower the tribal community to identify the livelihood opportunities themselves based on their experience, skills and local resources and effectively use them to enhance their incomes.
4. The developmental interventions supported under the projects is integrated and dovetailed with other ongoing programmes of the Government and its agencies to accelerate the pace of development and enable the scheduled tribes to maximize their benefits and alleviate the poverty.

Sectoral Performance Review towards Tribal Empowerment

Agriculture

In Visakhapatnam District, 87.38 % reported for getting income from agriculture, 82.57 % from agricultural labour,

66.45 % from food for work programme, 32.43 % from collection and sale of NTFP. Agriculture and forest produce put together constitute the major source of income to the people.

Total cultivable land in the agency area is 1,00,005 hac which is being used for cultivation of rain-fed crops as well as commercial crops. Rain-fed crops grown by the tribal includes Ragi, Maize, Sama, redgram, Rajma, Dry Paddy and Vegetables. Commercial crops are cultivated during khariff and Rabi season as well. The common commercial crops in the khariff season are Ground nut, Sugarcane, Marry gold, Maize, and Red gram with Rajma, Niger, Tubers crops in Rabi season.

The hilly terrain with a cool climate and annual average rainfall of 1200 mm primarily encourage the tribal to go for shifting cultivation. Shifting cultivation (Podu/Dandar Cultivation) is the age old practice and people are tuned to the traditional mode of agriculture. With an effort to maximize the agricultural productivity, ITDA has taken the initiatives of promotion of different methods of cultivation and introduction of modern technology of agricultural production.

In order to giving for the agriculture production subsidized seed and techniques are distributed to the farmers.

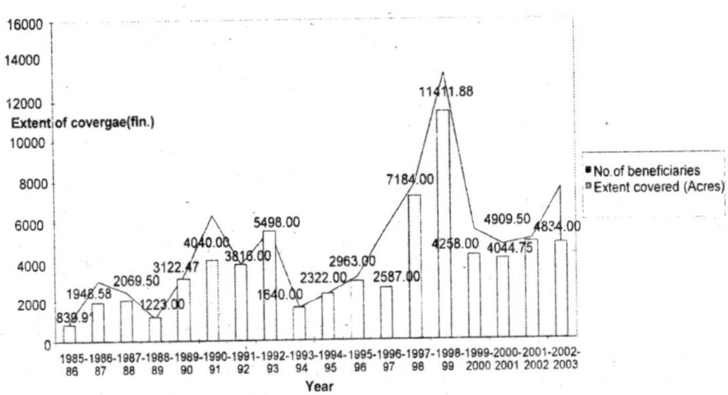

Figure 1. Coverage of Agricultural Seed Subsidy Since 1985-2003

Attempting to give boost to the traditional agriculture with modern techniques of production, ITDA has invested huge chunk of budget towards increasing capacity of the farmers through time to time training and demonstration programmes at agriculture research stations based in the agency and outside.

Nearly 45 % of the tribals draw livelihood from agriculture alone. The per acre paddy production in the agency area varies between 6-9 quintals against the State average of 25 quintals. However, due to introduction of System of Rice Intensification (SRI) in the paddy cultivation, and especially in the plain belts of Chintapalli, G.K.Veedhi, G.Madugula, the per acre paddy productivity is almost doubled. Farmers experienced less cost and high per acre yield in paddy cultivation. Subsidized seed and techniques of production have encouraged farmers to go for use of improved variety of seeds in cultivation and effective use of tiny patches of agricultural land for mixed cropping and attempted to keep the land under vegetative coverage for most part of the year. This has resulted in providing round the year income as well as meet the nutrient requirements of the tribal.

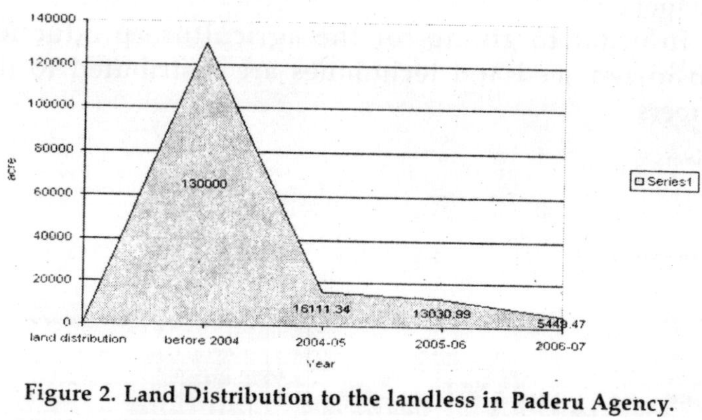

Figure 2. Land Distribution to the landless in Paderu Agency.

The targeted land distribution, the landless habitations falling under Remote and Interior Area Development programme, has benefited almost 1800 families to access and use land.

Community Initiated Grain Banks

Community grain banks have been set up in such areas from where the needy can borrow grain in times of need and repay the grain once the crisis is over. Following the special approach and focus to the villages falling under RIAD, there are 390 grain banks have been taken up for the tribal to arrest the seasonal food requirements and also ensure them healthy and ready to earn for the family.

Focused Intervention for Marginalized and the Vulnerable

Being guided by the Integrated Approach and System, and under the able guidance of the agency administration the agency has sincerely tried for up-liftment of marginal and vulnerable. Tribals in the agency are becoming vulnerable due to poor economic strength which later on coupled with low literacy is addition fuel to double exploitation by the external agents. Women in the agency are the worst sufferers. The economic soundness and low literacy altogether crippling their participation in decision making process at household and village development, perusing economic activities and also participation in development issues. Following the focused approach, the agency over the years emphasized empowering women as the Agents of Social change and development.

Multi-pronged Strategies have been adopted to tackle the issue which broadly aims at:

- To create an enabling environment for women to exercise their rights, both within and outside home, as equal partners along with men through early finalisation and adoption of "National Policy for Empowerment of Women"
- To expedite action to legislate reservation of not less than 1/3 seats for women in the Panchayat and thus ensure adequate representation of women in decision making.
- To adopt an integrated approach towards empowering women through effective convergence

of existing services, resources, infrastructure and manpower in both women specific and women related sectors.

- To adopt a special strategy of "Women's Component Plan" to ensure that not less than 30 per cent of funds/ benefits flow to women from other developmental sectors.
- To organise women into Self Help Group and thus mark the beginning of a major process of empowering women.
- To accord high priority to reproductive child health care.
- To universalise the on-going supplementary feeding programme- Special Nutrition Programme (SNP) and Mid Day Meals(MDM).
- To ensure easy and equal access to education for women and girls through the commitments of the Special Action Plan of 1998.
- To initiate steps to eliminate gender bias in all educational programmes.
- To institute plans for free education for girls up to college level, including professional courses.
- To equip women with necessary skills in the modern upcoming trades which could keep them gainfully engaged besides making them economically independent and self-reliant.

An integrated approach is adopted towards empowering women through convergence of existing services, resources, infrastructure and manpower available in both women-specific and women-related sectors with the ultimate objective of achieving the set goal. To this effect, through Indira Kranti Patham (IKP), a special strategy of `Women's Component Plan' is ensured. It also suggests a special vigil to be kept on the flow of the earmarked funds/benefits through an effective mechanism to ensure that the proposed strategy brings forth a holistic approach towards empowering women.

Education and Training

Education, being the most powerful instrument for empowering women, assumes special priority in the ITDA Annual Plan. Efforts in the ITDA Plan are, therefore, target-oriented in fulfilling the goal of `Education for Women's Equality' as laid down in the National Policy on Education (NPE), 1986 and revised in 1992. Towards this, special attention has already been paid to the identified low female literacy pockets and to the women and the girl children belonging to the socially disadvantaged groups, Minorities, Disabled, etc in each Mandals as they still lag behind the rest of the population with the lowest literacy rates ranging between 8 and 23 per cent, while the national average of female literacy stands at 39.3 per cent in 1991. Special incentive for women education is given through provisioning free education till 12th class. Adult education centers for women in Self Help Groups are promoted in the agency. This has brought a significant change in the day-to-day life of the women resulting in making daily counting of the transaction done, and approaching the bank on their own for transaction. 123480 women in the agency are pulled in to different groups and provided different support to make their own sustainability. 43387 women are engaged in preparation of Micro Credit Plan (MCP) for Income Generation Programmes (IGPs) and to the tune of Rs 693.83 crores have been injected into the economy which is revolving within the tribal women for creation of sustainable livelihood.

Vocationalisation of secondary education and vocational training for vulnerable women and men has accorded high priority and is one of the ultimate goals of empowering vulnerable is to make them economically independent and self-reliant. In this context, the existing network of NAC Construction Training, Sewing Training, Industrial Training at Guntur as well as Rajahmundry and Craft Training Centres (CTCs) is further strengthened with necessary improvements in the infra-structural facilities. Efforts are also made to encourage eligible women/girls with suitable incentives to join vocational education/training so that the facilities available at these exclusive Training Institutions. Introduction of part-time and short-term courses like tailoring and embroidery work is considered to meet the special needs and timings of working women/girls. Efforts are made to encourage women and girls with necessary incentives to opt for the emerging areas of technical education such as electronics, computer systems and applications, bio-engineering, bio-technology, food processing, fabric designing, beauty culture, communications, media etc, which have high employment potential.

Further, to encourage more and more girls to enter into the mainstream of higher education and thus ensure fulfillment of the commitment of `Education for Women's Equality', the ITDA is sponsoring children and thereby provisioning free education for girls upto college levels, including professional courses, so as to better empower women.

Work and Employment

Keeping in view the ultimate objective of fulfilling the 'Right to work for every citizen', special efforts are taken up to generate gainful employment through promotion/expansion of both wage and self employment opportunities for youths and women so as to make all potential women economically independent and self-reliant. In this context, the ongoing training-cum-employment-cum-income-generation programmes, viz., Integrated Rural Development Programme (IRDP), Training of Rural Youth for Self-Employment (TRYSEM), Nehru Rozgar Yojana (NRY), Jawahar Rozgar Yojana (JRY), Prime Minister's Rozgar Yojana (PMRY), Development of Women and Children in Rural Areas (DWCRA), Indira Mahila Yojana (IMY), Support for Training and Employment (STEP), Socio-Economic Programme (SEP) Indira Kranthi Patham (IKP) etc. are is expanded to create more and more of employment-cum-income generation opportunities and cover as many women as possible living below the poverty line. In these efforts, priority has been given to female-headed households and women in extreme/abject poverty.

Following the guidelines issued through G.O.Ms.No.76, 15385 units of economic support units have been taken up to address the income generation of the economically weaker sections of tribal community.

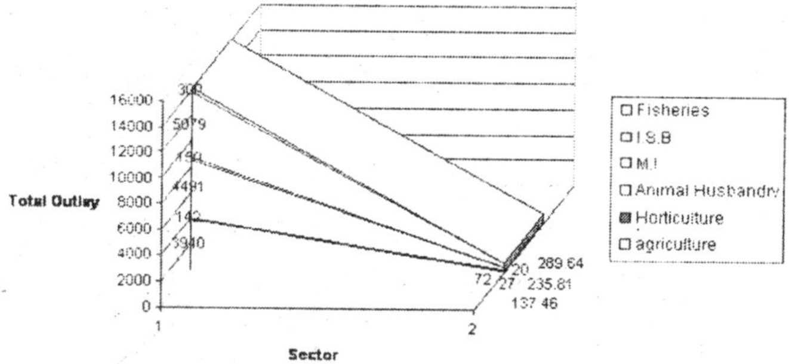

Figure 3. Decadal performance of Econ Suport Schemes in Paderu Agency

As in the past, special focus is on agriculture and its allied sectors. Special programmes have been devised for training women in soil-conservation, social forestry, dairy development and other occupations allied to agriculture like horticulture, livestock including small animal husbandry, poultry, fisheries, etc. across the agency. Initiatives of bio-nursery and vermi compost are taken up massively to address the issue of bio-fertilizers and hence making the farmers economically less dependant on market for purchasing chemical fertilizers.

Simultaneously, the extension services are strengthened to cover a larger number of farmers in agriculture and especially of women, keeping in mind, women's role as producers. Over the years, sensitization programmes have been taken up in coordination with the voluntary sectors to change the attitude, behavior and the mind set of the grass-root level government workers to serve the target clientele with devotion.

Women and Vulnerable Participation in Decision-making and Poverty Alleviation

As the representation of women in the decision-making levels has a direct bearing on all the affirmative actions directed towards their well-being and empowerment, every effort in the agency has an in-built component to ensure that women are in adequate numbers at the decision-making levels. To this effect, women are encouraged with special training facilities which provide them a direct entry into the path of decision-making levels. Women in the agency are no more engaged in the household chores. The horizon of involvement has expanded through strong visualization of the outer world and the maximum level of participation and involvement. 123480 beneficiaries across the agency are taken into several trainings, exposures, and social welfare activities, while special care has been taken for the disabled. Similarly, there is also a need for women to be active in public life and take part in the political decision-making process, as political decisions/ political will in favour of women can influence a lot in creating an enabling environment for women to empower themselves.

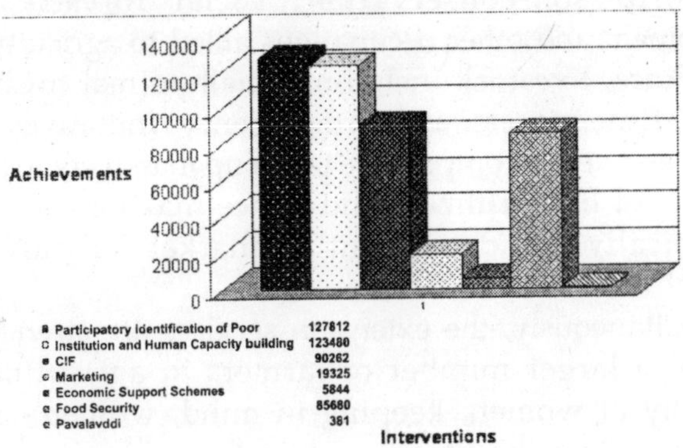

Figure 4. Focused Economic Intervetion for Women Empowerment by IKP During 2001-07

As economic empowerment of women is mainly related to their participation in decision-making with regard to raising and distribution of resources i.e., income, investments and expenditures at all levels, special efforts are made to enhance their capacity to earn besides enlarging their access to and control/ownership of family/community assets. With access to economic assets, women are encouraged to take up self-employment through various entrepreneurial ventures which are more convenient and allow them to play their dual role, within and outside home, effectively.

While organizing women into Self Help Groups marks the beginning of a major process of empowering women, the institutions thus developed would provide a permanent forum for articulating their needs and contributing their perspectives to development. Recognizing the fact that women have been socialized only to take a backseat in public life, affirmative action through deliberate strategies is initiated to provide equal access to and control over factors contributing to such empowerment, particularly in the areas of health, education, information, life-long learning for self development, vocational skills, employment and income generating opportunities, land and other forms of property including obtaining through inheritance of common property resources, credit, technology and markets etc. To this effect, the newly elected women members and the women Chairpersons of Panchayats and the Local Bodies are sensitized through the recently launched special training package to take the lead in ensuring that adequate funds/benefits flow towards the empowerment of vulnerable, disabled women and the girl child.

Remote and Interior Area Development Program (RIAD)

The RIAD wings of the Government of Andhra Pradesh has taken focused initiatives for the seasonally cut-off villages and provisioned to treat the habitation as contiguous area and made available all facilities and services under the capsule development package.

To this effect, 390 villages of Paderu agency spreading over 7 Mandals are identified as RIAD habitations and through package intervention basic amenities have been provisioned. Concentrated attention is bestowed upon to address the health and food security of the inhabitants. As a result, Mobile Medical Services are being placed to take care of the villages through regular interventions.

Table 1
Focused Intervention for RIAD Habitations

S. No.	Activities	01.01.2005 to 31.12.2005		01.01.2006 to 31.12.2006		After 01.01.2007		Total	
		No	Cost	No	Cost	No	Cost	No	Cost
1.	Roads			13	1031.80			13	1031.80
2.	MI - Check Dams	20	50.60	27	68.31	23	128.00	70	246.91
3.	Drinking Water	31	14.98	40	19.33			71	34.31
4.	ESS- Livelihood Enhancement.			5397	134.30			5397	134.30
5.	Food Security			4601	71.04			4601	66.00
6.	Grain Banks					276	34.01	276	34.01
7.	PHC Buildings			7	185.50	3	15.00	10	200.50
8.	Ambulances			6	36.00	5	37.50	11	73.50
9.	Housing	4750	354.83	877	67.17			5627	422.00
10.	Mini Anganwadi centres	144	10.00					144	10.00
11.	Providing DTH Units	20	3.49			9	3.82	29	6.22
12.	Electrification of Villages	214	444.50					214	444.50
13.	College Building, Chinthapalli					1	100.00	1	100.00
14.	Roads, R & B Department					1	233.00	1	233.00
15.	School Buildings	36	68.40	72	151.20			108	219.60
16.	Self Employment					225	31.03	225	31.03
17.	E-Seva					6	3.00	6	3.00
	Total	5215	945.71	11040	1759.61	549	585.36	16804	3290.68

Source: Statistics Department, ITDA, Paderu

Education and Tribal Welfare Schemes

Education being the prime force behind change of the people's life, livelihood, attitude, behavior and brings about a sustained change in the locality, the agency is mandated towards imparting quality education through residential schools. The tribal welfare schools are persistently shown impact in the agency. Though some missionary schools are running simultaneously, schools under the tribal welfare wings are taking care of the overall requirement of the tribal students for education and ultimately extending free education for all. In order to draw the attention of the students, several provisions for scholarships have been made to encourage students to go for higher education.

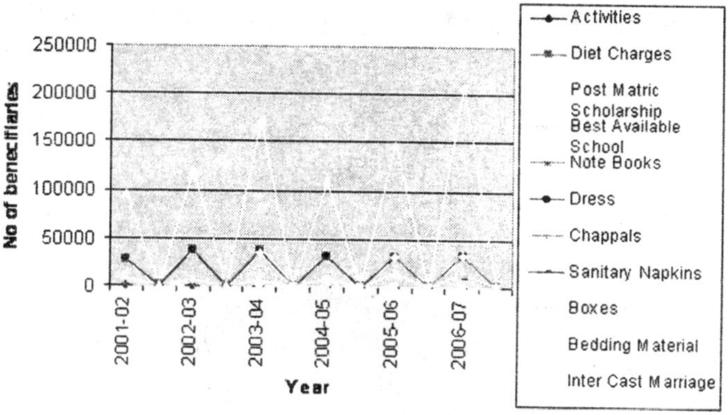

Figure 5. Welfare Activities for Tribal Students

The objective behind provisionary arrangement is to develop the people so that the area development would ultimately take care of, besides students having been linked to various technical agencies with ITDA fund support.

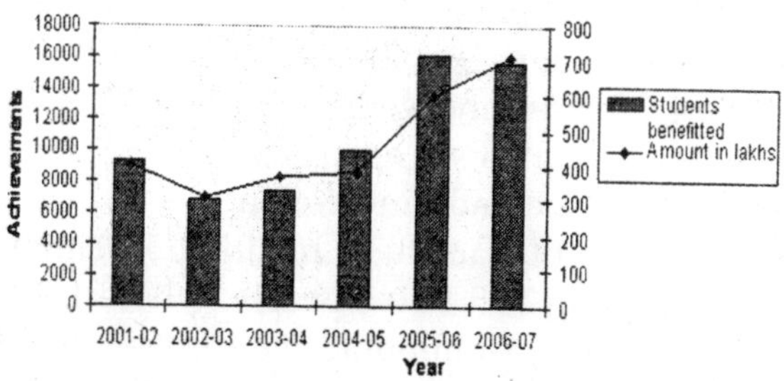

Figure 6. Post Matric Scholarship Status During 2001-07.

The focused intervention for the specific groups of people and also for a contiguous area, i.e., villages under RIAD, has been taken up as challenge to overcome the issues as identified by the people. Hence, development interventions in agency are more of participatory in nature, where the Project Officer owes the overall coordination for participation of departments with people.

Health-the All-round Challenge Ahead for the Agency

Outbreak of seasonal diseases in the Paderu agency area is common and frequently occurs in different forms due to

unfavourable ecological and epidemiological conditions. Major diseases prevalent in the agency area are Malaria, Diarrhea, Jaundice, Anemia, Typhoid, Chicken Pox, and General Fever with severe, body pains, Scabies, Respiratory infection. Strong prevalence of diseases and geographic spread of the agency and location of habitations is always a challenge for the health wings and the Agency administration.

The total area of Paderu is having 33 Primary Health Centers comprising 195 Sub-Centers, where transmissible diseases like Malaria, Communicable Diseases like Diarrhea, T.B., Viral Hepatitis, Acute Respiratory infections and Typhoid are being endemic. Health services are operational under the primary health care system. In Tribal area, the health services are monitored by the Additional District Medical & Health Officer and Malaria by the District Malaria Officer. The PHC'S are functioning at Mandal level and health delivery system is operational at village level through MPHA (M) & (F).

Inadequate staff and geographic spread in the face of seasonal sporadic outbreaks, therefore calls for a comprehensive, systematized and collaborative intervention to reduce the seasonal morbidity and mortality due to various diseases. Meticulous intervention would not only take care off reaching effective service delivery of the available health staff to un-reach habitation and community but also reduce the time requirement and fill the gap in timely and proper referral. Hence, all departments in the agency are working collaboratively with the voluntary organization to minimize the incidence of health outbreaks.

E.D.P.T. (Early Detection and Prompt Treatment)

Following the G.O. 76 Village Organisations of IKP and all Voluntary Organizations working in the agency would join

hand to extend the health services to the remote of the remotest habitations and help enable health department to respond quickly the referral cases. As per the mandate the Mandal Mahila Samakhya (MMS) would act as the platform to the respective mandal and on the schedule day of MMS meeting all departments would participate and solve the issues of the community. Each department would get a time slut for addressing the issues. The current arrangement has enabled the health department to provide quick response to the needy.

To address the health epidemics in the agency and following the convergence approach, a simple pamphlet has been printed by ITDA and circulated at the habitations. The pamphlet contains basic message on the common diseases with photograph. This has resulted in enough awareness within the community and hence generated demand for accessing services supplied at the habitation level. The simple approach of "collective involvement" of common with basic information on services available and the preventive measures has become a model for all other districts of Andhra Pradesh.

Water Borne Diseases

Primarily, people in Paderu agency depend on spring and stream for drinking and household purposes. The soil topography and location mostly pose the challenge to go for dug well or bore-well. However, ITDA had dug several wells and bore wells and kundies in almost every second habitation. Tribals because of traditional practice, generally use spring water. Spring and stream water during rainy season often get contaminated with man as well as animal wastes and hence, becomes the major source of outbreak of diseases where families and villages together get affected.

As a precautionary initiative and to avoid outbreaks of Diarrhea, Typhoid, Viral Hepatitis etc. primarily the waterborne diseases, the agency administration has taken adequate chlorination throughout the year with the help of the CHWs/AWW under close monitoring of the health staff and effective chlorination of water source by the Panchayat Secretaries/CHWs.

Similarly massive campaign on consumption of boiled water has been taken up at habitation and shandy points. This initiative has been taken up as a precautionary step for controlling waterborne diseases. This activity has been taken up in a big way throughout the year with constant motivation and is inculcated in the mind of the people. To achieve the desired level, all the intra and inter sectoral departments are involved for having constant watch on hotels and Ashram Schools where the implementation of activity is of prime importance.

ANAEMIA

Tribals in general and tribals in Paderu agency, in particular, are very strenuous and hardworking. Adequate nutritious food with strenuous work will enhance the energy level of the body and, hence, looks sound. Most of the pregnant, lactating mothers and children due to lack of adequate nutritious food become anemic. The supplementary nutrition programme under Reproductive and Child Health-II is serving the nutrition requirements to a certain extent. In order to arrest the situation, 24 hours MCH centers have been allotted to the agency. These centers would serve the twin objectives of nutrition counseling as well as check-up. Attention has been given for proper and timely distribution of Iron Folic Acid tablets and staff in Paderu agency have been warned of ensuring proper consumption at household level.

To address the food requirements of lactating and pregnant mothers, 1904 Grain Banks have been opened up in the villages to cater to the needs of the needy. The Grain Banks created at habitation level are run by the community members and are mandated towards serving the needs of the un-privileged women first. Additionally; provision is made for getting almost 3 months food to the lactating and pregnant families through Micro Credit Plan.

RESPIRATORY INFECTIONS AMONG CHILDREN

The seasonal growth and development of Parthenium weed is proved to be a notorious plant which causes respiratory problem among the children during flowering season due to widespread of pollen grains in the air. The flowering season is coinciding with the increase of fever incidence and respiratory problems during May, till August, wherever the dense growth of Parthenium is occurring. Awareness programmes through kalajatha and medical camps at habitation and shandy level are created to avoid use of Parthenium at home and in remote areas of the weeds before flowering.

MALARIA

Malaria in Paderu agency over the years has drawn the attention of media, State administration and country. The analysis of malaria incidence in Paderu shows the year 1999 is proved to be a bad year having more than 30,094. Malaria in the agency follows a three to five year cyclical pattern. However, it has shown a downward decreasing trend over the last three years i.e. 2005, 2006 and 2007 as well. Till April 2007, cases of Malaria reported are very minimal, i.e. 549 and, hence, may be the year 2007 would be rated as the best year in the agency.

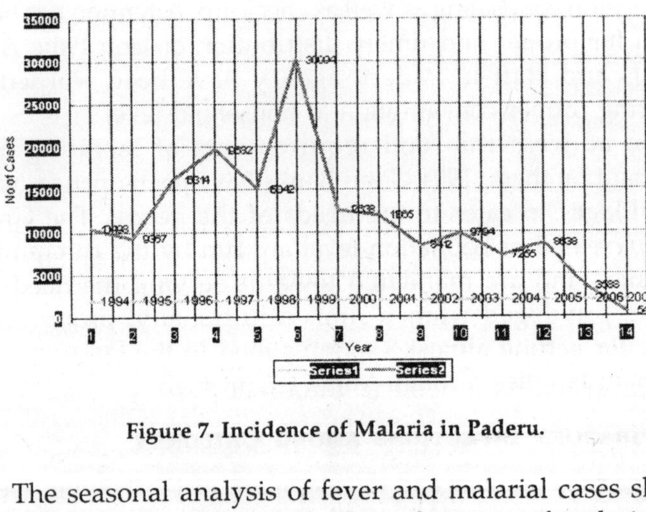

Figure 7. Incidence of Malaria in Paderu.

The seasonal analysis of fever and malarial cases shows that April-June is the period where the cases of malaria and fever are reported very high across the years (see table*).

Hence, warn the health department to take adequate precautions for prevention of the disease.

The remarkable reduction in the incidence is primarily because of the three-pronged perspective strategy, i.e. (a) creation of awareness through campaign, (b) Convergence with 14 line departments to complement each other in execution through proper timeline, and (c) Ensuring food security of the people during the lean season.

Table 2
Month wise Incidence of Fever and Malaria Cases

Sl. No.	Month	No. of Fever Cases			No. of Malaria Cases		
		2005	2006	2007	2005	2006	2007
1	January	21126	18051	16708	282	131	131
2	February	26175	20375	14678	440	190	120
3	March	36076	25243		597	279	
4	April	38682	26679		680	474	
5	May	67726	28534		1139	448	
6	June	74796	42258		1730	515	
7	July	73956	47605		1496	490	
8	August	61895	25933		904	259	
9	September	37484	21087		415	183	
10	October	33773	20990		262	202	
11	November	38802	19448		295	234	
12	December	25194	17466		208	183	
	Total	535685	313669	31386	8448	3588	251

Source: Statistics Department, ITDA, Paderu

At the community level, Community Health Workers (CHWs) use to access and deliver health services. 3200 CHWs acting visit which is planned in such a way that all habitation would be covered. Hence, CHWs ensure that all villages are touched periodically and information on village status is timely reported. The 966 Anganwadi Centers also added fuel in the drive of malaria evacuation in the agency. AWC became the center for awareness creation on consumption of boiled drinking water, village cleanliness, and village health and sanitation.

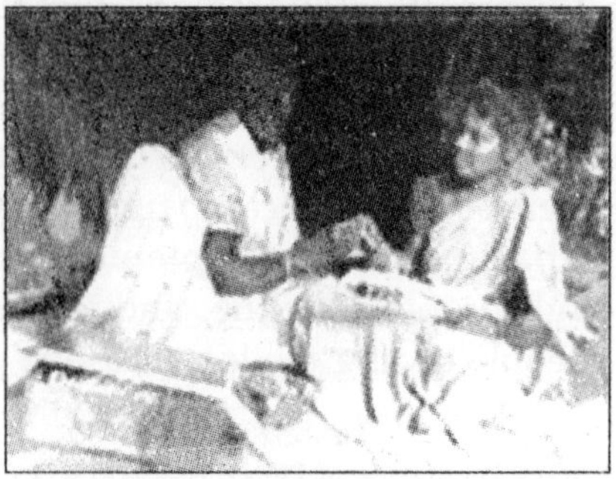

Consequently, the blood smear has also relatively decreased in the agency area. Statistics shows that over six years, i.e. 1999-2004, blood smears were widely collected and sent for testing. However, it has been reduced from 2004 and almost follows a downward trend. In fact, this is a good sign for well-being of tribals.

Table 3
Schemes and Beneficiaries under RCH-II in Paderu Agency Area

Name of the Scheme	*2001-02*	*2002-03*	*2003-04*	*2004-05*	*2005-06*	*2006-07*
NMBS Beneficiaries	1600	1000	1000	1000		
JSV Beneficiaries					2800	3670
Untied funds (Village Sanitation) Rs. in Lakhs					19.00	36.00
Hospital Development funds Rs. in Lakhs	13.5	13.5	15.30	15.30		54.30

Source: Statistics Department, ITDA, Paderu

Concerted effort is on reaching the services to each and every habitation. All the welfare schemes of Central and State Governments are reaching the targeted beneficiary. Agency administration has given a lot of focus on village health and sanitation and spends almost 51 lakhs towards encouraging village cleanliness and construction of garbage pits. Agency Health is no more in danger. The multi-pronged strategy as mentioned in the above paragraph is taking care of the requirement. The focused intervention through running of

Mobile Medical Units in the RIAD villages is absolutely a step forward to tackle the health issues of the unreached habitations.

Minor Irrigation

Plenty of water resources are available in the form of Rivers, springs and streams in the Paderu agency area. Agriculture is the major source of economic development of the community, but mostly rain fed, and in the lean season farmers practice stream cultivation, which is perennially fed by the springs. Second crop is only possible for those, whose fields are fed by the natural springs. This Traditional practice has enhanced by means of improved Irrigation facilities and optimum utilization of water surface water or sub-surface water. Hence, it is necessary to improve the Minor Irrigation facilities in the agency area.

The following are the different methods implemented in the agency area for providing irrigation facilities:

- By using sub-surface water
  - Irrigation wells
  - Drilling of Tube wells, Artisan wells
  - Lift Irrigation schemes
- By using surface water
  - Irrigation wells
  - Construction of Tanks, Kuntas
  - Construction of Check dams
  - Laying of canals, extension of canals.
  - Raising of Bunds

In 1980s, a massive programme has been taken up by the Govt. of India for Improvement of Minor Irrigation facilities to create a potential of 12,163 acres by providing Community Irrigation wells under JRY million wells programme. About 600 wells are constructed and motors have been provided to the beneficiaries in the agency area by spending about Rs. 20.00 crores.

The most successful method in the Minor irrigation sector in the agency area is construction of Check dams and diversion structures. There are as many as 1890 Minor Irrigation structures like check dams, Diversion structures and anicuts, which have been designed for a command ability of 27,370 hectors. The mandal-wise details of existing M.I structures are as follows:

Table 4
Mandal-wise status of M.I Structures

Sl. No.	*Name of the Mandal*	*No. of Sources*	*Ayacut in (Acres)*
1.	KOYYURU	193	10735
2.	CHINTHAPALLI	104	6608
3.	G.K.VEEDHI	72	3679
4.	G.MADUGULA	79	4396
5.	PADERU	123	4242
6.	HUKUMPETA	136	5388
7.	PEDABAYALU	110	3618
8.	MUNCHINGIPUT	92	3336
9.	DUMBRIGUDA	115	4121
10.	ARUKU	208	6155
11.	ANANTHAGIRI	310	7061
	Total	1,542	59,339

Source: Statistics Department, ITDA, Paderu

The MI structures constructed long back needs little renovation. The minor irrigation structures are beneficial to enhance their agro-economic status of the Tribes. Execution of minor irrigation structures has brought in to the notice of the departments the issues that need special care before execution of minor irrigation structures in the agency area.

Few Gaps are found in the implementation of the projects.

- Treatment of the catchment areas before constructing the structure;
- No mechanism was developed for the maintenance of the structures;
- Encroachments were made into the catchments of structures for agricultural purpose;
- Stream cultivation is practiced in entire agency area;
- Low or no ownership in execution and management;
- People's participation and contribution is not there in the process of construction of Minor projects.

HOUSING, ROADS AND NETWORKS

Since 1983, total 94843 houses were constructed under different schemes in Paderu tribal area. As per the instructions of the Government of Andhra Pradesh, 3268 houses were sanctioned under Remote Interior Andhra Pradesh focuses to provide houses for all the tribes living in ITDA jurisdiction of Paderu area of Visakhapatnam District as a special package for the next three years. Under this package, ITDA has planned to construct 36157 houses by using low cost permanent building material. In Paderu agency there are 2 ½ Assembly Segments getting clearly 2,500 houses under RPH programme. Thus we are getting minimum of 7,500 houses under RPH for the next 3 years. All the Mandal Revenue Officers to select the beneficiaries well in advance under SPR programme (In upcoming Housing scheme toilet is provided for each house hold).

PEOPLE'S PERCEPTION ON HOUSING

As per the recommendations of the Tenth Planning Commission, Gramsabha plays an important role in the entire process of identification and selection of beneficiaries, especially in Tribal area. AP Panchayatraj Amendment Act 1998 also focuses on GS mobilization. Hence GS must be prioritized in its true spirit. In order to address the issues, the department has attempted to ensure the following:

- Plastering of floor in the existing houses of the tribal area.

- Drainage facilities in and around the tribal households.
- Provide the material to construct the toilets instead of giving Rs. 2000/- worth of rice to tribals (let the department procure material for the construction of the toilets distributed only 50 kgs of rice to tribals) (Government uses to give Rs. 2700/- grant to construct toilets).
- Laying of roads/construction of CC roads in front of the households.
- Provide separate place for the cattle sheds for each household or common cattle shed for the village. by creating awareness among the tribes (NGOs/Civil society role).
- Provide water filters to each household (to provide safe drinking water to each household)/encourage traditional practices in purifying water.

Implementation of Housing programme in Agency area through 3 schemes as follows:

Table 5
Cost Details of Various Housing Schemes

Sl. No.	*Scheme*	*Unit Cost*	*Admn Fee*	*B.C**	*Subsidy*	*Loan from HUDCO*
1.	SPRH	7500	100	500	6900	
2.	I.A.Y	25000	100		24900	
3.	RPH	25000	100	500	7000	17500

* Beneficiary contribution

Source: Statistics Department, ITDA, Paderu

The actual construction cost is much higher in Agency area than in plain area due to:

- Transportation of building material,
- Lack of skilled labour and masons,
- Non availability of quality building material like sand, bricks and iron used in construction.

In plain areas, the beneficiaries most of the time do contribute their share by taking part in construction activity as a labour. Whereas in tribal areas, the beneficiaries may not involve in construction activity directly, because most of them are not aware of the work and it leads tribal people spending more money in the construction of their house.

Indira Avas Yojana (IAY) is a Central Government programme with full subsidy, and Rural Permanent Housing (RPH) with loan component from HUDCO, is facing difficulties in the sanctioning of houses. People have felt that one beneficiary in the same village enjoys full subsidy, and the other person is not. Person who gets house sanction under RPH has to pay loan component within the same habitation/ panchayat/village.

SPRH Programme

The implementation of various housing programmes in Tribal Areas like Semi Permanent Rural Housing (SPRH) housing, which is a state government programme (mud walls with tiled roof) with full subsidy. Right now the programme is executed for the interior villages of the ITDA. 13,104 beneficiaries have been benefited during the financial year 2006-07.

Rural Permanent Housing

Under this scheme the unit cost of Rs. 25,000/- is sufficient to complete the house in all respects in tribal area. The materials like chips, sand have to be procured from near by Anakapalli surroundings, which is 65 kms away from Paderu. The remaining additional cost from Rs. 10,000/- to Rs. 15,000/- has to be born by the beneficiaries themselves. 7567 beneficiaries are benefited till 2007.

IAY Housing

The programme is useful to tribal beneficiaries, comparatively with RPH scheme. In agency area, most of the villages are very interior and not having any infrastructure facilities. The sanctioned number of IAY houses, will not fulfill the requirement of eligible beneficiaries. As per the Government Order, 14 % district allocation under IAY, may be strictly implemented along with additional subsidy, as all the houses constructed in interior track. There are 1593 beneficiaries with an outlay of 309.68 lakhs are benefited.

Table 6
IAY Scheme

Year	*No of Physical Units*	*Outlay (Rs. Lakhs)*
2001-02	229	4.58
2002-03	471	9.42
2003-04	304	60.8
2004-05	385	7.68
2005-06	402	100.5
2006-07	806	201.5

Source: Statistics Department, ITDA, Paderu

MODEL COLONIES

Since the tribals are living in existing thatched houses, since last 20 to 30 years in kutcha areas without proper drainage facilities duly accommodating the goats and sheeps under the same roof, which leads for Malaria and other communicable decease. Therefore "Model Colonies" are taken up adjacent to the existing Thatched houses for providing roads, drainage and sanitation or in an open space close to their villages. 2734 households in 2006-07 have been brought under the model colony programme, while 806 houses were constructed for the flood damaged.

Table 7
Mandal wise Status and Requirement of Houses

Sl. No.	*Name of the Mandal*	*No. of Habi-tations*	*No. of House holds*	*House So far constructed*	*Houses Yet to be Provided*		
					Tiles	*RCC*	*Total*
1	Munchingiput	326	17632	13598	3750	284	4034
2	Pedbayalu	271	14625	10111	4000	514	4514
3	Hukumpeta	171	9266	6578	1500	1188	2688
4	Dumbriguda	87	4984	2936	1750	298	2048
5	Arakuvalley	170	9452	6987	1750	715	2465
6	Ananthagiri	291	15624	11564	2560	1500	4060
7	G.Madugula	306	16254	12674	2750	830	3580
8	Chinthapalli	238	12952	9426	3250	276	3526
9	G.K.Veedhi	174	9394	6910	2375	109	2484
10	Koyyuru	144	8092	5625	2375	92	2467
11	Paderu	231	12725	8434	2500	1791	4291
Total		2409	131000	94843	28560	7597	36157

Source: Dy. Engineer, ITDA office PADERU-2001 Census.

SECTION-III: CONCLUSION AND FUTURE ACTION PLAN

One way to examine the tribal development situation is to browse through the Report of the Working Group for Empowering the STs during the Tenth Five-Year Plan (2002-2007), under the Chairmanship of Dr. Ram Dayal Munda. However, the scenario of development of tribals could be well judged from the volume of work taken up by ITDA under its line departments. Each department in the agency area under the umbrella of ITDA claims for excellent performance and which is acknowledged many times by the State.

Agency area alone is a challenge for one and all, coupled with extremist activity and traditional culture, which often put the challenge to development agents and institutions. Execution of PESA, though, have been tried by many agents /institutions (NGOs), it has not really gone into the mind and blood of the elected peoples representatives to yield result and hence, became a distant dream to achieve community empowerment.

It is evident that apart from corrective measures being taken in the domain of the three elements ? institutions, delivery mechanisms and enabling policy framework ? the fourth element of 'Community Capacities' is an anchor for overall development. Only when the community has certain basic capacities it is possible for it to participate in the development process, as a subject rather than an object. The inadequacy of efforts to build these specific individual as well as collective capacities has led to exclusion or non-participation (or non-favorable inclusion) of individuals and community from various opportunities, institutions, delivery mechanisms, and an inability to take advantage of the enabling policy framework.

There is thus a genuine need to supplement and complement the current investments in development programs with processes that build capacities and provide opportunities to the millions of marginalized people to realize its potential, and enlarge available choices. This can be achieved by adopting a context-specific capacity building approach to empowerment and by institutionalizing these processes. An important aspect of empowerment is that it operates at both the individual and the community levels. At the individual level, it generates self-respect, esteem and confidence. At the community level, it enables individuals to organize themselves into groups and collectives, and mobilize themselves to achieve commonly-defined goals. Therefore, development interventions have to address empowerment at both the individual and community levels in order to bridge gaps in social sector outcomes and move rapidly towards the achievement of human development goals. In this regard, the ITDA along with the NGOs institutions can only facilitate this overall process of development and empowerment of the tribals in the agency area.

Bibliography

Anderson, Edward and Tammie O' Neil. "A New Equity Agenda?" Reflections on the (2006), World Development Report, the (2005) Human Development Report and the (2005) Report on the World Social Situation, WP 265.

Alex Ekka, Tribal Development and Empowerment, Responding to India's Social Challenges, Pages 54-67.

Baumann, Pari, Rajesh Ramakrishnan, Manish Dubey, Rajiv K. Raman, and John Farrington (2003), "Institutional Alternatives and Options for Decentralized Natural Resource Management in India", WP 230.

Berlin, I. (1969), "Two concepts of freedom", Four Essays on Liberty. Oxford: Oxford.

Clark, D.A. (2005), "Sen's Capability Approach and the Many Spaces of Human Well-Being", Journal of Development Studies, 41(8), 1339-1368.

Deb, Uttam Kumar, G.D. Nageswara Rao, Y. Mohan Rao and Rachel Slater (2002). "Diversification and Livelihood Options: A Study of Two Villages in Andhra Pradesh, India, 1975-2001". WP 178.

Deshingkar, Priya and Craig Johnson (2003), "State Transfers to the Poor and Back: The Case of the Food for Work Program in Andhra Pradesh", WP 222.

Deshingkar, Priya and Daniel Start (2003), "Seasonal Migration for Livelihoods in India: Coping, Accumulation and Exclusion", WP220.

Dollar, David and Aart Kraay (2000), "Growth is Good for the Poor", World Bank mimeo.

Dreze, J. (1990), "Poverty in India and the IRDP Delusion", Economic and Political Weekly, 25 (39): Mumbai.

Dreze, J. and A. Sen (1991), "Public Action for Social Security: Foundations and Strategy", in E. Ahmad, J. Dreze, J. Hills and A. Sen (eds.), Social Security in Developing Countries. Oxford: Clarendon Press.

Dreze, J. and A. Sen (1995), India, Economic evelopment and Social Opportunity. Delhi: Oxford University Press.

Dreze, Jean and Amartya K. Sen (1989), Hunger and Public Action, Oxford: Clarendon Press.

Dreze, Jean, and Amartya K. Sen (1995), India: Economic Opportunity and Social Development. New Delhi: Oxford University Press.

Fukuda-Parr, S. (2003), "The Human Development Paradigm: Operationalizing Sen's Ideas on Capabilities", Feminist Economics, 9(2-3), 301-317.

Gasper, D. (2002), "Is Sen's Capability Approach an Adequate Basis for Considering Human Development?", Review of Political Economy, 14(4), 435-461.

Ghosh, B. S. Marjit and C. Neogi (1998), "Economic Growth and Regional Divergence in India, 1960 to 1995", Economic and Political Weekly, June 27-July 3, Vol XXXIII, No 26, pp 1623-30.

Ghosh, J. (1998), "Assessing Poverty Alleviation Strategies for their Impact on Poor Women: A study with special reference to India", Discussion Paper 97. Geneva: UNRISD.

Gill, Gerard J., John Farrington, Edward Anderson, Cecilia Luttrell, Tim Conway, N.C. Saxena and Rachel Slater. (December 2003), "Food Security and the Millennium Development Goal on Hunger in Asia".

Goetz, A.M. and R.S. Gupta (1996), "Who takes the Credit? Gender, power and control over loan use in rural credit programs in Bangladesh", World Development.

GoI (2005), Economic Survey (2004-2005), New Delhi, India: Economic Division, Ministry of Finance, Government of India.

Haq, Mahbub ul (1995), Reflections on Human Development, Oxford: Oxford University Press.

Harriss, J. and P. De Renzio, (1997), "Missing link or Analytically Missing? The concept of social capital", Journal of International Development (9) 7, pp. 919-37.

Johnson, C. (2003), "Decentralization in India: Poverty, Politics and Panchayati Raj", Overseas Development Institute, London, WP 199.

Johnson, Craig, Priya Deshingkar and Daniel Start (2003), "Grounding the State: Poverty, Inequality and the Politics of Governance in India's Panchayats" WP 226.

Jos, Mooij. "Smart Governance? Politics in the Policy Process in Andhra Pradesh, India", WP 228.

J. Harrison and E. Freeman (1999), Stakeholders Social Responsibility and Performance. Empirical Evidence and Theoretical Perspectives., Academy of Management Journal, Vol. 42.

Kabeer, N. (1991), "Gender and Rural Poverty: Analysis from Bangladesh", Journal of Peasant Studies 18 (2): 241-62.

Kabeer, N. (1998), Money can't buy me love? Re-evaluating gender, credit and empowerment in rural Bangladesh. Brighton, UK: Institute of Development Studies, University of Sussex.

Kabeer, N. (2001), "Conflicts over Credit: Re-evaluating the empowerment potential of loans to women in rural Bangladesh". World Development 29 (1): 63-84.

Kabeer, N. (2002), "We don't do Credit": Nijera Kori, social mobilization and the collective capabilities of the poor in rural Bangladesh. Dhaka, Bangladesh: Nijera Kori.

Narayan, Deepa (1997), "Voices of the Poor: Poverty and Social Capital in Tanzania". Environmentally and Socially Sustainable Development Studies and Monographs Series 20. World Bank, Washington, D.C. ODI working papers.

Narayana, D. "Institutional Change and its Impact on the Poor and Excluded: the Indian Decentralization Experience", OECD Development Center, WP 242.

Nayak, Radhika, N.C. Saxena and John Farrington (2002), "Reaching the Poor: The Influence of Policy and Administrative Processes on the Implementation of Government Poverty Schemes in India".

National Institute of Rural Development (1999), India Rural Development Report 1999: Regional disparities in development and poverty. Hyderabad: National Institute of Rural Development (NIRD).

Planning Commission (2001), National Human Development Report, GOI.

Project Implementation Plan for Vulnerable Groups under RCH II (December 2004), Government of India, Department of Family Welfare, Ministry of Health & Family Welfare.

Prasanna K. Samal (1996), Tribal Development Options, proceedings of National Seminar (May 23-24), page, 363-367.

P. Krishnaiah (2003), Poverty Reduction, Self-help Group Strategy, UBI Publishers' Distributors Pvt. Ltd, page 77-117.

P. Kashyap and S.Raut (2006), The Rural Marketing Book, Biztantra, page 29-57.

Saxena, N.C. and John Farrington (2003), "Trends and Prospects for Poverty Reduction in Rural India: Context and Options", WP 198.

Saxena, Naresh C. "Policies for Tribal Development: Analysis and Suggestions".

Sen, A. (1985), "Well-being, Agency and Freedom: The Dewey Lectures 1984"; in: 64. UNDP. Nepal Human Development Report (2004).

World Bank (1999), The India Poverty Project: Poverty and growth in India, 1951- 94, Washington DC: World Bank.

World Bank (2000), India: Reducing Poverty and Accelerating Development. World Bank Report. Oxford University Press.

World Bank (2002), Empowerment and Poverty Reduction: A source book.

23

Political Empowerment of Rural Youth Through Youth Associations

Prof. R.D. Sampath Kumar
Paragati Venkateswarlu

Introduction

Youth constitute a large segment of the total population. Youth is a transition phase just as infancy gives way to childhood, youth gives way to adulthood. Youth is a period of physical, mental, ethical and emotional development. Elisentadt (1972) has defined youth as a period of transition from childhood to full adult status of full membership in society. In this period, the individuals no longer are considered as children, especially from a physical and sexual point of view, as they possess many attributes of adult characteristics besides fulfilling the adult roles.

United Nations and Demographers define youth chronologically as the population lying between the age-group of 15 to 24 years. The Ministry of Youth Affairs and Sports, Government of India, defines youth as the population in the age group of 15-35 years.

Youth Development

Youth development is aimed at providing skills, knowledge, attitudes, and behavior that enhances individual capacity as citizen. It is expected to provide young people to act with effectiveness and build abilities and inculcate public spirit so as to channelise their energies for the development of communities and institutions. Youth development creates opportunities for socialization of young people to face the challenges in life. Further, it provides support systems so as to develop their fullest potential, mind, heart, hands, and body. Programmes meant for youth development provide basic physical and social needs. It builds the individual assets and competencies in terms of knowledge, skills, relationships and values. (Virginia C. Gobeli (1995).

Education is one of the tools for youth development. Hence, there is a strong felt need that every one should have access to education. It provides a progression of activities promoting developmental growth and emphasizes learning strategies based on fun, play and action. They need teaching or life skills and soft skills rather than academic lessons (Mosher, 1979).

Youth as Member of Youth Clubs

Youth, of late, formed as associations to empower themselves. Youth clubs are considered as ideal agencies for inculcating positive qualities that will enable them to become good citizens (Varadaraju, 1991).

According to Sharma (1989) the youth clubs have six major objectives which help in the personality development of youth.

1. Development of scientific attitude towards farming and home making.
2. Development of qualities and skills of leadership.
3. Help them to learn better techniques of farming.
4. Train them in cooperative and community activities.
5. Help them to cultivate traits of healthy living, purposeful recreation and the intelligent use of leisure time and
6. Develop in them a sense of dignity

Empowerment

Empowerment is a means to an end and not an end itself. Empowerment in Indian context stands for transformation of people belonging to weaker segments: be it political, social, economic and cultural (Beteille, Andre, 1994).

Empowerment is a dynamic, multidimensional and democratic process of awareness and capacity building. Empowerment intends to transference or delegation of power and authority. Empowerment enhances the community capacity and increases personal, inter-personal and political power (Lorraine and Robert, 1991). Empowerment is a means by which people, communities and organizations achieve mastery over their affairs by realizing their full identity and power in all spheres of life. Empowerment believes in people's participation especially of deprived sections in decision making process (Rappaport, 1987).

Empowerment is a process of awareness and capacity building leading to greater participation, greater decision-making power and control, and to transform into action. The word 'empowerment' captures the sense of gaining control, participation and decision-making (Karl-1995).

Youth Empowerment

Leadership development is characterized by a spiral of learning and action that includes skill and knowledge. Participation of young people in different situations enables them to shoulder responsibilities, thus leading to empowerment (Virginia C. Gobeli, 1995).

Youth empowerment includes the participation of young men and women not only in decision making, but also in societal goals, through access to education, employment, health and resources such as land or credit. The concept of youth empowerment concentrates on the growing opportunities for young people and their achievements in society. However, much potential of youths is yet to be realized.

Youth played significant role in Freedom Movement and demonstrated their capacities to muster political power. After Independence, different youth wings of political parties such as - youth Congress, Yuva Janata, All India Youth Federation, The Democratic Youth Federation of India and a host of others mushroomed, advocating the recognition of the political power for the youth.

YOUTH–A CHALLENGE AND A RESOURCE

Challenges of youth is not a contemporary phenomenon, but it dates back as much as Indus civilization. As the resources are scarce and optimum utilization of resources is a challenge posed in all types of societies. Some of the challenges are: Inequities in social, economic and political conditions, gender discrimination, Insecure livelihoods, high levels of youth unemployment, armed conflict and confrontation, ethnic prejudice, social exclusion, homelessness, continuing deterioration of the global environment, increasing incidence of disease, hunger and malnutrition, changes in role of the family and inadequate opportunities for education and training.

NEHRU YUVA KENDRA

Nehru Yuva Kendra Samgatan (NYKs), an autonomous organisaiton of the Ministry of Youth Affairs and Sports, has its offices in 500 districts of the country. It has become one of the largest grass-root level organisaitons in the world, catering to the needs of more than eight million non-student rural youth enrolled in 19 million village based youth clubs. NYK organizes series of training programmes to the non-student rural youth. Some of the programmes of NYK are:

- Youth leadership training
- Sports & Games
- Vocational Training
- Adventure Programme
- Social Service

- Social Forestry
- Productional Units

For implementation of the programmes, every district NYK has a network of trained cadre of District Youth Coordinators, National Service Volunteers and youth leaders.

The training to youth is expected to empower them in social, economic, political and cultural areas. As such, the present study is taken up with the following objectives:

- To find out the age classification and their social status of the non-student rural youth
- To examine the extent of political empowerment gained by the members of youth clubs through NYK and lastly.
- To find out the impact of NYK programmes on youth political empowerment.

Study Setting

The study is conducted in three divisions of East Godavari District in Andhra Pradesh: They are Kakinada, Peddapuram and Amalapuram. Following table presents number of youth clubs associated with the NYK.

Divisions	*Youth clubs*
Kakinada	72
Peddapuram	78
Amalapuram	50
Total	200

Universe and Sample

20 youth clubs from each division is taken. Accordingly, 60 youth clubs from these three divisions were taken as sample.

Findings

1. *Social Characteristics*: The following table describes the social characteristics of the sample population.

Table 1
Social Characteristics

Variables	Youth Club (n=60)
Age (in years)	
< 25	18.4
25 - 35	73.7
> 35	7.9
Mean	29.37
Std. Deviation	5.635
Religion	
Hindu	82.5
Christian	17.5
Caste	
Scheduled Caste	58.8
Scheduled Tribe	1.8
Backward Community	22.8
Other Castes	16.7

A majority of the youth members (92.1) are found to be less than 35 years, which fits into the definition of youth as defined by the Government of India. The mean age of the respondents came to 29. As regards the social background of the respondents, a majority belong to Hindu religion, out of which more than half of the sample respondents hail from Scheduled Castes and the remaining were from Backward Communities and other castes.

2. *Political Empowerment*: The data indicate that 43 per cent of the youth club members have represented in various local government bodies. The following table explains division wise representations.

Table 2
Division-wise Political Representation

Division	Yes	No	Total
Kakinada	14	6	20
Peddapuram	7	13	20
Amalapuram	7	13	20
Grand Total	28	32	60

Out of the 3 divisions, it is found that more number of members of youth clubs from Kakinada division were found to be representing in the political bodies when compare to the other divisions. The following table discusses the category of political representation.

Table 3
Category-wise Political Representation

Divisions	*Ward Members*	*Sarpanch*	*MPTC*	*MPP*	*MLA*
Kakinada	20	1	4	-	-
Peddapuram	6	-	1	-	-
Amalapuram	9	2	-	1	1
Grand Total	35	3	5	1	1

Out of 14 youth clubs of Kakinada division, around 20 members of youth clubs became ward members, one sarpanch and four M.P.T.C. members. Similarly, in Peddapuram division, 7 members representing 7 youth clubs, 6 were ward members and one was M.P.T.C. member. As regards the Amalapuram division, out of 13 members representing 7 youth clubs, 9 were ward members, 2 sarpanches, one M.P.P. and one M.L.A. Thus, the data evidently show that the members of youth clubs could enter into political front of various political parties representing ward members, Sarpanch, M.P.T.C., M.P.P. and M.L.A.

3. *Association with Nehru Yuva Kendra*: As the study is focused on youth clubs which have affiliation to Nehru Yuva Kendra it is pertinent to find out the opinions of the respondents about the positive aspects gained in associating with the Nehru Yuva Kendra. The following table explains the same.

Table 4
Opinions of Positive Aspects Gained

Opinions	*Youth Clubs (n=60)**
Personality development	51.8
Acquisitions of Technical skills	46.5
Positive attitude	53.5
Leadership qualities	52.6
Development of capacities	51.8
Promotion of partnerships	51.8

* Multiple responses

The youth members opined that they could acquire positive attitude (53.5 per cent), leaderships skills (52.6 per cent) besides personality development, building the capacities and partnerships.

CONCLUSION

Therefore, there is a need to create positive environment where youth become empowered through the acquisition and development of skills that expand their personal traits. Young people are the leaders, decision makers, business people and parents of tomorrow, and therefore need the skills to empower them. It is a challenge for the government to provide the enabling environment which includes the economic and moral base, political will, resources, legal and administrative framework, equality, democracy, peace, knowledge, information, skills and values. It should provide opportunities for youth in building capacities and thereby empowerment. NYK should organize need and demand oriented programmes for youth.

The Government of India has recognized that youth empowerment more so the political empowerment cannot be achieved merely by government efforts and has recognised the role of multilateral agencies, educational and other institutions, civil society (e.g. family, kinship and community networks). There is great need that the NGOs, private sectors and media as stakeholders have to play a vital role in the process of youth empowerment.

There is less representation of members from the youth clubs in the local Government bodies. The investigations reveal that the senior political leaders do not wish to encourage the youth to taking political assignments as seniors have fear that they might lose positions if youth enter into politics. This is a wrong notion and second line leadership is essential for any political party to sustain. Hence, youth should be encouraged to take up political positions as they are the tomorrow's decision makers. NYK has to evolve such of those programmes which encompass the aspirations and desires of young citizens.

References

Beteille, Andre, 'Empowerment, Economic and Political Weekly, March 6-13, 1999, p. 590.

Chandra Gowda M.J. and G.M. Varada Raj, (1991), "Promoting village development through youth clubs: A Case Study". The Indian Journal of Social Work, LII. (2) (April).

Sharma, N.N. (1989), Accent on Empowerment news, 14 (4), 22 April.

Mohammad Hossen, (2005), Empowerment-Based Social Work Practice. The Indian Journal of Social Work 66, (2), April.

Lorraine, M. and Robert, O. (1991), Developing methods to empower Latinos: The importance of groups social work with groups, 14 (1), 24-25.

Rappaport J. (1987), "Terms of empowerment: Exemplars of Prevention-Toward a Theory for Community Psychology", American Journal of Community Psychology 15 (2), 121-145.

Govt. of India, Ministry of Youth Affairs and Sports, Annual Reports.

Gobeli, Virginia C. (1995), "Empowering youths through leadership development: Volunteers for the future", A video vicurity guide, Nebraska Co-operative extentives 4-H 303. University of Nebraska Lincoln, Nebraska, 1988.

24

Basic Education an Empowerment of Weaker Sections: Strategies for Social Work Intervention

Prof. M. Lakshmi Pathi Raju

Introduction

There are large groups in the Indian society,. Particularly the scheduled castes and scheduled tribes who suffer from social, educational, economic and cultural disabilities. They have not so far succeeded in securing for themselves what the Preamble to the Constitution has pledged. They have constitutional entitlement to social and economic justice, equality of opportunity, status and dignity. Even today, discrimination against scheduled castes persists. The society with its disabling environment that kept these depressed millions of Indians out of the mainstream and deprived them of their accessibility of intellectual, industrial, educational and cultural opportunities.

Dalits are subjected to social discrimination in respect of education. Though 83rd Amendment recognizes education as a fundamental right, there are disparities based on caste in India. The weaker sections, particularly scheduled castes and scheduled tribes are in a disadvantaged position in their accessibility to education.

There are high gaps between rural and urban areas and the probability of getting any education depends on gender, caste and income. Women, scheduled castes and tribes and the poor are based with barriers for getting basic education. Of the 200 million children in the age-group of 6-14, it is estimated that 59 million are out of school. Of these 35 million are girls.

According to 2001 census, the population of scheduled castes and scheduled tribes in India is 166,635,700 constituting 16.2 % of the population and 84,326,240 (8.2 %) respectively. The literacy rate of scheduled castes and scheduled tribes was 54.69 and 47.10 respectively. The gross enrolment rate has increased from 90 % in 2003-2004 to 98 % in 2004-05. The net enrolment rate has also increased from 72 % to 82 % Department of Education, 2006). The percentage of plan expenditure on elementary education has increased from 58% during 1951-56 to 66 % during 1997-2002.

In Andhra Pradesh the SC literates aged 7 years and above, according to 2001 census is 53.5% as against 60.5% for the State population as a whole. There is significant improvement during the decade 1991-2001. The literacy rate has increased by 21.9% from 31.6 in 1991.

Many factors contributed to the increase in enrolment rate of Dalit children. Among those factors may be mentioned, the Mid-day Meal Programme, Parent-Teacher Association (PTAs), Sarva Shiksha Abhiyan (SSA), and the Constitutional Amendment making compulsory education a fundamental right free for the children in the age group of 6-14 years.

So far the educational progress made by the weaker sections is not satisfactory when compared with the Non-scheduled castes and tribes. They lag behind considerable even after 60 years of Independence. Various studies have shown that the progress made by them is marginal, mainly confined to urban population. Dropout and Stagnation are the major problems faced by them. They enroll late, take longer time to complete and enroll into low standard educational institutions. Thus the educational problems of the weaker sections are two-fold; one at home level, and the second at school level (Wankade, 1999).

Social Exclusion

The scheduled castes voiced their grievances against their exclusion in international conferences like Durban. The National Campaign on Dalit Human Rights considered the issue of education, as one of the areas of social exclusion.

The concept of social inclusion is assuming importance, since there is increasing focus of the world on Non-discriminatory inclusive growth. Primary education was identified as one of the major factors contributing to the empowerment of Dalits. The dropouts of Dalit children and Dalit girl children constitute 54 % and 64 % respectively in the primary school stage. We are not able to provide basic education to 16 % of our population. International agencies like United Nations, World Bank and other agencies are emphasizing inclusive policies for integrated development of the country. Otherwise, the so-called development taking place today in our country becomes lop-sided and uneven. We cannot achieve growth with justice if large segments of the population are excluded in the development process. According to Kabir (2006), "Social exclusion reflects the multiple and overlapping nature of the disadvantages experienced by certain groups and categories of the population, with social identity is the central axis of their exclusion."

Social policy should focus on providing Universal benefits or "Reaching the poor" rather than social inclusion of the excluded. In Durban Conference, the deprived groups of various countries of the world debated on various forms of exclusion and evolved human rights approach to development. The shift of emphasis on human rights approach to development has implications for social exclusion in education. Social exclusion is not only a development issue but a human rights issue.

Article 46 of the Constitution states that, "The State shall promote with special care the educational and economic interests of the weaker sections of the people and, in particular of the scheduled castes and scheduled tribes and shall protect them from social injustice and all forms of exploitations. Articles 330, 332, 335, 338 to 342 and Sixth Schedule of the Constitution deals with special provisions for implementation of the objectives, set for them. These provisions need to be fully utilized for benefit of these weaker sections in our society.

After Independence, the Government of India has taken several steps to strengthen the educational base of the scheduled castes and scheduled tribes. The following special provisions for scheduled castes and scheduled tribes are incorporated:

(i) A primary school within one kilometer distance from the habitations of scheduled castes and scheduled tribes.

(ii) Abolition of tuition fee up to upper primary level for SC and ST children.

(iii) Incentives like free text-books, uniforms, stationery, school bags, etc for these students.

(iv) The Constitutional Amendment Bill, 2002, provides for free elementary education as fundamental right to all children in the age-group of 6-14 years.

(v) Sarva Shiksha Abhiyan (SSA): This scheme provides useful and quality elementary education to all children in the 6-14 age groups by 2010.

The government has also introduced various development programmes for benefiting SC and ST communities.

According to the National Common Minimum Programme (NCMP) among the six basic principles set by the government for governance and one of them is equality of opportunity, particularly in education and employment for scheduled castes and scheduled tribes. Under District Primary Education Programme (DPEP), there are specific strategies for girls and scheduled castes. The schools in DPEP districts had more than 60% students belonging to SC/ST communities. Mahila Samakhya (MS) addresses traditional gender imbalances in educational access of women from socially and economically disadvantaged and marginalized groups. National Programmes for Education of Girls at Elementary Level (NPEGEL) scheme is being implemented in educationally backward blocks (EBBS) where SC/ST female literacy is below 10 %. Kasturiba Gandhi Balika Vidyalayas are resident schools set up in different areas with boarding facilities at elementary level for girls belonging to the SC/ST population in the identified backward blocks. Jana Shikshana Sanstan (JSS) aims at improving the vocational skill and quality of life of SCs and STs women and girls and slum dwellers. Mid-day Meal Scheme aims to improve enrollment, retention and nutritional status of the children. Reservation of seats is provided for SC and ST students in Kendriya Vidyalayas (KVs), Navodaya Vidyalaya (NVs). Community polytechnics provide training to rural youths, SCs, STs, women, school dropouts and help them to obtain need based gainful employment.

Though the efforts are laudable, the proper quality of education is a major concern. There is no emphasis laid on making education more relevant. There are no activity based and child centered learning arrangements. There is no encouragement for learning by doing and learning by observation. Children mechanically go through the process of primary education without any creative abilities. The high rates of dropouts and low levels of completion rates of primary school reflect the poor quality of education. The Reproductive Child Health Survey II (2002-04) reveals that only 37.8% of children in 10-12 years age-group have completed five years schooling to Other Backward Classes (OBCs). The ST children are more disadvantaged than SCs in educational status.

The reasons for disparities in education between SC and ST children and other castes as identified by the Public Report on Basic Education (PROBE) are: the physical distance of the school from the habitations of SCs, "The Social Distance" in terms of their discriminatory treatment in the school by the teachers and the children of other castes (PORBE Report, 1999). Children of one hamlet will not attend the schools in another hamlet due to caste tensions.

The study conducted in 1995, revealed that SC/ST families live in colonies which are one kilometer away from main village (MODE Research, 1995). Teachers in India mostly belong to upper caste and show discriminatory treatment of SC children. Dalit children are assigned menial tasks like sweeping and cleaning the class-rooms. Higher rates of teacher absenteeism were reported in schools when the children are mostly from SC and ST communities. There is need for training of teachers for giving them necessary orientation for promoting positive attitudes towards SC children (Department of Education, 2006). Teachers from the disadvantaged background may be encouraged to develop empathy towards marginalized groups.

The Government of India realized the disadvantaged position of SC population in India. Hence, in its approach paper to 11th Five year plan, the government emphasized its commitment to remove the disparities in education between the castes. It also states that empowerment of disadvantaged groups is a constitutional commitment. It is also increasingly realized that education is an effective instrument of empowerment of SCs and STs.

It is necessary to go to the root of the problem and explore the reasons for low literacy rates and necessary measures may be taken during the 11th Plan (Planning Commission, 2006). What is required is a holistic approach towards the uplift of weaker sections. The remedial measures for social exclusion of a scheduled castes and scheduled tribes include involvement of these excluded groups in community life, providing them access to basic services, educating them for behavioral modification and attitudinal change, promoting skill development and employability, participation in decision making process. The kind of education that is required for these excluded groups is not mere primary education and formal education in schools. What they need is basic education which includes all elements of education i.e. a more comprehensive scheme of education covering besides primary education, vocational education, participation in community life and decision making process, involvement in the development programmes, continuing education and participation in local panchayats, and local self- governments.

Radical Changes Needed

A powerful campaign of education needs to be launched to educate people at all levels. The policies that have already been put into practice since the beginning of the Indian Constitution that need to be implemented must be explained to the people through a deliberate campaign to buildup political support for them. A powerful educational programme is needed for this purpose. Consideration of what needs to be done in this direction must deal with two sets of issues:

1. This concerns the 'targets' of such an educational programme.
2. The second relates to the content of the programme. The primary objective of process of education has to be elimination of poverty and impact social justice.

Prof. S. N Ranade suggests that 'social workers and educators have a special role and stake in helping to build up peace-movement. Such a movement cannot succeed unless policy-makers are made to realize that real defense and security lie in ensuring the well-being of the people, and not suppressing their discontent. Welfarism must be seen in terms of human rights. Both environment and human rights must envelope all mankind and social work must become part of the movement for the protection of both.

Dr. P.T. Thomas also advocates that the issue of peace must be recognized as a human relation skill namely, conflict resolution. The deteriorating, ecological environment, illiteracy, lack of access to opportunity, social conflict and dire poverty of disadvantaged groups need to be addressed.

The following areas need emphasis in the educational programme for the uplift of weaker sections:

1. Peace moments and peace studies.
2. Resolution of conflicts.
3. Social legislation and social action.

4. Policies, programmes and strategies for development of scheduled castes and scheduled tribes and other backward classes.
5. Social moments with particular reference to upliftment of backward classes.
6. Anti poverty programmes and their impact on poor and welfare programmes.
7. Panchayat Raj system to build participatory democracy from grass-roots upwards.
8. Communication and its effective use in educating people.

Strategies for Social Work Intervention

Social workers can take challenge to keep weaker sections in the education stream to fill the reserved posts. This would need permission to parents, providing of access to schools, developing hostel facilities, awarding fellowships, supplying free books, mid-day meals, arranging coaching classes and providing vocational and entrepreneurial training.

The mass-media must be used to make people, especially weaker sections, aware and conscious of their rights and duties. They continue to feel deprived and exploited as a group. Their lives were spent in a struggle for barest necessities of survival in the margins of society.

There are three types of changes-Developmental, Transitional and Transformational. Development change, simply, is an improvement upon the current way of operating. The aim is to do more and to do things better. Enhancing communication skills, enhancing technical expertise, building teams and expanding opportunities fall into this category.

Transitional change is the implementation of known new state and require rearranging or dismantling old social structure. Transitions usually occur over a set period of time. Transformational change is more profound and traumatic. It is somewhat out of direct control and it produces a future state that is largely unknown until it evolves. This type of change occurs when an organization (or society) reaches a plateau in its lifecycle and full prey to unwilling demands from the environment.

Special skills are needed to be developed in social workers to deal with transformational change skills in managing ambiguity and conflict, in leading deprived group towards a moving target and clearly communicating a change strategy and a vision. Transformational times are not just difficult on the bottom-line, they also wreck havoc on the large society. This is the most challenging task to be performed by the social worker to empower weaker sections. Training most provide and militate learner (social worker) to be successful in coping with the challenges of change while at the same time, serving the community as a whole.

SOCIAL WORKER TO ACT AS SOCIAL ACTIONIST

Social worker acts as a social actionist the attitudes of SCs, STs and the society as follows:

1. Present facts: Social workers and study groups compile, collate and publish relevant data for pointing out the inadequacy in legislation and suggest necessary amendments.
2. Articulation of professional opinion: Social workers can assist the policymakers to articulate their professional opinion and prepare memoranda on model draft amendments in legislation relating to SCs.
3. Communicating the findings: The social workers can present research findings on public platforms, agency forums and professional meetings so as to bring them to the notice of the public and the concerned authorities.
4. Feedback from beneficiaries: The professional social workers can promote a regular system of assessing the reactions of the beneficiaries to the legislation.
5. Lobbying (Social advocacy): Since the target groups cannot raise their voice, the social workers to take up the advocacy function.

6. Social Action: By collective efforts, the social workers can undertake a great deal of social action programmes.
7. Demonstration: The Social workers can implement the projects at the field level to demonstrate to the target population (SCs and STs).

Steps to be initiated by the Social Worker

1. Special drives/campaigns to observe 'fortnight week' for eradication of untouchability.
2. To find out ways and means to change the mental outlook and social attitudes of people.
3. Incorporating suitable reading material at the primary and middle school level.
4. Propaganda through mass media, TV, press, cinema, debates, seminars, symposia, padayatras to be undertaken.
5. Community feasts with SCs and STs inter-caste marriages may be arranged.
6. Houses not to be located away from the main village.
7. Land to be allotted to landless SCs and STs.
8. Economic rehabilitation would be successful when vulnerable groups come up educationally.
9. The National Commission for SCs and STs to undertake a comprehensive evolution to evaluate development programmes for SCs and STs.

The social worker can conduct training and orientation programmes for the community leaders, youth associations, employers organizations, student leaders in the following areas, by developing training modules:

1. Sensitization and awareness about various development programme intended for SCs.
2. Unity among different segments of poverty groups.
3. Transformation of poverty groups: Psychological, sociological and attitudinal change.

4. The social worker has to undertake educational and awareness programmes in the villages of educating and discriminating knowledge about various developmental programmes intended for SCs and STs.

The essential foundation for stimulating development lies not in super imposition of technologies for the development of material culture; rather, the first step must be the discovery of an effective method of working with people. The man belonging to the fourth state (wreaker sections or poor) or the common man of India or for that matter of the third world of today as well as of tomorrow and day after belong to rural and tribal India. To respite vitality to the Indian society and build up the future prosperity of the common man, it is necessary to strengthen and develop weaker sections, only then, and in that process, the well-being of the Indian people will be realized.

References

Bhargava and Avinash Samal (1998), Protective Discrimination and development of schedule castes: an alternative model for good governance, the Indian journal of public administration, July - September, no. 3.

Yangrade, K.D. (2005), Gandhian Approach to Development and Social Work, Concept Publishing Company, New Delhi.

MODE Research (1995), Attitudes study on Eliminatory Education in India: A Consolidated Report, Commissioned by UNICEF, New Delhi.

Narayana K.S. (1998), Drawbacks Impeding Success of Positive Discrimination, the Indian Journal of Public Administration, September, no. 3.

Planning Commission (2006), Towards Faster and More Inclusive Growth: An Approach to 17th Five Year Plan, Government of India, New Delhi.

PROBE Team (1999), India Education Report, Oxford University Press, New Delhi.

Registrar-General & Census Commissioner (2005), Census and You, Government of India, New Delhi.

Sen. Amartya (2000), Social Exclusion: Concept, Application and Something, Office of Environment, Asian Development Bank.

25

Urban–Rural Disparities in Literacy Rates in India: Some Dimensions

Prof. D. Pulla Rao

Introduction

Literacy is an important element of transformation and social, economic and political development. India today, in its critical stage of demographic evolution, badly stands in need of an accelerated pace of literacy transition which alone can serve the cause of continuing the menace of growing population which poses a serious danger to the progress of the country. A thrust on rural literacy assumes special significance in the context of India where more than 70 per cent of the India's population lives in rural areas. The number of rural illiterates in India is more than the total combined population of Japan, United Kingdom, Canada and Australia. India has undoubtedly recorded a phenomenal educational development since independence. Urban literacy, has, no doubt, improved significantly. However, the malaise still persists. Rural areas characterized by a literate majority continue to be primarily concentrated only in north east, north west and southern coastal areas while vast rural areas in the rest of the country have yet to free themselves from the curse of low rural literacy resulting in lower general literacy. In rural areas more than two-fifths of the population is still illiterate. Urban-rural literate ratio still calls for more vigorous efforts especially among the rural female population.

DEFINITION OF LITERACY

The definition of literacy varies from country to country depending upon its existing social and educational patterns and upon different needs of urban and rural life. Literacy has been commonly accepted as a skill through which an individual possesses mastery over symbols in written form or able to code or decode written messages that is knowledge and acquire ability to read and write. However, literacy goes much beyond this accepted definition. The International Liaison Committee for Literacy has explained, "Literacy is not the simple reading of a word or set of associated symbols of sounds, but an act of critical understanding of any situation in the World" (UNESCO 1972).

United Nations Development Programme defines literates as those who can with understanding; both read and write, a short, simple statement related to their everyday life. According to this definition, the least developed countries of the world had an average adult literacy rate (i.e. the percentage of people aged 15 and above) of 53.3 per cent in 2001 (U.N.2003). The developed and less developed countries presented a contrast with regard to levels of literacy. Although non-availability of comparable specific data on literacy of various countries restricts our analysis in this regard yet it is possible to state with reasonable confidence that while the developed countries are fortunate in having universal adult literacy, in case of the less and least developed countries the corresponding figures are depressingly low. Developed countries like U.S.A., Canada, Japan, Australia etc. achieved almost universal literacy and education with a negligible proportion of illiterates. Developing countries, on the threshold of development, exhibited an adult literacy rate of 74.5 percent (U.N.2003).

The most recent Indian census of 2001, however a registered a literacy rate of 65.20 per cent which varies considerably from the above mentioned U.N. figures. This is so because the 2001 India census defines literate as "a person aged seven and above who can both read and write with understanding in any language". A person, who can only read but cannot write, is not deemed to be literate. It is not necessary that to be treated as literate, a person should have received any formal education or passed any minimum educational standard. Literacy could also have been achieved through adult classes or through any non-formal educational system.

Trends of Literacy in India

All India average of percentage of literacy in the country was 5.36 per cent in 1901. The literacy ratio of male was 9.80 per cent and female less than one (0.60). In 1931 the average literacy rate was 9.51. During 30 years of period there was no more change in this rate. The drastic change started after 1941.

In the period from 1901 to 1931, the spread of literacy in India was almost stagnant. In 30 years, it is increased from 5.36 per cent to 9.51 per cent. After 1931, there was steady growth in the literacy percentage. In the period between 1931 and 2001, the literacy expansion was almost seven times i.e. from 9.51 per cent to 65.20 per cent. This positive trends can be seen both in, case of male as well as female literacy in the Table-1.

Table 1
Literacy In India (1901-2001)

		In Million			*In Percentage*		
Year	*Age Group*	*Population*	*Illiterate*	*Literate*	*Person*	*Male*	*Female*
1901	All	235.1	225.5	12.6	5.36	9.8	0.6
1911	All	248.2	233.5	14.7	5.92	10.6	1
1921	All	246.7	229	17.7	7.17	12.2	1.8
1931	All	273.4	247.4	26	9.51	15.6	2.9
1941	All	312	261.8	50.2	16.09	25	7.3

Contd....

		In Million			In Percentage		
Year	Age Group	Population	Illiterate	Literate	Person	Male	Female
1951	5 and above	316.1	300	60.19	19.04	27.2	8.9
1961	5 and above	372.84	267.3	105.52	28.3	40.4	15.3
1971	5 and above	468.6	307.1	161.41	34.45	45.95	22
1981	7 and above	581.78	340.7	241.03	41.43	56.5	29.8
1991	7 and above	688.16	328.8	359.28	52.21	64.1	39.3
2001	7 and above	869.15	302.44	566.71	65.2	75.8	54.2

Sources: Census India, Various Issues.

URBAN-RURAL LITERACY RATES IN INDIA

After independence, India has recorded a significant development in the field of literacy and education. Total eradication of illiteracy is an elusive goal in India. The overall literacy rate has shown a steady increase in every successive decade from 1951 to 2001 has rose from 18.33 per cent in 1951 to 65.38 per cent in 2001. Rural literacy in India increased from 12.10 per cent in 1951 to 59.40 per cent in 2001 (Table-2). A comparison of increase in overall and rural literacy rates during the second half of the 20th century is quite significant. Both have shown a steady increase in every successive decade. The overall and rural literacy rates in 1951 were 18.33 and 12.10 respectively. In 2001 they stood at 65.38 and 59.40 respectively. The urban character of the former British administration was fairly responsible for creating a wide gap between urban and rural literacy. The ratio between urban and rural literates which was 2.86 : 1.00 in 1951 has got reduced to 1.35 : 1.00 in 2001. The contrasts have been sharper in urban-rural female literate ratio than urban rural male literate ratio from 1951 to 2001. Urban-rural female literate ratio has experienced continuous decline since 1951 and it has come down from 4.58 : 1.00 in 1951 to 1.57 : 1.00 in 2001. The urban-rural gap in literacy is attributed to appalling poverty in rural areas, even when education is free to all children up to 14 years in India.

Table 2
Urban-Rural Literacy Rates and Ratios in India: 1951-2001

Year	*Males*	*Urban Rural Male Literate Ratio*	*Females*	*Urban Rural Female Literate Ratio*	*Persons*	*Urban Rural Literate Ratio*
1951		2.40:1.00		4.58:1.00		2.86:1.00
Rural	19.02		4.87		12.10	
Urban	45.60		22.33		34.59	
Total	27.16		8.86		18.33	
1961		1.92:1.00		4.01:1.00		2.42:1.00
Rural	34.30		10.10		22.50	
Urban	66.00		40.50		54.40	
Total	40.40		15.35		28.30	
1971		1.44:1.00		3.15:1.00		2.16:1.00
Rural	48.60		15.50		27.90	
Urban	69.80		48.80		60.20	
Total	45.96		21.97		34.45	
1981		1.55:1.00		2.59:1.00		1.87:1.00
Rural	49.60		21.70		36.00	
Urban	76.70		56.30		67.20	
Total	56.38		29.76		43.57	
1991		1.40:1.00		2.09:1.00		1.64:1.00
Rural	57.90		30.60		44.70	
Urban	81.10		64.00		73.10	
Total	64.13		39.29		52.21	
2001		1.21:1.00		1.57:1.00		1.35:1.00
Rural	71.40		46.70		59.40	
Urban	86.70		73.20		80.30	
Total	75.85		54.16		65.38	

Source: Census of India, 2001.

State Wise Urban-Rural Disparities in Literacy Rates in India

The average literacy rate of our country was 65.20 per cent in 2001. The literacy rate among male and female was 76 and 54 per cent respectively. But in Table-3 there are many disparities among the states. On the one side the Kerala has the highest literacy rate of 90.92 per cent followed by Maharashtra (77.27 %), Himachal Pradesh (75.915 %), Tamil Nadu (73.47 %), Punjab (69.75 %), west Bengal (69.22 %), Karnataka (67.04 %), and Gujarat was (66.43%). Rests of the states have literacy levels below than the national average. The lowest literacy level is in Bihar (47.53%) followed by Utter Pradesh (57.36%), Rajasthan (61.03%), Andhra Pradesh (61.11%), Madhya Pradesh (64.08%) and Assam (64.28%).

The national average of Literacy in urban areas was 80.06 per cent in 2001, the highest rate being in Kerala (93.38%) followed by Himachal Pradesh (89.63%), Assam (85.95%). Remaining other states had literacy rate below the national average.

The national average of literacy in rural areas in 2001 was 59.21 per cent, the highest literacy being in Kerala (90.05%) followed by Himachal Pradesh (74.38%), Maharashtra (70.84%), Haryana (68.82%), Tamil Nadu (66.66%), Punjab (65.16%), West Bengal (64.06%), Assam (60.92%) and Orissa (60.44%). The lowest literacy rate in rural India were in Bihar (44.42%), Utter Pradesh (53.68%) Rajasthan (55.92%) Madhya Pradesh (58.10%) and Gujarat (58.53%).

Table 3
State wise Urban-Rural Literacy Rate of Male and Female in India: 2001 Census

Census-2001	*Total*	*Male*	*Female*	*Rural*	*Urban*
Andhra Pradesh	61	71	51	55	76
Assam	64	72	56	61	86
Bihar	48	60	34	44	73
Gujarat	70	81	59	59	79
Haryana	69	79	56	69	80
Himachal Pradesh	77	86	68	74	90
Karnataka	67	76	57	60	81
Kerala	91	94	88	90	93
Madhya Pradesh	64	77	50	58	80
Maharashtra	77	86	68	71	86
Orissa	64	76	51	60	81
Punjab	70	76	64	65	79
Rajasthan	61	76	44	56	77
Tamil Nadu	73	82	65	67	82
Uttar Pradesh	57	70	43	54	71
West Bengal	69	78	60	64	82
All India	65	76	54	59	80

Source: Census of India, 2001.

Progress of Scheduled Caste and Scheduled Tribe Literacy in Urban and Rural India

Urban-rural disparity has been decreasing significantly among both the scheduled castes and scheduled tribes since 1961. The disparity has been decreasing both males and females in both the social groups. Among scheduled tribe population the urban- rural differential in female population has decreased most impressively. The urban-rural disparity among scheduled tribe females has decreased from 4.64: 1.00 in 1961 to 1.84: 1.00 in 2001 (Table-4). The decrease of the disparity is a positive sign. This situation may be due to so many policies and programmes implemented by the Government of India after independence to improve the literacy and enrollment of scheduled tribe population through concessions and reservations and awareness campaigns to improve the literacy of scheduled tribe population especially for the improvement of literacy among scheduled tribe females. It is most encouraging to find that in more recent times, the females from the rural poor have been awakened through public awareness campaigns and the disparity has reduced significantly.

Though a number of strategies have been used in India to meet the educational needs of the tribal students, yet they are inadequate. Therefore, there is a need to take effective measures on the following lines.

1. Provision of more schooling facilities, particularly model schools.
2. Undertake teacher training and orientation about tribal needs and educational programmes.
3. Re-orienting curriculum, content and medium of instruction suited to the tribal children.
4. Provision of teaching/learning materials.
5. Innovative methods to be developed for supervision of schools.
6. Micro planning and effective implementation.

Table 4
Literacy Rates of Schedule Caste and Scheduled Tribe Population by Sex and Residence in India: 1961 -2001

State/ Union Territory Literate	Schedule Caste Population				Schedule Tribe Population			
	Total	Rural	Urban	Urban Rural SC Literate	Total	Rural	Urban	Urban Rural Literate
Persons								
1961	10.27	8.89	21.81	2.45:1.00	8.53	8.16	22.41	2.75:1.00
1971	14.67	12.77	28.65	2.24:1.00	11.30	10.68	28.84	2.70:1.00
1981	21.38	18.48	36.60	1.98:1.00	16.35	14.92	37.93	2.54:1.00
1991	37.41	33.25	55.11	1.66:1.00	29.60	27.38	56.60	2.07:1.00
2001	54.69	51.16	68.12	1.33:1.00	47.10	45.02	69.09	1.53:1.00
Males								
1961	16.96	15.06	32.21	2.14:1.00	13.83	13.37	30.43	2.27:1.00
1971	22.36	20.04	38.93	1.94:1.00	17.63	16.92	37.09	2.19:1.00
1981	31.12	27.91	47.54	1.70:1.00	24.52	22.94	47.60	2.07:1.00
1991	49.91	45.95	66.06	1.45:1.00	40.65	38.45	66.56	1.73:1.00
2001	66.64	63.66	77.93	1.22:1.00	59.17	57.39	77.77	1.35:1.00
Females								
1961	3.29	2.52	10.04	3.98:1.00	3.16	2.90	13.45	4.64:1.00
1971	6.44	5.06	16.99	3.36:1.00	4.85	4.36	19.64	4.50:1.00
1981	10.93	8.45	24.34	2.88:1.00	8.04	6.81	27.32	4.01:1.00
1991	23.76	19.45	42.29	2.17:1.00	18.19	16.02	45.66	2.85:1.00
2001	41.90	37.84	57.49	1.52:1.00	34.76	32.44	59.87	1.84:1.00

Source: Censuses of India for various years.

State Wise Urban-Rural Disparities in Literacy Rates Among Social Groups in India

Table-5 presents distributions of persons aged 7 years and above by major social groups. The pattern of variation in the literacy rate was almost the same in rural as well as urban areas. However, in rural India, the literacy rate was the lowest for persons belonging to STs (42%) followed by persons belonging to SCs (47%). But in urban India, the literacy rate was the lowest for SC groups (66%) followed by ST Groups (70%). In both the sectors the literacy rate was the highest for persons belonging to group 'others' (Upper Castes).

The urban-rural bias can be seen in the literacy as is reflected in Table-5. Urban literacy extended in urban areas over the rural India. The urban literacy stood at 70 per cent where as it was just 42.2 per cent in rural area. The gap is explicit more in state like Tamil Nadu where in urban literacy stood at 95.7, which is far higher than just 50.8 per cent for rural Tamil Nadu.

Table 5

Percentage of Literate Persons Aged 7 Years and above in Rural and Urban Areas by Social Group Based On 55th Rounds

State	*ST*		*SC*		*OBC*		*Others*		*All*	
	Rural	*Urban*	*Rural*	*Urban*	*Rural*	*Urban*	*Rural*	*Urban*	*Rural*	*Urban*
Andhra Pradesh	26.1	57.5	39.4	67.3	42.5	68.8	62.3	82.2	45.8	74.5
Assam	71.6	85.3	69.7	69.2	72.9	80.1	66.7	89.7	69.0	86.1
Bihar	34.4	69.7	25.7	47.5	42.4	63.6	59.2	84.0	41.8	69.6
Gujarat	50.3	66.8	55.5	71.2	55.8	76.7	75.0	91.2	62.0	84.1
Haryana	48.3	93.7	50.7	53.4	58.1	75.5	67.7	84.6	61.2	76.6
Himachal Pradesh	73.1	85.4	67.7	81.2	81.1	78.9	74.2	93.3	73.4	90.2
Karnataka	41.3	53.9	44.3	65.6	56.6	79.6	65.2	88.9	55.9	82.1
Kerala	80.2	97.5	79.1	87.9	88.3	92.3	94.1	96.4	89.4	93.7
Madhya Pradesh	32.4	59.8	46.0	64.0	55.6	73.5	67.8	87.9	49.8	77.5
Maharashtra	49.9	79.4	63.5	80.1	69.0	83.0	72.2	88.3	66.5	86.0
Orissa	33.1	55.2	47.8	53.2	61.6	79.4	73.9	85.8	53.8	75.5
Punjab	69.2	75.5	51.9	60.1	63.5	80.3	70.4	87.2	62.5	78.9
Rajasthan	38.4	69.1	36.7	56.0	46.3	70.0	57.8	84.4	46.5	75.1
Tamil Nadu	50.8	95.7	55.9	74.1	66.3	84.0	81.7	92.9	63.8	84.5
Uttar Pradesh	47.7	78.5	40.7	58.1	47.6	59.3	64.9	79.7	51.1	70.1
West Bengal	41.6	63.2	57.1	67.4	74.6	81.2	64.7	86.2	61.7	82.2
All India	42.2	70.0	46.6	66.2	54.8	75.3	67.7	86.5	56.0	79.8

Source: NSSO Report No. 473: Literacy and Levels of Education in India 1999-2000.

State Wise Urban-Rural Disparities in Literacy Rates Among Religion Groups in India

The distribution of persons aged 7 years and above by each sector and religions are shown in Table-6. It is noticed that the literacy rate was lower in rural India for 'Islam' compared to other religions. Literacy rate for all the religious groups, as revealed again for the first time in 2001 Census, were very encouraging, shattering many myths earlier when such a data set was not available for the country as a whole. The literacy among Hindus (65.1%) was slightly better than the national average (64.8%) for all religious groups combined. Among

Muslims the literacy rate is 59.1 per cent, below the national average. The highest literacy rate is recorded among the Jains (94.1%), followed by Christians (80.3%), Buddhists (72.7%) and Sikhs (69.4%). Against the exiting popular perception, the female literacy rate among different religious groups does not show wide variations. Among the Muslims, for instance, the literacy rate among the females was stagnant 50.1 per cent, below the national average of 53.7 per cent. Slightly better is the females' literacy rate among the Hindus (53.2%), again below the national average. The highest literacy rate among the females was recorded among the Jains (90.6%), like their male counterparts. Female literacy rate among Christians was 76.2 per cent, followed by Sikhs (63.1%) (Census, 2001).

The 55th Round NSSO Report reveal the difference in literacy indifferent religions communities. The literacy rate in Christians is the highest both in Rural as well as urban areas. Hindus stand at the second place where as Muslim occupy the third place with 52 and 70 per cent literacy respectively in rural as well as urban areas (Table-6).

Table 6
Percentage Of Literate Persons Aged 7 Years And Above In By Religions Group Based On 55th Round

State	*Hinduism*		*Islam*		*Christianity*		*Others*		*All*	
	Rural	*Urban*	*Rural*	*Urban*	*Rural*	*Urban*	*Rural*	*Urban*	*Rural*	*Urban*
Andhra Pradesh	45.4	75.0	51.0	70.7	51.5	78.9	55.5	96.1	45.8	74.5
Assam	74.5	87.0	59.4	79.7	53.5	80.5	85.7	-	69.0	86.1
Bihar	42.6	70.7	36.1	61.1	44.7	83.5	41.3	96.0	41.8	69.6
Gujarat	61.8	83.7	69.1	82.7	62.5	94.2	-	-	62.0	84.1
Haryana	61.7	76.9	31.0	54.5	-	-	-	-	61.2	76.6
Himachal Pradesh	73.7	90.2	56.9	73.6	-	-	83.2	-	73.4	90.2
Karnataka	55.3	82.9	63.2	77.1	68.0	95.5	52.0	73.4	55.9	82.1
Kerala	88.4	94.2	87.2	91.0	95.1	95.8	-	-	89.4	93.7
Madhya Pradesh	49.1	77.5	60.3	73.6	66.5	89.1	-	61.3	49.8	77.5
Maharashtra	66.2	87.3	67.1	79.9	61.4	95.3	76.4	86.6	66.5	86.0
Orissa	53.7	76.6	67.1	56.7	48.5	63.7	62.6	-	53.8	75.5
Punjab	68.4	79.2	62.9	65.4	44.2	77.7	84.7	-	62.5	78.9
Rajasthan	46.7	76.0	38.4	64.9	-	100.00	47.8	92.6	46.5	75.1
Tamil Nadu	61.7	84.3	84.1	81.6	83.6	91.2	-	90.6	63.8	84.5
Uttar Pradesh	52.9	76.8	38.9	52.6	66.4	100.00	37.6	59.7	51.1	70.1
West Bengal	65.5	84.3	53.7	66.6	79.6	91.8	57.7	87.3	61.7	82.2
All India	55.7	81.1	52.1	69.8	73.7	91.1	54.2	87.1	56.0	79.8

Source: NSSO Report No. 473: Literacy and Levels of Education in India 1999-2000.

Conclusions

In India more than 70 per cent of the population is living in rural areas. The number of rural illiterates is more than the urban illiterates. There is no doubt that in India, there is a phenomenal development in education after independence. The population of literates in India increased from 12.6 millions in 1901 to 566.71 millions in 2001. The rural literacy in India increased from 12.10 per cent in 1951 to 59.40 per cent in 2001. The ratio between urban and rural literates which was 2.86 : 1.00 in 1951 has reduced to 1.35 : 1.00 in 2001. Kerala has the highest overall literacy rate of 90.92 per cent whereas the lowest literacy level is in Bihar (47.53%) as per 2001 census. The disparity of literacy rate has been decreasing in both males and females in both SCs and STs. In both urban and rural areas, the literacy rate was the highest for persons belonging to the 'Others' group (i.e. Other than SC, ST, and OBC). The literacy rate was lower in rural India for 'lslam' compared to other religions. The literacy rate in Christians is the highest in rural as well as urban areas.

We conclude that urban-rural literate ratio still calls for more vigorous efforts especially among the rural female population. Much still remains to be done. Rural women need to wake up and actively participate in the movement for universalisation of literacy. Special effort needs to be paid to promote rural literacy among various groups comprising SCs and STs especially among the female components of these groups.

References

Krishna G. and Shyam, M. (1978), "Regional Aspects of urban and Rural Differential in India, 1971", The Journal of Development Areas, Vol. 13, No.1, pp. 11-21.

Krishna, G. and Shyam, M. (1973), "Spatial Perspective on Progress of Female Literacy in India: 1901-71; Pacifi viewpoint, Vol. 13, pp. 22-36.

Mehta Arun C. (2006), Elementary Education in India, Analytical Report 2004-2005, Published by National Institute of Education

Planning and Administration and Ministry of Human Resource Development, GOI.

Singh, Nina. (1998), "Female Literacy in India: The Emerging Trends," Population Geography, Vol. 20. Nos. 1 & 2, June-Dec. 1998, pp. 23-26.

UNESCO. (1990), Final Report of World Conference on Education for All: Meeting Basic Learning Needs, 5-9 March, 1990, Thailand.

United Nations. (2005), Economics and Social Survey of Asia and the Pacific 2005, Economics and Social Commission for Asia and The Pacific, New York, 2005, pp.220.

United Nations Development Programme (2003), Human Development report, 2003, Oxford University Press, New York.

United Nations Development Programme. (2004), World Development Report, 2004, Oxford University Press, Oxford

UNDP. (2004), "Human development Report 2004", Cultural Liberty in Today's Diverse world, New York: Oxford University Press.

26

MDGS and Girl Child Basic Education: Some Issues and Perspectives

Dr. B. Ratna Kumari
Dr. T. Nirmala Jyothi

Introduction

Education is essential for the development of any state and this is evident from the above. Right to education has been considered as a human right which naturally accrues to any person by virtue of being born as a human. It is therefore the fundamental duty of all states to ensure this right to its people indiscriminately. In India women were deprived of basic education owing to various social, economic, political factors. So while creating measures for spreading education for all care has to be taken to evolve special procedure to solve the problem of Girl Child illiteracy and steps to be taken to bring them to the main stream. In this direction SAARC has declared the Year 1990 as the SAARC Year of the Girl Child and the decade of 1991-2000 was designated as the SAARC Decade of the Girl Child to sensitize the world governments towards girl child issues including education. All the efforts should converge at ensuring education for both genders equally.

The Articles in the Constitution have provided the justification for various judicial pronouncements in favor of right to education as a fundamental right. These have provided the platform for the Universal Elementary Education as basic human right. The Courts have gone a long way in promoting the right to education and making State responsible for the same which has led to the inclusion of right to education as the fundamental right in the long run. The Government of India has made an attempt to enhance the girl child's education.

Need of the Study

The girl child in the age group 0-18 years comprise nearly one fourth of the country's total population and 45% of the country's female population. Hence there is an urgent need to study the status of girl child in terms of the declining sex ratio, education and training and challenges under the globalization process with relate to India.

Objectives

The main aim of the present research study is to focus on the status of girl child and the challenges in India for their empowerment process with relate to MDGs. The objectives of the study are as follows:

- To study the sex ratio of girl child in India and the threats faced by girl child in our country.
- To review the goals of MDGs and X Five Year Plan regarding girl child's basic education in India in general and Andhra Pradesh in particular.
- To assess the situation of girl child education, schooling and
- To suggest the strategies for girl child 's basic education.

STATUS OF THE GIRL CHILD

The care and focus given to a child as a girl and as an adolescent with focus on her health and nutrition, education and economic potential determines her empowerment as a woman. A healthy, literate and empowered adolescent girl will be able to contribute positively to the society (GOI 2007).

DECLINING SEX RATIO

The sex ratio in India has been unfavorable to girls. The overall sex ratio was 927 in 1991 which improved to 933 in 2001. But for the 0-6 age group, it has fallen from 945 in 1991 to 927 in 2001. Life expectancy at birth has improved, both for males and females at all levels (63 for females and 61.3 for males in 2001). IMR has come down to 63 in 2002 (65 for females & 62 for males) & child mortality rate of 71.1 (2001) (71.6-70.5). However, at each age group, there are comparatively less number of girls than boys:

Table 1
Child Sex Ratio Over the Decade 1991-2001

Rank 2001	*States*	*Child Sex Ration* 2007	1991	*Difference 2001-1991*
1.	Punjab	793	875	-82
2.	Haryana	820	879	-59
3.	Gujarat	879	928	-49
4.	Himachal Pradesh	897	951	-54
5.	Rajasthan	909	916	-7
6.	Uttar Pradesh	915	928	-13
7.	Maharashtra	917	946	-29
	INDIA	927	945	-18
8.	Goa	933	964	-31
9.	Madhya Pradesh	933	952	-19
10.	Bihar	938	959	-21
11.	Tamil Nadu	939	948	-9
12.	Karnataka	949	960	-11
13.	Orissa	950	967	-17
14.	Manipur	961	974	-13
15.	Arunachal Pradesh	961	982	-21
16.	Kerala	963	958	5

Contd....

Rank 2001	*States*	*Child Sex Ration* 2007	1991	*Difference* 2001-1991
17.	Wes Bengal	963	967	-4
18.	Andhra Pradesh	964	975	-11
19.	Assam	964	975	-11
20.	Mizoram	971	969	2
21.	Tripura	975	967	8
22.	Nagaland	975	993	-18
23.	Meghalaya	975	986	-11
24.	Sikkim	986	965	21

Source: Calculated from Census of India, 2001, Rustagi 2003.

Legal action to stop female foeticide dates back to the Pre-Natal Diagnostic Technique (Regulation and Prevention of Misuse Act, 1994) which had been enacted in an attempt to reduce the imbalance in sex ratio. Keeping in view the emerging technologies, it has been further amended. The Pre-conception and Prenatal Diagnostic Techniques (Prohibition of Sex Selection) Act (2003) has broadened the existing ban on sex determination to prompt the use of preconception and pre-implementation gene diagnosis and other technologies for sex selection. Use other technologies for sex selection. Use of ultrasound machines has been brought within the purview of this Act. Other new provisions include maintenance of written records of procedures carried out (not previously required by doctors, and the vesting in state, district and sub district level authorities of powers equivalent to civil courts to ensure compliance with the law and to follow up reports on violation and misconduct.

Other relevant legislative enactments include amendment to the Medical Termination of Pregnancy Act 1971, (amended in 2002) which includes specific punishment of conduct of illegal abortions by unqualified persons and at places not approved by the concerned authority. Moreover, the authority has been decentralized to District Health Officers.

Mass communication and media are widely being used for disseminating messages condemning female foeticide. Government of India launched the 'Save the Girl Child Campaign' with a view to lessen son preference by highlighting achievements of young girls. Ms. Aruna Kesavan had been appointed as 'Brand Ambassadress' for the campaign for the year 2005. Ms. Sanya Mirza was the Ambassadress for the year 2004.

Responding to the declining sex ratio as a social problem, the Akal Takth-the highest seat of spiritual and temporal authority amongst Sikhs-issued a hukumnama (diktat) on April 6, 2001, prohibiting prenatal sex determination to stop the practice of female foeticide.

Strict enforcement of the act and monitoring by non-governmental organizations has resulted in the cancellation of the licenses of several local doctors and registrations of some ultrasound clinics.

The Janani Suraksha Scheme (revamped National Maternity Benefit Scheme) is a package of services geared at reducing maternal mortality female foeticide and gender disparity. It also aims at improving registration of births and deaths amongst most disadvantaged strata of population, by increasing access to institutional delivery. Under the scheme, pregnant women will get Rs. 500/- after delivery of a male child and Rs. 1000/- after delivery of female child.

A National Commitment Campaign was launched on the occasion of World Population Day on 11th July 2003 focusing on two key elements - Safe Motherhood and Adolescence. It included a signature campaign by students, politicians, sports persons and film stars in favour of the slogan, 'Beti ho ya beta, rakhein parivar chota', whether boy or girl keep family small'.

In addition to legal action and awareness campaigns, Balika Samriddhi Yojana was lunched in 1997 to help in raising the overall status of the girl child and bring about positive change in family and bring about a positive change in family and community attitudes. A cash grant of Rs. 500 is made to the mother of a girl (up to 2 per mother) and a further amount is invested in a financial instrument for education of the girl child and to make her economically independent. This will be paid to the girl when she attains the age of 18 years and remains unmarried till then.

The benefits and means of delivery were redesigned in 1999-2000. In addition, the girl child is entitled to receive a scholarship for each class of study successfully completed by her. The continuance of the scheme has been approved, and the Department proposes to make the scheme more attractive and easy to operate by decreasing the number of transactions and increasing the initial deposit.

Issues in Perspective

Demographic

Low Enrolment Ratios of girls in general and S.C. and S.T. girls in particular at Upper primary and Secondary levels. High dropout rates among ST girls at Primary level. High Dropout rate among girls at Upper primary level. Very High dropout rate among S.C. and S.T girls at Upper primary level.

Access

Parental fear of insecurity for out-station schooling of girls. Lack of suitable access for schooling of rural girls at secondary level of education. Lack of proper access for schooling of S.T. girls at Upper Primary and Secondary levels. Lack of proper access for schooling of out of school girls in work situations.

Enrolment and Retention

Low Enrolment Ratios of girls in general and S.C. and S.T. girls in particular at Upper primary and Secondary levels. High dropout rates among ST girls at Primary level. High Dropout rate among girls at Upper primary level. Very High dropout rate among S.C. and S.T girls at Upper primary level.

Child Labour

Lack of adequate machinery for the effective implementation of prevention of child labour Act and their schooling. Inadequate follow up of mainstreaming of the children attending RBCs and NRBCs. Lack of needed attention in the effective organization of alternative schooling system for mainstreaming of out of school children.

Quality

Increase in cadre strength of teachers due to provincialisation of services of teachers and increase administrative work load of the District Education Officers and Mandal Education Officers leaving little scope for academic supervision of schools and monitoring of school programmes. Massive educational program being handled by junior level officers who lack adequate managerial capabilities.

Table 2
Literacy Rate in Andhra Pradesh

Year	*Persons*	*Males*	*Females*
1961	21.19	30.19	12.03
1971	24.57	33.18	15.75
1981	35.66	46.83	24.16
1991	44.08	55.12	32.72
2001	61.11	70.85	51.17

Source: Census Abstract Andhra Pradesh, Series-29, Vol. 1

Table 3
Girls per 1000 Boys in Different Age Groups

	Rural		*Urban*		*Combined*	
Census Years	*0-4 Years*	*5-14 Years*	*0-4 Years*	*5-14 Years*	*0-4 Years*	*5-14 Years*
1991	983	948	965	959	978	951
2001	967	947	958	962	965	951

Primary Source: Census Abstract Andhra Pradesh, Series - 29, Vol.1

FEMALE LITERACY IN ANDHRA PRADESH-AT A GLANCE

In 2001, the female literacy level in Andhra Pradesh is recorded as 50.43% which is 17.71 points higher than the literacy level of 32.72% in 1991. The male literacy is 70.32% in 2001 while it was 55.13% in 1991. As stated above, the percentage increase of literacy level among male population (15.19 points) is lesser than among the female population (17.71) in the state. Nonetheless, the below table shows that fourteen out of the 23 districts records a variation of more than 20 points between male and female literacy level even in

2001. This shows the urgency to formulate specific strategies to improve female literacy in the state.

Table 4
Difference in Male/Female Literacy Levels Among Districts

Difference in Male/ Female Literacy Rate in Points	*Number of Districts*	*Districts*
0-10 Points (Range 9.06-10.24)	2	East Godavari, West Godavari
10-20 Points (Range 11.2-19.56)	7	Hyderabad, Krishna, Nellore, Guntur, Khammam, Ranga Reddy, Vishakapatnam
Above 20 Points (Range 21.84-26.29)	14	Chittoor, Vizianagaram, Srikakulam, Warangal, Prakasam, Karimnagar, Nalgonda, Adilabad, Mahabubnagar, Ananthapur, Nizamabad, Medak, Kurnool, Cuddapah

Source: Census Abstract Andhra Pradesh, Series - 29, Vol.1

Table 5
Area wise Literacy Rates

	1991 Census			2001 Census		
Area	*Male*	*Female*	*Total*	*Male*	*Female*	*Total*
Rural	47.28	23.92	35.74	65.35	43.5	54.5
Urban	75.81	56.41	66.32	83.19	68.74	76.09

Source: Census Abstract Andhra Pradesh, Series-29, Vol. 1

Table 6
Disparities in Literacy Rates Among Male & Female in Different Population Groups 1991 & 2001 Census

	Literacy Rates	
Category	*1991 Census*	*2001 Census*
Urban Male	75.81	83.19
Urban Female	56.41	68.74
Rural Male	47.28	65.35
Rural Female	23.92	43.50
SC Male	41.88	63.51
SC Female	20.92	43.35
ST Male	25.25	47.66
ST Female	8.68	26.11

Source: Census Abstract Andhra Pradesh, Series - 29, Vol.1

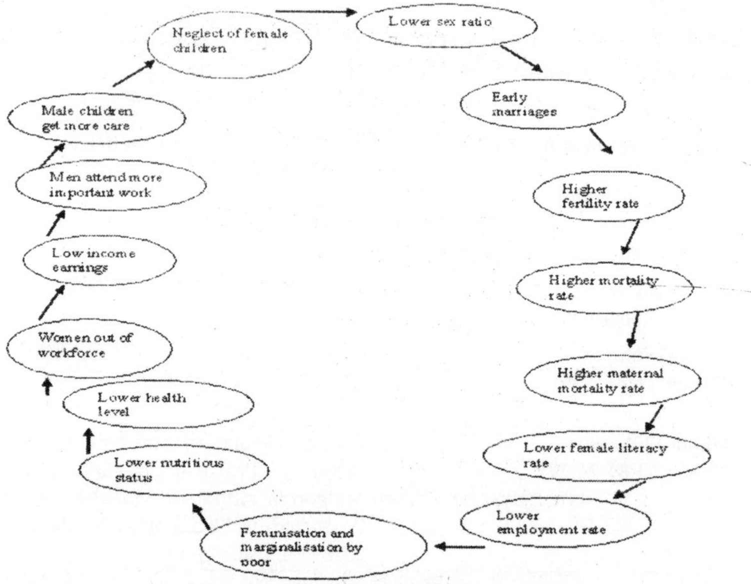

Figure 1. Vicious Circle of Girl Child's Life.

Millennium Development Goals

At the Millennium Summit in September 2000, 147 world leaders agreed to a global compact known as the Millennium Development Goals (MDGs). These consisted of eight goals and were backed by an action plan with 18 quantifiable targets combating poverty, hunger, disease, illiteracy, environmental degradation and discrimination against women. The MDGS consisted of the following:

- Eradicate extreme poverty and hunger.
- Achieve universal primary education.
- Promote gender equality and empower women.
- Reduce child mortality.
- Improve maternal health.
- Combat HIV/AIDS, malaria and other diseases.
- Ensure environmental sustainability.
- Develop a global partnership for development.

The MDG consisted of basic human rights-the rights of each person on the planet to health, education, shelter, and security. These goals have set target for the achievement of the above basic rights which are fundamental to all human beings irrespective of their nationality.

MDG's and Girl Child Basic Education

Achieving universal primary education is one of the important MDGs. The MDG's have set a universal target that by 2015 all children everywhere, boys and girls alike will be able to complete a full course of primary schooling. All the States have been urged to take steps in this direction to achieve the above target.

The MDG's has also set the promotion of gender equality and empowerment of women as one of the important goals. In most of the countries there exists blatant gender inequality leading to women deprived of most of their rights including their right to education. Considering this MDG's have set the following target for the achievement of goal of gender equality in education:

Eliminate gender disparity in primary and secondary education preferably by 2005, and at all levels by 2015.

In most of the developing countries children are unable to avail education due to poverty, which has been major or in fact the factor depriving children from their right to education. MDG's have set eradication of extreme poverty and hunger as the primary goal. Towards the achievement of the said goal the targets set are:

- Reduce by half the proportion of people living on less than a dollar a day.
- Reduce by half the proportion of people who suffer from hunger.

This will go a great way in improving the living standards of people across the globe thereby improving their quality of life by making them avail basic necessities in life. The eradication of poverty will lead to fulfilment of most of the other basic human rights including education, as poverty is one of the key hurdles in the achievement of the same.

Most of the MDG's are interconnected goals and cannot be held in isolation. They are basic human rights which every human being is entitled to and achievement of each goal is essential for the overall well being. The achievement of each goal will provide the basis for the achievement of the other.

Elementary Education: A Review

NPE proposed to set up new primary schools according to the norms in unserved Habitations. These schools were supposed to be opened by the State Governments following the norms specified under Operation Blackboard. The norms of OBB specified that there should be atleast two teachers in a primary school and one of them should be a woman teacher and each primary school should have at least two pucca classrooms. NPE also recommended the expansion of infrastructure at the upper primary level to increase enrolment at this stage. The norm of providing an upper primary school within 3 km walking distance has been relaxed to benefit the girl child.

Table 7

Area-wise Schooling Facilities (Total & Girl's schools) 1993-2002

Primary Schools

	1993		*2002*		*Growth % 1993-2002*	
Area	*Total*	*Girls*	*Total*	*Girls*	*Total*	*Girls*
Rural	44412	119	53883	614	21.33	415.97
Urbar	4729	93	7245	246	53.2	164.52
Total	49141	212	61128	860	24.39	305.66

Source: VI AIES, 1993 Report, VII AISES, 2002, Data Tables

Table 8

Upper Primary Schools

	1993		*2002*		*Growth % 1993-2002*	
Area	*Total*	*Girls*	*Total*	*Girls*	*Total*	*Girls*
Rural	4724	29	11904	149	151.99	413.79
Urban	1657	38	3191	65	92.58	71.05
Total	6381	67	15095	214	136.56	219.4

Source: VI AIES, 1993 Report, VII AISES, 2002, Data Tables.

Table 9
Secondary Schools

	1993		2002		Growth % 1993-2002	
Area	*Total*	*Girls*	*Total*	*Girls*	*Total*	*Girls*
Rural	4762	139	8280	414	73.88	197.84
Urban	2197	347	4085	407	85.94	17.29
Total	6959	486	12365	821	77.68	68.93

Source: VI AIES, 1993 Report, VII AISES, 2002, Data Tables

Table 10
Gender Parity in Enrolment

	Percentage of Enrolment to Total Enrolment					
	Primary Stage		Upper Primary Stage		Secondary Stage	
Year	*Boys*	*Girls*	*Boys*	*Girls*	*Boys*	*Girls*
1956	63.07	36.93	79.29	20.71	84.33	15.67
2000	51.12	48.88	55.26	44.74	57.15	42.85
2004	50.63	49.37	52.39	47.61	53.81	46.19
Target Year 2006	51	49	51	49	52	48
Target Year 2008	51	49	51	49	51	49

Source: Tables of Seventh All India Education Survey, 2002

Table 11
Percentage of Girls in School Enrolment 1956-57 to 2004-05

Year	*Primary (I-V)*	*Upper Primary (VI-VII)*	*Secondary (VIII-X)*	*Total (I-X)*
1956-57	37.08	20.71	15.67	34.22
2000-01	48.88	44.74	42.85	47.29
2004-05	49.37	47.61	46.19	48.34

Source: Tables of Seventh All India Education Survey, 2002

Table 12
Dropout Rates-2004-05

Category	*Primary Stage (%)*	*Upper Primary Stage (%)*	*Secondary Stage (%)*
ST Girls	56.94	78.37	85.11
ST Boys	51.27	72.69	81.16
SC Girls	34.4	61.65	72.59
SC Boys	32.77	56.92	68.42
All Girls	32.14	54.46	65.24
All Boys	31.77	51.96	62.30

Source: Selected Educational Statistics, 2004-05, Director of School Education, AP.

Gender Parity in Enrolment

The millennium development goal sets a target of achieving gender parity in primary and secondary levels by 2005. In terms of enrolment at primary level, Andhra Pradesh has achieved the target by 2004 itself. The growth rate of enrolment of girls at Upper primary and secondary levels is rapid and the current boy-girl ratios are 52: 47 and 54: 46 respectively. However, attaining gender parity at upper primary and secondary levels remain to be achieved. If the current trend of growth in girls' enrolment is maintained, particularly at upper primary (8% per annum) and secondary levels (13% per annum), gender parity can be achieved by 2008 positively.

The Tenth Five Year Plan - Gender Specific Programs for Achieving the UEE: A Review

The Tenth Five-Year Plan has planned the following programs for UEE. These programs are more oriented to reduce the gender disparity and bring in the drop out children especially girls back to the education system to achieve the goal of UEE. It can be rightfully asserted that the achievement of UEE is impossible without the inclusion of schemes for the promotion of girl child education which fact has been recognized by the tenth five year plan and has formed the basis for the same.

The tenth five year plan has also recommended gender specific programs to reduce gender disparity in education. To achieve the above, the plan has emphasized on the existing women centric programs such as Mahila Samakhya, and two new schemes, the Kasturba Gandhi Swantantra Vidyalaya (KGSV) and the National Programme for the Education of Girls at the Elementary Level (NPEGEL). The KGSV and NPEGEL were proposed to take the following features during the plan period:

- focus on educationally backward areas in girls' education;
- focus on girls from the disadvantaged sections like those belonging to SC/ST, minorities etc.;

- tackling gender-specific issues that prevent girls and women from having access to education;
- providing women and adolescent girls with the necessary support structure, and an informal learning environment to create opportunities for education;
- creating circumstances for larger participation of women and girls in formal and non- formal education programmes; and
- Helping girls to overcome socio-cultural and economic factors inhibiting their access to elementary education.

The tenth five year plan has laid down strategies for improvement of quality as the achievement of UEE will be hollow without ensuring quality education. In this regard the plan has stressed on Improving the quality of textbooks, Improving the quality of infrastructural facilities like toilets for girls, equipment and support services, playgrounds, classrooms. The main thrust of the tenth five year plan is to ascertain that all primary level schools have pucca buildings with all supporting infrastructural facilities.

The tenth five year plan has provisions for the improving the quality and performance of teachers education also. It has an elaborate strategy addressing the drop-outs too. The plan has identified that girls form the major chunk of the drop outs owing to various factors and has entrusted the duty of bringing them back while retaining the existing ones to various departments involved.

The tenth five year plan has laid immense importance on the UEE in general and girl child education in particular. The plan has clearly laid down strategies towards UEE. While there are general provisions applicable to both boys and girls towards UEE there are special provisions for girl child treating them as a special category.

Sarva Shiksha Abhiyaan

Under the tenth five year plan the SSA has to provide access and motivation to those outside the school system who are mostly girls, SCs/STs children, working children, urban deprived children, disabled children and children in difficult circumstances, without compromising on the quality of education.

The 'National Programme for Education of Girls at Elementary Level (NPEGEL)

NPEGEL has been formulated for education of under privileged/disadvantaged girls from class I to VIII as a separate and distinct gender component plan of Sarva Shiksha Abhiyan (SSA). This was started as an amendment to the scheme of SSA for providing additional components for education of girls at elementary level.

This scheme lays down a community based approached i.e. it involves actors at all levels following a participatory approach in its implementation. This scheme targets the out of school girls, drop outs, over aged girls who have not completed elementary education, working girls, girls from marginalised social groups, girls with low attendance and girls with low levels of achievement.

Objective

The primary objective of the NPEGEL is to reduce the gender gap in enrolment at elementary level especially among the SC/STs. The objectives of this scheme include:

- To develop and promote facilities to provide access and to facilitate retention of girls
- To ensure greater participation of women and girls in the field of education
- To improve the quality of education through various interventions and to stress upon the relevance and quality of girls' education for their empowerment.

KASTURBA GANDHI BALIKA VIDYALAYA (KGBV)

Kasturba Gandhi Balika Vidyalaya (KGBV) is being implemented by the Government of India by setting up upto 750 residential schools with boarding facilities at elementary level for girls belonging predominantly to the SC, ST, BC and minorities in difficult areas. The scheme will be coordinated with the existing schemes of Department of Elementary See generally Performance Budget 2006-07, Department of School Education, overnment of Andhra Pradesh Education & Literacy viz. Sarva Shiksha Abhiyan (SSA), National Programme for Education of Girls at Elementary Level NPEGEL) and Mahila Samakhya (MS).

Objective

The primary objective of the KGBV is to reduce the gender gap in enrolment at elementary level especially at the upper primary level in the rural areas and among disadvantaged communities. The objective of this scheme is to ensure access and quality education to the girls of disadvantaged groups of society by setting up residential schools with boarding facilities at elementary level.

Strategies

Between 500 to 750 residential schools will be opened in the country, in a phased manner over the 10th Plan period at an estimated cost of Rs. 19.05 lakh as recurring cost and Rs. 26.25 lakh as non-recurring cost, per school. Initially, the proposed schools shall be opened in rented or other available Government buildings after deciding the location. The district administration has to ensure that the residential schools are set up only in those backward blocks that do not have residential schools for elementary education of girls under any other scheme of Ministry of Social Justice & Empowerment and Ministry of Tribal Affairs.

Reaching the Girl Child

Access

"The concept of a National System of Education implies that, up to a given level, all students, irrespective of caste, creed, location or sex, have access to education of a comparable quality" says the Nation Policy on Education, 1986. It goes on to say "to promote equality, it will be necessary to provide for equal opportunity to all, not only in access, but also in the condition for success". This is quite the essence of the universalisation task, and means that needs of educationally disadvantaged groups would have to be given maximum attention.

The largest such groups are:

- Girls and women.
- Scheduled castes and Scheduled tribes.
- Minorities.
- The handicapped, and
- Other educationally disadvantaged groups i.e. working children, slum-dwellers, inhabitants of hilly, desert and other inaccessible areas, etc.

Issues in Perspective

MEO is the nodal officer responsible for monitoring and implementation of various schemes and programs along with regular academic responsibilities. Precedence over the former is leading to low quality of teaching. No direct recruitment in the cadre of Mandal Education Officer. Low percentage share of female teachers in rural areas at primary, upper primary and secondary stages of education. Lack of female teachers' in-position about 51 % of Primary schools, 25 % of Upper primary schools, 16% of secondary schools. Lack of at least 2 classrooms still (2002) in about 40% of primary schools which include 8% of schools with no classrooms. Lack of adequate sanitary facilities for girls at Upper primary and secondary levels. Lack of adequate teacher motivation to provide opportunities for girls. Lack of proper learning environment in teaching-learning situations due to overcrowded classrooms, lack of proper school buildings etc. Lack of adequate infrastructural facilities like teaching aids, furniture, equipment, games and sports material etc. Lack of adequate concern for children with special education needs. Lack of special attention to the enrolment, retention and learning achievements of children of focused groups like children of S.C., S.T., religious and linguistic minorities, street children etc. Inadequate involvement of the community in school programmes like enrolment, attendance, retention and pupil achievement.

STRATEGIES FOR GIRL CHILD EDUCATION

Demographic

Building up public awareness on the threats of declining girl child sex ratio and its impact on the social life. Awareness campaigns on educating girls at least up to class X. The fallout would be increase in the age of marriage and resultant decrease in maternal mortality rate which is a Millennium Development Goal. Encouraging competitions among populations of different habitations in achieving total literacy through monetary and other resource incentives including church. Giving boost to the total literacy programs in all areas of the state by involving the entire academic faculty from primary to university level at least for a period of 2 years in a concerted manner.

Access

Providing secondary school facility in each gram Panchayat having high SC population, within a radius of 3 km (in relaxation of the present norm of 5 Km) to enable the enrolment and retention of rural and SC girls in a phased manner. Provision of at least Upper primary facility closer to remote ST habitations through up gradation of GVVKs/ Primary schools/Alternative schools for the enrolment and retention of ST girls. Providing free bus service to all elementary school children and girls up to higher secondary by improving the bus connectivity and also the frequency. Building up public awareness on the need and importance of girls education through community mobilisation, awareness campaigns, media etc. Common school system and neighbourhood schools to be introduced.

Enrolment and Retention

Community mobilisation through awareness campaigns, enrolment drives and gram sabhas for the enrolment of the girls particularly at Upper primary and secondary levels. Parent Teacher Associations and School Committees to ensure that all girls in the village attend schools by enlisting the help of Self Help Groups and Mahila Mandals. Enrolment drive in June to mobilize enrolment of girls. The program to be repeated every year before reopening of schools. Special awards to schools/School Committees which achieve total enrolment and total retention of girls in the village. Preference to habitation/villages which have achieved 100% enrolment and retention of girls in Schools in sanction of public facilities like post offices/e-Seva centres/primary health centre/cooperative bank etc. The current policy of the State is bifurcation of Primary sections from Secondary schools as when they are upgraded in to secondary schools. Clubbing of Primary and Secondary schools which are functioning in the same premises to ensure total retention of girls. Capacity building for the officers of the education department who are designated as enforcement officers. All incentives provided for girls by different departments like education, social welfare, tribal welfare, women and child welfare, projects like SSA, Velugu, NCLP etc to be disbursed to the beneficiaries in the gram sabhas. Every Primary school to have a pre-primary section in villages where Anganwadi centres are not available, which will relieve the girl child of the sibling burden.

Quality

Restructuring of the district administration and upgradation of the post of District Educational Officer into Joint Director cadre who would be assisted by two District Educational Officers one in charge of Primary education (including SSA, Mid day meal programme) and the other for Secondary education. Direct recruitment in the cadre of Mandal Education Officer Capacity building courses to be offered to all officers Sensitizing functionaries on girl child education.

Teachers

To ensure atleast one female teacher in every Primary, Upper Primary and Secondary School. Sensitizing teachers on gender issues and steps to be taken by the teachers encouraging girls' student participation in the classroom activities, co-curricular activities to ensure equity in participation and attainment. Ensuring the availability of all subject teachers all through out the year.

Accountability

Norms of accountability for teachers to be formulated and implemented with incentives for good performance and disincentives for non-performance as laid down in NPE, 1986 and POA 1992. Ensuring women teachers in all schools. Introducing the clause of fixed tenure of 2 to 3 years for all newly recruited teachers in areas of low female literacy. Learning guarantee to be provided by the school at large to the children, parents and community.

Infrastructure

Infrastructural facilities to be enhanced for schools with high Girls enrolment. Provision of sanitation facilities in all Primary, Upper Primary and Secondary schools by convergence of various departmental initiatives like SSA, Indiramma, PMGY etc. A need based approach to be followed. Periodic review of the existing facilities in the residential schools and annual replenishment of the facilities.

Towards Better Learning Leading to Empowerment of Girls

Teachers to be made responsible. Tutorial classes. School level physical education activities are to be organized. Launching of confidence developing measures through various monetary level. Cash incentives to SC/ST girls with more than 80% aggregate

Social Audit

The school charter to be displayed Periodic evaluation of the performance of the school by the community. Participatory appraisal of the performance of all the schools is to be taken up at mandal level. Panchayats and Self Help Groups (SHGs) conducive school environment for girl child etc.

Schemes

- Andhra Pradesh Primary Education Project (APPEP).
- Operation Blackboard (OBB).
- District Institutes of Educational Training (DIET).
- District Primary Education Programme (DPEP).
- National Programme of Nutritional Support to Primary Education (School Meal Programme)(NPNSPE).
- Sarva Shiksha Abhiyan (SSA).
- The National Programme for Education of Girls at Elementary (NPEGEL).
- Kasturba Gandhi Balika Vidyalaya (KGBV).

References

Census of India (2001), Provisional Population Totals Paper-2 of 2001 series-29.

"From Girl Child to Person", (1995), UNESCO.

Human development Report (2005), UNDP.

India Education Report, (2002), A Profile of Basic Education, NIEPA.

Jain, (2003), M.P. "Indian Constitutional Law".

National Policy Education, (1986).

NFHS-2, (1998-99), Andhra Pradesh.

27

Rural Empowerment Through Science and Technology

Ch. Subha Kumar

Introduction

The growing billions of citizens around the world, especially the poor and the disadvantaged no longer believe that the responsibility of goods and macro societies (National/ Government) as well as micro societies (Organizations) is the exclusives responsibility of Government. The language of development is fast changing to mean. Co-governance, coline governance, partnership ventures networking. Among elected, the burning issues of individual and community rights entitlements and empowerment are beginning, negotiation on-all aimed at partnership and networking based support for sustainable development and rural development.

India has a long and distinguished tradition in Science and Technology from the ancient times to great achievements during this century. The later half point to independence has been related long to pure research. The time of independence, our scientific and technological infrastructure was neither strong nor organized as compared to the developed world. This had resulted in our being technologically dependent on the skills and capability largely commensurate with meeting national needs has been created minimizing our dependence on other countries. Large countries from smallest sophisticated has been established covering a wide range of utilities, services and goods. There is no reservoirs and expertise well acquitted with most modern advances in basic and applied areas that are equipped to make choice between available technologies, to absorb readily new technologies and private framework for future.

In the process of rural development, science and technology must necessarily play a crucial role. Rural India has abundant human resources mostly upon unskilled nature also rural developments are traditional bound and cautious in adopting new method and approaches. They have problem of lack of capital and low capacity to bear the risk of any loss. Therefore, intermediate technology or software technology, which is need-based within the available means and which suits well the aspirations, environment and culture of the people.

Science and Technology

The word 'technology' means different things to different people. Technology refers to a particular type of techniques or method of doing something with special skills or knowledge. The knowledge used in doing a thing may not necessarily be one written in a book based on scientific theory. A person may acquire knowledge with practice. His own experience in particular work states that technology is not primarily public knowledge, available in written form and easily transformable from one country to another, but know-how, learned in the doing by trail and error, the practioner's skill rather than the scientists theory. A technology is always embodied in a set of factors of production used both on applications of growing knowledge of science and scientific theory as well as on certain skills or arts evolved out of experience is well recognized.

India has the third largest man power of scientists engaged and technologists after USA and the erstwhile Russia. There have been many achievements of Indian science and in agriculture in Medicine, electronics and communications in atomic energy and defence also the green revolution, Pockron implosion space satellites and missiles are few examples where the Indian scientists have established that giving necessary political and financial support, time target programmes can be successfully implemented.

Appropriate Technology in Rural Development

There is need for an appropriate technology in different aspects of rural development is as discussed below:

Appropriate Technology in Agriculture: Agricultural situations vary from region to region. There are areas with assured irrigation and abundant capital but with scarce labour. In such situation, widespread use of high yielding variety of technology or capital intensive nature becomes appropriate. The affluent sections of the farm community in such areas substitute capital for labour. However, a major part of cropped area in the country is rain dependent and the problem in one of both land and capital scarcity with lot of uncertainty. Associated with farm production in such situation, land augmenting technologies with labour use becomes necessary.

Animal Husbandry

Artificial insemination technology is an important factor in improving the quality of the cattle wealth. In the field of dairy, economical method of manufacturing milk products under rural conditions have been developed. The shortage of large quantities of milk is now possible by the setting up of chilling plants in rural areas. The modern technology in the field of dairy has already resulted in white revolution in select places for transformation of rural economy. Dairying technology must be popularized in different areas. In the field of poultry development, balance poultry feed have been evolved, strains of birds have been developed with high rate of egg production. Methods have also found for defertilization of eggs with a view to increasing their keeping quality.

Appropriate Education

To facility the rural illiterate in adopting appropriate technology in different aspects of development, appropriate education becomes crucial. The education in rural masses must be at such a type, which could import to them a variety of skills appropriate for their occupation and day-to-day life. Engineers and technologists and extension agents in different fields have to be first trained well in appropriate technology before there are called upon important appropriate technology of rural development.

A vision of science and technology in rural development. In the context of rural development and employment generation activity, it will be desirable not only to have a vision but also to set some priorities. The following prioritized objectives are presented.

1. Greater diffusion and user friendly access of technology and development to alleviate problems of food scarcity, nutrition and health for rural development.
2. Provision of modern infrastructural services of agency, transport and telecommunications especially to the un-reached people in the far flung rural areas which are not otherwise connected.
3. Optional sifting of finite natural resources from a lower to higher productivity level and better yield by provision of state of art technologies.
4. Wide-spread adoption and promotion of technologies of waster prevention through designs of Cyclical processing - and less consumption of raw materials in order to maintain in vital balance and avoid degradation of the economic system.
5. Effective improvement of process technology for optimal use of natural resources with special care.

The section which needs attention on priority basis with special reference to rural areas should be the following:

1. Agricultural and allied sectors and Agricultural based industries development of sustainable crop nutrients and crop conservation materials.
2. Dissemination of Development technologies for rural areas to ensure land management and water management and energy resources of the sustainable development of rural areas.
3. Wide spread utilization of energy conservation and technology, including alternative fuels which are renewable and non-conventional energy.
4. Development and dissemination of technologies relevant to preventive and community health care systems for rural areas.
5. Utilization technologies for betterment of infrastructural facilities such as transport, communication, housing to rural community on priority basis.
6. Ensure betterment of living condition of rural areas through materials, development, biotechnology, electronics and communication in rural areas.
7. Agriculture processing technology with special emphasis on fruits, vegetables, marine products, spices and medicinal plants.
8. Utilization of new materials like polymers, ceramics and composites for utilization in rural constructions.

Conclusion

Effective utilization of science and technology demands that the technologies would find ready acceptability at the lowest tier of rural areas-viz. the gram panchayathi only, if the technologies are user-friendly, eco-friendly and are economically viable. It has been established that for every instrument made in the use of science, technology utilization can occur only if the returns show financial giants to rural poor.

All efforts in the development process in the rural areas, including science and technology, efforts would never successes unless there is wholesome participatory involvement of the people. It also follows that the premises of transporting technology should be for rural beneficiaries. It will not succeed unless the wisdom, experiences with consonance of local percepts of management, in general, is integrated suitability in the process.

References

Arora R.C., (1986), Indian Rural Development, S. Chand & Co.

Bihari L., Patel, (1986), Biogas technology and Rural India, Kuruskutra; Vol. XXXIV, no. 6.

Kumar (1986), Sources Technological in Informal Inventions.

Shukla P.R. (1992), Strategies and Rural Development, Akasdeep Publication, New Delhi, India, 2007, p. 729

Journal of Rural Development, (Oct-Dec 2001), Vol. 20.

28

Basic Education for Empowerment of Weaker Sections

K.J. Sudheer
N. Sony Havilah

Causes and Consequences of Poverty

Illiteracy could be one of the cause and consequence of poverty. Causes can also be distinguished as primary and secondary. What can, however, be safely stated is that there is no single cause that explains poverty fully. The major causes of poverty in the Asia-Pacific region have been identified as high population pressure, unemployment and under employment, low human capital development, lack of assets such as landlessness, lack of access to credit, natural calamities (Tan, Poochang). On other hand it is argued that the basic causes of poverty is ignorance, Lack of Knowledge, skills, and attitudes which are needed for working and living together. But ignorance itself may be due to illiteracy and lack of literacy makes the people weak in the ability to communicate with others and causes their alienation from the society.

Basic Education for Empowerment of the Weaker Sections:

To "empower" a person, literally speaking, is to give power to the person. 'Power' here does not mean a mode of domination over others but a sense of internal strength and confidence to face life, the right to determine one's choices in life, the ability to influence the social processes that affect one's life and the direction of social change. The concept is employed with reference to individuals, population groups, institutions and organizations. Empowerment of women, for example, is to equip women with power. The underlying assumption is that women or whosoever is being empowered are lacking the requisite knowledge and skills to pursue desired goals or to effectively deal with inhibiting situations or circumstances. These goals could be in the spheres of securing gender justice or in fighting social customs that restrict development or in living oppression-free lives. Empowerment has, therefore, to be with concrete reference to the pursuit of a perceived goal or overcoming constricting forces in the way of leading a fulfilling life.

"Empowerment" of the weaker section is equipping the poor with power. In a broad sense, one can say that the poor need to be empowered in order to fight the many constraining afflictions of poverty. These afflictions could be illiteracy, poor health, illness, malnutrition, low income, destitution, low productivity, marginalized social position, low self-esteem and so on. However, although all weaker sections generally share common characteristics and face similar problems, the specific nature of the problems they have to contend which differs according to region, gender, caste, ethnicity and other factors. For example, the poor who are victims of caste hierarchy face social isolation and discrimination in the community The social customs relating to child rearing, education, marriage, occupation and other aspects of life inhibit the growth of women as free human individuals and make them the worst sufferers of poverty.

The empowerment of the poor has many dimensions to it depending upon how one defines poverty and standard of living. A purely quantitative and materialistic view of poverty as "inability to attain a minimal standard of living" may point to their empowerment with reference to income, housing, health, nutrition, and other basic needs. On the other hand if 'poverty' is not restricted to not having enough money or access to material goods and extended to other deeper aspects of life relating to basic human values, culture and spirit, the empowerment of the poor has to bring under its purview a much wider range of goods having to do with the full flowering of the human potential in all its dimensions-physical, intellectual, social, cultural, moral, aesthetic and spiritual. The poor, in this perspective, need empowerment not just in increasing income levels and access to material goods but also in spheres related to their total development as persons.

Education contributes to the changing of human individuals not just in the managerial sense of developing human capitals but in the deeper sense of making new persons out of them, characterized by a heightened awareness of the human conditions, positive and constructive out look of life and a sense of commitment to human values. In other words education acts as a force that leads to empowerment of human values.

How Basic Education Empowers the Weaker Sections

Attacking Ignorance

Implied in the concept of empowerment as acquisition of power to do something one wants to do are two fundamental assumptions. The first is that one knows how to go about achieving one's goal. The other is that at present one does not have the required power (resources) to achieve the goal. A prerequisite to empowerment, whether of individuals or groups, is therefore the eradication or at least reduction of ignorance. Ignorance among the poor about the many aspects of the physical and social world around them may arise mainly from lack of access to information due to illiteracy. The poor may not know, for example, basic rules of health and hygiene, how to make use of basic services, what their basic human rights and freedoms are and how to exercise them, how to make use of cooperatives, credit and savings, and what methods to adopt to increase farm or animal productivity. They may be unaware of the protection given to them under laws governing labour, land reforms, marriage and of the various measures instituted to alleviate their poverty in the form of anti-poverty projects and programmes. A first necessary step in such a case would be to provide such information and knowledge to the poor as would help them in availing of services, increasing their productivity, and organizing themselves to fight against exploitation. Empowerment of the poor entails the provision of access to such information and knowledge. But mere possession of information would not by itself give power to the poor. What is also needed is the capacity to convert information into usable knowledge for solving concrete problems.

Building Skills

Helping the poor to know the 'what' and 'why' of things that affect their lives (for example production and marketing of goods) are a necessary but not a sufficient condition for their empowerment. What the poor also need is the necessary skills and other material and non-material resources required to attain their goals. Poor farmers may know the reasons for their poverty or why they are not able to increase the farm yield. They may know that they have to change their traditional practices and adopt new technologies. But they may not have acquired the skills to use new farm practices. They may also not have access to fertilizers and high quality seeds. More than all, they may not have the required capital to buy their requirements. What is needed in such a situation is the possession of skills-not just the technological ones but also skills related to effective management and resource generation-and the availability of other financial, material and non material resources required to attain the ends. Empowerment of the poor to fight their poverty should therefore include both these aspects of awareness building, and skill development and supply of resources.

ATTITUDES AND VALUES

One of the important causes of poverty (and a major constraint in combating it) is the negative attitudes and value system of the poor. The poor accept their poverty as inevitable, with resignation and fatalism. The poor are unorganized, suffer from low self-esteem and do not know how to work collectively, cooperatively. They are unaware of their rights and afraid to assert their claim to justice. Empowerment would imply, under these circumstances, building of positive attitudes and values like self-confidence, and cooperation and emboldening the poor to collectively fight against exploitation.

MEETING THE LEARNING NEEDS OF POVERTY GROUPS

In more specific terms, basic education contributes to the empowerment of the poor by addressing their very special learning needs. Research findings on the economic, sociological, cultural and psychological dimensions of poverty and the critical analysis of poverty characteristics, causes and consequences point to these needs as: Literacy, numeracy, problem solving and productivity skills to enhance capacity for labour and to creatively respond to income earning opportunities.

29

Rural Agricultural Development Green Revolution: Proposals for Future Plans

Prof. Fathima Kutty Kapil

Introduction

This paper is focused on developing agriculture, water resources, bringing waste lands into productive use, Manures and proposals for future plans. More than 50 million of Andhra Pradesh people live in rural areas. They represent 70 per cent of the states population and its work force and work mainly in agriculture. Agriculture almost the only resource of employment. Individuals are unable to fully realize their potential due to lack of resources, technology, high population growth rate and poor health indicators.

Despite efforts made by the government over the past few decades rural poverty in India continues to be significant. The poverty alleviation/eradication programmes have been strengthened by the government in successive years. In percentage terms of poverty levels have reduced from around 56 per cent of India's population in 1973-74 to around 34 per cent in 1998-1999. The number of rural poor however, has more or less remained static and is estimated to be about 244 million persons. In post colonial India the Rural Development (RD) programmes began with sectoral approach.

Developing Agriculture

Developing agriculture is the key to bringing prosperity to rural Andhra Pradesh and to the States economy. The approach to developing this sector will focus on transforming agriculture from means to subsistence livelihood into a dynamic sector of the economy. Achieving transformation desired will require the following actions: harnessing water resources, integrated development of rain-fed areas, bringing waste and marginal lands into productive use; focusing on high growth sectors; and ensuring policy reform.

Harnessing Water Resources

Harnessing all available water resources is critical to achieving the targeted levels of agricultural growth. This will require a three pronged effort: realizing the maximum irrigation potential of the state; improving the efficiency of the existing irrigation network; and managing water resources through stakeholder participation.

Water Resources

To realize the full potential of surface and ground water resources, the state will construct and complete all feasible major and medium irrigation projects. Where there is no potential for major projects, for instance, in upland areas, it will promote minor irrigation and lift irrigation schemes. This effort has already begun through the implementation of existing irrigation schemes and mobilization of funds from the World Bank, The Overseas Economic Cooperation Fund (OECF) Japan, the National Bank for Agricultural and Rural development (NABARD) and the flotation of 'Irrigation bonds" to complete ongoing projects.

To improve irrigation efficiency the state will improve the maintenance of irrigation systems and introduce new technologies to enhance productivity of water use. Improving maintenance will require a focus on operations and maintenance (O&M), an area that has suffered due to low recovery of operating costs. It will also draw on the assistance of water users themselves to improve irrigation efficiency. This will be the part of state's effort to involve stakeholders in the management of water resources.

New technologies will be another imported element of improving irrigation efficiency. These will include using an irrigation information system to ensure timely and adequate water supply as well as water conservation technologies such as dynamic control systems, sprinkles and drip irrigation.

Finally the state will standardize canals, drains and field channels to close the gap between irrigation potential created, the actual and drip irrigation.

To involve stakeholders in the management of water resources, the state will continue to encourage and support the Water Users Associations (WUA), water resources by raising funds for maintenance, supervising works, deciding on water allocation and improving services. The state will also look to them to encourage water conservation and spread awareness of alternate irrigation systems such as drip and sprinkler systems for horticulture.

Bringing Waste Lands into Productive Use

The state will need to bring waste lands and fallow lands into productive use. This will require substantial investments and the state will have to think through various innovative mechanisms to develop these lands. One method could be to create a business entity in which the government has an equity share to develop these wastelands. The government equity could be distributed among landless labourers.

Proposal for Future Plan

Another method of developing waste lands for the weaker sections will be by allotting wastelands to weaker sections for cultivation and also providing modern methods of agriculture like tractor for a group of people at a nominal rented price. The nominal rent also can be recovered after the harvest because the poor may or may not be in a position to pay the nominal rent also. Green Revolution can be achieved by giving good seeds, irrigation facilities, etc. After one or two harvests the government can start giving loans at a lower interests.

Food Security and Poverty Eradication

Food security and poverty eradication will be achieved in two ways (1) the focus on increased agricultural production will increase food security for rural people engaged in agriculture allied and other activities; (2) For people below the poverty line food and income security will be ensured through a well designed public distribution system, employment generation schemes providing minimum wages and social security measures such as old age and disability pensions. To ensure the effectiveness of social security programmes, the government will involve local communities in their management and encourage them to contribute their local resources to strengthen these programmes.

Criticism

The government is giving agricultural loan. Only the lower middle class and upper middle class are able to take the loan and improve their status. The poor man is not able to take because he has no marginal money to invest. The poor man below the survival status has no land to cultivate. That's why the waste lands to be given to the poor, who are below survival level.

Manuring

Twigs and Leaves are used for manuring. Over a large part of Madras, Coimbatore, the spreading of wild shrubs, such as wild indigo madar avara kolinji, convolvulus and the shoots and leaves of Pangamia glabra and other trees is used much on 'wet' lands. Principally on rice fields the shrubs and leaves are spread green on the fields and then trodden in by foot. The twigs and leaves are spread on the land where rice is to be sown; canal water is let on, and the twigs are trodden into the soil with foot. It is worthy to note that though served by canal irrigation, the compartments or beds in which the water is enclosed are here quite small just as in garden cultivation.

Associated with the use of twigs, leaves for manure is the system of seed-bed cultivation termed rab. This system is employed mainly in the Bombay presidency throughout the districts of heaviest rainfall. The crops for which it is chiefly used are rice and millet called nagli. The word rab literally means 'cultivation'. The process consists in heaping on the spot selected for the seed bed successive layers of cow dung, tree loppings, shrubs, leaves and grass with earth on the top to keep all down; the heap is made about three feet high and then the whole is set fire to. Another system of manuring is that by using silt, tank mud or by the mixing of soils of different character in order to improve the texture of the land.

Nitre or Salt peter (Nitrate or Potash) is a salt with which the soil in many parts of India is impregnated. The accumulations of the salt in all probability have their origin in natural process of nitrification (production of nitrate) which is the solid and liquid excrete of cattle and men as well as vegetable and other refuse have undergone. Wood and other vegetable ashes supply potash in the form of carbonate potash. The potash in the soil itself, more especially, when the soil is clay in nature, no doubt contributes also to production of Nitre. Nitre as a manure is used little owing to its high price. Experiments in the government farms show that it gives considerable increase in the out-turn of cereals and other crops.

Fish manure, which may be considered partly phosphoric manure is prepared in Mangalore and is transported in land within certain distances. This is used by the coffee planters of Coorg and Mysore.

Bone Manure

Bones are practically the only source of supply of phosphates of the soil. Bones are very extensively explored from India, and are but little used in the country itself. The collectors of bones are mostly coolies of Chamar caste. The bones are roughly broken with a hammer conveyed to the nearest station and then left for removal by train. These bones are crushed in mills in Thana near Bombay. The cost of it in the year 1890 was Rs.45/- per ton.

Bones are in most countries regarded as valuable manure for almost all cultivated crops. In almost every where in India the value of bones for manure is disregarded by the cultivator. This is due partly to religious and caste prejudices, partly to the Indian soils. They are however, employed with useful effect by tea and coffee planters.

Year	*Tons*
1884-85	*18,000*
1885-86	22,000
1886-87	18,000
1887-88	26,000
1888-89	33,000
1889-90	44,000

Town Waste as Manure

The manure which could be obtained from towns would if fully utilized, help Andhra Pradesh agriculture very materially. Sanitation is improving and town sweepings and night soils are now used as a manure to a larger extent. In some places a considerable impetus has been given to the cultivation of irrigated crops by the use of pondrette or the contents of trenches in which night soil has been mixed on earth. The pondrette system of disposing of night-soil is from an agricultural point of view eminently satisfactory. It is in no way antagonistic to native usages and if properly carried out, produces a manure which can be carried to some distance by cart.

Proposals For Future Plan in Manuring

I. Twigs and leaves used for manuring in Madras and Coimbatore to be followed in Andhra Pradesh (Report on the Indian Agriculture).

II. Production of Nitrate or Salt Peter which is the solid and liquid excrete of cattle, vegetables and other refuse.

III. Fish manure which is prepared in Mangalore and transported to inland within certain distances also can be followed in coastal Andhra.

IV. Bone Manure, which was prepared in Thana near Bombay and exported to other countries as the static shows 1984 to 1990 can also be used in Andhra Pradesh after raising no objection.

V. Town waste manure which could be obtained from towns and villages if fully utilized help Andhra Pradesh agriculture very much materially.

References

Kutala Lahiri, (2002), Dutt and Gopa Samantra, "State initiatives for Empowerment of Women of rural Communities", Community Development Journal, Oxford University Press, p.137.

Community Development Journal Vol. 37 No. 2 AP-2002, PP 138-156.

Dynamic, Self-Reliant Rural Communities. www.aponline.gov.ac.in

Development of Women and Children in Rural areas Water users Associations Chief Minister's Empowerment of Youth Vana Samrakshana Samitis.

Ibid.

Dynamic, Self Reliant Rural Communities. www.aponline.gov.ac.in

Proposals of Prof. Fathima Kutty Kapil for agricultural development.

Report on the Improvement of Indian Agriculture, p.95.

Fathima Kutty Kapil, (2003), Agrarian Policy in India-East Godavari District, 1925-1947, Andhra University Press, pp.86-87.

Report on the Improvement of Indian Agriculture, p.111

Ibid., p.113

Ibid., p 113-117

Imperial Gazetteer of India, The Indian Empire, Vol. III Economic, Oxford Clarenden Press, 1907 p. 20-22.

Ibid.

Proposals of Prof. Fathima Kutty Kapil for Manures.

Section – IV

30

Women Empowerment: A Case Study of Self Help Groups in Andhra Pradesh

Prof. B. Ramakrishna Rao
Mr. K.V. Somanadh
Dr. P. Hanumantha Rao

Introduction

India has made tremendous progress in various spheres of life during the last five and half decades. Its economy has expanded and diversified, society has become cohesive and polity democratized. It has also been facing many problems, some of which have successfully been solved, but many others still remain unsolved. Poverty is one such challenge India has been facing today. To fill the gaps in the implementation of this erstwhile self-employment programme known as Integrated Rural Development Programme, the Central Government announced a holistic programme called Swarna Jayanti Gram Swarozgar Yojana which is based on group approach to rural development where the rural poor were organized into Self-Help Groups (SHGs) provided micro-credit and took up viable economic activities on their own.

While most of the development programmes address themselves to alleviating the conditions of the poor who live below subsistence levels, women who form the single largest disadvantaged section of gender oppression to the already existing caste and class oppression are seldom given priority in such programmes. Majority of these women come from the lowest strata of the caste/class hierarchy. Their caste affiliation restricts their mobility, their class membership limits their access to productive resource, while their gender role minimizes their economic participation, it being limited to only extensions of domestic orders. As such, they are marginalized as workers, are found in situations of immense exploitation and victimization and are therefore forced to a status of invisibility and powerlessness. Despite their invisibility in the labour force and their powerlessness in the family, it is their meager but substantial income that sustain and meets the needs of the family. This is particularly the case when unemployment among men is high and where the major item of expenditure is alcohol and gambling.

Empowerment of Women

Women constitute about 48 per cent of the total population of the country as per the 2001 census; they suffer many disadvantages as compared to men in terms of literacy rates, labour participation rates and earnings. In order to address issues relating to social and economic advancement of women, the Department of Women and Child Development under the Ministry of Human Resource Development has been implementing various schemes. The National Policy of Employment of Women was adopted in the country in 2001 with the ultimate objective of ensuring women their right.

The major strategies of Women Empowerment include- social empowerment, economic empowerment and gender justice i.e. to eliminate all types of discrimination against women and the girl child. Social empowerment of women is designed to create an enabling environment by adopting various affirmative policies and programmes for development women, besides providing them easy and equal access to all the basic minimum services to enable them to realize their full potential. Education being an important tool for social empowerment of women, specific schemes to provide incentives to promote education, especially amongst girl children and reduce the school dropout rates are being implemented. Two important schemes viz. 'Sarva Shiksha Abhiyan' and 'Mahila Samakhya' is being implemented by Department of Education as a special effort to stretch the reach of education especially to the girl child. In addition, the Department of Women and Child Development (DWCD) implements the schemes of 'Condensed courses for educated and vocational training' and 'Distance Education programme for Women' supplementing the efforts of the Department of Education.

WOMEN ENTREPRENEURSHIP IN INDIA

Women have a unique position in every society. Real development cannot take place if it bypasses women, who not only represent one half of a country's population but also the kernels around which societal revolution take place. Entrepreneurship enhances financial independence and self esteem of women. Around 50 per cent of India's population is women, yet business spheres such as trade, commerce and industry is still considered a male preserve. Entrepreneurial work has also been predominantly a man's world in India. This is based on the fact that only seven per cent of the total entrepreneurs in India, are women. Among the states, Gujarat, Maharashtra and Karnataka have more women entrepreneurs. Indian women are in no way inferior to men in all walks of life and they can be good entrepreneurs as men in the country. Therefore, it is essential to exploit the potential of Indian women. Women's participation in trade, industry and commerce, requiring entrepreneurship is still poor, mainly because of the problems associated with their gender roles. Therefore, promotion of entrepreneurship and economic empowerment of women poses a challenge to the government, funding agencies and non-government organizations. It is important for these people to focus on the limitations faced by the women and to plan supporting systems to enhance the women entrepreneurship in India.

Objectives of the Study

(i) To study the profile and nature of enterprises owned by women.

(ii) To evaluate the performance of business enterprises carried by rural women entrepreneurs.

(iii) To offer suggestions for promoting empowerment among rural women.

METHODOLOGY

Srikakulam and East Godavari Districts in Andhra Region, Chittoor and Kurnool in Rayalaseema Region and Warangal and Khammam in Telangana Region have been selected on the basis of number of Self-Help Groups linked to the banks as on 31-03-2003, in the first stage of sampling. The selection of mandals in each of the selected district is the second stage of sampling. The selection of the villages in each of the selected mandal is the third stage of sampling. The sample groups are selected in the final stage of sampling on a random basis from the villages selected.

Based on the information furnished by the Office of DRDA, the mandals and subsequently villages were selected based on the number of group members actively carrying income generating activities. In selecting the groups, it is felt to select only those groups in the village which are cooperative. Accordingly the following 133 SHGs have been finalized from each selected village.

Warangal	:	28
Khammam	:	22
Kurnool	:	07
Chittoor	:	10
East Godavari	:	40
Srikakulam	:	26
Total	:	133

From each group three members have been selected on random basis making the sample 400 members. Data have been collected from the members of the group with the help of interview schedule. One of the primary objectives of Self Help Groups is that each number should undertake income generating activity. The groups which availed of assistance for individual activities have chosen a wide spectrum of income generating activities, which are by and large are area-specific. The following are income generating activities selected by the respondents under study.

1. Dairy; 2. Powders and Pickles; 3. Garments; 4. Kirana and Tea Stall; 5. Vegetables; 6. Adda leaf, Agarbatti and Candles; 7. Construction Material; 8. Coconut and Coir; 9. Handicrafts; 10. Sweets and Bakery, 11. Dry Fish 12. Lace and Leather Bags.

FINDINGS

Education is a boon to mankind, while lack of education to a person is a bane now-a-days. The confidence of illiterate women is generally low in comparison to literate women. The study revealed that out of 400 respondents in the sample, 62 members (15.50 per cent) are illiterates. Such illiterates are found more in Warangal (20.24 per cent) Kurnool (19.05 per cent) and East Godavari (17.50 per cent) districts.

The table further shows that 207 respondents (51.75 per cent) have studied between First and Fifth class while 98 respondents (24.50 per cent) studied between Sixth class and Ninth class. There are however a few respondents who have studied SSC (6.50 per cent), Intermediate (1.25 per cent), Degree (0.50 per cent). Respondents with Intermediate and Degree education were found in Warangal, Khammam, Kurnool and East Godavari Districts only. On the whole, it can be concluded that majority of the respondents have studied below Ninth class only.

The possession of consumer durables such as Television, Radio, LPG, Mixi, Fan, Gold Ornaments, Moped, Refrigerator and Telephone etc. reflects the standard of living as well as life style of an individual. Larger the number of these consumer goods possessed by an individual, higher is the standard of living and vice versa. The ownership of these consumer durables is the function of individual's discretionary income. Higher the discretionary income, larger the number of consumer duables under the possession of an individual and vice versa.

The study revealed that a little over 95.75 per cent of the members have possessed either Table Fan or Ceiling Fan, 88.00 per cent have possessed LPG, 44.25 per cent possessed different gold ornaments, 44.00 per cent possessed Television and 40.75 per cent possessed Radio. There are a few members who possess Telephone as well as Refrigerator. The same phenomenon is found among all the members belonging to the six districts under study. Thus it can be inferred that the standard of living as well as life style of the SHG members under study is satisfactory.

An attempt is made in the study to find out the usual habits of the women under study and the information is presented in Table-1. It is clear from the table that out of 400 sample SHG members only 24 women (6.00 per cent) read daily news papers, 176 women (44 per cent) watch television, 395 members (98.75 per cent) visits cinemas, 387 members (96.75 per cent) visit bank premises and 378 members (94.50 per cent) visit government offices. It is common phenomenon that though some of the group members do not possess television, they used to watch their neighbors' television. Thus it can be concluded that barring reading news paper habit, majority of the SHG women members have been in the habit of watching television, seeing cinemas, visiting bank premises and visiting government offices. The predominance of illiteracy and meager education is the primary reason for absence of news paper reading habit among the women under study.

The study revealed that as many as 363 members accounting for 90.75 per cent have joined in the group in order to get eligibility for availing government schemes followed by 329 members (82.25 per cent) who joined in the group to avail Bank loans at low interest rates. 163 members (40.75 per cent) have joined in the group to avail internal loans to meet the domestic needs. 260 members (65.00 per cent) have joined in the group to get self satisfaction; 230 members (57.50 per cent) joined as member to cultivate savings habit. On the whole it can be concluded that whatever may be the reason the members have joined the group as member with a good intention and the two dominating reasons are to avail government schemes and to avail Bank loan at lower interest rates.

Table 1
Distribution of SHG Members by Their Habits

	Nature of Habits					
District	*Reading News Papers*	*Watching TV*	*Seeing Cinemas*	*Visiting Bank Premises*	*Visiting Govt. Offices*	*Total*
Warangal	03 (03.57)	38 (45.24)	83 (98.81)	80 (95.24)	56 (66.67)	84 (100.00)
Khammam	01 (01.52)	27 (40.91)	66 (100.00)	66 (100.00)	46 (69.70)	66 (100.00)
Kurnool	04 (19.05)	12 (57.14)	21 (100.00)	21 (100.00)	17 (80.95)	21 (100.00)
Chittoor	02 (06.67)	14 (46.67)	30 (100.00)	30 (100.00)	23 (76.67)	30 (100.00)
East Godavari	12 (10.00)	55 (45.83)	116 (96.67)	115 (95.83)	86 (17.67)	120 (100.00)
Srikakulam	02 (02.53)	30 (37.97)	79 (100.00)	75 (94.94)	50 (63.29)	79 (100.00)
Total	24 (06.00)	176 (44.00)	395 (98.75)	387 (96.75)	378 (94.50)	400 (100.00)

Figures in brackets are percentages to their respective samples.

One of the main objectives of SHG movement is that a member should undertake income generating activity by choosing a business venture of her own choice. Table 2 shows the reasons for starting the business by the women under study. The members have given more than one reason. It is clear from the table that 137 members (34.25 per cent) started the business as a result of encouragement received from husband and others, 126 members (31.50 per cent) started business out of frustration with earlier job and 121 members (30.25 per cent) started business to get financial liberty. The same phenomenon is found among the members belong to the five districts under study. On the whole it can be concluded that the members have started the business with a good intention to earn money to supplement the family income.

Table 2
Reasons for Starting the Business

Class	*Warangal*	*Khammam*	*Kurnool*	*Chittoor*	*East Godavari*	*Srikakulam*	*Total*
To earn money	38 (45.23)	26 ((39.39)	09 (42.86)	12 (40.00)	62 (51.67)	31 (39.24)	178 (44.50)
Interest to do the business	16 ((19.05)	21 (31.82)	04 (19.05)	07 ((23.33)	37 (30.83)	14 (17.72)	99 (24.75)
Frustration with previous job	30 ((35.71)	21 (31.82)	03 ((14.29)	05((16.67)	42 (35.00)	25 (31.65)	126 (31.50)
To utilize leisure time	22 (26.19)	25 ((37.88)	06 (28.57)	10 (33.33)	31 (25.83)	16 (20.25)	110 (27.50)
To get financial liberty	26 (30.95)	18 (27.27)	07 (33.33)	09 (30.00)	40 (33.33)	21 (26.58)	121 (30.25)
Not willing to work eslewhere	15 (17.86)	10 (15.15)	01 (04.76)	02 (06.67)	22 (18.33)	11 (13.02)	61 (15.25)
Encouragement from husband and others	32 (38.10)	27 (40.91)	08 (38.10)	11 (36.67)	36 (30..00)	23 (29.11)	137 (34.25)
To develop ideas	09 (10.71)	12 (18.18)	04 (19.06)	05 (16.67)	18 (15.00)	07 (08.86)	55 (13.75)
Total	84	66	21	30	120	79	400

Figures in brackets are percentages to their respective samples.

Table 3
Distribution of SHG Members by Business Activity

Class	*Warangal*	*Khammam*	*Kurnool*	*Chittoor*	*East Godavari*	*Srikakulam*	*Total*
Dairy	12 (14.29)	09 (13.64)	04 (19.05)	03 (10.00)	08 (06.67)	09 (11.53)	46 (11.50)
Pickles and Powders	11 (13.09)	14 (21.21)	01 (04.76)	06 (20.00)	17 (14.17)	08 (10.25)	57 (14.25)
Garments	07 (08.33)	11 (16.67)	05 (23.81)	04 (13.33)	13 (10.83)	10 (12.82)	50 (12.50)
Kirana and Tea stalls	14 (16.67)	08 (12.12)	02 (09.52)	-	10 (08.33)	11 (14.10)	45 (11.25)
Vegitables	08 (09.52)	04 (06.06)	02 (9.52)	03 (10.00)	06 (05.00)	13 (16.66)	36 (09.00)
Addaleaf, Agrarabatti and Candles	06 (07.14)	06 (09.09)	-	02 (06.67)	03 (02.50)	04 (05.12)	21 (05.25)
Construction material	-	02 (03.03)	-	02 (06.67)	06 (05.00)	02 (02.56)	12 (03.00)
Coconut and Coir	05 (05.95)	-	-	05 (16.67)	14 (11.67)	09 (11.53)	33 (08.25)
Handicrafts	08 (09.52)	04 (06.06)	04 (19.05)	04 (13.33)	12 (10.00)	05 (06.41)	37 (09.25)
Sweet and Backery	-	-	-	-	16 (13.33)	-	16 (04.00)
Dry Fish	04 (04.76)	-	-	-	07 (05.83)	07 (08.97)	18 (04.50)
Lace and Leather Bags	09 (10.73)	08 (12.12)	03 (14.29)	01 (03.33)	08 (06.67)	-	29 (07.25)
Total	84 (100.00)	66 (100.00	21 (100.00)	30 (100.00)	120 (100.00)	78 (100.00)	400 (100.00)

Figures in brackets are percentages to their respective samples

Table 3 shows distribution of category-wise respondents by type of economic activity. It is clear from the table that comparatively larger number of members is found in economic activities such as Powders and Pickles (14.25 per cent) followed by Garments (12.50 per cent) Dairy (11.50 per cent) Kirana and Tea stalls (11.25 per cent) Handicrafts (9.25 per cent). The presence of forward caste members are found in economic activities such as Dairy, Powders and Pickles, Kirana and Tea Stalls and Sweets and Bakery, while the presence of members belonging to backward caste are found in activities such as Garments, Vegetables, Handicrafts, Coconut and Coir etc. It is surprising to note that members belonging to SC and ST communities are also found in economic activities such as Dairy, Kirana and Tea Stalls, Adda Leaf, Agarbatti and Candles etc. None of the forward caste members in the sample has taken Dry Fish activity. Among the forward caste members, the members who are running Kirana and Tea Stalls are none other than Vysya community people. On the whole, it can be concluded that majority of the sample members have chosen Powders and Pickles, Garments, Dairy, Kirana and Tea Stalls and Handicraft activities.

Savings are the backbone of success of Self Help Groups, as cultivation of the savings habit among the members is ultimate objective of the SHG Scheme. Table 4 shows district-wise accumulated savings of the Self Help Group members as on date of enquiry. It is seen from the table that the accumulated savings of the members under study amount to Rs. 24,64,500. In other words on an average accumulated savings of each member as on date of enquiry amount to Rs.6,161. The accumulated savings comprises of 1) Penalties 2) Interest on Bank Savings 3) Interest on Internal loans and 4) Resource persons fees. The table further shows that the average accumulated savings of the members belonging to East Godavari District is the highest (Rs. 7,183/-) while that of Khammam district is the least (Rs. 5,212/-) among the six districts under study. On the whole, it can be concluded that the savings performance of the Self Help Group members under study relating to the six districts is appreciable.

The study revealed that as many as 166 members accounting for 41.50 per cent have availed group loans three times while 138 members accounting for 34.50 per cent have availed two times. There are however 65 members representing 16.25 per cent who have availed group loans four times. Among those members who availed internal loans four times, members belonging to Kurnool, Chittoor, Srikakulam and East Godavari districts represent maximum number while among the members who availed group loan three times those belonging to Warangal, Khammam, Srikakulam and East Godavari districts account for larger in number. Thus it can be concluded that majority of the members under study have availed group loans more than thrice ever since they became group members.

The investment made by the respondents in different business activities as on date of enquiry is shown in Table 5. It is clear from the table that the total investment made by all the respondents as on date of enquiry amounts to Rs. 84.45 lakhs with an average investment of Rs. 21,113. The average investment varied between Rs. 12,788 and Rs. 28,866. As can be seen from the table average investment is the highest in the case of Sweets and Bakery business followed by Lace and Leather Bags (Rs. 28,840), Construction material (Rs. 28,088), Garments (Rs. 23,562) and Handicrafts (Rs. 23,532). The average investment is comparatively lesser in business activities such as Vegetables and Dolls (Rs. 12,788); Adda Leaf, Agarbatti and Candles (Rs. 14,119), Kirana and Tea Stalls (Rs. 15,743) and Dry fish (Rs. 16,211). On the whole the investment in each business activity carried by each SHG member is mediocre and is within the reach of each member as the banks are coming forward in providing loans to these members under bank linkage programme.

As a whole, it can be concluded that the repayment performance of members in the sample is not seen as a serious problem. From the business venture they have been generating sufficient income to enable them to repay the above loans. The few members who are irregular are found in business activities such as Adda Leaf, Agarbathi, Candles, Dry Fish,

Vegetables, Dairy, Kirana and Tea Stalls etc., while the few members who are irregular in repayment of bank loan are found in Vegetables, Kirana and Tea Stalls, Dairy, Powder and Pickles, Handicrafts and Dry Fish (Table.6).

The study revealed that as many as 75.00 per cent of the members are selling their products in local markets followed by 29.00 per cent who sell in DWCRA bazaars, 22.25 per cent who sell in Exhibitions, Melas and Pushkaras, 14.75 per cent who sell in Rytu Bazaar. Local Markets are the major sources of marketing for business activities such as Kirana and Tea Stalls, Dairy, Pickles and Powders. DWCRA bazaars are also major source of marketing for business in the case of business activities like Pickles and Powders and Handicrafts. There are group members carrying Pickles and Powders, Vegetables and Coconut and Coir who sell their products in Rytu Bazaars. On the whole, it can be concluded that local markets, DWCRA Bazaars and Exhibitions, Melas and Pushkaras are the major source of marketing for the SHG members under study.

The study also revealed that. Inadequate capital is the problem mostly found in Pickles and Powders, Dairy, Kirana and Tea Stalls and Handicrafts while lack of publicity is the main problem mostly in the case of Garments and Handicrafts. Marketing is a major problem mostly found in business activities such as Handicrafts, Pickles and Powders, Vegetables and Garments. On the whole the major problem facing the members under study are inadequate capital, lack of publicity and low purchasing power of the rural people.

Table 4
District-wise Accumulated Savings by SHG Members as on Date of Enquiry

District	*No. of Members*	*Total Accumulated Savings in Rs.*	*Average Accumulated Savings in Rs.*
Warangal	84	4,72,500	5,625
Khammam	66	3,44,000	5,212
Kurnool	21	1,39,000	6,619
Chittoor	30	2,06,500	6,883
East Godavari	120	8,62,000	7,183
Srikakulam	78	4,34,800	5,575
Total	400	24,64,500	6,161

Table 5
Activity-wise Investment of the SHG Members as on Date of Enquiry

Activity	*No. of Members*	*Total Investment in Rs.*	*Average Investment in Rs.*
Dairy	46	8,55,200	18591
Pickles and Powders	57	14,23,150	24,968
Garments	50	11,78,100	23,562
Kirana and Tea Stalls	45	7,08,450	15,743
Vegetables and Dolls	36	4,60,350	12,788
Adda leaf, Agarbathi and Candles	21	296500	14,119
Construction Material	12	337050	28,088
Coconut and Coir	33	725600	21988
Handicrafts	37	870700	23,532
Sweets and Backery	16	461850	28,866
Dry Fish	18	291800	16,211
Lace and Leather Bags	29	836350	28,840
Total	400	8445000	21,113

Insufficiency of internal loans is the major problem expressed by the majority of members carrying all the twelve business activities. Some members have expressed more than one problem. While competition for internal lending is the major problem in the case of majority of the members carrying business activity such as Construction Material, Adda Leaf, Agarbathi and Candles, Dry Fish, Lace and Leather Bags and Vegetables. The problem of distribution of bank loans not according to the needs of the members is expressed by more number of members carrying Adda Leaf, Agarbathi and Candles (33.33 per cent), Sweets and Bakery (25.00 per cent) and Garments (22.00 per cent), while the problem of partiality of group leaders is expressed by more number of members carrying business activities such as Dry Fish (27.78 per cent); and Dairy (15.22 per cent). Getting benefits by a very few is the problem expressed by members carrying Dry Fish (22.22 per cent) and Vegetables (16.67 per cent) traders. The problem of inability to maintain records and accounts is the major problem expressed by more number of members carrying Dry Fish (44.44 per cent), Coconut and Coir business (30.30 per cent), Vegetables (25.00 per cent) and Dairy (19.57 per cent). Thus it can be concluded that all the members in the sample have facing one problem or the other.

Table 6
Distribution of Activity-wise SHG Members by Loans Repayment Performance

Activity	No-of Members	Group Loan		Bank Loan	
		Regular	*Irregular*	*Regular*	*Irregular*
Dairy	46 (11.50)	39 (09.75)	07 (01.75)	45 (11.25)	01 (0.25)
Pickles and Powders	57 (14.25)	51 (12.75)	06 (01.50)	56 (14.00)	01 (0.25)
Garments	50 (12.50)	44 (11.00)	06 (01.50)	50 (12.50)	–
Kirana and Tea stalls	45 (11.25)	39 (09.75)	06 (01.50)	43 (10.75)	02 (0.50)
Vegetables	36 (09.00)	30 (07.50)	06 (01.50)	34 (08.50)	02 (0.50)
Addaleaf, Agarbatti & Candles	21 (05.25)	17 (04.25)	04 (01.00)	20 (05.00)	01 (0.25)
Construction material	12 (03.00)	11 (02.75)	01 (0.25)	12 (03.00)	–
Coconut and Coir	33 (08.25)	30 (07.50)	03 (0.75)	33 (08.25)	–
Handicrafts	37 (09.25)	31 (07.75)	06 (01.50)	36 (09.00)	01 (0.25)
Sweet & Backery	16 (04.00)	14 (03.50)	02 (0.50)	16 (04.00)	–
Dryfish	18 (04.50)	15 (03.75)	03 (0.75)	17 (04.25)	01 (0.25)
Lace & Leather Bags	29 (07.25)	26 (06.50)	03 (0.75)	29 (07.23)	–
Total	400 (100.00)	347 (86.75)	53 (13.25)	391 (97.75)	09 (02.25)

Figures in brackets are per centages to 450.

The efficiency of a business activity is measured in terms of its income generating capacity. Towards this end, an attempt is made in the study to find out the amount of income derived by the members from each income generating activity. Table 7 shows the average monthly income of the members from each business activity. It is seen from the table that the income generated by each business activity varied between Rs.1,850 (Sweets and Bakery) and Rs.819 (Vegetables). Activities such as Sweets and Bakery, Construction Materials, Lace and Leather Bags, Powders and Pickles, Garments and Handicrafts are yielding more income to the members compared to other business activities. Thus a vast majority of the members with the financial assistance under bank linkage programme have improved their economic condition.

Decision-making in a family for the purpose of present analysis has been categorized as:

1. Husband dominated decisions.
2. Wife dominated decisions.
3. Joint decisions.

It is commonly observed that in a family some decisions are exclusively taken by the husband i.e. head of the family, some decisions are exclusively taken by the house wife, while some decisions are taken jointly by both husband and wife. There are some other decisions, which are exclusively taken by other members in the family viz., the children, and elders in the family etc. The more the number of decisions in the family is exclusively taken by the housewife, the more the freedom she enjoys in the family and vice versa. Against this background an attempt is made in the study to find out the extent the family members are taking buying decisions.

Table 8 shows involvement of the respondent, her husband and others in the domestic decisions and business decisions. As can be seen from the table for domestic decisions, the role of husband is apparent while in the case of business decisions the role of wife is evident. Joint decision making is found more among members in the case of business decisions. Wife's role in the purchase of domestic items as well as business items is paramount among respondents relating to Warangal, Kurnool and Chitoor districts while the role of husband for domestic items and business item is paramount in other districts. Joint decision making in the purchase of business items is found among all the members belonging to all the districts under study. Thus it can be concluded that the involvement of husband is more common for all types of decisions among all the group members under study.

Conclusion

Poverty alleviation is the ultimate goal of any nation. Towards this end, delivery of micro finance to the micro enterprises plays a significant role. Rural women with low income and lack of knowledge of available banking facilities can do little for the growth of banking habits on their own. For this a concrete effort is needed to be taken up by society, the government and by bankers themselves to enhance the standard of rural women with regard to banking habits. Imparting training to rural women in the realm of marketing and production go a long way in ameliorating their socio-economic lot. The Government has emerged as a major catalyst by way of providing training incentives and other facilities to succeed particularly in rural areas to empower the rural women.

Table 7
Averapge Monthly Net Income of the Membersfrom Each Business Activity

Activity	*No. of Members*	*Total Net Income Per Month Rs.*	*Average Net Income Per Month Rs.*
Dairy	46	54800	1,200
Pickles and Powder	57	91200	1,600
Garments	50	75500	1,500
Kirana and Tea Stalls	45	45400	1,008
Vegetables	36	29500	819
Addaleaf, Agarbatti and Candles	21	19000	905
Construction Material	12	21600	1,800
Coconut and Coir	33	46500	1,409
Handicrafts	37	55800	1,508
Sweets and Backery	16	29600	1,850
Dry Fish	18	18700	1,038
Lace and Leather Bags	29	53600	1,848
Total	400	541200	1 ,353

Table 8
Involvment in Domestic and Business Decisions by Family Members

District	Domestic Decisions					Business Decisions				
	Self	*Husband*	*Joint*	*Others*	*Total*	*Self*	*Husband*	*Joint*	*Others*	*Total*
Warangal	33 (39.29)	21 (25.00)	25 (29.76)	05 (5.95)	84 (100.00)	29 (34.52)	08 (09.52)	47 (55.96)	-	84 (100.00)
Khammam	20 (30.30)	23 (34.85)	16 (24.24)	07 (10.61)	66 (100.00)	20 (30.30)	15 (22.73)	29 (43.94)	02 (03.03)	66 (100.00)
Kurnool	08 (38.10)	06 (28,57)	07 (33.33)	-	21 (100.00)	08 (38.10)	03 (14.28)	10 (47.62)	-	21 (100.00)
Chittoor	10 (33.33)	07 (23.33)	13 (43.34)	-	30 (100.00)	08 (26.67)	05 (16.67)	17 (56.66)	-	30 (100.00)
East Godavari	29 (24.17)	54 (45.00)	24 (20.00)	13 (10.83)	120 (100.00)	32 (26.67)	22 (18.33)	55 (45.83)	11 (09.17)	120 (100.00)
Srikakulam	21 (26.58)	33 (41.77)	19 (24.06)	06 (07.59)	79 (100.00)	26 (32.91)	16 (20.25)	34 (43.04)	03 (03.80)	79 (100.00)
Total	121 (30.26)	144 (36.00)	104 (26.00)	31 (07.75)	400 (100.00)	123 (30.75)	69 (17.11)	192 (48.00)	16 (04.00)	400 (100.00)

31

Empowerment of Rural Women Through DWACRA

D. Vanaja

Introduction

The empowerment of women became necessary as they are almost fifty percent of the population and are being discriminated at all fronts. The moral inferiority of Indians, was supposed to be demonstrated by the barbaric practices followed against women.

Present days problems like bride burning, domestic violence, suicides of wives, daughters and sisters, the origins were laid by our ancestors out of ignorance. Hence, the solution lies in empowering women to eliminate the Economic Inequalities, Social Inequalities, Physical Inequalities and Political Inequalities. Economic Inequalities of women may be in terms of inheritance of property, salary, contribution to the maintenance of the family etc. Women have no right to inherit the property on equal basis on par with her brothers as per Dharma Sastras. This social deformity resulted in the raise of Dowry System in the Hindu Society. Social Inequality means inequality in terms of literacy, education in which women are not on par with men.

The political inequality is at high degree, which is visible to the naked eye, and can be seen by observing the number of women representatives in the legislatures. Women have been politically marginalized in our country and most of them live extremely restricted lives. They are not allowed to have much of a voice even within their community or family's decision-making processes, live alone a meaningful say in the national politics. Not just politicians but also even many intellectuals are angrily rejecting the idea of reservations for women and calling it a retrogressive move even in societies where women exercise relatively more freedom in day-to-day living.

Rural Women and DWACRA

Empowerment of women started from the South in India that too rigorously from Andhra Pradesh. The women Prime Minister and the women Chief Ministers failed to instill any kind of the sense of confidence among women in India. Here the policies matter not personalities. A change, which is radical, has taken place in the family life of the women of rural Andhra Pradesh because of the scheme of DWCRA, presently, 4, 20,000 DWCRA groups are working only in Andhra Pradesh that is major portion of total DWCRA groups in India. The main highlights of the DWCRA are the women members of DWCRA form a group of 10 to 15 women at the village level for delivery of services like credit and skill training, cash and infrastructure support for self-employment. Women save one Rupee a day and after watching the performance of a group over nine to twelve months, that group is given a one time grant of Rs.25,000 /- as a Revolving Fund, shared by Central and State Governments in 50:50 ratio towards infrastructure, purchase of raw materials, marketing, child care and so on. The DWCRA groups formed in Andhra Pradesh cover more than 2 million women and their savings have crossed Rs. 15 million so far. It is assumed that the DWCRA has created a sense of confidence among the women of rural Andhra Pradesh and they are moving towards autonomy in decision-making at all fronts which reflected in the reduction of population growth rate in the State. The State of Andhra Pradesh has every right to claim the credits of the statistics of Census of India, 2001 for its performance regarding the population control as it is in the forefront of empowering women in the state by means of DWCRA. The ignorance of DWCRA women in utilizing their saved money to be checked by providing adequate guidance. What will happen, if these DWCRA women started asserting their voting power? The political equations will tilt. What will happen, if these women threaten all the governments... not to vote if govt., has not given the reservations in the legislatures? These women can even demand legislation in the Parliament for inheritance of Equal Property. But somebody should educate them in this direction. And they will ultimately give a final blow to the male domination in the parliament and politics. Yes, it is this DWCRA woman that can initiate a change in this direction in India.

There are several socio-cultural, economic and political factors for this second class status of the Indian women. They are second class citizens in the sense they do not have autonomy in the decision-making process, leave alone at political level, not even in their family, particularly on their reproductive rights. Even after witnessing a women Prime Minister, women Chief Ministers and women dignitaries, the Indian women failed to get the moral boost, and remained indifferent to their reproductive rights. Hence, Indian population crossed the One Billion mark, though India initiated the Family Planning Programme way back in 1951. What remain constant are the low economic, social, cultural and political values accorded to the work performed primarily by the women in the conditions of exploitation, no job security, and violations of Human Rights against them, which reflected in the growth of the population. Of late, it is identified that the empowerment of women is necessary to check the population growth for sustainable development.

Many schemes launched by Government of India and State governments failed to attract the attention of Indian women, resulted in partial success only, and failed to imbibe the sense of confidence among women, except the Central Government's scheme, DWCRA (Development of Women and Children in Rural Areas).

Benchmarking of DWACRA

Best practices in SHGs are being evolved continuously based on experiences for example:

- Regular meetings.
- Continuous savings.
- Internal rotation of savings.
- Conduct of meetings with specific agenda.
- Thrift and credit operations taking place in the group meeting.
- Rotation of leaders.
- Transparent and democratic decision making.
- Non-exploitation of members' needs.
- One for all and all for one.
- Urge for increase of corpus.
- Determination for economic and social development.
- Training and Capacity building.

Bankable, Creditworthy

Once the DWACRA completes six months and members continuously practicing thrift, rotating the corpus generated, it becomes eligible to get bank loan. The loan amount ranges from two times of savings amount (including amount under rotation) to four times. Leadership of NABARD in Andhra Pradesh today has made bankers very positive towards DWACRA. Bankers are viewing DWACRA as a bankable option. Constant orientation programs to bankers, and also developing positive attitude with the groups on repayment has helped to scale up the DWACRA-bank linkage program. Totally around Rs. 1900 crores of credit has been mobilized for the DWACRA women.

Marketing

Marketing support is provided to the SHGs through DWCRA Bazaars (Market outlets), which have been set up in all the districts, and permanent DWCRA Bazaar is nearing completion at Hyderabad. Products worth more than Rs. 100 crores were sold through DWCRA Bazaars in the last two years. Training and Technology Development Centres (TTDC) have been established in each district to introduce innovative technologies for the qualitative improvement of products made by the DWACRA.

The DWACRA are assisted in many districts to develop branding of their products ex: Stree Prakasham in Ongole disrict, Mahila in Adilabad district etc., women are encouraged to participate in fairs taking place at national level and in other states. Collaboration with Hindustan Lever Ltd., has been secured by SHGs of Nalgonda district where MACS have been appointed as stockist points and groups as sales points for marketing DWCRA products. Leading super bazaars like Food World, Trinetra came forward to tie up with SHGs and market DWCRA products. Some DWCRA products have very good demand. Pickle producing SHGs of Guntur district got orders worth Rs. 6.00 lakhs and lace groups of West Godavari district got export orders.

Institutional Building

SHGs are encouraged to come together as Cooperative Societies at the village level and Mandal level by federating them under Mutually Aided Cooperative Societies Act 1995. Nearly 250 societies have been formed so far. These societies will be accessing credit from financial institutions, donor agencies, DRDAs and Voluntary organizations and help the members of women SHGs in availing bigger loans for economic activities and also helps in collective bargaining in marketing of products, purchasing raw materials etc. there is perceptible improvement in socio-economic status of rural women as a result of this movement. Women have become very active, assertive and are concerned with the issues relating to them and their surroundings.

Suggestions

1. It is important to promote role and status of rural women towards development. The problems of rural women should be given importance.
2. The government and NGOs should play key role in uplifting the women's economic conditions.
3. To empower women by providing equal opportunities, liberty and justice.
4. Alternative strategies and remedial measures should be taken from time to time to empower the women.

Conclusion

It is evident that DWCRA is playing a very important role in empowering the rural women. Especially in their social and economic conditions of life. Undoubtedly a unique successful development strategy for empowerment of women is DWACRA. So it helped the women to develop economy, self reliance, courage and vision for better future.

References

Women, Poverty and Productivity in India, (1992), all 3 versions, L. Bennett.

Gender Perspective, (1999), Participation, Empowerment and Development A.D. Mishra, Radha Publications.

Women Empowerment, (2007), M. Lakshmipathi Raju.

32

Empowerment of Rural Women Through Self Help Groups

R. Srinivasu

Introduction

The concept of SHG serves to underline the principle "for the people, by the people and of the people". The origin of SHG is from the brain child of Gramin Bank of Bangladesh, which was founded by Prof. Mohammed Yunus of Chittagong University in the year 1975. This was exclusively established for the poor. Self help group is a small economically homogeneous and affinity group of rural poor which voluntarily agrees to contribute to a common fund to be lent to its members as per group decision, which works for group solidarity, self and group awareness, social and economic empowerment in the way of democratic functioning.

"Self-help" means the improvement of a person or group by his/her or its own contributions and efforts and largely for his/her or its own benefit. Self-help is thus the opposite of charity. A citizen group that solicits contributions or gifts from well-to-do outsiders or secures them, with no contributions of its own from the government is not engaging in self-help, even though it might be complimented for its industry. Such services as sewing, child-care, and literacy classes can be considered self-help if the group contributes some share of the money for the teachers, the equipment, or the building facilities. They may also be considered self-help if they are sponsored by the group and arranged for and carried out at its invitation.

Our Constitution in its Fundamental Rights has provision for equality, social justice and protection of women. These goals are yet to be realized. Women continue to be discriminated, exploited and exposed to inequalities. By empowerment, women would be able to develop self-esteem, confidence, realize their potential and enhance their collective bargaining power. Women's empowerment can be viewed as a continuum of several interrelated and mutually reinforcing components.

Awareness building about women's situation, discrimination and rights and opportunities is a step towards gender equality.

- Capacity building and skill development, especially the ability of plan, make decision, organize, manage and carryout activities; to deal with people and institutions in the world around them would empower the women.
- Action to bring about great equality between men and women.

Empowering women contributes to social development. Economic progress in any country whether developed or under developed could be achieved through social development. Women constitute equal share with men in total population of our country. Women's empowerment cannot be ignored while devising various policies for rural and socio-economic development. Women participation is significant one in rural employment. They put their entrepreneurial skills in all the rural employment activities such as agricultural operations, poultry, sheep rearing, dairy, fire wood cutting and selling, sale of agricultural produce etc. The self help group disburses micro credit to the rural women of the purpose of making them enterprising women and encouraging them to entrepreneurial activities. Credit needs of the rural women are fulfilled totally through the self help groups. The self help groups enhance equality of status of women as participants, decision makers and beneficiaries in the democratic, economic, social and cultural spheres of life. Self help groups encourage women to take active part in socio-economic progress of our nation.

Though they put their heart and soul in rural employment activities, their economic status is not improved. Their livelihood is poor. So, they need financial assistance. Providing micro credit to the rural women in an organized set up will make them enterprising women. Regional banks, Cooperative Banks and Commercial Banks are not successful in providing rural micro credit. Overdue rates are increasing and recovery percentage is coming down in the rural credit agencies.

The self-help group generally has members not exceeding 20 and each group selects among its members a leader called animator. The animator conducts two to three meeting every month in the evening hours. The group members save a regular amount of Rs. 20 to Rs. 100 every month. The group rotates the money to the needy members for various purposes at a specified interest rate. As the repayment is cent per cent and the recycling is very fast, the savings amount increases faster owing to the accumulation of income from interest. Saving habit helps the members to escape from the clutches of money lenders. Saving habit paves the way for the empowerment of women and builds confidence in them that they could stand on their won feet. After the group stabilize over a period of six months or more in the management of its own funds, it conduct regular meetings, maintains savings and gives loans to members on interest. The SHG's are being linked with the banks of the external credit under the projects of rural development. The joint appraisal teams consisting of bank managers, rural development officers, NGO's project implementation units visit the groups and select the beneficiaries proposed by the women groups for providing financial assistance to the respective entrepreneurial activities.

Banks provide financial assistance for various entrepreneurial activities such as setting up of petty shops, vegetable shops, tailoring units, charcoal making units, dairying, etc. (The Hindu, 1st November 1999).

Self Help Groups undertake entrepreneurial activities at smaller level with minimum capital requirements. In future, the inbuilt strength of the self help groups will pave the way to undertake mega projects, like projects performed by joint stock companies, public sector enterprises, etc. Self help groups have the power to create socio - economic revolution in the rural areas of our country. Self help groups heave proved that they could indeed bring about a change in the mindset of the very conservative and tradition bound illiterate women in rural areas. Self help groups have made the rural women to contribute for the socio-economic progress of the country.

Dr. C. Rangarajan, the former Governor of the Reserve bank of India has rightly pointed out that initiation and monitoring the credit programmes for the poor can be made more effective and less costly if banks make attempts to organize the poor in self-help groups to ensure proper utilization of the credit and prompt repayment of loans. The self help groups can also contribute towards improving the quality of lending by offering loans in a prompt and simple manner, ensuring need-based loans and keeping the loan size within the repaying capacity of the borrowers. Undoubtedly, self-help groups have the advantage of better knowledge about their members as compared to the bank staff.

Self help groups enhance the equality of status of women as participants, decision maker and beneficiaries in the democratic, economic, social and cultural sphere of life in all stages of economic and social activities, involvement of women becomes essential. The encourage women to take active part in the socio-economic progress of our nation. Mahatma Gandhi, father of our nation has stated that "women are the noblest of God's creation, supreme in their own sphere of activity", the SHG's bring out the supremacy of women in moulding the community in right perspective and explore the initiative of women in taking up entrepreneurial ventures.

The District Rural Industries Project has been introduced by the NABARD to develop rural non farm sector industries. In the first phase in 1993-94, five districts were identified in the whole country to implement this project. In the second phase, seven districts have been identified. This project seeks integrated approach to banks. Government departments, NGO's and other agencies. Specific SHG's may be created to implement the NABARD's project successfully for the growth and development of non farm sector industries. The Swarnajayanti Gram Swarozgar Yojana, a new credit linked poverty alleviation programme which envisages bulk of the subsidy and credit to flow through SHG's.

The NABARD organizes training programme for members of the self-help groups like programme on entrepreneurship development, financial management, book keeping and skill development in the non-farm sector. The training programme for bankers is also sponsored by the NABARD. The SHG Bank linkage is the felt need of the hour to provide micro credit to the deserved and un-reached rural poor. This linkage must be considered as a corporate strategy of banks.

Self Help Groups-Multiple Roles

It is working to improve the health, education, and social welfare of people living below the poverty line in rural communities. It empowers women to improve their quality of life and the economic and social conditions of their families and communities.

1. Preventive Health, our community health workers participate in the monthly self-help groups meetings and disseminate information on reproductive and child health, and prevention of various diseases such as cholera, anemia, scabies, filarial, primary complex, etc.
2. Self help groups may raise education among the rural people by promoting literacy programmes in its service areas.
3. Self help groups may also organize rural library and collect various types of books relating to agriculture,

health, education, literature, justice, stories, spiritual, etc.

4. The self-help groups may build relationship and networking with various NGO's International NGO's, service clubs, volunteers and Government Departments to root itself in a number of villages making a visible impact in their programmes.
5. Women self help groups are playing an increasingly important role in the community radio stations like "Mandakini Ki Awaaz" (the voice of Mandakini) located in Bhanaj, Rudraprayag district, Uttarkhand, India which started its operation in 2004.
6. In February 2007, a women self-help group in the village of Machkadi opened a post office savings account to collect funds for the repair and maintenance of the satellite radio receiver that their group has received from UNESCO.

Self Help Groups Work towards Economic Independence of Women

The country envisions a future in which Indian women are independent and self reliant. Their participation in remunerative work in the formal and non-formal labour market has increased significantly in the past decade. Women's income is becoming very necessary to households of all types in the wake of globalization and changing economic structures.

It is estimated that India is home to 92 Million working women though 90% of them are working in the unorganized sector. The female work predication rate increased from 14.2% in 1971 to 22.3% in 1991. Women's share in the organized sector mean while, increased from 11 % in 1991 to 15.9% in 1997. The requisite steps have to be taken to recognize this and take cognizance while framing economic policies and programmes.

The department of rural Employment and Poverty Alleviation of the Ministry of rural Development has initiated several schemes in which 30 - 40% of the benefits are reserved for women below the poverty line. The underlying philosophy of these schemes is to encourage entrepreneurship and self-help among women.

Swarna Jayanthi Gram Swarogar Yojana Scheme (SGSY), the attended and merged version of the erstwhile Development of Women and Children in Rural Areas (DWCRA), Integrated Rural Development Programme (IRDP) and Training of Rural Youth for Self Employment (TRYSEM), was launched in April 1999. It is a holistic credit-cum-subsidy programme covering all aspects of self employment.

The National Bank for Agriculture and Rural Development (NABARD) links banks with self help groups with the objective of meeting the credit needs of the poor. As many as 85 % of the groups linked with the banks are women's groups.

Indira Mahila Yojana (IMY) was lunched in 1995 in over 200 blocks in India for the holistic empowerment of women. IMY is being implemented in 238 blocks and till now, 40,000 women's groups have been formed under the scheme. Of these, 3000 groups were formed in 1999-2000.

Rural women's development and empowerment project (Swashakthi project) was launched in 1998 for strengthening the process of empowerment of women in six states through the establishment of self-help groups.

Rashtiya Mahila Kosh (RMK) a national credit fund extends credit facilities to poor and needy women. The RMK has extended loans to 20,000 self help groups of women and has a membership of over 3,00,000. It is instrumental in encouraging women to take control of their own development, and has helped build confidence and political awareness.

The LIC of India has also been assigned to scale of Janashree Bima Yojana to cover all women self-help groups that are credit linked to the banks. There is an allocation of Rs.500 crore for this purpose.

A task force has been constituted in 1999 to review all existing legislation and government schemes with a view to enhancing the access of women to national resources and ensuring that they take their rightful place in the mainstream economic development. The task force will also chalk out specific programmes for observing the year 2001 s "Women's Empowerment Year". This is one of the most crucial areas of work that has been taken up by the government. The primary aim is to make women economically independent and help them gainful confidence in themselves. [Source: PIB FEATURES, 2000].

The major forms of microfinance in India is that based on women's self help groups which are small groups of 10-20 members. These groups collect saving from their members and provide loans to them. However, unlike most Accumulating Savings and Credit Associations (ASCAs) found in several countries, these groups also obtain loans from banks and lend them to their members. By 2003, over 7,00,000 groups had obtained over Rs. 20 billion (US $ 425 million) in loans form banks benefiting more than 10 million people. Delinquencies on these loans are reported to be less than 5%. Savings in these groups are estimated to be at least Rs. 8 Billion (US $ 170 million).

Despite these consider Table achievements, sustainability of the SHGs has been suspected because several essential services required by the SHGs are provided free or a significantly subsidized cost by organizations that have developed these groups.

The Self Help Groups Movement-Women in Local Governance-Arli village

Arli village women is situated in the tribal dominated Pandhrkawad block of Yavatnal district. Arli is an outstanding example of how women have taken advantage of their unified identity under the SHG banner to assert their political rights in the Panchayat Raj system. Such initiatives by women also set a constructive trend in local governance processes which otherwise disregard the concerns of common people. With strong backing from the SHG members, Babytai kumbre, their group leader, could also successfully contest the Gram

Panchayat elections. Working as a member for five years gave her a chance to raise women's issues at the Panchayat level. She could bring out topics like village sanitation, cleanliness programmes. More importantly this political experience has fortified her confidence about women's collectives. "A lot can be done if women come together and support each other".

School Monitoring and Leadership

School monitoring and leadership in local governance are just a few of the examples in a series of activities that rural women in Yavatmal district have taken up after having formed SHGs. Based on the concept of Government Community Action (GCA) the empowerment programme was initiated in Yavatmal district since 2001 by the District Rural Development Agency with support from local NGOs and UNICEF. At present, over 1,860 SHGs have been formed in 465 villages of the district as a means to facilitate economic, social and political empowerment of women.

As an initial step, village women are mobilized through SHGs also referred to its thrift and credit groups. Once the savings become regular and the monthly meetings a habit, the facilitators prepare the women for a greater social and political role in the villages. They work as collective building linkages with their schools government offices and more importantly, among themselves.

As a further step SHGs are also establishing linkages with the Gram Panchayats are taking active part in local decision making processes, like Babytai, have also been elected as member in local gram panchayats. As the experience of Aarli women indicate very often SHGs metamorphose into more than just a savings group. It leads women to take active part in public sphere and influence decisions in their favour. [Source: UNICEF/India/Vidya Kulkarni, 2006].

Need for Social Intervention

As revealed from the research studies, most of the self help groups are not functioning well and they suffer from limitations. The loan facilities are not extended to all the groups. There is differential treatment between self-help groups supported by ruling party and other groups belonging to other political parties. Most of the self help groups are not able to save and deposit their share of contributions in the banks regularly as per the stipulated time schedule and they may become sick units.

In view of the above limitations and short comings there is need for social work intervention for educating and motivating the self help groups to function successfully by observing the norms, rules and regulations. In this regard, the professional social worker plays the role of animator for promoting the thriftiness, regular savings and entrepreneurship among the members of self help groups. Social worker may also conduct the meetings of self help groups for discussing various issues pertaining to monitoring of the groups, bank procedures, self employment schemes, etc.

The social worker may also conduct orientation and training programme for promoting leadership qualities, entrepreneurship and thriftiness, savings, vocational training and income generating programmes in collaboration with NGOs, Janasiksha Samsthan, polytechnic colleges and other training institutions.

The professional social worker may also involve the SHGs for creating awareness in the community about various social and health issues i.e. HIV/AIDS, sanitation, public health, hygiene, nutrition, child labour, dowry, domestic violence, human trafficking and prohibition of alcoholism, narcotic drugs, etc.

While working with the self help groups the social worker will utilize the professional knowledge of social work and the methodology of social work interventions of working with individual, groups and communities.

References

Economic Empowerment of Rural Women in India, (2003), edited by Rita Bhakshi, M.S., Rathore, Meenu Agarwal and Manjula Tyagi, Jaipur, RBSA, 166 p, $ 20 ISBN-81-7611-184-8.

Social Structure and Change, Volume 2, Women in India Society, B.S. Baviskar, E.A., Ramaswamy, Sage Publications, New Delhi.

SGSY Training Series-III, Ministry of Rural development, Govt. of India.

Women and Rural Entrepreneurship in India-DD Sharma, S.K. Dhameja, Abhishek Publications, Chandigarh-160017.

Women and Technology, S.C. Jain, Rawat Publications, Jaipur.

33

Empowerment of Rural Women: Sociological Study of Self Help Groups

A Study on Guntur District

Ch. Janaki

Introduction

In recent decades, there is a huge change observed in the thoughts of women. Women almost entered every field in the world. They change their attitude and life style to fulfill their needs. Women not only entered into jobs, but also into business and stocks and shares. Some are in politics and some are CEO's (Chief Executive Officers) of several multinational companies. These changes are not only for the educated and urban background women but also for the rural and uneducated women. But some women are helpless and never see the lights of development and are still crushed between the iron hands of money-lenders, and are not getting their basic needs. To empower these rural undeveloped women the Government provides several programs like S H Groups which play a major role.

S.H. Groups

Aim: The main aim of SH groups is to help themselves by saving money and circulating between them to fulfill their needs, which are not fulfilling through their daily wages for obtaining education and health, etc.

The Main Objectives of S.H. Groups

1. *Group*: The gathering of individuals is called S H group.
    - These are formed to do a work by all the people.
    - Group is formed to do a work which is impossible to do by a single person.
    - Ten to fifteen members are necessary to form a group.
2. *Rules to Form a Group*:
    - Every group has its specific name.
    - They must have to stay in the same village and in the same place.
    - They have the same needs and same necessities to fulfill.
    - They must have the same social status.
    - They must have unity between members to withstand the group for a long period.
    - Those who are working and of more than fifteen years age are eligible to join in this group.
3. Uses by forming a Group:
    - Group is more powerful than individuals.
    - One for all and all for one rule is strengthened within a group.
    - To improve self confidence among the people.
    - To know the rights and responsibilities and to achieve them.
    - To improve strengths and skills among the people.
    - To develop saving of amount and uses its when critical conditions takes place.

4. President or Leader:
   - The leader plays very important role to form a group and to lead it in a right way.
   - The leader is elected by all the individuals in the group.
   - The skillful and responsible person has to be elected as president.
   - The group must conduct a meeting and prepare AGENDA and the work is done as per the AGENDA.
5. Records and Registers:
   - The economical process must be recorded in records.
   - Savings, revolving fund, paid interest and spending money must be recorded.
   - The records must be recorded under the observation of members in the group.
   - Savings must be recorded in the bank pass books and installments are recorded in the individuals pass books.
6. Banks helping S.H. Groups:
   - Bharateeya china tharaha abivruddi Bank.
   - Mahila vikasa nidhi.
   - Bank of India.
   - State Bank of India Priya Darsini Yojana.
   - And other small scale Banks.

S.H. Groups were first introduced in 1994. The DRDA plays the important role in conducting these S.H groups, State and Central Governments provide funds to the DRDA to conduct these programs.

PURPOSE AND CONCEPT

The self help groups help themselves by forming a group and revolving money with the help of government support. In the beginning, the started fund is called "Revolving fund".

Ex:

Ten Individual persons

↓

Formed a group-with one president and Secretary

↓

Each person pays 30/- per month.

↓

There are 300/- are gathered per month

↓

1800/- are saved from 6 months

↓

→ These amount deposited in Banks.

↓

The person need of money taken thousand to 1200/- from the Bank.

↓

This concept is written as " THERUMANAM" between president an individuals

↓

The individuals pays 100/- + 30/- monthly amount + 20/- Interest and
all other monthly pay of 30/- from other persons.

↓

→ And all these amount again saved in banks.

Flow Chart for Concept of Revolving Fund and Installs in S.H. Groups

Ten to Fifteen persons are gathered and form into a group and these people deposit Rs. 30/- as a minimum of amount in the name of group. This saving amount is Rs. 300/- per month and when saved up to six months, the amount is Rs. 1800/-. The needed individual takes Rs. 1000/- to Rs. 1200/- from the saving amount in the bank and the individual returns Rs. 100/- and Rs. 30/- of monthly pay and Rs. 20/- interest = 150/- to the bank with the amounts of other members monthly pay of Rs. 30/- is again deposited in banks. There is a return of statements between the President and individual member, which is called "Therumanam". And again the money revolves and the needed persons fulfill their needs by this amount. This process continues in every S.H. Group.

From 1999

From 1999, the bank issued loans as per their percentage to the responsible S.H. Groups so that the groups get Rs. 12,500/- from the bank. This amount is sponsored to the bank by DRDA (District Resource Development Agencies).

From 2004

From 2004, all S.H. groups which have completed 6 months of repayment of bank loans are eligible for pavala vaddi. The DRDA will obtain details of self help group repayment for the purpose of interest subsidy, twice in a year, that is in September 30 and in March 31. In that interest of 75% is paid by DRDA and 25 % only by the beneficial.

Need of Study of Guntur District: (S.H. Groups)

Guntur District stands first in S. H. Groups from 1994. Many groups are showing good performance and get financial support to their families. The groups are going to several places with spread of these groups in many places. These people are the active participants in "Dwakra Bazars" held at several places.

Dwakra Bazars

The exhibition of S.H. Group products is called "Dwakra Bazars". Upto now, there are 10 country wide Dwakra Bazars which are held at Hyderabad. This is a 12 day camp and the accommodation is provided by the Commissioner of DRDA and the TA and DAs are provided by district-wide DRDA. Approximately one crore is funded to State-wide DRDA to commence this Dwakra Bazars from the assistance of Central Government. Through Dwakra Bazars, the Government is providing market to the S.H. groups to exhibit their products.

Some products of Dwakra Bazars: Pickles, Sarees, handicrafts, soaps, leather goods, etc

Data of Guntur District

Total Number of Groups ⟶ 38,392 groups.
Total Number of Members ⟶ 4,23,694 members.

Statistical Data of Guntur S H Groups Distributed in Pavala Vaddi

Year	O.B	Funds Received from Govt.	Other Receipts	Total Funds Available	Expen-diture As on Data	Balance Funds Available
2005 - 06	0.00	94.54	29.25	123.79	123.79	0.00
2006 - 07	0.00	349.12	6.21	355.33	280.80	74.53
2007 - 08	74.53	281.74	0.00	356.27	332.75	23.52

The following is the year wise expenditure under interest Subsidy.

Sl. No.	Year	Total Groups	Interest Subsidy (Pavalavaddi) Disbursed (Rs. In Lakhs)
1.	2005 - 06	9,766	123.79
2.	2006 - 07	14,933	280.80
3.	2007 - 08	13,863	332.75

Source: From DRDA

Total Groups Availed Pavalavaddi: in the District — 21,785
Total Amount Disbursed: — Rs. 737.35 Lakhs

In 2005-2006

- Repalle mandala got the highest groups of 466 SH groups are formed with the total amount of Rs. 5,87,438.00 sectional by the government.

Next to the Repalle Mandal the Highest is

Pedakakani	385 groups	4980091/-
Bapatla	382 groups	394189/-
Amaravathi	373 groups	435447/-

- The total number of groups in this particular year are 9766.
- The total amount of funds sanctioned by the government in this year is 12379851/-.

In 2006-2007

- Kollipara mandal got the highest number of groups of 641 with the total amount of Rs. 13,84,765/-.
- There is rise of 247 groups than the previous year.
- The total number of groups in particular year are 14,933.
- The total amount of funds sanctioned in these years are Rs. 2,80,80,010/-.

In 2007-2008

- Tadikonda mandal got the highest number of groups of 427 with the total amount of Rs. 129618/-.
- The total number of groups in particular year are 13,863.
- The total amount of funds sanctioned in these years are Rs. 33,275,393/-.

Social Category Wise S.H. Groups Received Pavala Vaddi

Year	*Total SHGs received Pavala vaddi*		*S.Cs*		*S.Ts*		*Disabled*		*Minorities (BC+OC)*		*Others*	
	Group	*Amt*	*Group*	*Amt*	*Group*	*Amt*	*Group*	*Amt*	*Group*	*Amt*	*Group*	*Amt*
05-06	9,766	123.7	2485	31.4	423	5.12	5	0.12	610	7.72	6248	79.46
06-07	14933	280.8	4189	76.74	543	10.21	7	0.16	834	15.68	9367	178.1
07-08	13863	332.7	3882	79.8	693	16.63	9	0.25	970	23.22	8309	212.7

Source: From DRDA.

SCs

- In 2005-06 year, 2,485 groups are formed under SC category with the total amount of 31.49 lakhs.
- In 2006-07 year, 4189 groups are formed under SC category with the total amount of 76.74 lakhs and a raise of 1704 groups than the previous year.
- In 2007-08 year, 3882 groups are formed under SC category with the total amount of 79.86 lakhs.

STs

- In 2005-06 year, 423 groups are formed under ST category with total amount of 5.12 lakhs.
- In 2006-07 year, 543 groups are formed under ST category with total amount of 1021 lakhs and a rise of 1200 groups than the previous year.
- In 2007-08 year 693 groups are formed under ST category with total amount of 16.63 Lakhs and a rise of 150 groups than the previous year.

Physically Challenged

- In 2005-06 year, 5 groups are formed with total amount of 0.12 lakhs sanctioned by the government.
- In 2006-07 year, 7 groups are formed with total amount of 0.16 lakhs sanctioned by the government with a rise of 2 groups than previous year.
- In 2007-08 year, 9 groups are formed with total amount of 0.25 lakhs than the previous year.

Minorities

- In 2005-06 year, 610 group are formed with total amount of 7.72 lakhs sanctioned by the government.
- In 2006-07 year, 834 groups are formed with total amount of 15.68 lakhs sanctioned by the Government and there is a rise of 224 groups than the previous year.
- In 2007-08 year, 970 groups are formed with total amount of 23.29 lakhs sanctioned by the government and there is rise of 136 groups than the previous year.

Others (BC + OC)

- In 2005-06 year, 6248 groups are formed with total amount of 7946 Lakhs sanctioned by the Government.
- In 2006-07 year, 9367 groups are formed with total amount of 178.17 lakhs sanctioned by the government and huge rise of 3119 of groups than the previous year, This rise is the highest when compared to all others.

- In 2007-08 year, 8309 groups are formed with total amount of 212.72 lakhs are sanctioned by the government and there is a 34.55 lakhs mine amount is sanctioned by the government than the previous year.

Statement Showing the List of Elected Women Representatives in S.H. Groups in Guntur District

	Ward Members	*Sarpa*	*M.P.T.C.*	*Z.P.T.C.*	*M.P.P*	*Total*
SC	394	38	45	4	1	482
ST	42	5	6	0	0	53
BC	294	33	39	3	2	371
GEN	422	39	45	5	4	515
Total	1152	115	135	12	7	1421

Source: IKP (Indira Kranthi Padhakam)

Ward Members

Ward members are highly involved in SH groups than all other people's representative. The people in the general category an participating more than SC, ST, BC's to the general category 394 SC category people are commencing this ST Group Higher than all 1152 women ward members out of 1421 as participated in SH groups.

Sarpanches

- Out of 115 women sarpanches, general category are more with 39 members next to the general category SCs category people stands next with 38 member.
- There are 115 women sarpanches out of 1421 women people's representatives who are involved in S.H groups.

M.P.T.C's

- In MPTC's both general and SC category people stand equal number of members with 45 members out of 135 M.P.T.C's.
- M.P.T.C's are the next highest people representatives involved with SH Groups.

- BC stands next to the SC and general category with 39 members in SH Groups.

Z.P.T.C.

- There are 5 Z.P.T.C. from general category particularly in SH Groups out of total 12 Z.P.T.C.
- 4 members from SCs and 3 members for STs category are involved in S.H group.

M.P.P

- 9 M.P.P from group category involve in SH group out of 7 M.P.P. from SC and 2 from BC.

Totally

482–SCs category women public representatives involve out of 1421 of total women representatives.

53–STs category women public representatives involve out of 1421 of total women representatives.

371–BCs category women public representatives involve out of 1421 of total women representatives.

512–General category women public representatives involve out of 1421 of total women representatives.

CONCLUSION

By this statistical data we can clearly see that S H Groups play the major role in the empowerment of Women around Guntur district. Up to now 423694 women members are getting benefit by SH groups. Especially, SC women are the active participants in this SH group. Government providing training to women members for better participation and development.

DRDA other rural development institution are providing funds. Now there is no place without these groups and these groups are rising from year to year and getting the maximum benefits. Hence we hope that in the future years, 'SH Groups' stand as the major source of income to the backward women.

34

HEALTH STATUS OF RURAL WOMEN IN VIZIANAGARAN DISTRICT OF ANDHRA PRADESH

DR. K. VENKATANAIDU

INTRODUCTION

Women are high risk population from health point of view. However, it is only since the women's development decade of 1970s and Alma Ata declaration of health for All by 2000 AD, issues relating women's health, have attracted the attention of academics, policy-makers and international organizations. At present, there is growing awareness about women's low social status and gender-based discrimination which have serious adverse implications on women's health. Women's health and nutritional status are on a national as well as individuals welfare concern, as these also affect the next generation, through their impact on children and women's economic productivity. The status of Indian women in identifying areas for further investigation, which coincides with the UN Decade for Women (1975-85) indicating thereby growing concern for the health status of Indian women.

Despite the significance of women's health as national and individual welfare concern, there are many gaps in information relating women's health. The World Bank's 1994 Survey on women's health observed, that women's health status is affected by complex biological, social and cultural factors that are highly interrelated. The interrelationship between women's work and the growing scarcity of energy resources for survival show their impact on women's health and nutrition. The above study found that there is a deficit of nearly 1000 calories per day per woman, whereas a man has an intake surplus of nearly 800 calories. The study concludes that women's deprivation occurs at three levels:

1. Socio-environment level,
2. Environmental level and
3. Service programme level.

There is an urgent need for restructuring and expanding the scope of the existing health and nutrition programmes to reach out to all women and to draw them into its network. A review of earlier research examined the ways in which women's role leads to gender differences in health and survival. The high maternal and infant mortality in rural India take place owing to early marriages. It is further observed that out of 4.5 million marriages that take place every year in India, 3 million brides are children. It is further observed that the high mortality rate for girls under 16, calls for greater attention to ante-natal and post-natal care in pregnancy.

The Rural Health Care Services in India noted that those living in the interior and rural area have limited access to health care services and rapid expansion diluted quality of services. This is resulted in the erosion of creditability of health staff among the rural people. The possible reason for different digress of utilization have also been discussed and its implications for Nutritional health Policy are being identified. But these studies are silent on the gender aspect of utilization of health services.

The National Institute of Public Cooperation and Child Development observed that 'the neglect of maternity and child health services and general public health services through over concentration on efforts for family planning had their adverse affects on maternal and infant mortality rates defeating the ultimate objective of the family planning programme.

OBJECTIVES

- Health Status of Rural Women in Vizianagaram district, based on secondary data.
- Health status of Rural Women and their socio-economic background characteristics.
- Health status of Rural Women and their socio-economic determinants.
- The Rural Women's awareness about Health care programmes and their approach to medical and for different types of diseases.
- Rural women's access to PHC services by women.

THE HEALTH STATUS OF RURAL WOMEN IN VIZIANAGARAM DISTRICT BASED ON SECONDARY DATA

Demographic Factors

(i) Density of the population;
(ii) Literacy rate;
(iii) Work participation rates;
(iv) Sex ratio;
(v) Age at marriage;
(vi) Health infrastructure facilities.

Table 1
Literacy Rate by Sex During 1961-2001 in India, Andhra Pradesh and Vizianagaram District

	India		*Andhra Pradesh*		*Vizianagaram*	
Year	*Male*	*Female*	*Male*	*Female*	*Male*	*Female*
1961	34.44	12.95	30.19	12.03	21.47	5.49
1971	39.45	18.72	33.18	15.75	27.37	9.87
1981	46.89	24.82	39.26	20.99	32.65	13.82
1991	52.68	32.52	55.13	32.72	45.92	22.47
2001	60.74	41.63	64.15	40.67	52.89	28.39

Source: Amulya Ratna Nanda, Census of India 2001, Series 1, India, Paper 1 of 2001, provisional population totals. The Registrar General and Census Commissioner, India.

Census of India, 2001, Andhra Pradesh, Director of Census operations, Andhra Pradesh (1991-2001) Census Report, Vizianagaram District.

Table 2
Work Participation Rate by Sex During 1961-2001 in India, Andhra Pradesh and Vizianagaram District

	India		*Andhra Pradesh*		*Vizianagaram*	
Year	*Male*	*Female*	*Male*	*Female*	*Male*	*Female*
1961	57.6	27.93	62.22	41.32	23.13	18.41
1971	57.75	14.22	58.38	28.04	29.34	13.42
1981	52.65	19.77	57.68	33.54	59.90	37.13
1991	51.52	22.69	55.44	34.81	59.03	41.91
2001	53.61	24.66	59.54	37.72	61.12	45.73

Source: Singh R, P., Director of Census operations, Andhra Pradesh. Census of India 2001, Series 2, Andhra Pradesh, Paper 1 of 2001

Table 3
Sex Ratio (Females per 1000 Males) During 1961-2001 in India, Andhra Pradesh and Vizianagaram District

Year	*India*	*Andhra Pradesh*	*Vizianagaram District*
1961	941	981	1037
1971	930	977	1025
1981	934	975	1006
1991	929	972	1000
2001	933	976	1002

Source: Premi, M. K. 2001 in India's Population Heading towards a billion. An analysis of 2001 census, provisional results, B. R. Publishing Corporation, New Delhi, Census of India 2001, Andhra Pradesh

Table 4
Age at Marriage by Sex During 1961-2001 in India, Andhra Pradesh and Vizianagaram District

Year	*India*		*Andhra Pradesh*		*Vizianagaram*	
	Male	*Female*	*Male*	*Female*	*Male*	*Female*
1961	21.3	15.5	21.1	15.3	14.4	13.9
1971	22.4	17.2	22.7	16.2	18.9	15.3
1981	23.3	18.3	23.0	17.3	21.7	16.5
1991	24.5	19.7	25.1	19.1	24.5	18.2
2001	26.8	20.9	28.7	22.4	27.8	20.5

Source: Census Report of India and Andhra Pradesh during 1971, 1991 and 2001, District Census Handbook, 2001, Vizianagaram District

Table 5
Health Facilities in Andhra Pradesh and Vizianagaram District During 2000-2001

Health Facilities	*Andhra Pradesh*	*Vizianagaram District*
1. Population per dispensary		
(a) Allopathy (primary health centers)	46,771	38,381
(b) Ayurveda	99,414	95,952
(c) Unani	3,39,326	10,55,471
(d) Homeopathy	2,31,735	1,31,934
2. Population per Doctor		
(a) Allopathy	7,969	11,535
(b) Ayurveda	1,22,257	1,17,275
(c) Unani	4,26,333	10,55,471
(d) Homeopathy	2,30,131	1,31,934
3. Population per hospital bed in Allopathy dispensaries		
(a) Male	3,292	9,177
(b) Female	3,568	9,596
4. Percentage of population treated to rural population		
(a) Ayurveda	9.24	14.93
(b) Unani	2.32	0.39
(c) Homeopathy	2.74	4.44

Source: Directorate of Economic and Statistics, Government of Andhra Pradesh, Statistical Abstract of Andhra Pradesh During 2000-2001.

Health Status of Rural Women in Vizianagaram District of Andhra Pradesh

Health status is usually measured in terms of mortality indicators like crude death rate. Infant mortality rate, expectation of life at birth, age-specific death rate and mortality indicators like prevalence rate, fatality rate and causes of death at the district level.

Table 6
Death Rate by Sex During 1961-2001 in India, Andhra Pradesh and Vizianagaram District

	India		*Andhra Pradesh*		*Vizianagaram*	
Year	*Male*	*Female*	*Male*	*Female*	*Male*	*Female*
1961	20.5	23.4	25.2	26.4	9.14	8.6
1971	17.3	18.6	14.6	15.9	5.7	6.3
1981	15.0	15.2	13.8	12.5	13.2	12.0
1991	10.8	10.9	9.1	10.3	9.7	9.0
2001	8.7	8.15	8.3	9.7	9.2	9.4

Source: Census of India 1991 and 2001, Andhra Pradesh

Table 7
Infant Mortality Rate by Sex During 1961-2001 in India, Andhra Pradesh and Vizianagaram District

	India		*Andhra Pradesh*		*Vizianagaram*	
Year	*Male*	*Female*	*Male*	*Female*	*Male*	*Female*
1961	153.2	138.3	139.0	114.1	105.3	94.3
1971	130.1	128.4	143.0	135.0	112.3	103.8
1981	147.0	157.2	102.0	82.2	158.0	116.0
1991	105.3	112.5	115.1	99.2	115.2	104.9
2001	116.8	171.6	113.4	102.6	119.5	108.2

Source: The Registrar, General, Vital Statistics Division, Infant Mortality in India, sample registration scheme, Analytical series no. 1, 1981, Census, New Delhi. Recent literary trends in India, occasional paper no. 1 of 1997 by OP Sharma, Robert D Retherford, the Registrar, General and Census Commissioner of India, Ministry of Home Affairs, Government of India, New Delhi.

Census of India, 2001, A Handbook of Population Statistics by Verma, V.S. The Registrar General and Census Commissioner of India.

Health Status of Rural Women, Socio-economic Background Characteristics

(i) Age of women;
(ii) Literacy level of rural women;
(iii) Family status of rural women;
(iv) Economic status of Rural women;
(v) Work status of rural women;
(vi) Women's earnings in rural family.

Health Status of Rural Women, Socio-economic and Social Determinants

(i) Environmental cleanliness;
(ii) Fuels needs for cooking;
(iii) Personal hygiene:
  (a) regular bath, (b) change of clothes regular,
  (c) Intake of food regular.

Rural Women's Awareness About Health Care Programmes

In rural areas the Government of India and the Government of Andhra Pradesh have implemented in the rural areas of Andhra Pradesh. Health care programmes understanding women's awareness about various types of health care and utilization of medical aid both for prevention and cure of diseases.

Women's perceptions of their own health, their utilization of full range of health services from Ayurvedic to Allopathic and their service preference for utilization of medical aid for various types of ailments, particularly in respect of rural women, are as given below.

Women's Awareness About Various Types of Health Care Programmes in Vizianagaram District of Andhra Pradesh

1. Immunization Programmes:
   (i) Polio; (ii) BCG; (iii) DPT;
   (iv) Measles; (v) DT; (vi) TT;
   (vii) Vit. A solution,
   (viii) Iron polic-acid tablets;
   (ix) Iron Polic Acid liquid; (x) Typhoid.
2. General Health Programmes:
   (i) National programme for control of blindness;
   (ii) Malaria; (iii) Leprosy; (iv) Tuberculosis;
   (v) Eye care; (vi) Conjunctivitis;
   (vii) Squint; (viii) Steroid; (ix) Viral fever;
   (x) Bruise.

3. Communicable diseases in Health programmes:
   (i) Chickenpox; (ii) Diphtheria; (iii) Mumps;
   (iv) Polio; (v) Typhoid; (vi) Tonsillitis;
   (vii) Tetarus; (viii) Measles;
   (ix) Whooping cough.
4. Miscellaneous Health Programmes:
   (i) Allergy; (ii) Anemia;
   (iii) Appendicitis; (iv) Bleeding;
   (v) Bowlegs; (vi) Burns;
   (vii) Cerebral palsy; (viii) Chocking;
   (ix) Cloudy urine; (x) Colour blindness;
   (xi) Asthma.
5. Maternal Health Care Programmes:
   (i) Antenatal care of mother
      (a) Sufficient rest, (b) Physical exercise,
      (c) Nutritional diet
   (ii) Post natal care
   (iii) Immunization to mother and child against tetanus
   (iv) Nutrition supplementation
   (v) Family planning

Rural Women to Assess on PHC Services by Women

The basic function of PHC services in the rural area:

(i) Providing medical and in rural areas;
(ii) protection of maternal and child health and family welfare;
(iii) promotion of health among school children;
(iv) propagation of modern ideas of health and sanitation among rural people;
(v) prevention of epidemics.

Rural Health Care Services-Suggestions

1. The number of PHC sub-centre and CHC need to improve the quality of primary health care services in villages.
2. The management and control of PHC sub-centers and CHCs should be handed over to Panchayatiraj institutions at the village, mandal and district level.
3. Top priority should be given to improve rural sanitation, hygiene and water supply, pollution of water, air and soil should be prevented.
4. Food and nutrition support should be provided to all the children upto 11 years, especially those belonging to rural poor.
5. Health education and information should be intensified in rural ares, using mass media like TV, cinema, videos, song, drama, etc.

Conclusion

Women's health and nutritional status are of national as well as individual welfare concerns because they also affect the next generation, through their impact on children and women's economic productivity. The status of women in India highlights the seriousness of the health status of India women in identifying areas for further investigation. The demographic factors are highlighted in the rural areas regarding health facilities available in Vizianagaram district of Andhra Pradesh inclusive of health status of rural women in Vizianagaram district which highlighted in the sources of secondary data. Rural women's socio-economic characteristics as also health determinants and rural women's awareness on health-care programmes. Rural women's access to PHC services are projected fro Vizianagaram district of Andhra Pradesh.

References

Basu, A.M., (1995), "Women's Roles and Gender Gap in Health and Survival' in Monical Das Gupta et. al. (ed.) Women's Health in India, Oxford University Press, Madras.

Brijesh C. Purohit & Tasleem A. Siddiqui, (1994), "Utilization of health Services in India", Economic and Political Weekly, Vol. XXIX, No. 18, April, pp. 10-79.

Bose Ashish, (1991), "Demographic Diversity of India, 1991 census state and district level data B.R. Publishing Corporation, New Delhi.

Das Gupta Monica et. al., (1995), "Women's Health in India, Risk and Vulnerability, Oxford University Press, Bombay.

Anrudh, K. Jain & Pravin Visaria (ed) (1988), Infant Mortality in India Differentials and Determinants, New Delhi.

Director of Health, Andhra Pradesh, (1997), Handbook of Health and Family Welfare Statistics of Andhra Pradesh, Hyderabad.

Germain Andreinne, (1995), Gender and Health, Form Research to Action in Das Gupta Monica et al, pp. 28-31.

Monjurana & Beena Yadav, (1991), "Mothers Awareness of Children's Health and Hygiene", Journal of Social Welfare, Vol. XXXVIII, No. 7, October, pp. 32-33.

Malcolms Adiseshiah, (1993), "Sex Ratio", Kurushetra, Vol. XIII, No. 1, October, p. 12.

Monica Sharma, (1991), Women and Health Problems and Issues in Dak, T.M. (ed), pp. 196-216.

World Bank, (1994), Social Determinants of Women's Health.

Srinivas, S., (1994), Management of Rural Health Care Services in India: An Overview, Journal of Rural Development, Vol. 13, No. 4, October-December, pp. 51-55.

Singh R.P., (1991), Census of India-1991, Series-2, Andhra Pradesh, paper 1 of 1991, Supplement, Director of Census Operations, Andhra Pradesh.

Suma Chitni's and Srilatha Batliwala, (1988), The Health Status of India Women-A Reader, Unit for Women's Studies, Tata Institute of Social Sciences, Bombay.

Marina Pinto, (1995), Women's Health Development through Empowerment of Women in India" Kurukshetra, Vol. XIIII, No. 11, August, pp. 11-12.

35

REPRODUCTIVE HEALTH NEEDS OF THE RURAL WOMEN

DR. V. HARI BABU
DR. M. MARY

INTRODUCTION

The programme of action of the International Conference on Population and Development, held at Cairo in September 1994, defined reproductive health as "A state of complete physical, mental and social well-being and not merely the absence of disease or infirmity, in all matters relating to the reproductive systems and to its functions and process". Reproductive Health, therefore, implies that people must have a satisfying and safe sex life and that they have the capability to reproduce and the freedom to decide if, when, and how often to do so. Implicit in this last condition are the rights of men and women to be informed and to have access to safe, effective, affordable and acceptable methods of Family Planning of their choice for regulation of fertility which are not against the law and the right of access to appropriate health care services that will enable women to go safely through pregnancy and childbirth and provide couples with the best chance of having a healthy infant.

In line with the above definition of reproductive health, reproductive health care is defined as "the constellation of methods, techniques and services that contribute to reproductive health and well being by preventing and solving reproductive health problems. It also includes sexual health, the purpose of which is the enhancement of life and personal relations and not merely counseling and care related to reproduction and sexually transmitted diseases". Keeping in mind the above definition, reproductive rights embrace certain human rights that are already recognized in National laws, International Human Rights Documents and other consensus documents. These rights rest on the recognition of the basic right of all couples and individuals to decide freely and responsibly the number spacing and timing of their children and to have the information and means to do so, and the right to attain the highest standard of sexual and reproductive health.

It also includes the right to make decisions concerning reproduction free of discrimination, coercion and violence, as expressed in the Human Rights Documents. In the exercise of this right, they should take into account the need of their living and future children and their responsibilities towards the community. The promotion of responsible exercise of these rights for all people especially for tribals should be the fundamental basis for government and community supported policies and programmes in the area of reproductive health, including Family Planning. As part of their commitment, full attention should be given to the promotion of mutually respectful and equitable gender relations, particularly for meeting the educational and service needs for adolescents to enable them to deal positively and responsibly with their sexuality.

This approach to reproductive health contrasts with various previous approaches dealing with reproduction. The earlier approaches focused on specific aspects of reproductive health like providing information and services on contraception, promoting the health of mother and their young children, the need to ensure that pregnant women receive adequate prenatal care, safe delivery and postnatal care and sought to address the high risks that women in many contexts face in relation to child-bearing.

The United Nations (1995) reports that Reproductive Health was eluding many of the people due to different factors as: inadequate levels of knowledge about human sexuality, inappropriate or poor-quality reproductive health information and services, the prevalence of high-risk sexual bahavious, discriminatory social practices, negative attitude towards women and girls, and the limited power many women and girls have over their sexual and reproductive lives.

Reproductive Health is based on the premise that the health status of individuals at any given time is affected by their earlier experiences. The Reproductive Health of men and women of childbearing age reflects not only their current experience but also their health status during infancy, childhood and adolescence. Similarly, their health status beyond the reproductive ages may reflect their earlier reproductive experiences. The experiences of one generation also have implications for the health of the next generation.

In this background, the dearth of information on reproductive health status of different Rural population groups necessitates micro level studies in this area. A number of studies have been undertaken covering various aspects of reproductive health. However, comprehensive studies covering all aspects of reproductive health are very few. As such micro level studies on reproductive health giving information about the needs of various target groups are very much needed. The present study is an attempt in this direction.

Objectives

- Understanding the Reproductive Health needs of Rural Women of Visakhapatnam Rural region of Andhra Pradesh.
- To study the socio-economic, demographic background of the respondents and their educational status.

- Understanding issues associated with the Reproductive Health.
- Study of factors associated with infant and abortion.

Study Area and Sample

The study was carried out in the Pendurthi, Anandapuram and Nakkapalli Rural Mandals of Visakhapatnam district in the state of Andhra Pradesh. For the purpose of this study 100 Rural women were taken and nearly half of them are illiterates.

Development of the Interview Schedule

The interview schedule was prepared covering the items relating to the various variables indicated in the objectives of the study. The items were of multiple choice, 'Yes' or 'No' type and open ended. The interview schedule was pre-tested (to avoid ambiguity if any in the items) and finalized before administering to the respondents of the sample.

Data Collection

The data was collected by trained woman investigator. Rapport was established by the investigator with the respondents before administering the interview schedule. The respondents were explained about the purpose of the study and were requested to extend their full co-operation. The investigator collected the information required from the respondents by meeting them at pre-fixed appointments.

Statistical Techniques

The data collected was subjected to simple statistical analysis for easy interpretation. Frequencies and percentages were used to interpret the data.

Profile of the Sample Respondents

Socio-economic and demographic variables are considered to be the most important factors influencing the quality of population in a community. The quality of life depends upon the prevailing socio-economic situation in the community.

These variables should be examined to know their effect on demographic process of the community.

Reproduction is a rational behaviour influenced by the status of women. In view of this, the social, economic and demographic profile is expected to indicate not only the characteristics features of the respondents, but also from methodological point of view a definite relationship between these characteristics and reproductive behaviour of women in a more explicit and meaningful manner. The variables included for the understanding of the respondents profile are age, clan, occupation, income, type of family and type of house.

Table 1
Profile of the Sample Respondents

Sl. No.	*Character*	*Variable*	*Illiterate*	*Literate*	*Total*
1.	Age	16 years below	18 (33.96)	20 (42.55)	38 (38.00)
		17 - 20	12 (22.64)	23 (48.93)	35 (35.00)
		21 - 25	13 (24.52)	4 (8.51)	17 (17.00)
		25 and above	10 (18.86)	-	10 (10.00)
2.	Clan	Bagatha	13 (24.52)	11 (23.40)	24 (24.00)
		Valmiki	15 (28.30)	14 (29.78)	29 (29.00)
		Kondakapu	8 (15.09)	9 (19.14)	17 (17.00)
		Mannedora	17 (32.07)	13 (27.65)	30 (30.00)
3.	Occupation	Agriculture	21 (39.62)	18 (38.29)	39 (39.00)
		Daily wage earner	19 (35.84)	12 (25.53)	31 (31.00)
		Seasonal Work	10 (18.86)	12 (25.53)	22 (22.00)
		House Wife	3 (5.66)	5 (10.63)	8 (8.00)
4.	Income	Below Rs. 5000/-	36 (67.92)	39 (82.97)	75 (75.00)
		Rs. 5001-10000/-	14 (26.41)	6 (12.76)	20 (20.00)
		Above Rs. 10000/-	3 (5.66)	2 (4.25)	5 (5.00)
5.	Type of Family	Nucleus	18 (33.96)	25 (53.19)	43 (43.00)
		Joint	35 (66.03)	22 (46.80)	57 (57.00)
6.	Type of House	Thatched	27 (50.94)	13 (27.65)	40 (40.00)
		Tailed house	8 (15.09)	10 (21.27)	18 (18.00)
		Slab house	2 (3.77)	1 (2.12)	3 (3.00)
		Kaccha house	16 (30.18)	23 (48.93)	39 (39.00)

Reproductive Health Profile

Reproductive Health (RH) is the term which covers all aspects of women's health from child hood and adolescence through reproductive age, menopause and beyond. It is influenced by gender equity, education including health education, sexual behaviour, fertility control, maternity care and reproductive tract infections. It covers all aspects of Reproductive Health across a life span (from the cradle to the grave, childhood to adolescence, reproductive period to menopause and elderly age). Female illiteracy, gender inequality, malnutrition, uncontrolled fertility, poor maternity care services and Reproductive Track Infections (RTI), all adversely affect RH resulting in high reproductive morbidity and mortality rates a common occurrence in the developing world.

Age at Menarche

Menarche is a biological phenomenon which gets expression in women at a particular stage of her biological development. Thereafter, the woman goes on to have the same experience every month at an interval of four weeks or so. The age at which a woman experiences her menstruation for the first time is known as her age at menarche.

Table 2
Percentage Distribution of Respondents by Age at Menarche

Sl. No.	*Age at Menarche*	*Illiterate*	*Literate*	*Total*
1.	≥ 13 years	42 (79.24)	40 (85.11)	82 (82.00)
2.	Around 14 years	11 (20.76)	7 (14.89)	18 (18.00)
3.	15 years and above	-	-	-

From the above table observed that majority 82 (79.24 per cent illiterate and 85.11 per cent literate) percent of the sample respondents attained menarche around the age of 13 years, remaining 18 (20.76 per cent illiterate and 14.89 per cent literates) attained the menarche around the age of 14 years. On the whole, all the respondents of the sample attained menarche by the time they were 15 years old.

Menstrual Cycle

Table 4
Percentage Distribution of Respondents by Awareness about Menstrual Cycle

Respondents	*Regularity of the Periods*		*Interval of menstrual cycle*		
	Regular	*Irregular*	*Below 28 days*	*28-30*	*Above 30 days*
Illiterate	40 (75.47)	13 (24.52)	11 (20.75)	26 (49.05)	12 (22.64)
Literate	42 (89.36)	5 (10.63)	7 (14.89)	30 (63.82)	7 (14.89)

The data indicated that 82 per cent of the rural women had regular menstrual cycle. The remaining 24.52 per cent illiterate and 10.63 per cent literate women had irregular periods. Further, variation existed in the interval of menstrual cycle among the respondents. Majority 56 of the sample rural women (49.05 per cent illiterate and 63.82 per cent literate) had regular menstrual cycle at an interval of 28-30 days. About one-fifth illiterate and 14.89 percent literate had a menstrual cycle of less than 28 days interval. The remaining nearly one-fourth of illiterate and 14.89 per cent literates' respondents had menstrual cycle at an interval respondents had menstrual cycle at an interval beyond 30 days. Some of the respondents can not give information in this regard.

Duration of Menstrual Period

Table 5
Percentage Distribution of Respondents by Awareness About Duration and Flow of Menstrual Period

Respondents	*Duration of menstrual period*			*Menstrual flow*		
	3 days	*4-5*	*Above 5*	*Scanty*	*Normal*	*Profuse*
Illiterate	10(18.86)	30(56.60)	13(24.52)	6(11.32)	33(62.26)	14(26.41)
Literate	7(14.89)	36(76.59)	4(8.51)	4(8.51)	29(61.70)	14(29.78)

The above table reveals that for about two third sample respondents (56.60 per cent illiterate and 76.59 per cent literate) the menstrual period lasted for 4-5 days. About 18.86

percent illiterate women and 14.89 per cent literate women respondents had menstrual period for about 3 days. For the remaining illiterate and literate women respondents the menstrual periods lasted beyond 5 days.

Majority 62.26 per cent of illiterate and 61.70 per cent literate respondents had normal menstrual flow. Among 11.32 per cent illiterate and 8.51 per cent literate respondents' women the menstrual flow was scanty. The remaining 26.41 per cent literate and 29.78 per cent illiterate had profuse menstrual flow during their periods.

Type of Pads and Attendance to Work

Table 6
Percentage Distribution of Respondents by Type of Pads Used by Them During Menstrual Period and By Their Attendance to Routine Work During the Period

Respondents	*Type of Menstrual Pads Do You Used*		*Attendance to Routine Work During Menstrual Period*	
	Home Made Cloths	*Sanitary Napkins*	*Attend to Work*	*Stopped One Day*
Illiterate	45 (84.90)	8 (15.09)	53 (100.00)	-
Literate	12 (25.53)	35 (74.46)	40 (85.11)	7 (14.89)

Most of literate women respondents of the sample (74.46 per cent) had used sanitary napkins during menstrual periods. In contrast, there were only 15.09 per cent of the women respondents among illiterate who used sanitary napkins. The rest of the illiterate respondents used hand/home made or cloth pads during menstrual period.

All the respondents of the sample (with the exception 7 (14.89 per cent) literate) attended to their regular routine work during menstrual period also. The 14.89 per cent literate respondents' count not attends to their routine work for one day during the menstrual period. However, the other respondents also indicated that there work efficiency was effected to some extent during the menstrual period compared to normal days.

Age at Marriage

Age in general and age at marriage are widely acknowledges as having considerable relevance in the study of reproductive behaviour. Generally, marriages are performed at an early age in India. Currently as is the case in most of the countries of the world, the minimum age at marriage for both male and females has been laid down by law and is not left to custom. As such, the average age at marriage for women during the last few decades is on the rise. By and large considerable variations in the age at marriage are seen in diverse socio-economic and population groups.

Table 3
Percentage Distribution of Respondents by Age at Marriage

Sl. No.	Age at Marriage	Illiterate	Literate	Total
1.	Below 15 years	20 (37.74)	15 (31.92)	35 (35.00)
2.	15-18	33 (62.26)	30 (63.82)	63 (63.00)
3.	18 years and above	-	2 (4.26)	2 (2.00)

Women reproductive span range from 15 to 45 years, the total period being 30 years. If a woman marries at higher age, it cuts her reproductive span and thereby reducing fertility. Thus one of the factors that determine the number of children that women will have during her reproductive period is the age at which she gets married. Majority 63 (62.26 per cent illiterates and 63.82 per cent literates) per cent of women respondents were married in the age between 15 to 18 years, one third of the respondents (37.74 per cent illiterate and 31.92 per cent literate) are married below fifteen years. Only 2 (4.26 per cent) literate women respondents are married at the age of 18 years. All most all the respondents are married at below 18 years this is against constitution.

Interval between Marriage and First Birth

Table 4
Interval between Marriage and First Birth

Sl. No.	First Motherhood	Illiterate	Literate	Total
1.	1 year below	4 (7.54)	-	4 (4.00)
2.	1 - 2	37 (69.81)	25 (53.19)	62 (62.00)
3.	2 - 3	12 (22.64)	22 (46.81)	34 (34.00)

The percentage distribution of even-married women according to interval between age at effective marriage and age at first motherhood and mean interval are presented in the table. This table reveals that 4 (7.54 per cent) illiterate mothers have their first child within one year from the date of their marriage. Whereas 62 (69.81 per cent illiterate and 53.19 per cent literate) women respondents having motherhood within 1 to 2 years. The percentage of mothers who have the interval of 2 to 3 years between age of effective marriage and age at first maternity is 34 (22.64 per cent illiterate and 46.81 per cent literate) percent.

Interval between Birth and Birth

Table 5
Time Period of Interval between Birth and Birth

Sl. No.	Interval	Illiterate	Literate	Total
1.	1 year below	-	-	-
2.	1 - 2 years	45 (84.91)	20 (42.55)	65 (65.00)
3.	2 - 3 years	7 (13.21)	20 (42.55)	27 (27.00)
4.	Single baby	1 (1.88)	7 (14.90)	8 (8.00)

To show the trend in the interval among marriage, first birth and second birth of women. This table shows that 65 (84.91 per cent illiterate and 42.55 per cent literate) percent mothers have their second child within 1 to 2 years from the date of first birth, where as 27 (13.21 per cent illiterate and 14.90 per cent literate) per cent women within 2 to 3 years.

There are 8 (1 illiterate and 7 literates) per cent women have only one child.

Number of Children

Table 6
Number of Children

Sl. No.	Number of children	Illiterate	Literate	Total
1.	1 child	1 (1.88)	7 (14.90)	8 (8.00)
2.	2 children	10 (18.86)	25 (53.19)	35 (35.00)
3.	3 children	39 (73.58)	15 (31.91)	54 (54.00)
4.	4 and above	3 (5.66)	-	3 (3.00)

The above table reveals that the number of surviving children, we find that 97 per cent of women had 3 or less number of children living. Out of these 8 (1.88 per cent illiterate and 14.90 per cent literate) percent women had only one child. Majority 54 (73.58 per cent illiterate and 31.91 per cent literate) per cent had 3 children. Only 5.66 per cent illiterate women reported that they had four and more children. This is need on the part of health officials to propagate small family norms in the area especially among illiterate women.

Infant and Childhood Death

Table 7
Infant and Childhood Death

Sl. No.	Childhood Death	Illiterate	Literate	Total
1.	Yes	8 (15.09)	3 (6.38)	11 (11.00)
2.	No	45 (84.91)	44 (93.62)	89 (89.00)

During the process of development of a baby from the date of delivery to completion of early childhood period differential morality was noticed at different periods of life i.e. neo-natal, post-natal and early childhood. An attempt was made to find out whether the childhood death occurred or not. It was found that 11 (15.09 per cent illiterate and 6.38 per cent literate) percent of the women respondents reported that their children death at childhood during the delivery time due to different reasons.

Abortion

Table 8
Percentage Distribution of Respondents by Abortion and Number of Times

	Abortion		*Number of times*	
Respondents	*Yes*	*No*	*One*	*2 or more*
Illiterate	10 (18.86)	43 (81.13)	4 (40.00)	6 (60.00)
Literate	3 (6.38)	44 (93.62)	3 (100.00)	-

The women whose last their pregnancy terminated into abortion were asked about the abortion. An attempt was made weather the abortions made or not. 13 (18.86 per cent illiterate and 6.38 per cent literate) percent of the women respondents reported that they have got abortion during the pregnancy period. The women respondents asked to how may times are abortions? And they are informed that only one time (4 illiterate and 3 literate) is happened. 6 illiterate women respondents noticed that they have two times abortions.

Implications of the Study

The study provided significant information about the knowledge and experience of the sample subjects on various issues of reproductive health. In addition, the study also provided information on the sample subjects perceptions and experiences relating to infant and abortion. Based on the data, the following measures are suggested for attaining a higher quality of reproductive health status.

- Steps should be taken for adequate ante-natal, natal and post-natal care. Attention should be focused on neo-natal health care and nutrition.
- Information and education campaigns should focus on promotion of small family norm and for raising awareness by emphasizing the significant benefits of fewer children, better spacing, better health and nutrition and better education.

- Radio and television serve as the most powerful media for disseminating relevant socio-demographic messages. Government should make appropriate regulations and even legislations, if necessary to mandate the broadcast of social message during prime time.
- Knowledge about spacing methods is inadequate and patchy which is breeding and perpetuating myths and misconceptions.
- Counseling and advocacy have to be provided after the birth of child about contraception to encourage adoption of a reversible or a terminal method. This will also contribute to the health and well being of both mother and child.
- A constant review and evaluation of community needs has to be taken up for effective programme delivery with good management practices and with newly emerging technologies.
- Women need support for obtaining access for essential obstetric care. Lack of necessary support form men to seek preventive and promotive interventions is resulting in poor utilization of pre-natal, natal and post-natal services by pregnant women. Hence, there is need to cognize men on this aspect.
- Promotion of empowerment of women will ensure women's understanding of their needs and to assert their rights in general and reproductive rights in particular.
- Community education about pregnancy and childbirth and making health service more respective to the needs of women will go a long way in seeking services with confidence and without delay.

BIBLIOGRAPHY

Kesarwari, (1989), Fertility and Differential Fertility, Common Wealth Publishers, New Delhi.

Reproductive and Child Health Project repaid house hold survey report conducted by Population Research Centre, (2001), Andhra University, Visakhapatnam.

United Nations, (1994), Report of the International Conference on population and development, Cairo, Egypt, 5-13th September 1994.

Viswanadha Gupta et al, (March 2006), Impact of the Literacy on Reproductive Health Status of Rural Women" Indian Journal of Population Education, No. 32, p.p. 14-25.

Women and World Development Series, (1995), Women and Health, Zed Books Limited, London.

36

EMPOWERMENT OF RURAL GIRL CHILD (WOMAN OF THE FUTURE) BY IMPROVING HEALTH & EDUCATION

MRS. P. USHA
DR S. PULLA RAO

INTRODUCTION

In India the status of girl child 'the woman of the future', reflects serious gender based differences, inequalities and discrimination both in the house and society. Preference for son in the society and discrimination against girl child are interlinked due to inter play of different religious and social factors. These vulnerabilities are stronger in rural areas, where poverty, traditions and lack of social infrastructure prevail.

In rural society of India, girls suffer from the beginning of their life. Child mortality rates in rural India are at its height, the female child mortality rate causes more concern. Truly, the children in rural areas do not get proper medical treatment and nutrious food due to which they become sick and die as infants. Over and above this fact, the girl child becomes a neglected child for the parents in rural India. Rural girl children spend their time in cooking, cleaning, fetching food and water, caring for children and working in different agriculture works like sowing, transplanting and weeding. In fact, girl children contribute over 20 percent of total work at home. In this paper an attempt is made to present systematically review of literature on different aspects of rural girl child in India.

The objectives of the paper are to review literature relating to

(a) the living conditions of rural girl child.
(b) health dimensions and educational aspects of rural girl child with a view to assess the prospects for their empowerment.

Though India is the world's tenth largest economy, in rural areas, women are generally not perceived to have any meaningful income generation capacity due to their illiteracy. There is a social disapproval of education for girls. Also the inadequacy of schools, costs of buying books, uniforms and transportation to the school prevent parents to enroll girl children in schools. Development and welfare of the rural women has become a major concern of the government the women in the rural areas are still found in a deplorable condition. Illiteracy, ill health, malnutrition, lack of land ownership rights, unemployment, and underemployment, lack of bargaining power, low wages, low social status and above all physical exploitation still continue to be the chronic maladies of the women folk of the rural India society. A young girl's status is related to her mother's status. Girl children are considered an economic liability in child care costs, dowry costs and marriage support. Rural children lack the advantages of modern amenities and facilities such as transportation, electricity, media, hygiene, health care and access to education.

The government has undertaken serious efforts to ensure better status to the rural women, to utilize their untapped potential for national development and as such to bring them into the mainstream of the process of development. The government has undertaken a multi dimensional approach to bring down this gender bias. These include provisions of affording education, ensuring health services, providing income-generating activities.

The sex composition of the total population, by age groups is vital for studying the demographic trends of young population, particularly, the status of the girl child. At the census 2001, sex ratio of the population in the age group 0-6 years has been registered as 927 in India, declining from 945 in 1991 and 962 in 1981. The national average for child sex ratio in the case of rural population is higher at 934 if compared to 906 of urban population. This has registered a decline of compared to 1991 when it was 948.

The child sex ratio (0-6) in the country in villages and UAs/Towns is low when compared to the sex ratio of the total population reflecting prevalence of bias against the girl child in certain parts of the country both in villages and towns. In 122,517 villages, the child sex ratio is less than 800, while in the case of overall sex ratio; only 33.876 villages are in this group. Nearly 40 per cent villages in the country which have more than 50 per cent population in the age group 0-6 below 900 in census 2001. There are 690 UAs/Towns which have registered child sex ratio below 850 while for the total population as a whole this is 471 UAs/Towns in this group.

Report on the UN Committee on the rights of child, every year 12 million girls are born 3 million of who do not survive to see their 15th birth day. About one third of these deaths occur in the first year of life and it is estimated that every sixth female death is directly due to gender discrimination. Gender inequality is now receiving greater atrtention. Women and children represent 67.7 per cent of country's total population. More worrisome however in the drastic fall in the CSR (Child Sex Ratio) for the age group 0-6 years. A recent study by the United Nations Fund for Population Activities (UNFPA), India recorded more than 50 point decline in the CSR in 70 districts, in 16 states and UTs between 1991 and 2001. The overall sex ratio is naturally no better. As per the 2005 data, India had 107.5 males per 100 females, the highest girl child deficit being reported from Northern states many of which have high female literacy levels and are in the front line of economic progress.

1991-2000 was observed as the decade of the girl child. The National plan of Action for the Girl Child (1992) recognizes the right of the girl child to equal opportunities, to eliminate all forms of violence perpetuated against the girl child and to provide inputs for personality development of the girl child.

In rural areas boys and girls play key roles in family farming and through their economic activities generate incomes that improve rural livelihoods for the poor. The livelihoods of poor farmers for instance, depend on child labor, at least seasonally and schooling is often not available or accessible for all children. The Government of India developed an action plan in 1992 for developing the girl child. In 1994, India passed a universal female education bill that offers parents incentives for access and punishment for keeping a girl out of school.

UNICEF says that in India girl children tend to be taken to health centers less frequently than boys, receive less food than boys, and are given less education than boys. In rural India the situation is even worse regarding educating the girl children. India, which is estimated to have some 432 million illiterate people, must give top priority to compulsory elementary education for social and economic growth to occur 64 percent of Indian men are literate, but fewer than two out of five women can read and write. About 41 percent of Indian girls under the age of 14 do not attend school.

UNICEF Report says that education of girls is their human right. Girls must enjoy the right to freedom, right to education and right to birth. They are biologically stronger than boys and must receive adequate nutrition, health care facilities and education. They must be given opportunities to explore themselves and prove their capabilities. As mothers, they are responsible for imparting values cultural beliefs and manners in their children. Hence they must be educated spiritually, emotionally and intellectually.

In India, very conspicuous gender disparities persist in all the educational indicators, especially in regard to enrollment and retention at the primary, upper primary and higher levels of school education. The situation is much worse in rural and tribal areas due to social attitudes, poor access to education and family oriented role and responsibilities of the girl child. The incidence of dropout and stagnation for girls is much higher than that of boys at primary and upper primary stage. Access to education continues to be a major problem, especially for rural girls. Female literacy is closely associate with reduction in fertility rates, population growth, IMR and USMR shows positive association with age at marriage, life expectancy, women's participation in development process.

As a result of education programmes, by the end of 2000, 94 per cent of India's rural population had primary schools with in one km. and 84 per cent had upper primary schools with in 3 km. Special efforts have made to enroll SC/ST and girls. The enrollment in primary and upper primary schools has gone up considerably since the first five year plan. So the number of primary and upper primary schools has increased. The Haryan government has decided to institute a cash award of Rs.1 lakh for the panchayats which ensure the enrollment of 100 per cent girls in the age group of 6 to 14 years in schools. Moreover to provide medical checkup facility to girls, all girl students up to the age of 18 years will now be issued health cards. The provision of proper immunization coverage, treatment of anemia. Dewarming, testing of eyes and dental checkup facilities would be ensured through these cards.

Girl's education has been a high priority with the Government of India. The National commitment to provide free and compulsory education to all children in the 6-14 years of age group is now a fundamental right of every child in India after the passing of the constitution (86th Amendment) Act in December 2002. Sarvasiksha Abhiyan or 'Education for All' programme recognizes that ensuring girls' education requires changes not only in the education system but also in societal norms and attitudes. A two-pronged gender strategy therefore been adopted to make the education system responsible to the needs of the girls through targeted interventions which serve as a pull factor to enhance access and retention of girls in schools and on the other hand, to generate a community demand for girls education through training and mobilization.

The Indian Government in its mission to universalize elementary education, over the years has been able to increase the rate of enrollment but has failed to arrest the dropout rate. Only 47 of the 100 children enrollment in class I reach class VIII putting the dropout rate in primary and elementary schools at 52.79 per cent. According to official sources, the dropout rate at the primary level (class 1 to V) for girls is 33.72 per cent. Dropout rates are even more alarming at the elementary level (class I to VIII) where 53.45 per cent of girls and 52.28 per cent of boys dropout of school.

Malnutrition as another indicator of poverty is captured through measuring child mal nutrition. Studies show that there is an important co-relation between income levels and child mal nutrition. i.e. households with income below the poverty line usually have acute problems of mal nutrition. The Ministry of Human Resource Development made a comparative study of Infant Mortality Rate (IMR) among girls is only 88 out of 1000 births, it is 156 in rural India. If a girl child gets sick in the village, the parents expect the illness to pass of naturally. If a girl does grow up there are fewer health cares facilities for her. India has the highest maternal mortality rates in rural areas world wide.

Socio-cultural and economic factors continue to inhibit women from gaining adequate access even to the existing public health facilities. This handicap does not merely affect women as individuals it also has an adverse impact on the health, general well-being and development of the entire family, particularly children.

Infant Mortality Rate (IMR)

The country has observed a continuous decline in IMR. It stood at 192 during 1971, 114 in the year 1980 and 60 in 2003. The decline in IMR has been noticed both for male and female during the period. However, the rate of decline is more pronounced in the case of male as compared to female.

Infant Mortality Rate by Sex

(Per 1000 Live Births)

Year	*Male*	*Female*	*Total*
1980	113	115	114
1985	96	98	97
1990	78	81	80
1993	73	75	74
1996	71	73	72
2000	67	69	68
2003	57	64	60

Source: Ministry of Health & Family Welfare.

On account of child health interventions, the infant mortality rate in the country has gone down from 114 in 1980 to 60 in 2003. While looking at the IMR of the country, it is observed that there is a continuous decline both in rural as well as in urban areas although urban areas of the country are observing rapid decline in IMR as compared to be rural areas attributing this change to better health care facilities easily accessible urban areas. The table below shows the IMR according to rural urban residence status.

Infant Mortality Rate by Rural-Urban

(Per 1000 Live Births)

Year	*Rural*	*Urban*	*Total*
1980	124	65	114
1985	107	59	97
1990	86	50	80
1993	82	45	74
1996	77	46	72
2000	74	43	68
2003	66	38	60

Source: Ministry of Health & Family Welfare

The principal causes of Infant Mortality in India are prematurity, diarrheal diseases, acute respiratory infections, vaccine preventable, inadequate maternal and new born care, mal nutrition contributing to over 50 per cent of child death. Low birth weight (30%) and birth injury.

Better Socio-economic and Educational Status of Women Reduces IMR & MMR

Infant Morality Rate (IMR) and Maternal Mortality Rate (MMR) is influenced by a whole range of socio-economic determinants. The status of women with low level of education, cultural misconceptions, economic dependency and lack of access to services influences the maternal mortality and morbidity. Hospital based data reveals that states like Kerala, Tamilnadu, Maharashtra, Andhra Pradesh, Punjab and Haryana which have relatively better socio-economic and educational status have lower MMR than the other states. Thus besides improving the maternal health care services, Government is committed to improve the social status of women including the education standard to reduce the current level of MMR.

For the holistic development of the child, various programmes/schemes have been under taken which inter-alia include most unique out reach programme of the Integrated Child Development services programme (ICDS) which aims to provide integrated package of health, nutrition and educational services to children up to six years age pregnant women and nursing mothers, besides schemes for improving health and nutrition levels of the child, schemes like pre-school education and crèches/day care centers for children below 5 years belonging to weaker sections of society are also provided. Earlier the mother of girl child born on or after August 15, 1997, in a family below the poverty line rural and urban areas was given a grant of Rs. 500. The Government of India developed an action plan in 1992 for developing the girl child. In 1994, India passed a universal female education bill that offers parents incentives for access and punishment for keeping a girl out of school.

Low literacy rates and lack of employment opportunities in rural areas contribute to economic deprivation and overall under developed status of women. Child marriage practices, lack of the women's control over the births and an overall dependence on male members in a generally patriarchal society contributes immensely towards the low social status of women especially in rural India. Education system in India does little to impart life skills and prepare adolescent girls to face the challenges of womanhood and motherhood.

In order to encourage and enthuse villages to become more sensitive to the girl child's needs and facilitate her welfare, development and empowerment, it is suggested that villages be given a set of parameters/indicators to monitor and such villages that comply with all the indicators be declared 'Girl child friendly'. An illustrative list of girl friendly indicators grouped into three categories, viz. health and nutrition, education and protection is provided.

Health and Nutrition

- pregnancy registration
- immunization for mothers
- nutrition supplements for mother
- institutional delivery
- regular health check up
- accessibility of health centre
- availability of health worker
- availability of medicine
- regular monitoring of health of child
- immunization records of the girl child
- supplementary nutrition of the girl child
- micro nutrients supply.

Education

- Preschool education and supplementary nutrition facilities.
- Enrollment of girl child in school.
- Primary education facility.
- Availability and accessibility of elementary and secondary education facility.
- Number of teachers.

- Provision of mid-day meal/supplementary nutrition.
- Availability of school books/stationary/school uniform.
- Pucca school buildings.
- Toilet/sanitation facility in school.
- Sports facilities.
- Extra curricular activities in schools.
- Special provisions for SC/ST/OBC.
- Special education for disabled.

Protection

- birth registration of the girl child.
- protection from child abuse.
- protection of child marriage.
- protection from sexual exploitation and trafficking.
- prevention of child labor.
- care for street children.

Based on the number of indicators fulfilled the state government/district administration may like to reward those villages/clusters with awards/recognition etc., Based on the number of village/clusters declared 'Girl child friendly 'the concerned state may also be recognized for its efforts at the nutritional level for which the Ministry of women and child development make constitute a special award.

The major policy initiatives under taken by the government in the recent past for welfare of women include:

- Balika Samridhi Yojana (BSY).
- National Commission for Children (NCC).
- Adoption of National Nutrition Policy (NNP).
- Integrated Child Development Services Scheme (ICDS).
- Kishori Shakti Yojana an intervention for adolescent girls (11-18) was launched in 2000-01 as part of the Integrated Child Development Services Programme.

- BSY launched in 1997 with the specific aim to change the community's attitude towards the girl child has been further recast in June 1999.
- The Ministry of Women and Child Development (WCD), Integrated Child Development Protection Scheme (ICPS) to protect girls among all children.
- It also set up the National Commission for Protection of Child Rights (NCPCR) to implement chits related legislation and now it has announced a radical "New Cash transfers Scheme" for families to allow their daughters to live and flourish.

As a result of the Government policies to ensure facilities for schooling and extend special care to the girl child and expansion of nutrition programmes particularly for the girl child, from 1950-51 to 2001-2002, the participation of girls has increased many fold in the Primary, Middle, Secondary/ Higher Secondary stages as well as in Higher Education, from 28.1% to 44.1%, from 16.1% to 41.8%, from 13.30% to 39.5%, and from 10.0% to 39.9% respectively.

References

Primary Census Abstract India, (2001), Census of India.

UNICEF Report, (2001).

Annual Report-Department of Women & Child Development.

The progress of the Nation, (2000), UNICEF Organization Report.

The Hindu, (Feb. 21, 2005).

Reducing Vulnerability of the Girl child in poor Rural areas by Maria-Hartl, Technical adviser, gender and Social Equality-IFAD.

Working Group on Development of Children for the Eleventh Five Year plan 2007-2012 A Report.

Ministry of Health & Family Welfare.

37

ACCESSIBILITY TO HEALTH CARE WITH SPECIAL REFERENCE TO RURAL WOMEN

CH. MINA KUMARI

INTRODUCTION

India has a population of 989 millions. It is most populous country and in world-wide it is second. Of that number, 120 million are women who live in poverty. India is one of the few countries where males significantly outnumber females, and this imbalance has increased over time.

There seems to be a consensus that higher female mortality between ages one and five and high maternal mortality rates result in a deficit of females in the population.

Women bear the primary responsibility for actions needed to end hunger and promote education, nutrition, health and family income.

Women's health status is basic to their advance in all fields of endeavour. Any serious attempt to improve the health of women must deal firstly with biased social customs and cultural traditions that have an impact on their health status. Though the health problems of women have been identified for priority attention and efforts made for maternal and child services since the beginning of planned development in India, much remains to be done to improve health care for women both in qualitative and quantitative terms.

India has exceptionally high rates of child malnutrition, because tradition in India requires that women eat least throughout their lives even when pregnant and lactating; malnourished women give birth to malnourished children, perpetuating the cycle, Nutritional status of women is a major determinant of the health and development of the community. In developing countries like India the incidence of malnutrition among women is very high. Maternal nutrition is major determinant of intrauterine development of fetus and major influence on outcome of pregnancy Ex: Ijitra uterine death, Still birth 20%, born to low birth weight babies. Undernourished mothers are more likely to have undernourished children. Ex: Marasmus, Kwashiorkor, Malnutrition during pregnancy complicated by stunted growth and infections carries high mortality of mothers. ICMR identified the maternal nutritional risk factors to reduce the maternal death during the course of life.

1. If maternal age is less than 18 years.
2. If maternal weight is less than 40 kgs.
3. if height of mother less than 145 cm.
4. If weight gain during pregnancy less than 5kgs.
5. If birth interval is less than 2 years.
6. If body mass index is less than 16.

There is need for increased requirements of Iron during pregnancy otherwise, there are dangers of anemia to pregnant women. If women are anemic (HB<11 g/did) or she has pallor, give her two IFA tablets for three months. Women with severe anemia (Hob<7 g/did) or those who have breathlessness and tachycardia due to anemia, should be referred to Gynecologist.

Even women who have had difficulty with previous pregnancies are usually treated with home remedies only for the reasons that the decision that pregnant women seek rests with the mother in-law and husband; financial considerations; and fear that the treatment may be more harmful than the malady. It is estimated that pregnancy- related deaths account for one quarter of all fatalities among women aged 15 to 29, with well over two-thirds of them considered preventable; for every maternal death in India, an estimated 20 more women suffer from impaired health; one village-level study of rural women determined on the basis of physical examinations that some 92 per cent suffered from one or more gynecological disorder.

Families are far less likely to educate girls than boys, and far more likely to pull them out of school either to help at home or from fear of violence. Women and girls receive far less education than men, due both to social norms and fears of violence. India has the largest population of non-school-going working girls. India's constitution guarantees free primary school education for both boys and girls up to age 14. This goal has been repeatedly reconfirmed, but primary education in India is not universal. Over all, the literacy rate for women is 39 per cent versus 64 per cent for men. Reduction in government expenditures on higher education and encouragement to private colleges will reduce women's opportunities for higher education since privatization in education promotes only male-dominated professional and technical courses, as they are lucrative.

Maternal health status is assessed through measurement of mortality, morbidity and growth, development. According to world scenario WHO estimates about 4,95,000 maternal deaths occurred during the year 2000 globally.

East Mediterranean countries	2,43,000
European countries	20,000
South East Asia	65,000
European Countries	3,000
South East Asia	1,43,000
Western Pacific	19,000

According to WHO, a maternal death is defined as "the death of a woman while pregnant or within 42 days of termination of pregnancy irrespective of the duration and size of pregnancy, from any cause related to aggravated by the pregnancy or its management but not from accidental or incidental causes".

FINDINGS

Maternal mortality rate–MMR is expressed as a rate per 1000 live births.

MMR ratio in selected countries 2000.

Country	*MMR Per 100,000 Live Births*
India	407
Nepal	540
Bangladesh	350
Srilanka	60
China	55
USA	8
Japan	8
Singapore	6

Life time chances of maternal death in the world is	1 in 75
In least developed countries	1 in 16
In developing countries	1 in 60
In industrialized countries	1 in 4100

Most maternal death is preventable. Low status of women in society added to their low literacy rate prevents them from taking antenatal care even if services are available.

Tragic situation in India most of these deaths are not due to disease but occurred during or after a natural process of delivery; most of deaths occurred at reproductive age group of women in many parts of the world.

Reproductive age means-15 to 49 years; this period can be divided into adolescent age, antenatal, natal and post-natal.

A woman may become pregnant by failure of contraceptive method. Women who have become pregnant because of not use of any contraceptives, unmarried women or widow or victim of rape who became pregnant can terminate their pregnancy legally, under safe clean condition by qualified doctors. Eleven percent of maternal deaths are due to unsafe and septic abortions. Sepsis leading to life threatening conditions like peritonitis, septicemia, renal failure and death. Excessive vaginal bleeding resulting in death. Injury to bladder resulting in death, perforation of intestine is common.

Suggestions

Women's health concerns cover a wide spectrum. While many health conditions affect both men and women, a number of health issues affect only women and some are more prevalent in women. In addition, a number of medical conditions may cause different symptoms in women, affect women differently than men, and may require different treatment or prevention protocols.

Besides conditions such as menopause, ovarian and cervical cancer, and pregnancy, which are unique to women and other medical conditions play a large role in women's health. Breast cancer and osteoporosis are thought of as women's health concerns, although they occur in men. Heart disease is a serious disturbance at home, a break on new career, death of close friend or relative or excessive and rapid weight loss; certain medicines can also cause this as tumor of the brain.

Heavy periods may be due to changes in hormones, infections or intrea-uterine devices.

Pre-menstrual tension may cause variety of symptoms like painful breast, nausea headache, anxiety, instability and some time depression. These symptoms are more severe in the days before menstruation. Prolapsed of the uterus may happen due to Abnormal positions of the womb.

Conclusions

There is need for increased requirements of Nutritious food items for women due to the large genital surface area and sharpness of female urethra. So genitalia is prone to bacterial fungal and virus infections. Urinary incontinence, dribbling of urine and urinary tract infections are more frequent in women.

Obesity usually occurs in most of the women due to their sedentary household life, sometimes in usage of birth control methods, hormone treatment.

Obesity women are highly prone to cardiovascular diseases. Type two Diabetes is also common in obese women globally.

20% of the pregnancies end as spontaneous abortions before 28th week. Some times pregnancy may premature as entopic pregnancies [outside the uterus]; genetic abnormal pregnancies are doomed to failure.

INDEX

D

H

I

M

S